THE ROLE OF
ARGUMENT STRUCTURE
IN GRAMMAR

CSLI
Lecture Notes
No. 62

THE ROLE OF
ARGUMENT STRUCTURE
IN GRAMMAR
EVIDENCE FROM ROMANCE

ALEX
ALSINA

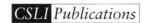

CENTER FOR THE STUDY OF
LANGUAGE AND INFORMATION
STANFORD, CALIFORNIA

Copyright ©1996
CSLI Publications
Center for the Study of Language and Information
Leland Stanford Junior University
Printed in the United States
00 99 98 97 96   5 4 3 2 1

Library of Congress Cataloging-in-Publication Data

Alsina i Keith, Alex, 1958–
    The role of argument structure in grammar / Alex Alsina.
        p.   cm. – (CSLI lecture notes ; no. 62)
    Rev. and expanded version of ch. 2–6 of the author's dissertation
(1993).
    Includes bibliographical references (p. 281) and index.

    ISBN 1-57586-035-X (hardback : alk. paper).
    ISBN 1-57586-034-1 (pbk. : alk. paper)

    1. Grammar, Comparative and general–Syntax. 2. Grammar,
Comparative and general–Verb phrase. 3. Romance languages–Syntax.
I. Title. II. Series.
P295.A38 1996
415–dc20   96-4006
                                                        CIP

CSLI was founded early in 1983 by researchers from Stanford University, SRI International,
and Xerox PARC to further research and development of integrated theories of language,
information, and computation. CSLI headquarters and CSLI Publications are located on the
campus of Stanford University.

CSLI Lecture Notes report new developments in the study of language, information, and
computation. In addition to lecture notes, the series includes monographs, working papers,
and conference proceedings. Our aim is to make new results, ideas, and approaches available as quickly as possible.

∞The acid-free paper used in this book meets the minimum requirements of the American
National Standard for Information Sciences—Permanence of Paper for Printed Library Ma-
terials, ANSI Z39.48-1984.

Contents

Acknowledgements   ix

Cross-References and Abbreviations   xi

1   Introduction   1
  1.1   Some Puzzles   1
  1.2   Argument Structure   4
  1.3   The Emergence of Argument Structure   7
  1.4   The Autonomy of A-Structure   9
  1.5   Contents   12

2   The Theoretical Framework   15
  2.1   C-Structure and F-Structure   16
      2.1.1   Internal Organization   17
      2.1.2   Pairing of C-Structures and F-Structures   21
      2.1.3   Assignment of Grammatical Functions   27
      2.1.4   An Example of Function-Category Mapping   30
  2.2   A-Structure   34
      2.2.1   The Prominence Ranking of Arguments   35
      2.2.2   The Proto-Role Classification   38
      2.2.3   Mapping to Grammatical Functions   43
  2.3   Active/Passive Alternation   48
      2.3.1   The Active Structure   48
      2.3.2   Passive   50
      2.3.3   The Passive Oblique   53
      2.3.4   Obliques   55
  2.4   Nonargument Functions   57
      2.4.1   Discourse Functions   58
      2.4.2   Raising Functions   62
      2.4.3   Expletive Functions   72

2.5 Summary   77

3   **The Romance Reflexive Clitic**   **81**
   3.1 Two Current Approaches   81
   3.2 Valence Reduction   85
      3.2.1 NP Extraposition   85
      3.2.2 Case Marking in Causative Constructions   86
      3.2.3 Nominalizations   89
      3.2.4 Past Participle Agreement   94
      3.2.5 Conclusion   97
   3.3 Reflexivized Verbs are Unaccusatives   98
      3.3.1 Auxiliary Selection   98
      3.3.2 Causatives of Reflexivized Verbs   99
      3.3.3 Participial Constructions in Italian   100
      3.3.4 Summary   102
   3.4 Reflexivized Verbs are not Unaccusatives   103
      3.4.1 Bare Plural/Mass NP   104
      3.4.2 *En*-Cliticization   107
      3.4.3 Modifiers of the Logical Subject   109
      3.4.4 Subject Selection with Ditransitives   111
   3.5 The Paradox   113

4   **Solving the Paradox**   **115**
   4.1 A-Structure Binding   116
   4.2 Explaining the Facts   121
      4.2.1 Valence Reduction   121
      4.2.2 The Unaccusative Behavior   123
      4.2.3 The Unergative/Transitive Behavior   129
      4.2.4 Conclusion   134
   4.3 Is Reference to the External Argument Needed?   135
      4.3.1 Passives   135
      4.3.2 Raising Verbs   139
      4.3.3 Unaccusative Verbs   140
      4.3.4 Summary   143
   4.4 Comparison with Other Theories   144

5   **Objects and Case Marking**   **149**
   5.1 Indirect Objects are Direct Functions   150
   5.2 Morphological Case   160
      5.2.1 Dative: The Marked Case Value   161
      5.2.2 Overt Realization of Case   164
      5.2.3 The Dative Object as a PP   166
   5.3 Case Assignment   169

5.3.1 Two Competing Generalizations 170

5.3.2 Case Assignment Convention 174

5.3.3 Case and Reflexivized Predicates 177

5.3.4 No Dative Subjects in Romance 179

5.4 Implications 182

6 Causatives 185

6.1 The A-Structure and F-Structure of Causatives 186

6.1.1 A Complex Predicate 188

6.1.2 Morphological Case Alternation 190

6.1.3 Object/Oblique Alternation 193

6.1.4 Summary 199

6.2 The C-Structure of Causatives 200

6.2.1 A Functionally Double-Headed C-Structure 201

6.2.2 Word Order in Causative Constructions 203

6.3 The Causee is not a Grammatical Subject 207

6.3.1 Absence of Subjecthood Properties 209

6.3.2 The Causee and Floating Quantifiers 213

6.3.3 The Causee and Quantifier Binding 217

6.3.4 Reflexivized Causatives 220

6.3.5 Summary 223

6.4 The Causee is a Logical Subject 223

6.4.1 A Logical Subject Reflexive 224

6.4.2 Control into Adverbial Clauses 227

6.4.3 Conclusion 232

6.5 Conclusions 233

7 Two Types of Binding 237

7.1 Syntactic Anaphors 237

7.2 The Reflexive Clitic as Clitic Double 242

7.3 Further Consequences 248

7.4 Reciprocal Readings with "Inversion" Verbs 255

7.5 Discussion 263

8 Conclusions 265

8.1 The CURT, the PEAR, and the 1-1 Match 265

8.2 For an Autonomous Argument Structure 267

8.3 Autonomous Levels of Representation 275

Bibliography 281

Index 295

Acknowledgements

This work contains most of chapters 2, 4, 5, and 6 of my dissertation (Alsina 1993), thoroughly revised and expanded. I am very grateful to the members of my dissertation committee, Joan Bresnan, Sam Mchombo, Peter Sells, Tom Wasow and Annie Zaenen, for their detailed comments and criticisms. In addition, detailed comments on earlier versions of the manuscript were provided by Joan Bresnan, Maria Teresa Espinal, K. P. Mohanan, Peter Sells, Tom Wasow, and two anonymous reviewers, whose suggestions have helped me improve the present version. The research on which this work is based was supported in part by NSF grant No. BNS-8919880 to Joan Bresnan.

Cross-References and Abbreviations

Cross-References

Numbered items such as examples and principles are referred to by their number alone in the chapter in which they appear, and by their number preceded by the number of the chapter in which they appear when the reference is made in a different chapter. Thus, examples (3) and (12b) of chapter 2 are referred to as (3) and (12b) in chapter (2) and as (2.3) and (2.12b) in any other chapter.

Abbreviations

In glossses in Catalan examples:

1	first person	INF	infinitive
2	second person	M	masculine
3	third person	NOM	nominative
ACC	accusative case	P or PL	plural
DAT	dative case	RF	reflexive clitic
F	feminine	S or SG	singular

In glosses in Bantu (Kichaga and Chicheŵa) examples (following Bresnan and Moshi 1990 and Alsina and Mchombo 1993):

Numbers (1, 2, 3, etc.) indicate gender classes.

AP	applicative	PS	past
FV	final vowel	RCP	reciprocal
PAS	passive	S	subject marker
PR	present		

1

Introduction

This book has two main goals. One is theoretical: to contribute towards our understanding of the nature of argument structure and its relation to other levels of representation in the grammar. The other is descriptive: to provide analyses of phenomena in the Romance language Catalan that have traditionally posed analytical problems within Romance linguistics. The two goals complement each other: the theoretical proposals are supported by the descriptive analyses, and the analyses are made possible by the theoretical proposals.

In this chapter, I start out by introducing some of the empirical problems that this study deals with, in section 1.1, and go on to give an intuitive idea of the notion of argument structure, in 1.2. I then outline the emergence of argument structure (or *a-structure*) in linguistic theorizing, in section 1.3, pointing out that it is not generally assumed to be a level of syntactic representation. In 1.4, I present the view of argument structure that this study adopts as a fully autonomous level of syntactic structure. In section 1.5, I outline the contents of this book.

1.1 Some Puzzles

The empirical problems that this book is concerned with have to do mostly with the correspondence between syntactic expressions and semantic roles. For example, is it a one-to-one correspondence or can it be many-to-one? What constraints apply to the correspondence between semantic roles and types of syntactic expressions?

The first of these questions must be addressed when dealing with "reflexivized" constructions in Romance. In Catalan, as in other Romance languages, transitive sentences like (1a) can normally alternate with reflexivized sentences like (1b), which include a reflexive clitic and have a reflexive or reciprocal interpretation.

1

(1) a. La directora defensa l'estudiant.
'The director defends the student.'

   b. La directora es defensa.
the director RF defends

'The director defends herself.'

The two sentences in (1) are not only different semantically, as the English translation indicates; they differ syntactically in one important way: (1a) has a subject and an object, whereas (1b) has a subject, but no object. This claim is supported by several kinds of evidence. For example, only intransitive verbs, those that don't take an object, can undergo nominalization of their infinitive form. Interestingly, the reflexivized predicate in (1b) can be nominalized, as in (2):

(2)   El defensar-se enèrgic de la directora
the defend-RF energetic of the director

'The director's energetic self-defense'

If the reflexivized sentence (1b) has a subject but no object, we should ask ourselves how the two semantic roles of the predicate are expressed in this example. In (1a), the subject *la directora* expresses the defender role, and the object *l'estudiant* expresses the defendee role. However, in (1b), which is argued not to include an object, there is a mismatch between semantic roles and syntactic expressions: there are two semantic roles, but only one corresponding syntactic expression. There are three alternative ways of analyzing this mismatch, schematized in (3). The subject *la directora* in (1b) may correspond to: (a) the defender, with the defendee having no syntactic expression, as in (3a); (b) the defendee, with the defender having no syntactic expression, as in (3b); or (c) both the defender and the defendee, as in (3c).

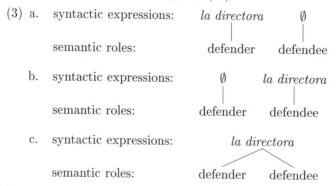

(3) a. syntactic expressions: *la directora*   ∅

        semantic roles: defender   defendee

   b. syntactic expressions: ∅   *la directora*

        semantic roles: defender   defendee

   c. syntactic expressions: *la directora*

        semantic roles: defender   defendee

Most conceptions of the syntax-semantics interface assume that there must be a one-to-one match between expressed semantic roles of a predicate and syntactic expressions that correspond to those roles. This assumption immediately excludes the representation in (3c) because it has two expressed semantic roles corresponding to one syntactic expression. This reduces the choice of representations to (3a) and (3b), as in each case there is only one expressed semantic role corresponding to one syntactic expression, which preserves the one-to-one match.

However, when it comes to choosing between (3a) and (3b), serious difficulties arise. The syntactic properties of expressions are known to be determined, in part, by the semantic properties of the roles they express. Thus, an expression that corresponds to the defender role, as in (3a), is expected to have different syntactic properties from an expression that corresponds to the defendee role, as in (3b). It turns out (see chapter 3) that the sole nominal expression in a reflexivized construction like (1b) (*la directora* in this case) has many of the syntactic properties that are expected if it corresponds to the same role as the subject of the nonreflexivized form: this supports (3a). But it also turns out that reflexivized predicates exhibit some syntactic properties that can only be explained if their sole nominal expression corresponds to the same semantic role as the object of their nonreflexivized counterparts: this supports (3b). Neither of the representations in (3a) and (3b) can explain all of the properties of reflexivized constructions.

I argue in chapter 4 that the only way to solve this paradox is to abandon the requirement of the one-to-one match between semantic roles and syntactic expressions and to assume that (3c) is the correct representation of reflexivized constructions in Romance. From such a representation it follows that the sole nominal expression in a reflexivized construction has the syntactic properties expected of each of the two semantic roles that it corresponds to.

Another of the puzzles dealt with in this book concerns the variable syntactic expression of semantic roles, which is most clearly illustrated with the alternation between a verb and its causative form, as in the Catalan examples (4a) and (4b)

(4) a. El nen   llegeix la carta.
       'The boy reads   the letter.'

    b. He   fet   llegir la carta   al nen.
       I have made read the letter to-the boy

       'I made the boy read the letter.'

The reader role is expressed as the subject, *el nen*, in the noncausative construction (4a), whereas it is expressed as an object (an indirect, or dative, object) in the causative (4b). The observation made earlier that the semantic properties of roles determine in part the syntactic properties of the expressions that correspond to those roles faces a problem with examples such as (4). How can semantics constrain syntactic expression, while still allowing alternations in the syntactic expression of semantic roles such as that illustrated in (4)?

A prevalent strategy in theoretical linguistics has been to assume a uniform assignment of grammatical functions to semantic roles. The existence of problems for this assumption, such as (4), has led researchers to claim that this assumption holds only at a level of representation that does not directly reflect the overt expression of syntactic elements. Thus, the reader role of the verb *llegir* 'read' is always represented as a subject at that level, not only in examples like (4a), where this role is expressed as a surface subject, but also in examples like (4b), where it is not expressed as a surface subject. The claim is, then, that the NP *(a)l nen* in (4b) is a transformed subject: a subject that has been transformed to look like something else. There is, however, an alternative approach that does not require each semantic role to be assigned a fixed grammatical function. According to this approach, the reader role is expressed as a subject in (4a), but not in (4b), where it is not even a subject in disguise; it is what it looks like: an object. When the two strategies are compared, it becomes clear that assuming that the NP *(a)l nen* in (4b) is a subject has no explanatory advantage and creates serious problems, as will be argued in chapter 6.

This is not evidence against the claim that semantic properties constrain syntactic expressions, but only against a rigid interpretation of this claim, namely, the hypothesis of the uniform assignment of grammatical functions. The view that emerges from the facts analyzed in this book, such as the causative/noncausative alternation in Romance, is one in which semantics does impose constraints on syntactic expressions, while allowing for a certain amount of syntactic alternation.

1.2   Argument Structure

This section tries to give the reader an intuitive understanding of the notion of argument structure, which figures prominently in the analyses presented in this book. A predicate expresses a relation (or relations) among participants; these participants are called the *arguments* of the predicate. Consider the following examples:

(5) a. The director placed the document in the drawer.

    b. She defended the proposal.

    c. The committee laughed.

In these examples, the predicates we will be concerned with are the verbs: *placed* in (5a), *defended* in (5b), and *laughed* in (5c).[1] The participants *the director*, *the document*, and *in the drawer* in (5a) each correspond to one of the arguments of *placed*. Likewise, *she* and *the proposal* in (5b) correspond to the two arguments of *defended*, and *the committee* in (5c) corresponds to the single argument of *laughed*. Comparing these examples with the following ungrammatical ones, we see that the predicate determines the number of arguments it takes:

(6) a. *The director laughed the document in the drawer.

   b. *She placed the proposal.

   c. *The committee defended.

The number of participants in (6) does not match the number of arguments specified in the argument structures of the predicates, which renders the sentences ungrammatical. Thus, *laugh* takes only one argument, but (6a) includes three different participants; *place* takes three arguments, but it appears in (6b) with only two participants; and *defend* takes two arguments, but it appears in (6c) with only one participant.

In addition, the correspondence between grammatical functions (subject, object, prepositional oblique, etc.) and the arguments of a predicate is neither random nor totally unpredictable. Whether an argument is expressed as a subject or as an object, for example, is partly determined by the semantics of the predicate. If we interchange the subject and the object of (5a), the resulting sentence (7) does not have the same interpretation, in which the director causes the action expressed by the verb and the document undergoes a change of location. Instead, (7) can only have the pragmatically impossible (or the nonliteral, metaphorical) interpretation in which the document causes the action and the director undergoes the specified change of location.

(7)   The document placed the director in the drawer.

Not only is the correspondence between arguments and grammatical functions highly constrained for each predicate, but it is constrained in a similar way for large classes of predicates: it follows general principles. These principles are so general that any verb that we invent will have to conform to them. If we should invent the verb *obliquate* to mean

---

[1] Here and in what follows, only verbs are used as examples of predicates. In fact, the present study focuses on the argument structure of verbal predicates. This does not mean that only verbs are predicates. On the contrary, all lexical items of the four major syntactic categories can be considered to be predicates, and therefore to take arguments. See Williams 1981, Higginbotham 1985, Di Sciullo and Williams 1987, and Grimshaw 1990 for the proposal that all nouns have an argument structure, including nouns such as *dog* or *exam*.

"build or place in an oblique position or direction," we would use it in sentences like (8a), but not in sentences like (8b), if we intend Jim to be the builder.

(8) a. Jim obliquated the door of the closet.

    b. *The door of the closet obliquated Jim.

Thus, in order to capture these regularities, we must factor out the syntactically relevant information that is peculiar to each predicate, placing it in argument structure, from that which is general to large classes of predicates, encoded as correspondence principles relating arguments to grammatical functions. Since the argument structure is sensitive to semantics, we can say that the syntactic frame of a predicate (the number and type of grammatical functions that it takes) is—indirectly— constrained by its semantics.

Another area in which the notion of argument structure is pertinent involves morphologically related forms of a verb with different syntactic frames, such as the active and passive forms. Comparing an active and passive pair such as (9a) and (9b), it is clear that the semantic relations expressed by the predicates are the same in the two examples. In both cases, the predicate takes two arguments, one corresponding to the "defender" and one corresponding to the entity being defended. However, whereas the defender is the subject in (9a), it is not in (9b), where, instead, the entity defended is the subject.

(9) a. The director defended the proposal.

    b. The proposal was defended by the director.

We would like to say that, in spite of the important differences in surface syntax between an active sentence and its corresponding passive, the two sentences have a common syntactic representation underlying their surface structures. This common syntactic representation is argument structure. The argument structures of an active verb and its passive form are essentially the same. The two argument structures differ only as a result of the information added by the passive morphology to the passive form, which is absent in the active form. One of the tasks of linguistic theory is to determine what this information is so that from its presence or absence the difference between an active and a passive form will follow, given general principles.

Argument structure is then the minimal information of predicates necessary for deriving their syntactic frame, or subcategorization, and for deriving their alternative syntactic frames when an alternation exists as with the active and passive pair. Having established what argument structure is in a pretheoretical sense and what it is needed for, we need to address such questions as: (a) exactly what information it includes; (b) how this information is represented; (c) how it relates to semantics and to other syntactic levels of representation; (d) what principles establish the correspondence between argument structure and the actual syntactic frame of its predicate; (e) how alternative correspondences arise for the same predicate; etc. This book addresses these questions and proposes specific answers, some of which differ in important ways from the solutions most commonly accepted in the field.

1.3   The Emergence of Argument Structure

Argument structure was introduced into linguistics in work such as Bresnan 1978 and Williams 1980, 1981 as a type of grammatical information found in the lexical entry of predicates. In most transformational approaches to syntax, such as the framework of Government-Binding (GB) (Chomsky 1981, 1982, 1986), argument structure has remained in the lexicon. At the lexical level, what an active sentence and its passive counterpart have in common is the argument structure of their predicate. However, in the syntax, the role of expressing this commonality is reserved for d-structure. The prominence that a-structure has acquired in recent years in work within the GB framework by Grimshaw (1990), S. Rosen (1989), among others, influenced by work outside this framework, such as Jackendoff 1990, raises questions about the roles of a-structure and d-structure. D-structure is claimed to be a " 'pure' representation of θ-structure" (Chomsky 1986), but that is exactly what a-structure is. Is it necessary for linguistic theory to include both a-structure, representing the prominence relations among arguments (Grimshaw 1990:10), and d-structure, recasting these prominence relations in phrase structure terms? If a-structure is adopted as a syntactic level of representation, following the arguments that have been made in the literature for this position, is there any need for d-structure?[2]

Grimshaw (1990), S. Rosen (1989), and others working within the GB framework argue convincingly for the level of a-structure, but are very cautious about indicating whether it displaces any other level of representation. Preserving standard assumptions within GB, Grimshaw

---

[2]Recent versions of GB, such as Chomsky 1993, propose to dispense with d-structure as a formally independent level of representation. However, d-structure, understood as the canonical phrase structure representation of arguments, is still present in Chomsky 1993. In this version, d-structure is represented as the VP-internal structure, which is visible at LF thanks to traces or other empty categories. The VP-internal structure is the phrase structure representation of argument structure, i.e., d-structure. Therefore, the observations to be made below about d-structure apply to Chomsky 1993 as much as to older versions of GB.

(1990:1) presents a-structure as the interface between the lexicon and the syntax: "Argument structure is projected from lexical semantic structure, and d-structure is projected from argument structure and principles of X-bar theory." This view of the position and role of a-structure within the grammar can be represented as in (10).

(10)

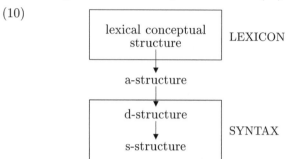

According to this, all of the lexical information that the syntax needs is represented in the a-structure. Furthermore, a-structure is only relevant for determining d-structure configurations. This idea is defended by Belletti and Rizzi (1988:294–295), who propose that, once θ-structures (i.e., a-structures) fulfil their role of determining d-structures, "reference to such entities is excluded in formal grammar." In other words, within this view, any phenomenon that takes place in the mapping of d-structure to s-structure or any principle that applies at s-structure (or subsequent levels) cannot refer directly to a-structure information, but can only be sensitive to phrase structure configurations. (Not included in (10) are the syntactic levels of Phonetic Form, or PF, which provides the input for phonetic interpretation, and Logical Form, or LF, which provides the input for semantic interpretation. Both PF and LF are assumed to be derived from s-structure independently of each other.)

The view represented in (10), which reflects a consensus among GB theorists (see, for example, Belletti and Rizzi 1988, Baker 1988a, 1988b), entails that all of the syntactically relevant information in the a-structure must be encoded in phrase structure terms at d-structure. Any information in the a-structure that failed to translate into phrase structure configurations would, ipso facto, fail to have any relevance for syntax. Thus, under this view, a-structure and d-structure are *nondistinct* as far as the syntactic component is concerned. While the a-structure may be a type of information necessary within the lexicon (for morphological or lexical processes) and as the interface between the lexicon and the syntax, once the d-structure is generated, the a-structure is ignored.

However, this view is not the one endorsed (perhaps only implicitly) by Grimshaw (1990) and other proponents of a-structure as a level of representation distinct from phrase structure: a-structures are not mapped onto d-structures in such a way that all the information present at a-structure is preserved at d-structure. For Grimshaw (1990), there are a-structure notions that are uniquely represented at a-structure and are not recoverable from d-structure configurations, for example, the notion "thematically most prominent argument," which does not always correspond to the structurally most prominent argument at d-structure. That notion is shown to be relevant for anaphoric phenomena, namely, binding of anaphors (see also Kiparsky (1987), Joshi (1989, 1993), Dalrymple (1993), among others); since binding by the thematically most prominent argument is argued to take place at s-structure (see Grimshaw 1990:162ff), it follows that s-structure processes may refer directly to a-structure. Therefore, the picture in (10) is not the view that Grimshaw (1990) proposes of the relation among the syntactic levels of representation; rather, it is better illustrated in the diagram in (11) (corresponding to the syntactic portion of (10)).

(11)
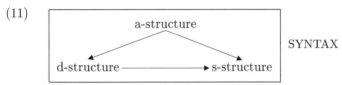

SYNTAX

Thus, in Grimshaw's view, the a-structure is not only the interface of the lexicon and the syntax, as is standard in GB, but is also a level of representation in the syntax *independent* of other levels such as d-structure and s-structure, in the sense that the information it expresses is not recoverable in those other levels, and *parallel* to these other levels, in the sense that the information it contains is accessible to the other levels.

1.4   The Autonomy of A-Structure

Grimshaw's proposal constitutes an important departure from standard GB assumptions. By making a-structure a level of representation that can access s-structure directly, the dispensable nature of d-structure is highlighted. Notions such as "external argument" and "internal argument," which were traditionally represented at d-structure, are defined and represented only at a-structure in Grimshaw 1990: there is not a one-to-one correspondence between these a-structure notions and d-structure positions.[3] For example, although external arguments (except

---

[3]Williams (1980, 1981), who introduced the notion of external argument, proposed to represent this notion both at the level of argument structure as a distinguished

when suppressed) are always realized as d-structure subjects, not all d-structure subjects are external arguments (see Grimshaw 1990:31–37). It is clear that, under this conception, a-structure takes over the role of d-structure and that there are no reasons, except for theory-internal inertia, to continue assuming the existence of d-structure.

In this study I intend to take the hypothesis of a-structure as an independent and parallel level of representation to what seems to me to be its logical consequence. Thus, I will not assume that the arguments in a-structure are mapped onto phrase structure positions at a deep level of structure, which is subsequently modified to yield the surface forms of those arguments. Instead, I will assume that the mapping of arguments in the a-structure onto their morphosyntactic expressions does not involve any other level of phrase structure than that in which these surface forms are represented. Following an important body of research in a variety of frameworks, I assume that this mapping of arguments onto morphosyntactic expressions is licensed by a set of categories that we can refer to as *syntactic functions*, such as "subject," "object," and "oblique," one of whose functions is to link arguments with their surface forms, as indicated in (12).

(12)

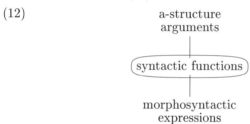

The conception schematized in (12) characterizes a class of theories that can be generically referred to as "linking theories," such as Foley and Van Valin 1984, Kiparsky 1987, Bresnan and Kanerva 1989, Jackendoff 1990, among others.[4]

One of the salient features of linking theories that distinguishes them from GB approaches is the absence in the former of d-structure and con-

---

argument, which is notated by means of underlining, and at the level of d-structure as the NP argument that is external to the predicate or VP.

[4]Not all "linking" theories use the term *syntactic functions* (or synonymous terms such as *grammatical functions* or, simply, *functions*) to designate the categories by means of which arguments are assigned overt expression. For example, Kiparsky (1987) uses the term *linkers* for this purpose: *linkers* refer to morphosyntactic properties of the realization of arguments (such as case features, agreement, phrase structure adjacency, etc.), but they play the same role in the theory as syntactic functions in other theories because they make the same abstract distinctions (between direct and indirect functions, and between subject and objects).

sequently of the assumption that each argument or θ-role of a predicate is uniformly represented in phrase structure terms. This assumption follows in GB from the Projection Principle, "which requires that lexical properties be represented by categorial properties in syntactic representation" (Chomsky 1986:82), coupled with the assumption that there is a canonical structural realization of each semantic category selected by a head (Chomsky 1986:87). This means that, if a verb takes a patient, it must take an object NP, the canonical realization of a patient, even when the patient is overtly realized as a subject, as in a passive form: this is possible because such a form is assumed to be derived by moving the object NP to the subject position. In linking theories, in contrast, nothing requires each argument or θ-role to have a uniform phrase structure representation and therefore there is no level of structure (such as d-structure) that encodes this representation. Linking theories are characterized by allowing variable associations between arguments and syntactic functions (and therefore with morphosyntactic expressions); these associations are not random, but are constrained by principles that are sensitive, among other things, to the representation of the a-structure.

I will adopt the idea characteristic of the framework of Lexical-Functional Grammar (LFG) (Bresnan 1980, 1982a, Kaplan and Bresnan 1982) that each of the grammatical categories in (12) is represented in a separate and formally different level of structure. Standard LFG has developed a precise formalism for the representation of syntactic functions, at the level of functional structure, or *f-structure*, and for the representation of morphosyntactic expressions, at the level of constituent structure, or *c-structure*. Likewise, I will assume that arguments are represented at a different level of syntactic description, argument structure, or a-structure. Each of these levels is related to the others by correspondence principles. These principles constrain the possible pairings of different structures that describe a well-formed sentence.

The conception of grammar that I am proposing can be schematized as in (13). This diagram indicates that a-structure is both in the lexicon, as part of the lexical entries of predicates, and in the syntax, where it constrains the surface realization of arguments. There are constraints applying in the mapping between arguments, at a-structure, and syntactic functions, represented in f-structure, and in the mapping between syntactic functions and morphosyntactic expressions, represented in c-structure. These two kinds of mapping relations will be presented in detail in chapter 2. This model also allows for direct mapping constraints between a-structure and c-structure, although this possibility will not be developed in this study (see Alsina 1994a, 1994b for evidence of direct mapping between a-structure and c-structure).

(13)

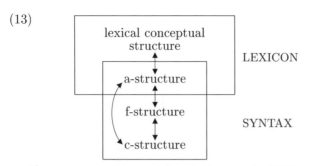

If we compare this model with the standard GB model given in (10), we see that a-structure in (13) corresponds to both a-structure and d-structure in (10), thus eliminating the redundancy that these two levels of structure create in the system. F-structure in (13) corresponds to s-structure in (10), since both structures represent surface grammatical relations. And c-structure, which encodes the phonologically interpretable syntactic information, corresponds in GB to PF, which is not included in the diagram in (10). (As for LF, also not included in (10), we will not be concerned here with determining whether semantic interpretation should be read off a syntactic level explicitly designed for this purpose, such as LF, or whether it should be related directly to the other levels of syntactic structure.) The main point to be emphasized is the conceptual simplification achieved in the model in (13) by having one single level of structure (a-structure) play the role that two different levels of structure have in (10), namely, a-structure and d-structure.

1.5 Contents

Chapter 2 presents the main theoretical assumptions of this work: the content and representation of the different syntactic structures assumed, in particular, of a-structure, and the mapping principles governing the correspondences between these structures. The representation of a-structure includes a hierarchical ranking of arguments and a representation of the notions of *logical subject, external argument,* and *internal argument,* which are relevant for determining the syntactic realization of arguments and the operation of processes that are sensitive to a-structure. The mapping principles that relate arguments with syntactic functions must allow for alternations in syntactic functions, such as the subject/object alternation found in active/passive pairs. Such alternations are derived without resorting to operations that change syntactic functions. Syntactic function alternations result from the creation of a derived predicate through the merging or composition of two predicates; because the derived predicate is different from the base predicate on which it is formed, the application of the mapping theory may yield a different set of associated syntactic functions for the two cases.

Chapter 3 examines the facts of reflexivized constructions in Romance. The evidence presented reveals that none of the commonly accepted analyses is capable of accounting for the whole range of facts of reflexivized constructions in a natural way. First, it shows that a reflexivized sentence has one syntactic function less than its nonreflexivized counterpart. It also argues for analyzing the subject of a reflexivized sentence as being the expression of the same argument as the object of the nonreflexivized form. However, a third set of facts shows that the subject of the reflexivized form is the expression of the same argument as the subject of its nonreflexivized counterpart. What these facts show is that a single syntactic function in a reflexivized construction is the expression of two different arguments of the predicate. The conclusion that two arguments may be expressed as one syntactic function is a paradox for most current theories, which assume a one-to-one correspondence between arguments and syntactic functions.

Chapter 4 proposes to analyze the Romance reflexive clitic as a morpheme that specifies binding of two arguments of a predicate at the level of a-structure. The theory developed in this work requires that two arguments that are bound (at a-structure) map onto, or correspond to, the same syntactic function. Thus, by positing this minimal operation on the a-structure, it follows that a reflexivized form based on a dyadic predicate is intransitive and that the single syntactic function associated with it is the expression of both arguments of the predicate, accounting for why this syntactic function displays behavior attributable to either of the arguments it corresponds to. Given this, all of the properties of reflexivized constructions are explained by independently required principles. It is only in a theory in which the representation of arguments (at a-structure) is autonomous from the representation of the syntactic functions that express those arguments (at f-structure) that we can expect to find mismatches between categories at the two levels.

Chapter 5 focuses on the analysis of objects and case marking in Romance. It establishes the existence of two types of objects in Romance, traditionally labelled "direct" and "indirect," arguing that all that distinguishes these two kinds of objects is a difference in morphological case, from which other differences follow. Furthermore, I show that case assignment is very often determined on the basis of the hierarchical a-structure. Dative case is assigned to the thematically more prominent of two direct functions that is not mapped onto the external argument, leaving nondative as the default case feature for direct functions. Thus, the different properties of objects need not be attributed to abstract distinctions, such as abstract Case in GB, but follow from the morphological case distinction, which, in turn, is sensitive to a-structure.

Chapter 6 analyzes causative constructions in Romance, which are problematic for theoretical approaches that assume a uniform assignment of syntactic functions to the arguments of a predicate. In the present theory, Romance causative constructions are analyzed as involving the composition of two a-structures, that of the causative verb (i.e., *fer* in Catalan) and that of the embedded verb. As the a-structures involved in a causative and its noncausative counterpart are different, the syntactic structures that correspond to them are predictably different. One of the salient features of this analysis is the monoclausality of causative constructions. This property explains, among other things, the fact that the causee (the logical subject of the base verb in the causative construction) is not expressed as the subject, but as an object or as an oblique. Various facts reveal the inadequacy of assuming that the causee is a grammatical subject and argue for analyzing it as a logical subject. The conclusion is that the a-structure of a causative construction is complex, but is contained in a single f-structure, which is further evidence for the autonomy of the two levels.

Chapter 7 resumes the topic of a-structure binding, comparing this phenomenon to anaphoric binding. The present study argues that a reflexivized construction differs from a structure involving a syntactic anaphor such as *himself* or *herself* not only syntactically, since the former lacks the object that is expressed by the anaphor in the latter, but also semantically, as reflected in elliptical constructions. This difference argues against reducing the binding relation in reflexivized constructions to a special type of anaphoric binding in which the syntactic anaphor is phonologically null, since this would not provide an account of that semantic contrast. The clitic-doubling use of the reflexive clitic is analyzed, as an alternative to its a-structure binding use, deriving important consequences. Finally, the a-structure binding analysis predicts the range of reciprocal interpretations that reflexivized constructions give rise to.

Chapter 8 presents the main conclusions of this study, which concern the role of a-structure in grammar. This study shows that the arguments of a predicate have a uniform representation, not in the phrase structure, but at a-structure, a level of representation that is autonomous, that is, nonisomorphic with any other level. This autonomy allows for mismatches of various types between arguments and syntactic functions.

2

The Theoretical Framework

> **Warning**: Readers with a low tolerance for formalism
> should skip this chapter, or read only sections 2.2 and 2.3
> (pages 34–57), and refer back to it as the need arises.

In this work I adopt central ideas of the framework of Lexical-Functional
Grammar (LFG), a syntactic model that originated in work by Joan
Bresnan and Ronald Kaplan (see Bresnan 1980, 1982a, Kaplan and
Bresnan 1982). This formal framework, as reflected in its name, em-
phasizes the centrality of the lexical module and of syntactic functions.
It is a *lexicalist* theory, understood in the sense that it assumes a strict
division between the lexicon, as the word-formation component, and the
syntax, as the phrase-formation component, and does not allow syntactic formation rules to take part in the formation of words (see Bresnan
and Mchombo, 1995, and T. Mohanan 1995 for recent formulations of
the "Lexical Integrity Hypothesis"); and it is a *multilevelled* theory,
which, by factoring different types of grammatical information into formally different levels of representation related to each other by principles
of correspondence, represents syntactic functions independently of the
phrase structure and accounts for alternations in syntactic functions (so-
called "grammatical function changes") not by derivational changes in
syntactic structure, but by allowing alternative correspondences among
units at the various levels.

The theory that I present in this chapter and that is assumed in the
remainder of the book shares these ideas with previous versions of LFG,
as well as many aspects of the formal representations. However, it also
differs from those versions in many ways. In order to keep the exposi-
tion simple, I will avoid making detailed comparisons with alternative
conceptions and formalizations within LFG, and will just give point-
ers for the interested reader to refer to. The first section presents the

15

levels of syntactic representation that are standardly assumed in LFG, namely, the c-structure and the f-structure, advancing a new proposal for the correspondence between them. In section 2.2, I introduce the a-structure, and present a proposal for its internal representation and for its mapping to other levels of structure, in particular, the mapping of arguments to syntactic functions. Section three brings in the topic of grammatical function alternations, exemplifying this phenomenon with the active-passive alternation. Section 2.4 outlines a proposal for the treatment of non-argument functions, such as discourse functions, raising functions, and expletive functions.

2.1 C-Structure and F-Structure

The syntactic information of any grammatical utterance is factored into three levels of representation: constituent structure, or c-structure, which encodes the surface arrangement of syntactic constituents, functional structure, or f-structure, which represents the syntactic functions (subject, object, etc.) of a clause, and argument structure, or a-structure, which expresses the information of a predicate relevant for its subcategorization. These levels are related to each other by correspondence principles or mapping principles. The well-formedness of any string of words depends on its being assigned a representation at each of these levels, which must satisfy not only the principles that apply internally to each level, but also the mapping principles—the principles that relate one level to the other. The sentence in (1), for example, is represented by the three structures shown in (2).

(1)   The girls read a novel in the garden.

(2) a. a-structure: 'read ⟨ Arg1 Arg2 ⟩'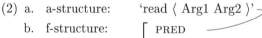

b. f-structure:
$$
\begin{bmatrix}
\text{PRED} & \rule[0.5ex]{2em}{0.4pt} \\
\text{TENSE} & \text{PAST} \\
\text{SUBJ} & \begin{bmatrix} \text{DEF} & + \\ \text{NUM} & \text{PL} \\ \text{PRED} & \text{'girl'} \end{bmatrix} \\
\text{OBJ} & \begin{bmatrix} \text{DEF} & - \\ \text{NUM} & \text{SG} \\ \text{PRED} & \text{'novel'} \end{bmatrix} \\
\text{OBL} & \begin{bmatrix} \text{PRED} & \text{'in} \langle \text{Arg} \rangle \text{'} \\ \text{OBJ} & \begin{bmatrix} \text{DEF} & + \\ \text{NUM} & \text{SG} \\ \text{PRED} & \text{'garden'} \end{bmatrix} \end{bmatrix}
\end{bmatrix}
$$

c.   c-structure:

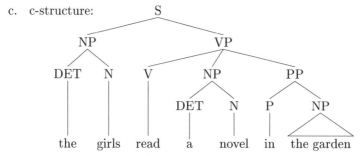

As we shall see, the representation at some of these levels, in particular, a-structure, will have to be made more elaborate as we proceed. Unlike a-structure, which has only recently been introduced as a formal level of representation, c-structure and f-structure have been an integral part of LFG since the appearance of this formal framework. I will therefore have little to add to what is standardly assumed about c-structure and f-structure, although I will propose changes in the representation of grammatical functions, in 2.1.1, and will propose a new theory for the mapping of these two levels of structure in the remainder of this section. In 2.1.2, I propose a formal representation for the pairing of c-structures and f-structures, and in 2.1.3 I propose principles for the assignment of gramatical functions on the basis of c-structure information; an illustration of this theory is given in 2.1.4.[1]

2.1.1   Internal Organization

As can be seen in (2c), c-structure is a representation of dominance and precedence relations among syntactic constituents, such as NP, V, S, etc., formalized as a familiar phrase structure tree. C-structure is formed according to X$'$ theory. I assume a maximally simple X$'$ theory in which there are only two levels of projection: X^0 and XP. According to this theory, every lexical item of a major category (N, V, A, and P) is immediately dominated by a phrasal constituent whose categorial information is determined by its lexical daughter. This lexical item, or X^0, is the head of a phrasal constituent, or XP. XPs may have either a lexical category X^0 or a phrasal category XP as their head daughter. In addition, there is a phrasal category S, which is not the projection of any lexical head; for this category we need a special rule that licenses it as the mother of NP and VP in languages like English. Most of what needs to be said about c-structure concerns the mapping of c-structure to f-structure, which will be dealt with in the next subsections.

---

[1]The development of this theory owes a lot to discussions with K. P. Mohanan, although he may not agree with specific aspects of the theory.

F-structure is represented as an attribute-value matrix that expresses information such as the grammatical functions (subject, object, oblique, etc.) of a sentence and the syntactic features relevant for agreement, case, etc.[2] In earlier versions of LFG, grammatical functions were generally assumed to consist of atomic labels, that is, unanalyzable attributes: the grammatical function attributes SUBJ or OBJ had the same status as the grammatical feature attributes NUM or DEF in that they were all atomic. However, it can be shown that it is necessary to make generalizations over groups of grammatical functions and that these clusters of grammatical functions behave alike for a variety of syntactic phenomena, which justifies decomposing grammatical functions into features that define natural classes of grammatical functions.

The idea that syntactic functions are decomposed into primitive features originates in work by Simpson (1983) and Levin (1986) and has enjoyed much acceptance in recent work in LFG. The proposal articulated here, however, departs from the version of decomposition found in works such as Bresnan and Kanerva 1989, Bresnan and Moshi 1990, Bresnan and Zaenen 1990, Alsina and Mchombo 1993, Alsina 1992a, to appear, etc. The criterion used to establish the set of features that make up syntactic functions is that each feature should divide the set of syntactic functions into two natural classes that behave homogeneously with respect to an important number of grammatical processes. Thus, the featural decomposition of syntactic functions should capture the natural classes of direct and indirect functions, on the one hand, and of subject and nonsubjects, on the other hand, both of which groupings have been recognized in many theories. (See Alsina 1993 for cross-linguistic evidence supporting these natural classes.)

The existence of a large number of phenomena across languages that refer to both subjects and objects, opposing them to obliques, indicates the need to define the class of *direct functions* (or *terms*). (*Term* is the expression used in the Relational Grammar (RG) literature (e.g., Perlmutter and Postal 1974, 1983) and in Kiparsky 1987 to designate this class.) The direct/oblique distinction plays a role in many phenomena cross-linguistically: binding, control, agreement, affixal or null pronominalization, case/prepositional marking, etc.[3] This distinction correlates

---

[2]An f-structure is a function in the mathematical sense, since every attribute takes a unique value. Thus, the formal representation of grammatical functions is a mathematical function. See Kaplan and Bresnan 1982:182 for the double sense of the term *function* as a mathematical notion and as a grammatical notion.

[3]Examples of such phenomena include the following: reflexive binding in Albanian, where a direct function, unlike an oblique, can only be anteceded by a direct function (see Sells 1988); control in English and Marathi, where only a direct function can

with whether or not a syntactic function expresses a specific semantic role independently of the verb or predicate it occurs with. As noted in Andrews 1985:81–82, direct grammatical functions "tend to express a wider range of semantic roles," whereas obliques (or indirect functions) "can for the most part be identified with their semantic roles." Likewise, many phenomena cross-linguistically single out the subject among the direct functions, opposing it to all other grammatical functions.[4] This points to the need to make a formal distinction between the subject and other grammatical functions, grouping the latter as nonsubjects. As we shall see in what follows, the principles that map grammatical functions to c- and a-structure categories appeal to the four proposed natural classes of grammatical functions.

These natural classes of grammatical functions can be formally captured by means of two binary valued features: the feature [obl(ique) ±] distinguishes between direct functions ([obl +]) and indirect functions or obliques ([obl −]), and the feature [subj(ect) ±] characterizes subjects ([subj +]) and nonsubjects ([subj −]). These two features group grammatical functions into the classes shown in (3) and define specific grammatical functions through the combinations of feature values indicated by connecting lines in (3).

(3)
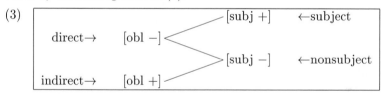

So, for example, direct functions may be either subject or nonsubject (i.e., object) depending on whether the feature [obl −], which characterizes direct functions, combines with the feature [subj +], yielding a subject, or the feature [subj −], yielding an object. As the diagram in (3) indicates, the feature [subj +] can only combine with the feature [obl −], expressing the claim that subjects are necessarily direct

---

be a controller (see Bresnan 1982a and Joshi 1993 respectively); verbal agreement in Ojibwa and Southern Tiwa, which is triggered by all and only direct functions (see Rhodes 1990 and C. Rosen 1990a respectively); etc.

[4] The following properties are recurrently found to be exclusive of subjects: the ability to trigger grammatical agreement on the verb (see Bresnan and Mchombo 1987 for Chicheŵa), the ability to antecede reflexives (see K. P. Mohanan 1982 for Malayalam), occupying a position external to the VP (in languages for which this constituent is motivated, such as English), being the unexpressed constituent of clausal complements of raising and control verbs, showing *that-trace* effects (for example, in English), etc. (See Keenan 1976 for a survey of properties that characterize the grammatical function subject.)

functions.[5] Hence, the possible combinations of specifications of the two features yield the three types of grammatical functions shown in (4).

(4)

$$\begin{bmatrix} \text{subj} + \\ \text{obl} - \end{bmatrix} (= \text{SUBJECT}) \qquad \begin{bmatrix} \text{subj} - \\ \text{obl} - \end{bmatrix} (= \text{OBJECT}) \qquad \begin{bmatrix} \text{subj} - \\ \text{obl} + \end{bmatrix} (= \text{OBLIQUE})$$

As a consequence of this, the f-structure attributes SUBJ, OBJ, etc., are no longer atomic labels, as is standard practice, but are attribute-value matrices. I will, nevertheless, sometimes use those labels as abbreviatory conventions, replacing the corresponding feature matrices.

There is an asymmetry between the subject and the other grammatical functions. On the one hand, a clause nucleus (a predicate and its associated grammatical functions) may not include more than one subject, although it may include more than one object and more than one oblique. This is the uniqueness of the subject, a property of subjects that is acknowledged by all grammatical frameworks. On the other hand, a clause nucleus that corresponds semantically to a proposition must include a subject, although it need not include any other grammatical function. This is the obligatoriness of the subject, which is embodied in the "Final 1 Law" of RG (Perlmutter and Postal 1974, 1983), in the "Extended Projection Principle" of GB (Chomsky 1981), and in the "Subject Condition" of earlier LFG (Baker 1983).[6] These two requirements, which apply exclusively to subjects, can be stated as the following *Subject Condition*:

(5)   *Subject Condition*:

An f-structure with propositional content must include a subject (as one of its grammatical functions) and no f-structure may include more than one subject.

It might appear that the uniqueness of the subject should be independently required by the general condition of *Uniqueness* (or *Consistency*)

---

[5]The specification [subj −] is predictable in a grammatical function specified as [obl +] (an oblique), and the specification [obl −] is predictable in a grammatical function specified as [subj +]. However, these predictable specifications are not redundant, as they allow us to refer to the natural class of nonsubjects, consisting of objects and obliques, and to the natural class of direct functions, consisting of subjects and objects, by means of the feature values [subj −] and [obl −] respectively. As we shall see, there are principles that make use of these feature values and they apply to all grammatical functions with the appropriate specification, even when predictable.

[6]The claim that the obligatoriness of the subject is an absolute universal has been questioned (for example, by T. Mohanan (1994), Bennis (1986), and Zaenen (in preparation)). I shall take it to be, if not an absolute universal, at least the unmarked parameter setting.

(see Bresnan 1982a, Kaplan and Bresnan 1982, etc.), which f-structures must satisfy. Uniqueness requires that every f-structure attribute must take a unique value. However, I am assuming that grammatical functions are distinguished by their mapping to argument structure, so that two grammatical functions that correspond to different arguments are treated as distinct attributes even if they have the same featural composition in terms of (4), and therefore they don't violate Uniqueness. A way to distinguish formally the attributes of grammatical functions that map onto different arguments is proposed in section 2.2.3. Thus, a clause structure may include two or more objects, grammatical functions defined by the feature structure [obl −, subj −]. The reason why the subject is unique, therefore, cannot be due to the general condition of Uniqueness, but must follow from an explicit requirement to that effect, as in (5).

I take here the strong position that, leaving aside the discourse functions (TOPIC and FOCUS), the only distinctions in terms of grammatical functions that the theory allows are those shown in (4). Every in-clause grammatical function must belong to one of the three types given in (4). This means that distinctions that in previous versions of LFG were made in terms of grammatical functions are assumed here to be made at other levels of representation, which makes it unnecessary to replicate the distinction at the level of grammatical functions. For example, objects are all OBJ, i.e., [obl −, subj −]: for the distinction formalized in earlier LFG between OBJ and OBJ2/OBJ$_\theta$, see chapter 5 for the Romance languages, and Alsina 1993 also for other types of languages. The expressions that were previously distinguished as OBL and ADJ are here all OBL, although the distinction is still made, more appropriately, at another level (see 2.3.4). Similarly, the categories COMP, XCOMP, and XADJ of earlier LFG are absorbed into the three grammatical function types in (4).

2.1.2 Pairing of C-Structures and F-Structures

It is clear that f-structures and c-structures do not exist in isolation, but come in pairs. We have just seen that there are principles that operate internally to each level. Now we shall see how the correspondence between nodes in the c-structure and feature structures in the f-structure are constrained. Previous approaches to this problem propose a highly elaborate procedure for mapping c-structures onto f-structures according to which each c-structure node is annotated with equations that indicate the mapping of that node onto an f-structure in relation with the mapping of the immediately dominating c-structure node (see, for example, Kaplan and Bresnan 1982). In this way, an f-structure representation is derived from an annotated c-structure tree by following the instructions on the c-structure. While normally one thinks of mapping principles as constraints on the correspondence between levels of representation that have themselves no place in the formal representation, the functional annotations in standard LFG are mapping constraints attached to one of the levels of representation. I wish to propose a view of the mapping between c-structure and f-structure in which the mapping principles are not formally included in either of the two structures or in an intermediary level such as the annotated c-structure of earlier LFG, but are simply constraints that license the correspondence between pieces of the c-structure and pieces of the f-structure. In earlier LFG, the c-structure formation rules, that is, the rules that generate c-structures, such as X′ theory, include the correspondence principles between c-structure and f-structure, in the form of functional equations. By having the same set of rules perform two functions (formation and mapping), we fail to uncover, or, at least, to express in a perspicuous way, the generalizations about each of the two functions. I propose to factor out these two functions: this allows us to indicate clearly which regularities in the mapping of c-structure to f-structure are inviolable universals, which are recurrent universals, and which are language-particular statements.

Much of the information in both the c-structure and the f-structure comes from the lexical entries of the lexical items used. Lexical entries include c-structure information, such as the phonological representation and the syntactic category of the lexical item, and f-structure information represented as an attribute value matrix or f-structure. Let us assume that the c-structure and the f-structure information of a lexical entry is linked. The linking or correspondence between pieces of different formal structures can be formally represented in different ways. One way is to have a line connecting the two pieces of structure: a line connecting an f-structure to a c-structure node represents a correspondence between the two structures. Another way is to coindex the two pieces of structure: identity of indices on an f-structure and a c-structure node represents a correspondence between the two structures. The lexical entries of the items in the noun phrase *the girls* of sentence (1) are given in (6) using these alternative notations.

(6) a. the: DET_1 $\begin{bmatrix} DEF & + \end{bmatrix}_1$ $\quad$ $DET \text{---}\begin{bmatrix} DEF & + \end{bmatrix}$

$\quad$ b. girls: N_1 $\begin{bmatrix} NUM & PL \\ PRED & \text{'girl'} \end{bmatrix}_1$ $\quad$ $N \diagdown \begin{bmatrix} NUM & PL \\ PRED & \text{'girl'} \end{bmatrix}$

It should be clear that a pairing of c-structure and f-structure can have its correspondence signalled either by coindexation or by connecting lines, as shown by the alternative representations in (6). The two notations are equivalent, that is, notational variants. The choice between the two is, thus, not an empirical issue, but a matter of visual clarity. It is for this reason that the coindexation device is chosen here. If the device of connecting lines were used instead, it is easy to see that, as the structures become molt complex, the number of lines increases and the representation becomes very hard to interpret.

When a lexical entry is used in the syntax, its c-structure information is represented in c-structure and its f-structure information is represented in f-structure directly, without going through the intermediate step of representing the f-structure information in an annotated c-structure (as in Kaplan and Bresnan 1982:185). Coindexation (or connecting lines), as in (6), is a means of keeping track of the correspondence between the f-structure representation and the c-structure representation of the same lexical item. A well-known property of the mapping of c-structures and f-structures is that the f-structure does not show all the hierarchical relations of the c-structure. The head of a phrase (at c-structure), as well as minor categories such as determiner, maps onto the same f-structure as the phrase it is the head of. We can represent this correspondence of different c-structure nodes to the same f-structure (or *co-linking*) by having each c-structure node involved either joined by a line or coindexed with a single f-structure. (7a) and (7b) illustrate these two alternative representations for the NP *the girls*, which includes the information provided by the lexical entries in (6).

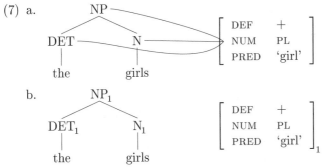

Once again the two notations are shown in (7) to emphasize their formal equivalence. In addition to being easier to interpret in complex structures, the coindexation notation has another advantage over the device of connecting lines: it represents co-linking, that is, the mapping of several units at one level of structure to a single unit at another level, on the c-structure alone. If two c-structure nodes have the same index, we don't need to represent the f-structure in order to know that they map onto the same f-structure. With connecting lines, on the other hand, it is necessary to have the c-structure and the f-structure side by side in order to represent co-linking.

One property that the paired c- and f-structures in (7) represent is that the information in a given f-structure may be provided by two different lexical entries and therefore correspond to different terminal nodes in the c-structure. The information in the f-structure in (7) is the result of unifying the f-structure information of the lexical entries of *the* and *girls*, given in (6a) and (6b). Two sets of f-structure features may combine into one single feature matrix, or f-structure, as long as no featural inconsistency arises. The principle of Consistency, or unification, must be satisfied—see Pollard and Sag 1987 and Shieber 1986 for the notion of unification. What (7) shows is that there is not a one-to-one correspondence between units in the c-structure and units in the f-structure: two or more c-structure nodes may correspond to one single feature matrix (or f-structure) in the f-structure. We assume two asymmetries in the mapping between c-structure and f-structure: (a) every c-structure node must have a correspondence in f-structure, while every f-structure need not have a correspondence in c-structure, which allows for the possibility of grammatical functions with no overt expression, and (b) the mapping to f-structure is unique, whereas the mapping of f-structure to other levels such as c-structure is not required to be unique. This is expressed by the following two principles:

(8)   *C- to F-Structure Mapping*:

Every c-structure node maps onto f-structure.

(9)   *Uniqueness of F-Structures*:

Each f-structure is uniquely identified by its index.

By (9), no two f-structures may have the same index. This entails that a given c-structure node cannot map onto two different f-structures, because, in order to map onto the same c-structure node, the two f-structures would have to have the same index, which violates the Uniqueness of F-Structures. This principle is relevant not only for the mapping of c-structures to f-structures, but, as we shall see, also for the mapping of a-structures to f-structures.

The combination of principles (8) and (9) derives the standard assumption that the mapping of c-structure to f-structure is a function in the mathematical sense (Bresnan 1994b): a (mathematical) function yields a unique value for each argument it is applied to. Given the notation of coindexation to indicate mapping of c-structure to f-structure, it follows that, since every c-structure node is coindexed with some f-structure, in accordance with (8), and two distinct f-structures cannot have the same index, by (9), every c-structure node must map onto one and no more than one f-structure.

For every phrasal node in the c-structure we have a choice whether to assign it the same mapping to f-structure as one of its daughter constituents or a different mapping. I assume that we don't need any ad hoc principle to constrain this choice, but rather that this choice is determined by independently required principles that license f-structures. We observe, for example, in a structure such as the one given in (7), that the NP node is assigned the same mapping to f-structure as its two daughter constituents, the determiner and the head noun. This reflects a general pattern of the mapping of c-structures to f-structures, namely, that a maximal projection maps onto the same f-structure as its lexical head and that minor categories such as determiners must also map onto the same f-structure as the lexical head of the phrase they are daughters of. It appears that this result can be achieved without ad hoc principles enforcing this correspondence. In a well-formed f-structure, every f-structure must be the value of a grammatical function, unless it is the matrix f-structure (corresponding to the root S node). If the two daughters of NP in (7) mapped onto different f-structures, the f-structure corresponding to the determiner would lack a PRED feature and would not be licensed as the value of a grammatical function. If the NP node was assigned a different mapping to f-structure from its daughters, the f-structure (or f-structures) corresponding to its daughters would not be licensed as the value of a grammatical function. What grammatical function may correspond to a given c-structure node will be discussed in the next subsection.

A maximal projection is sometimes assigned the same index (i.e., the same mapping to f-structure) as its mother node and sometimes not. This, once again, depends on general well-formedness conditions on f-structures. Consider the mapping to f-structure of the NP *the girls* in relation to its mother node in example (1). This NP, as shown in (2c), has a VP as its sister. This VP, for the reasons just indicated, must be coindexed with its head verb (i.e., must map onto the same f-structure). Since both the NP and the VP have a different PRED specification, provided by their lexical heads, they cannot map onto the same f-structure, as the two PRED features cannot unify. Thus, the NP *the girls* and its sister VP in (2c) must have different indices, that is, different mapping to f-structure. Now, their mother node S could not have a different index from each of its daughters, because, if it did, its f-structure correspondent would lack a PRED, and, thus, the f-structures corresponding to each of its daughters would not be licensed. If the S had the same index as its NP daughter, the f-structure of the VP would not be licensed as a grammatical function and it would not satisfy the Subject Condition (5) because it would lack a subject. Therefore, the only mapping that woud satisfy all f-structure well-formedness conditions is the one in which the S and its VP daughter have the same index, which is different from that of the NP daughter, as shown in (10).

(10)

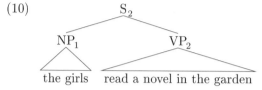

So, here we see that a maximal projection, the VP daughter of S, is assigned the same index as its mother, whereas another maximal projection, the NP daughter of S, is assigned a different index from its mother. This result is achieved without any specific indexing principle.

When an f-structure is constructed alongside a c-structure, the part-whole relations in the c-structure are partially preserved in the f-structure. This requirement of parallelism in the part-whole relations of the two structures can be formally stated as in (11):

(11)   *Part-Whole Parallelism*:

> If c-structure node α dominates c-structure node β, the f-structure coindexed with β is included[7] in the f-structure coindexed with α.

In order for a c-structure such as the one in (10) to satisfy the Part-Whole Parallelism in its mapping to f-structure, it may map onto an f-structure such as (12a), but not onto f-structures such as (12b–c), where GF stands for any grammatical function.

(12) a. $\begin{bmatrix} \\ \text{GF} \quad [\ ]_1 \\ \end{bmatrix}_2$ b. $^*\begin{bmatrix} \\ \text{GF} \quad [\ ]_2 \\ \end{bmatrix}_1$ c. $^*\begin{bmatrix} \text{GF} \quad [\ ]_1 \\ \text{GF} \quad [\ ]_2 \end{bmatrix}$

The pairing of (10) and (12a) satisfies the Part-Whole Parallelism (11) because the f-structure that maps onto the mother node S includes the f-structures of the daughters of S: the f-structure of the NP is a subsidiary f-structure and the f-structure of the VP is the same f-structure as that of S. The pairing of (10) and (12b) does not satisfy this principle, because the part-whole relations are reversed, and the pairing of (10) and (12c) does not satisfy the principle either, because the part-whole relations of (10) are not preserved in (12c).

---

[7]F_1 includes F_2 iff all of the information in F_2 is represented in F_1. Consequently, either F_2 and F_1 are the same f-structure or F_2 is a subsidiary f-structure of F_1.

2.1.3   Assignment of Grammatical Functions

The previous subsection has presented a formalism for the pairing of c-structures and f-structures such that every node in the c-structure corresponds to a feature matrix (or f-structure) in the f-structure. As I have mentioned earlier, every f-structure except for the one that corresponds to the root S must be the value of a grammatical function. The assignment of specific grammatical functions, such as subject or object, to the f-structure correspondents of particular c-structure nodes is not random. (In what follows, I refer to this, for short, as the assignment of grammatical functions to c-structure nodes.) The principles that constrain this assignment are sensitive, in some languages, to morphological properties such as case, and, in other languages, to properties of the c-structure or to a combination of both kinds of properties. In a language with a system of rich morphological case, such as Hindi-Urdu, the morphological case of a constituent constrains the grammatical function that it is assigned: for example, simplifying somewhat, if an expression has ergative case, it must be the subject, and, if it has accusative case, it must be an object (see T. Mohanan 1994, and Butt 1993). Often, in this kind of language, configurational properties of the c-structure play no role in the assignment of grammatical functions to constituents. Unlike what happens in *configurational* languages such as English, the distinction between subject and object in *nonconfigurational* languages like Hindi-Urdu does not correlate with a consistent testable distinction in the surface position of the corresponding constituents.

Configurational languages such as English exhibit an asymmetry between subjects and nonsubjects in the phrase structure encoding of these grammatical functions. The configurational asymmetry between subjects and nonsubjects, represented in (13), establishes that the sister of the VP head of a sentence maps onto the subject, whereas a sister of a lexical head corresponds to a nonsubject function.

(13)   *Configurational Subject/Nonsubject Asymmetry*:

a.

$$
\begin{array}{c}
C_2 \\
\diagup\,\diagdown \\
XP_1 \quad , \quad VP_2
\end{array}
\quad\longrightarrow\quad
\left[\ [\text{subj} +]\quad [\ \ ]_1\ \right]_2
$$

b. $XP_1 , Y \quad\longrightarrow\quad \left[\ [\text{subj} -]\quad [\ \ ]_1\ \right]$

XP stands for any maximal projection, C stands for any category, and Y stands for the lexical head of a major category (V, N, A, or P). The c-structure representations in (13) only indicate the immediate dominance and sisterhood relation of two categories, not their linear order: so, "XP , Y" signifies that the two phrases are sisters (i.e., immediately dominated by the same node), regardless of the order they may appear in. (13a) establishes that the f-structure correspondent of the XP sister of a VP coindexed with its mother is a subject. (13b) allows an XP sister of a lexical head to map only onto a nonsubject. The use of the feature [subj ±] in the decomposition of grammatical functions allows us to refer to subject and nonsubject in a maximally simple way. By specifying the grammatical function in (13b) only as [subj −], we allow it to be any nonsubject function, that is, either an object or an oblique; whether it is one or the other depends on other principles of the theory (for example, (14)).

These constraints are stated as unidirectional implications; in other words, not all subjects map onto an XP sister of VP, and not all nonsubjects map onto an XP sister of a lexical head. This is because there are grammatical functions that do not map onto any c-structure node: for example, the anaphorically controlled null subject of tenseless clauses in English and other languages, phonologically null grammatical functions in languages with so-called "pro-drop", etc. Catalan, like other Romance languages such as Spanish, Portuguese, and Italian, freely allows the subject of tensed clauses to be phonologically null, thanks to the pronominal function of the verbal subject agreement morphology. In such cases, a phonologically null subject is a gramatical function (represented as such at f-structure) that corresponds to no c-structure constituent. However, assuming a maximally simple X′ theory in which all (argument) XPs are introduced as sisters of a lexical head except for the daughters of S, which (in languages like English) takes a VP as its head, it will follow that, if a subject maps onto a c-structure node, it maps onto an XP sister of VP, and, if a nonsubject maps onto a c-structure node, it maps onto an XP sister of a lexical category.

A further constraint that has been noted on the correspondence between c-structure nodes and grammatical functions is that, in the unmarked case, a nominal category (N or NP) maps onto a direct function and a prepositional category (P or PP) maps onto an oblique function. This asymmetry in the f-structure correspondence of nouns and prepositions is captured in (14):[8] (14a) states that a noun maps onto a direct function, and (14b) states that a preposition maps onto an oblique,

---

[8]Bresnan (1994c:104) states a principle similar to (14a) as follows: "If C is a c-structure position restricted to subjects or objects, then C is nominal." Such a principle presupposes a classification of c-structure positions as being restricted either to subjects and objects or not. This is undesirable, since the purpose of principles such as (14) is precisely to determine whether a c-structure position is a position of direct functions (subject or objects) or of obliques.

provided the preposition and its XP sister have a different mapping to f-structure, i.e., different indices.

(14)   *C-structure Encoding of Direct and Indirect Functions*:

    a. $N_1 \longrightarrow \begin{bmatrix} [\text{obl} -] & [\ ]_1 \end{bmatrix}$

    b. $P_1 , XP_2 \longrightarrow \begin{bmatrix} [\text{obl} +] & [\ ]_1 \end{bmatrix}$

The reason why a preposition is only required to map onto an oblique if its sister has a different index is to allow for semantically empty prepositions that function merely as case-markers: the PP headed by such a preposition will (in the default) map onto a direct function, as will be argued in 5.2 to be the case with dative objects in the Romance languages. The constraints in (14) make crucial use of the feature [obl $\pm$], which classifies grammatical functions into direct and indirect (or oblique) functions. In the absence of such a featural decomposition of grammatical functions, the natural classes of direct and indirect functions would have to be designated by a list or a disjunction of labels.[9]

The principles in (14) should be viewed as default principles, which can be overriden by more specific constraints. For example, it can be argued that in languages with rich systems of morphological case noun phrases can map onto oblique functions provided they bear an appropriate case specification (an oblique case feature). In such languages, the requirement that an NP with an oblique case feature map onto an oblique function will override principle (14a), which has the effect of mapping an NP onto a direct function. In languages without morphological case distinctions, an NP can sometimes map onto an oblique function, provided it occupies a special c-structure position. In the Bantu languages Runyambo (Rugemalira 1993) and Haya (Duranti and Byarushengo 1977), the passive oblique is expressed as an NP immediately following the verb: in these languages, a rule licensing precisely this correspondence will override principle (14a). Thus, the principles in (14) can be viewed as expressing the generalizations that an NP is the unmarked c-structure

---

[9]The featural decompositions of grammatical functions of Bresnan and Kanerva 1989, Bresnan and Moshi 1990, Alsina 1992a, Bresnan 1994c, among others, fails to capture these natural classes without disjunctions. The class of direct functions consists of the grammatical functions that in the works cited are designated as SUBJ, OBJ, and OBJ$_\theta$. SUBJ and OBJ have in common the feature [−r] (unrestricted), and OBJ and OBJ$_\theta$ have in common the feature [+o] (objective), but there is no feature common to SUBJ and OBJ$_\theta$. Since there is no single feature common to these three functions, they must be referred to by the disjunction of the features [−r] and [+o]. Similarly, there is no single feature that refers exclusively to obliques, which must be referred to as [+r, −o].

realization of a direct function, and a PP is the unmarked c-structure realization of an oblique.[10]

A point that needs to be emphasized about the principles just proposed for the mapping of c-structures and f-structures (unlike the functional annotations in standard LFG) is that they are not language particular stipulations, but they are universal principles that are subject to cross-linguistic parametrization. Principles (13) and (14) are not valid only for English, but for a wide variety of languages: they are therefore parametric universal principles. If a language is argued to lack a VP node, as Malayalam is in K. P. Mohanan 1982, not surprisingly this node cannot be used to distinguish between subjects and nonsubjects, and thus the principles in (13) will be assumed to be inactive (not to apply) in such a language. In place of these principles, this language will have other principles to encode the distinction between subjects and nonsubjects.

2.1.4   An Example of Function-Category Mapping

We are now in a position to illustrate the operation of the function-category mapping principles proposed in this section. Let us take the f-structure and c-structure in (2a) and (2b) respectively, which describe the sentence in (1), and see what the correspondence between them is. For expository reasons, we will proceed in a step by step manner, starting with one piece of structure and adding more structure as we go along. (But note that there is no procedure involved in the generation of syntactic structures.) We first need the lexical entries of all the lexical items involved in the sentence, which are given in (15).

(15) a. the: DET_1 $\begin{bmatrix} DEF & + \end{bmatrix}_1$

     b. girls: N_1 $\begin{bmatrix} NUM & PL \\ PRED & \text{'girl'} \end{bmatrix}_1$

     c. read: V_1 $\begin{bmatrix} PRED & \text{'read}\langle \text{ Arg1 Arg2 }\rangle\text{'} \\ TENSE & PAST \end{bmatrix}_1$

---

[10]Bresnan 1994c argues that the preposed locative in inversion constructions in English such as *Into the room walked the man* is linked to the subject function, although this linking is not licensed by its occupying the position of NP daughter of S (i.e., the subject position), but because it occupies a position in which it is assigned a discourse function such as TOPIC, which allows it to fill the subject function. In order to accommodate this analysis, we would have to assume that PPs of the kind under discussion would have to have their mapping to f-structure licensed either as an oblique, by principle (14b), or as a discourse function. In the latter case, principle (14b) would not have to be satisfied and the PP would be allowed to map onto a direct function such as the subject. See section 2.4 for a proposal for the treatment of discourse functions.

d. a: DET_1 $\begin{bmatrix} \text{NUM} & \text{SG} \\ \text{DEF} & - \end{bmatrix}_1$

e. novel: N_1 $\begin{bmatrix} \text{NUM} & \text{SG} \\ \text{PRED} & \text{'novel'} \end{bmatrix}_1$

f. in: P_1 $\begin{bmatrix} \text{PRED} & \text{'in} \langle \text{Arg1} \rangle \text{'} \end{bmatrix}_1$

g. garden: N_1 $\begin{bmatrix} \text{NUM} & \text{SG} \\ \text{PRED} & \text{'garden'} \end{bmatrix}_1$

We have already seen in (7) what the c-structure representation of the NP *the girls* is and what its correspondence to f-stucture is. In connection with (10) we saw that the root node S, which immediately dominates this NP, must have the same index (i.e., the same mapping to f-structure) as its daughter VP, which, in turn, must have the same index as its lexical head. So, ignoring for the moment everything except for the part of the c-structure that is coindexed with the root S, we obtain the following paired c- and f-structures:

(16) S_1 $\begin{bmatrix} \text{PRED} & \text{'read} \langle \text{Arg1 Arg2} \rangle \text{'} \\ \text{TENSE} & \text{PAST} \end{bmatrix}_1$

         $|$

        VP_1

         $|$

         V_1

         $|$

       read

(16) is constructed using only the information of the lexical item *read*, which is given in (15c). The c-structure information of this item is that it is a verb; as such it must project a VP, according to the X' theory. In addition, this VP is the daughter of S. For the reasons given earlier, the three c-structure nodes shown in (16) must be coindexed, that is, they map onto the same f-structure. This f-structure (so far) contains only the information provided by the single lexical item used in (16).

The NP *the girls* of sentence (1) occupies the position of daughter of S and must have a different index from its mother, as shown in (10). If we include this NP in the representation we are constructing, we shall combine the paired structures in (7b) with the paired structures in (16), yielding the (incomplete) representations in (17). For the reasons stated in connection with (10), the NP in (17) must have a different index from its mother S and, thus, must map onto a different f-structure. Given the Part-Whole Parallelism (11) that must hold between c-structures and f-structures, the f-structure correspondent of the NP, with index 2 in this example, must be included in the f-structure correspondent of the S, with

(17)

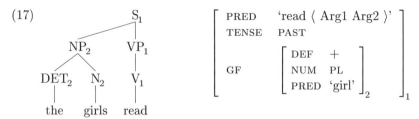

index 1 in this example, as it is in (17). The f-structure correspondent of the NP has to be the value of a grammatical function (GF), as it is not the matrix f-structure. This grammatical function is left unspecified in (17); what its full specification should be follows from the c-structure constraints on grammatical function assignment presented in 2.1.3.

The verb *read* in sentence (1) is followed by an NP, *a novel*, and a PP, *in the garden*. By the same kind of reasoning as has been given earlier in connection with the NP *the girls*, these two constituents have a different index from their mother node (and from the verb), which means they map onto different f-structures, as we see in (18). For the moment, the content of the NP and PP sisters of the verb both at c-structure and at f-structure is not represented. These two constituents, like the NP *the girls*, map onto f-structures each of which is the value of a grammatical function. In (18), these grammatical functions are specified, in accordance with the principles (13) and (14).

(18)

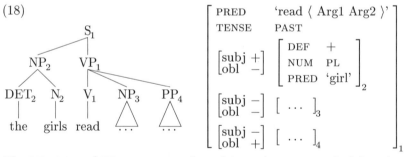

The NP sister of VP maps onto the subject, the grammatical function defined by the features [subj +] and [obl −]. This is required by the principles given above: (13a) requires the NP sister of the main VP in a sentence to map onto a subject ([subj +]) and principle (14a) requires a nominal category to map onto a direct function ([obl −]). The NP sister of V maps onto an object function, defined as [subj −] and [obl −]: principle (13b) requires a category sister of a lexical category to map onto a nonsubject, [subj −], and principle (14a) requires a nominal category to map onto a direct, [obl −], function. The PP sister of V maps onto an oblique function, [subj −] and [obl +]: as a sister of the lexical category V it must be a nonsubject, by (13b), and as a PP (whose daughter NP has a different index) it maps onto an indirect function, by (14b).

We will now include, in (19), the structures associated with the NP and the PP following the verb in the representation in (18). The paired c-structure and f-structure of sentence (1) are shown in (19), using the coindexation notation to indicate linking between the two structures. Here and subsequently, for greater visual clarity, the grammatical function names SUBJ, OBJ, etc., are used instead of the corresponding feature matrices, such as [subj +, obl −].

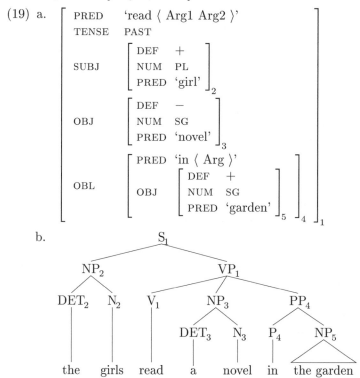

The f-structure of the NP *a novel* is the result of unifying the f-structure information of the two lexical items that compose this NP, whose entries are given in (15d) and (15e). In order for the f-structure information of these two lexical items to be represented as the same f-structure, they must map onto the same f-structure: in other words, the corresponding c-structure nodes are coindexed. The PP *in the garden* maps onto an f-structure whose information is determined by that of the head P *in*, which is given in (15f); therefore, the PP and the head P are coindexed.

The NP daughter of this PP has its c- and f-structure determined by its component lexical items, the determiner *the*, (15a), and the noun *garden*, (15g). This NP maps onto an object function, as required by the GF assignment constraints (13b) and (14a). And, by the Part-Whole Parallelism (11), the f-structure of this NP is included in the f-structure of the PP.

We have just seen how we can construct the c-structure and the f-structure of a sentence side by side. Although this has been shown in a step by step manner for expository purposes, there is no procedure involved in the generation of c-structures and f-structures. In addition to the well-formedness conditions applying internally to each of the structures, every pair of c- and f-structures corresponding to a linguistic object must satisfy constraints on the linking or association between the two types of structures. This section has focused mainly on these linking constraints. We have seen, for example, that the NP sister of the main VP of a clause maps onto the subject function. Thus, the NP *the girls* in (19) is (i.e., maps onto) the subject of the clause. What we have not yet provided an account of is why the subject in (19) is interpreted as the 'reader', rather than the 'thing read', whereas the object is interpreted as the 'thing read', rather than the 'reader'. We know that, by the Subject Condition (5), the f-structure in (19a), which has propositional content, must include one and only one subject. But, given the matrix predicate information in (19), must the corresponding f-structure include an object? Can it include more than one object? In order to answer these questions, we need to provide principles relating the argument structure of predicates to their semantic representations, on the one hand, and to their associated f-structures, on the other hand. These are the issues addressed in the next section.

2.2   A-Structure

Argument structure, or a-structure, is the information of predicates provided in their lexical entries that is necessary for constraining the syntactic structures in which they may appear and that underlies their alternative subcategorization frames. The a-structure is a level of representation that is related, on the one hand, to the semantic (or lexical-conceptual) representation, and, on the other hand, to the representation of grammatical functions (or f-structure). The a-structure of a predicate is constrained (and partially determined) by the semantics of the predicate; in its turn, the a-structure constrains the grammatical functions that the predicate may take. The present study adheres to the hypothesis that the a-structure is the interface between the lexical semantic representation of predicates and their syntactic subcategorization in terms of grammatical functions. In spite of its importance in the development of LFG as a linguistic framework, a-structure (sometimes referred to as "predicate argument structure" or PAS in earlier work, as in Bresnan 1980, 1982b, among others) has remained a relatively unstructured level of representation even in this framework until recently.

In this section I will propose the formal representation of a-structure that will be adopted in this study and the principles that associate arguments (the units at a-structure) with grammatical functions. This representation involves a ranking of arguments, presented in 2.2.1, and a classification of arguments into three types, in 2.2.2. Both the ranking and the classification of arguments are determined by semantic properties of the arguments. We can thus say that there is a set of mapping constraints relating the semantic representation of predicates, which specifies the semantic entailments of predicates, to their a-structure, which includes no semantic information. At the same time, the a-structure constrains the realization of arguments in terms of grammatical functions: the principles governing the correspondence between arguments and grammatical functions is presented in 2.2.3.

2.2.1   The Prominence Ranking of Arguments

A-structure contains the information of lexical entries that is relevant for determining the set of syntactic functions associated with a predicate and the correspondence of syntactic functions to semantic arguments. It expresses that which is invariant across morphologically related forms of the same predicate. While an active form and the corresponding passive, for example, may differ considerably in the syntactic functions that they take and in the semantic roles associated with their syntactic functions, the a-structure that underlies the two forms is largely the same: the passive morphology adds a specification to one of the arguments (the one that would normally be the subject in the active form) that will prevent it from being the subject.[11] This change in the argument structure triggers a different association of arguments to syntactic functions from the one that obtains in the active form.

Certain regularities have been found to hold in the correspondence

---

[11] Here and in what follows, I use the term *argument* in a very restrictive sense, to refer only to the units of the a-structure. An *argument* is what has also been called an *argument role*, a *lexical role*, an *argument slot*, a *thematic role* or *θ-role*, etc. I do not use the term "argument" to refer, for example, to a constituent in the c-structure. Arguments are elements of the a-structure, just as syntactic functions are elements of the f-structure and constituents are elements of the c-structure. Thus, there are no arguments in the c-structure, only constituents that may correspond to arguments.

between arguments and syntactic functions that have motivated grouping semantically similar arguments into types of arguments, or *thematic roles*. For example, take a predicate whose thematic roles are agent (a participant that causes an event, and/or controls it, and/or is volitionally involved in it) and patient or theme (a participant that is affected by the event, and/or undergoes a change of state or location). It has been observed (as early as in Gruber 1965 and Fillmore 1968) that, for such a predicate, the agent is associated with the subject function, while the patient or theme is associated with the object function, as a default, in an active form in syntactically accusative languages. This has suggested to many researchers that arguments in an a-structure should be represented as thematic roles in order to express generalizations about the correspondence between arguments and syntactic functions.

However, the existence of regularities in function assignment, in patterns of agreement, noun incorporation, idiom formation, etc., holding across a-structures involving different thematic roles has been taken to indicate that the specific thematic role of an argument is not as relevant as its position in relation to the other arguments in the a-structure. This motivates the proposal of organizing arguments at a-structure according to a Universal Hierarchy of Thematic Roles. An early proposal concerning this hierarchy can be found in Jackendoff 1972, and it has subsequently been developed in Ostler 1979, Foley and Van Valin 1984, Givón 1984, Mithun 1984, Kiparsky 1987, Bresnan and Kanerva 1989, Jackendoff 1990, etc. The version of the hierarchy adopted here, given in (20), follows Bresnan and Kanerva 1989, 1992.[12]

(20)   *Thematic Hierarchy:*

$$ag > ben > goal/exp > ins > pt/th > loc$$

This hierarchy imposes its ordering on all a-structures, so that any two roles in an a-structure reflect the prominence ranking determined by this hierarchy: an agent is more prominent than a goal, a beneficiary is more prominent than a patient, etc.

One of the consequences of having the arguments at a-structure ranked by prominence is that it allows us to identify the most prominent argument in an a-structure. All predicates that have at least one argument have a maximally prominent argument: this argument is referred to as the *logical subject*,[13] as in Kiparsky 1987, Bresnan and Kanerva

---

[12]The abbreviations used in (20) and elsewhere for thematic roles are: *ag* for "agent," *ben* for "beneficiary," *exp* for "experiencer," *pt* for "patient," *th* for "theme," and *loc* for "locative."

[13]The term *logical subject* should not be taken to mean "the expected subject" from an English-speaking or Eurocentric perspective, implying that those languages whose

1989, and others. The notion of logical subject has been shown by Kiparksy 1987, Joshi 1989, 1993, T. Mohanan 1994, among others, to be needed independently of the notion of grammatical subject for determining syntactic phenomena, such as the antecedent of reflexives, the controller in certain control structures, etc.

I assume, following K. P. Mohanan 1989, T. Mohanan 1994, and Grimshaw 1990, among others, that, although arguments are ordered in the a-structure according to their thematic role, thematic role information is not represented at a-structure. This is for two reasons: nonredundancy and restrictiveness. In the first place, as argued in K. P. Mohanan 1989 and T. Mohanan 1994, among others, if thematic information is represented in the lexical semantic representation of predicates, it would be redundant to replicate this information elsewhere, as in the a-structure. In the second place, a theory that claims that the syntactic properties of arguments are determined without direct reference to thematic information, as has been hypothesized by Belletti and Rizzi 1988, Grimshaw 1990, and other work, is more restrictive than a theory that does not hypothesize the inaccessibility of thematic information to syntax.[14]

While it seems desirable for linguistic theory to include the hypothesis of the inacessibility of thematic information to syntax, there are clear cases in which syntax is constrained by semantic information such as thematic roles. For example, certain case morphemes and adpositions are sensitive to thematic roles or other semantic information such as animacy, definiteness, etc. However, it seems reasonable to subsume such instances under "semantic selection," the phenomenon by which a lexical unit (word or morpheme) requires some semantic property on the constituent it combines with (either in the syntax or in the morphology). If we assume that only lexical units, including case morphemes and adpositions, may impose semantic selectional restrictions, we are making the claim that direct constraints of semantics on syntax must be signalled

---

grammatical subject diverges more or less systematically from the logical subject are less "logical" than languages like English. The adjective *logical* in the expression "logical subject," as well as in other expressions found in the literature such as "logical relations," "logical form," etc., is used in opposition to *grammatical*, as in "grammatical subject," and is roughly synonymous with "thematic" or "semantic."

[14]The inaccessibility of thematic information to syntax has sometimes been disputed, as in Alsina and Mchombo 1991, where thematic information is argued to make a greater contribution to a-structure and, consequently, to syntax than is often acknowledged. However, the phenomenon discussed in Alsina and Mchombo 1991 is shown in Alsina 1993 not only to be consistent with the hypothesis of the inaccessibility of thematic information to syntax, but, in fact, to be inconsistent with the assumption that syntactic principles may refer to thematic information.

by overt morphology. Elsewhere, where no morphology is involved, syntactic principles, such as mapping principles, are barred from accessing semantic information, and thus can only refer to the a-structure, which contains no semantic information such as thematic information. The claim being made is, then, that a semantic effect on syntax is either reflected in the a-structure or in the morphology. For example, given the assumption that thematic roles are not part of the a-structure, it follows that a principle relating arguments to grammatical function cannot refer to thematic roles *unless* it is a morphologically encoded principle. Thus, subject selection can be sensitive to thematic roles *only* if the predicate is marked with some overt morphology whose function is to signal the thematic role of the subject, as is the case in Tagalog (see Kroeger 1993). This predicts that there cannot be a principle without any associated morphology stating "the predicate's goal or beneficiary is the subject," which seems to be correct.

I thus assume that a-structure is a level of representation (or a type of information) that is derived from the lexical semantic representation by abstracting away and adding information in a principled way: a-structure retains from the lexical semantic representation the information about the number of arguments of a predicate, on which an ordering is imposed according to the thematic hierarchy. As in Grimshaw 1990, the thematic hierarchy plays a role in the mapping from the lexical semantic representation, where thematic information is expressed, to the a-structure, where arguments are ordered according to the thematic hierarchy, but where there is no thematic information. In addition, arguments are further classified in a way that is constrained by their semantic properties, as we shall see now.

2.2.2 The Proto-Role Classification

I adopt the assumption here that the argument structure information is represented as the value of the PRED feature in the f-structure.[15] Given the view of a-structure presented here, the lexical entries for *come* and *give* would have their a-structures represented as follows:

(21) a. come: V_1 [PRED 'come $\langle$ Arg1 Arg2 $\rangle$']$_1$

　　 b. give: V_1 [PRED 'give $\langle$ Arg1 Arg2 Arg3 $\rangle$']$_1$

The representation in (21a) does not indicate that the first argument of *come* is a theme and the second one a locative, nor does the represen-

---

[15]While previous versions of LFG have generally assumed that the PRED value includes an array of fully specified syntactic functions, the present proposal does not include any specifications of syntactic functions in the PRED feature. In the present approach, syntactic functions are represented only as attributes in the f-structure.

tation in (21b) indicate that the first argument of *give* is an agent, the second one a goal, and the third one a theme. All that these representations indicate is the number and ordering of the arguments. However, the number and ordering of arguments in an argument structure is clearly not sufficient for determining the assignment of syntactic functions. If this were all we had, the a-structure of *come* would be identical to that of *read*, and the a-structure of *give* would be identical to that of *put*, which would grossly underdetermine their syntactic properties. For example, on the basis of the number and order of arguments, it would be impossible to know that *come* does not passivize, while *read* does, since both have two arguments, or that the third argument of *give* (the theme) is expressed as an NP object, while the third argument of *put* (the locative) is expressed as a prepositional oblique.

It follows that the a-structure needs to be enriched. We need to be able to determine which arguments will be expressed as direct functions (subject and objects) and which will be expressed as obliques. Among the arguments that are normally expressed as direct functions, we need to distinguish between those that can normally alternate between subject and object, which we can refer to as *internal arguments*, and those that are invariably expressed as the subject of an active sentence in a language like English, which we can call *external arguments*.[16] The argument expressed as an object in an active transitive sentence in English is an example of an internal argument: it is realized either as an object (in the active form) or as a subject (in the passive form). The argument that corresponds to the subject of the active form of such a verb is an example of an external argument: it cannot normally alternate with an object function. The notion of external argument is similar, but not identical, to that of *logical subject* (see 2.2.1). The logical subject is determined solely on the basis of the hierarchical ordering of arguments: it is the highest argument in an a-structure. Thus, all argument-taking predicates have a logical subject. However, not all logical subjects are external arguments: for example, the distinction within

---

[16]The term "external argument" was first proposed by Williams (1980, 1981) to designate a diacritically distinguished argument in a sense roughly equivalent to that of grammatical subject. Subsequent work (by Belletti and Rizzi (1988), Rappaport and Levin (1989), Grimshaw (1988, 1990), etc.) has reinterpreted this term, assuming that whether an argument is external or not is, at least in part, determined by the semantics. Originally, the term "external argument" was chosen to indicate that the argument in question was represented in the phrase structure (at d-structure) as an NP *external* to the predicate or VP. In the present work, as in other current theories, such as Bresnan and Zaenen 1990 and Grimshaw 1990, that term is retained although it is not assumed that the external argument is represented as a specific phrase structure configuration.

intransitive verbs between unaccusatives and unergatives (first proposed in Perlmutter 1978a) can be reduced to the idea that the logical subject of an unergative is an external argument, whereas the logical subject of an unaccusative is an internal argument.

It is thus necessary to distinguish at a-structure among: (a) the external argument, the argument that in so-called nominative-accusative languages like English is invariably expressed as the subject in simple active clauses, (b) internal arguments, which alternate between the subject and object functions, and (c) other arguments, which are neither external nor internal and are typically expressed as obliques. In what follows I propose to adopt and modify some ideas in Dowty 1991 so as to capture these syntactically relevant distinctions among arguments on the basis of their semantic properties. Dowty 1991 proposes that arguments can be classified as more or less prototypical *Proto-Agents* or *Proto-Patients* depending on the number of semantic entailments characteristic of either *Proto-Role* (or *P-Role*) that each argument has. Rather than treating the proto-role scale as a gradient or continuous one, as in Dowty (1991), I propose to treat it as providing three discrete categories: arguments are classified as either *P-A* (for Proto-Agent), *P-P* (for Proto-Patient), or neither, depending on whether each argument has or doesn't have key semantic properties of either P-Role. Thus, the P-Role classification of arguments can be seen as a classification by means of a feature that can be positively or negatively specified, as well as unspecified. (See Zaenen 1993, for another adaptation of Dowty's (1991) ideas.)

Let us assume that, if an argument is an "incremental theme" (that is, the argument of a telic predicate—an achievement or an accomplishment—that serves to measure the completion of the event), or "undergoes a change of state," or "is causally affected by another participant," it is necessarily classified as a P-P. On the other hand, the properties of "causing an event or change of state in another participant" and "volitional involvement" seem to be determining properties of the P-A classification; a third property, "sentience (and/or perception)," also appears to be relevant for the P-A classification, but only if the argument has none of the P-P entailments mentioned. Arguments that have none of these key properties are unspecified for the P-Role classification. The chart in (22) schematizes the relation between the semantic entailments of arguments and their P-Role classification:[17]

---

[17]There are in all probability other properties that need to be taken into account for determining the P-Role classification, and languages may vary somewhat in the choice of key P-Role properties. For example, Joshi (1993) proposes "nonentailment of sentience" as a Proto-Patient property, which seems to be necessary to predict the "objecthood" of certain arguments that would otherwise have no P-Role properties in

(22) Proto-Role Classification of Arguments:

	P(roto)-A(gent)	P(roto)-P(atient)
Primary Properties	causer volitional involvement	incremental theme undergoes change of state causally affected
Secondary Property	sentience/perception	

There is, in addition, an asymmetry between P-A arguments and other arguments in that the P-A argument of a predicate, if it has one, is the most prominent one in the a-structure. This condition may not have to be explicitly stated in the theory, as it probably follows from the way the thematic hierarchy (20) interacts with the P-Role classification of arguments: if any argument has the P-A classification, it has to be the most prominent argument.[18] (This does not mean that the most prominent argument has to be P-A, since there may be no P-A argument in an a-structure.) A consequence of this is that a predicate may have at most one P-A argument: if it had two, one of them would not be the most prominent argument in the a-structure. On the other hand, nothing excludes an argument having multiple P-P or unspecified arguments. In this connection, it is important to note that prominence ranking of arguments only holds among co-arguments, that is, arguments of the same minimal predicate. The relevance of this becomes apparent when dealing with complex predicates such as causatives, where more than one predicate is involved and each may have its own P-A argument.

An important function of the P-Role classification of arguments is to define the notions of *direct argument* (and its opposite *indirect argument*) and of *external* and *internal argument*. Arguments with a P-Role classification are direct arguments, whereas those that lack a P-Role classification are indirect arguments. This distinction is important because only direct arguments are accessible to operations and principles that refer to a-structure, such as binding and suppression and the mapping principles. In a sense, then, indirect arguments occupy a very marginal position in a theory of argument structure, since they hardly play any

---

Dowty's (1991) system, such as the stimulus of perception verbs. In addition, Joshi 1993 shows that, in Marathi, the equivalent of the P-A classification in the present system is determined solely by the entailment of volitional involvement. The present proposal should be taken as an approximation to deriving syntactically relevant distinctions from semantic properties.

[18] Dowty 1991 outlines a proposal for deriving the thematic hierarchy from the Proto-Role entailments of arguments; according to this proposal, an argument with more Proto-Agent entailments than another argument outranks the latter.

role at all. The distinction between P-P and P-A arguments serves to define the former as internal arguments. As for the external argument, although in simple cases it always corresponds to the P-A argument, it cannot be defined simply as a P-A argument, because of the existence of complex predicates with more than one P-A argument where, nevertheless, only one of the P-A arguments is the external argument. For this reason, the external argument is defined as the P-A argument of the most inclusive (or least embedded) a-structure. (In a complex a-structure, an a-structure is more inclusive than another one when the latter is contained entirely in the former; thus, in a structure such as $\langle a \ldots \langle b \ldots \rangle\rangle$, the a-structure labelled "a" is more inclusive than the a-structure labelled "b.") The notion of external argument is important for the principles that map arguments to functions, as well as for other syntactic properties of arguments. The three a-structure notions just mentioned are defined in terms of the P-Role classification, as shown in (23), where the symbol "X" represents any predicator.

(23)   *Direct argument*:   [P-A] and [P-P]

          Internal argument: [P-P]

          External argument: 'X $\langle$ [P-A] ...$\rangle$

Adding the P-Role classification of arguments to the a-structures in (21) we obtain the PRED values shown in (24).

(24) a. come: V_1 [PRED 'come $\langle$ [P-P] [ ] $\rangle$']$_1$

     b. give: V_1 [PRED 'give $\langle$ [P-A] [(P-P)] [P-P] $\rangle$']$_1$

The logical subject of *come* is classified as a P-P: it is an incremental theme (the argument that serves as a measure for the completion of the event). This defines the predicate as an unaccusative—a predicate whose logical subject is an internal argument. The second argument of *come* (the locative) is not classified as either P-P or P-A, as it has none of the semantic entailments that determine either of these classifications: it is therefore an indirect argument. The logical subject of *give* (the agent) is classified as a P-A: it causes an event, and is typically sentient and volitionally involved. As the P-A argument of the most inclusive a-structure, it is defined as an external argument. The second argument of *give* (the goal) receives an optional P-P classification depending on whether it is interpreted as causally affected by another participant or not: by the principles to be discussed in the next sections, this difference determines whether it is expressed as an object or as an oblique *to*-phrase.[19] The third argument of *give* (the theme) has P-P entailments, including incremental themehood, which make it a P-P or internal argument.

In sum, the a-structure, which is the value of the PRED feature of argument-taking predicates, encodes the number and ordering of arguments. A-structure does not include thematic information, but, instead, the P-Role classification of arguments, which is constrained by their semantic properties. This classification plays a crucial role in function-argument mapping, as we shall see next.

2.2.3 Mapping to Grammatical Functions

Syntactic functions have the role of linking arguments to morphosyntactic expressions. Arguments are mapped onto syntactic functions, which in turn correspond to particular morphosyntactic realizations. Syntactic functions are, therefore, interface categories between arguments at a-structure, which connect syntax with semantics, and overt expressions at c-structure, which connect syntax with phonology. The theory that deals with the correspondence between arguments and syntactic functions is the *Functional Mapping Theory* (FMT).[20]

The principles of the FMT are constraints on the correspondence between arguments and syntactic functions. Since the a-structure is the value of the feature PRED of the f-structure, the principles of the FMT can be seen as constraints operating internally to the f(unctional)-structure (hence the adjective "functional" in "*Functional* Mapping Theory"), relating two different types of units of the f-structure: arguments, which are part of the feature PRED, and syntactic functions, which are represented as f-structure features. This correspondence or linking between arguments and grammatical functions will be notated by means of the

---

[19] As noted by Jackendoff (1990:199), "the Goal is easier to construe as Beneficiary" when expressed as an object than when expressed as an oblique. A beneficiary is a special kind of patient in Jackendoff's (1990) system, and a patient is defined as an affected argument. Thus, it is likely that whether the goal is interpreted as an affected argument or not determines its P-Role classification and consequently its expression as a direct or an oblique function.

[20] The FMT has a lot in common with the *Lexical Mapping Theory* (LMT), developed in Bresnan and Kanerva 1989, Bresnan and Moshi 1990, Bresnan and Zaenen 1990, Alsina 1992a, Alsina and Mchombo 1993, and other recent work within LFG. Nevertheless, the two mapping theories differ in many ways: regarding the decomposition of syntactic functions, the representation of a-structure, and the correspondence between arguments and functions. In addition, the LMT was originally conceived as effecting the assignment of syntactic functions to arguments in the lexicon; in the present theory, this assignment is assumed to take place entirely in the syntax since lexical items exit the lexicon with PRED features such as those in (24) containing no information about syntactic functions.

same kind of indices that have been used in the previous section to signal the correspondence between grammatical functions and c-structure nodes.[21] Argument ARG and grammatical function GF are said to be linked or to map onto each other when the index of ARG is the same as the index of the f-structure value of GF, as in the following representation:

(25)
$$\left[\begin{array}{ll} \text{PRED} & \text{`X}\langle \dots [\,]_1 \dots \rangle\text{'} \\ \text{GF} & [\,]_1 \end{array} \right]$$

The mapping principles have to express the following two generalizations: that the external argument is realized as the subject, and that internal arguments are realized as direct functions. These principles are formalized in (26) and (27) respectively, where the symbol 'X' represents any predicator.

(26) *External Argument Mapping Principle:*

$$\left[\text{PRED } \text{`X}\langle [\text{P-A}]_1 \dots \rangle\text{'} \right]_2 \longrightarrow \left[\begin{bmatrix} \text{obl} & - \\ \text{subj} & + \end{bmatrix} [\,]_1 \right]_2$$

(27) *Internal Argument Mapping Principle:*

$$\left[\text{PRED } \text{`X}\langle \dots [\text{P-P}]_1 \dots \rangle\text{'} \right]_2 \longrightarrow \left[[\text{obl} -] \; [\,]_1 \right]_2$$

These principles are stated as conditional implications that are to be interpreted in the following way: any f-structure that satisfies the f-structure schema in the antecedent of the conditional must be subsumed by the feature structure in the consequent. Thus, the External Argument Mapping Principle (26) says that an f-structure whose PRED value contains an external argument must include a subject coindexed with the external argument; and the Internal Argument Mapping Principle (27) says that an f-structure whose PRED value contains an internal argument must include a direct function coindexed with that internal argument. The decomposition of grammatical functions into the features [subj ±] and [obl ±] allows us to formulate these mapping principles by referring to underspecified grammatical functions, as in (27). This principle maps a P-P argument onto a direct function, which can be either a subject

---

[21] In fact, the same indices can be assumed to signal the mapping to *semantic structure* (or *s-structure*), which represents the semantic information of sentences. See Halvorsen 1983 and Dalrymple 1993 for proposals about s-structure in LFG. Given the assumption made here that the information in a-structure is semantically motivated, it follows that every argument at a-structure has semantic content and, therefore, maps onto a piece of structure in a semantic representation (s-structure). Thus, the indices on arguments, which signal this mapping, can be thought of as referring to their semantic representation.

([subj +]) or an object ([subj −]); in other words, either a subject or an object satisfies mapping principle (27).

Any theory has to guarantee that the subcategorization requirements of a predicate are satisfied, namely, that the syntactic structure include all the grammatical functions required by the predicate and no spurious ones. This is partly accomplished by the mapping principles: as they are stated as conditional implications, whenever the a-structure contains the right type of argument (external or internal), there must be a corresponding function of the right type (subject or object).[22] Thus, the mapping principles ensure expression in terms of grammatical functions for all external and internal arguments, unless there is a stipulation to the contrary. However, nothing so far excludes the possibility of syntactic functions that have no correspondence to a-structure. In fact, this possibility should not be excluded entirely, but should not be allowed without restriction either. Oblique functions occur quite freely in syntactic structures where they have no correspondence to a-structure: they are adjuncts. And there are direct functions that are not licensed by mapping onto an argument of the a-structure, such as expletives (see section 2.4).

Notice that the mapping principles given in (26)–(27) only refer to direct functions: there is no principle that maps an argument onto an oblique function. This absence is not accidental, but follows from a fundamental distinction between direct and indirect functions, namely, that whereas the semantic role of a direct function is determined solely by its governing predicate, the semantic role of an oblique, or indirect function, is determined, at least in part, by some element other than its governing predicate—typically, an adposition or a case marker. This suggests that direct functions must be licensed by their predicate, that is, by mapping onto an argument of their governing predicate, whereas obliques don't even have to map onto an argument of their predicate. Thus, we can assume that a direct function is licensed only if it satisfies

---

[22]The mapping principles, stated as (26)–(27), allow us to dispense with the wellformedness condition of *Completeness* of standard LFG, which ensures that all subcategorized functions are represented in the f-structure. In the present model, Completeness does not have to be stipulated as it follows from the FMT mapping principles, as far as direct functions are concerned. As for oblique functions, as we shall see, the FMT treats them as optional in the default case. In order for an indirect argument to be obligatorily expressed, we need to override this default by lexically stipulating the obligatoriness of the argument. Conversely, the expression of internal and external arguments is treated as obligatory in the default; we thus need to allow the possibility of lexical stipulations licensing such arguments to be unexpressed for those cases in which they are optional.

one of the mapping principles. This is stated in the well-formedness condition *Coherence* in (28).[23]

(28)   *Coherence*:

Every direct function must be licensed by a mapping principle.

Thus, the mapping principles of the FMT have the double role of assigning direct functions to arguments and, by Coherence, of licensing direct functions. For example, an f-structure containing an object that maps onto an internal argument of the predicate is well-formed because it satisfies (a) the requirement imposed by the Internal Argument Mapping Principle (27) that an internal argument must map onto a direct function and (b) the requirement imposed by Coherence (28) that a direct function, such as an object, must be licensed by a mapping principle. However, an f-structure with an internal argument in its PRED feature but with no direct function coindexed with that argument is ill-formed (unless a marked specification allows this absence of mapping), because it fails to satisfy mapping principle (27). Likewise, an f-structure containing an object that does not map onto an argument of the predicate is ill-formed, because it violates Coherence as the object is not licensed by a mapping principle.

Coherence does not affect oblique functions, which, therefore, can be used with any predicate whatsoever, subject only to semantic compatibility. Any verb can take a locative phrase, a temporal modifier, a manner adjunct, etc., provided there is no semantic inconsistency, and the semantic contribution of the phrase is signalled by the adposition or case marking of the phrase. The coindexation between an oblique and an argument is not governed by any mapping principle, but only by semantic adequacy or by morphological requirements of the oblique, as with the passive oblique (see section 2.3.2).

Many grammatical theories assume that the pairing of arguments and syntactic functions must be in a one-to-one correspondence, enforced by principles such as the "Theta-Criterion" of Chomsky (1981), and "Function-Argument Biuniqueness" of Bresnan (1980). This study will show that it is wrong to require a biunique correspondence between syntactic functions and arguments, even allowing for the possibility of unexpressed arguments (arguments that don't map onto any syntactic

---

[23]Coherence in earlier LFG (Bresnan 1982a and Kaplan and Bresnan 1982) is stated as a condition on the set of "governable functions," a heterogeneous list of functions that can vary somewhat from language to language. In the present formulation, the set of governable functions is coextensive with the set of direct functions, which constitutes a natural class formally characterized by the feature [obl −]. We ignore here nonthematic functions, but, as we shall see in section 2.4, nonthematic functions have special licensing conditions that require a redefinition of Coherence.

function) and nonthematic functions (syntactic functions that don't map onto any argument): the correspondence can be one-to-many in both directions. The principles just mentioned rule out correspondences such as the following between arguments and grammatical functions:

(29) a. 'X⟨ ... ARG1   ARG2 ... ⟩'   b. 'X⟨ ... ARG ... ⟩'

                          GF   GF1   GF2

I will argue that both of these correspondences are attested. A large part of this study is devoted to showing that the correspondence schematized in (29a) in which two arguments map onto the same grammatical function must be allowed in linguistic theory, as it is required for the right analysis of the Romance reflexive clitic, among other constructions. Although arguing for the correspondence represented in (29b) is not such a central aspect of this study, I will propose it as part of the analysis of certain constructions with expletive subjects (see 2.4).

One of the main theoretical points that the present work will make is that linguistic theory should not require a one-to-one correspondence between arguments and functions. The bulk of the argument for this claim is based on empirical adequacy: a theory that requires such a correspondence is unable to give an adequate analysis of many facts that will be discussed in subsequent chapters. In addition, a theory that dispenses with a theoretical principle is preferred on grounds of simplicity over a theory that includes the principle in question. In the present theory, "Function-Argument Biuniqueness" is not replaced by another (possibly less restrictive) principle; it simply disappears. Some of the effects that might be attributed to Function-Argument Biuniqueness follow from the Uniqueness of F-Structures (9), which is independently required and is assumed in standard LFG as part of the algorithm for mapping c-structures onto f-structures. This is true of the situation represented in (29b), in which two grammatical functions map onto one argument. In this situation, the two grammatical functions must have the same f-structure as their value: since they map onto the same argument, their values must have the same index as the argument they map onto; by the Uniqueness of F-Structures (9), there cannot be two distinct f-structures with the same index, but they must be the same f-structure.

The formal problem raised in 2.1.1 in connection with the possibility of having multiple instances of the same type of grammatical function, for example, two objects, can be formally solved by assuming that the index that is part of the f-structure value of a grammatical function is copied as part of the attribute of a grammatical function. For example, in an f-structure containing two objects (i.e., two grammatical functions

whose attribute is made up of the same features, [obl −, subj −]), each
of the two objects has a different index as part of its attribute, that of its
f-structure value, which allows them to take different values. Thus, the
structure does not violate Uniqueness, which requires each f-structure
attribute to take a unique value. So, OBJ_3 and OBJ_4 are allowed to
cooccur in the same f-structure because they are different attributes
and therefore take different values.

2.3 Active/Passive Alternation

Having spelled out the principles that make up the FMT, we can now
illustrate how this theory operates in constraining the correspondence
between a-structure and grammatical functions. Of particular interest
is to show what the effect of passive morphology is on an a-structure
and how the mapping theory predicts the correct alternation of syntactic
functions in pairs of active and passive sentences. We will first exemplify
the FMT with an active sentence, in 2.3.1. In 2.3.2, we will see the effect
of the passive morphology on the same a-structure and, through the
FMT, on the mapping to grammatical functions. We will discuss the
passive oblique in 2.3.3 and obliques in general in 2.3.4.

2.3.1 The Active Structure

At the end of section 2.1 the mapping between c-structure and f-
structure was illustrated for example (1), in (19). In order to complete the syntactic representation of this sentence we need to give its
a-structure with the linking to grammatical functions; we will then have
the three syntactic structures, a-, f-, and c-structure, linked to each
other. The a-structure of the predicate of (1), *read*, is given in (30),
where it is shown as the value of the f-structure feature PRED.

(30)   read: V_1 [PRED 'read $\langle$ [P-A] [P-P] $\rangle$']$_1$

This a-structure includes an external argument (the P-A argument) and
an internal argument (the P-P argument). The External Argument Mapping Principle (26) requires the external argument to be coindexed with
the subject. The Internal Argument Mapping Principle (27) requires
the internal argument to be coindexed with a direct function, an [obl−]
function. Either a subject or an object satisfies this mapping requirement; however, since the structure must include a subject coindexed
with the external argument, there cannot be another subject coindexed
with the internal argument, because the Subject Condition (5) rules out
a structure with two subjects. Therefore, the internal argument must
be coindexed with an object.

Thus, the f-structure that contains the PRED feature (30) must include a subject linked to the external argument and an object linked to the internal argument. In addition, there cannot be any other direct function: by Coherence (28) it would have to be licensed by one of the mapping principles and therefore would be coindexed with one of the arguments in (30); by the Uniqueness of F-Structures (see (9)), its f-structure value is unique and therefore would be the same as that of any other direct function linked to the same argument. As we shall see in section 2.4, if two grammatical functions have the same value, one of them must be nonthematic. Thus, since each argument maps onto at most one f-structure and an f-structure is the value of only one thematic function, it follows that each argument maps at most onto one thematic function. We shall also see in section 2.4 that an f-structure with the PRED value in (30) does not license any nonthematic function. As for indirect functions, they may occur freely in such an f-structure, subject to semantic compatibility with the main predicate. Indirect functions are not subject to Coherence and therefore need not map onto an argument of the predicate.

In conclusion, the f-structure of sentence (1), with the a-structure in (30) and specifying the mapping between a-structure and grammatical functions, is shown in (31).

(31)

$$
\begin{bmatrix}
\text{PRED} & \text{'read} \langle \, [\text{P-A}]_2 \ [\text{P-P}]_3 \, \rangle \text{'} \\
\text{TENSE} & \text{PAST} \\
\text{SUBJ}_2 & \begin{bmatrix} \text{DEF} & + \\ \text{NUM} & \text{PL} \\ \text{PRED} & \text{'girl'} \end{bmatrix}_2 \\
\text{OBJ}_3 & \begin{bmatrix} \text{DEF} & - \\ \text{NUM} & \text{SG} \\ \text{PRED} & \text{'novel'} \end{bmatrix}_3 \\
\text{OBL}_4 & \begin{bmatrix} \text{PRED} & \text{'in} \langle \, [\text{P-P}]_5 \, \rangle \text{'} \\ \text{OBJ}_5 & \begin{bmatrix} \text{DEF} & + \\ \text{NUM} & \text{SG} \\ \text{PRED} & \text{'garden'} \end{bmatrix}_5 \end{bmatrix}_4
\end{bmatrix}_1
$$

(31) shows that the external argument of 'read' maps onto the subject function, and the internal argument maps onto the object. The oblique function in (31) does not map onto any argument of 'read': it is an adjunct. If we put this f-structure beside the corresponding c-structure, shown in (19b), we see that, since arguments map onto grammatical functions complying with the FMT and grammatical functions map onto

c-structure nodes complying with the principles of function-category correspondence, there is also a correspondence between arguments and c-structure nodes. Although these two sets of mapping constraints don't relate arguments directly with c-structure nodes, the transitivity of the mapping relation allows us to say that, if argument A maps onto grammatical function G and grammatical function G maps onto c-structure node C, argument A maps onto c-structure node C. Furthermore, this relation is clearly indicated in the present notation through identity of indices. For example, the external argument in (31) is coindexed with the NP 'the girls' in (19b). This, together with the constraints relating a-structure to lexical semantic representations, allows us to assign the semantic role of 'reader' to this NP.

2.3.2 Passive

It is well-known that, in English and many other languages, many verbs, such as *read*, can appear in either an *active* or a *passive* structure. The active use of this verb is illustrated in example (1), with the syntactic representation given in (19) and (31). An example of its passive use is given in (32).

(32)   A novel was read in the garden.

A central topic of interest in theoretical linguistics has been how to express the commonalities and differences between an active sentence and its passive counterpart. It is clear that the semantic roles of the verb are the same in the active as in the passive construction and that these semantic roles are expressed by different syntactic constituents in the two constructions. For example, in the case of *read*, the "reader" role is expressed by the NP immediately preceding the verb in the active form, *the girls* in (1), but is unexpressed in the passive form, as in (32). (It could also be expressed as a *by*-phrase in the passive, as we shall see later.) And the role of the thing read is expressed by the NP immediately following the verb in the active form (1) and by the NP preceding the verb in the passive form (32). How can these alternative correspondences between semantic roles and morphosyntactic expressions be accounted for in a restrictive theory of grammar?

In the present theory, the principles that relate the various levels of representation (c-, f-, a-structure, and semantic structure) are the same for the active and the passive constructions. The reason why the two constructions have different syntactic structures is that the morphology associated with the passive adds a certain instruction to the a-structure that affects how the FMT applies to it. All morphemes, including the passive morpheme, carry information about their representation at the various levels of structure: semantics, c-structure, f-structure, and a-structure. When a morpheme combines with a stem to form a new lexical item, the derived form is the result of combining the information about the different levels of representation provided by the morpheme and by the stem. I assume that the passive morpheme includes in its lexical entry an underspecified a-structure that composes with the a-structure of a predicate to yield the passivized form of the predicate. The a-structure of the passive morpheme specifies the *suppression* of the logical subject.[24] In this theory, a suppressed argument is inaccessible to *f-structure internal* principles, including the principles of the FMT. An f-structure internal principle is a principle that operates on the f-structure (for example, relating an argument in the a-structure with a grammatical function) without regard to the c-structure realization of the arguments or functions involved. I propose to represent suppression formally by circling the index of the suppressed argument, signifying that the index cannot be referred to by f-structure internal principles. Thus, the a-structure of the passive morpheme indicates that its logical subject is suppressed (that is, has its index circled), as shown in (33).

(33) *Passive:* $\left[\ \text{PRED} \ \text{`P*} \ \langle \ [\ \ ]_{①} \cdots \rangle\text{'} \ \right]$

Passive is an incomplete predicate, which is indicated because its PRED value includes an unspecified predicator, notated with the symbol P^*, and an underspecified a-structure. As an incomplete predicate, it must undergo *predicate composition* with a complete predicate to yield a derived predicate, where the unspecified predicator of the incomplete predicate is replaced by the predicator of the complete predicate, and the two a-structures unify. Since the a-structure of the passive morpheme only specifies suppression of the logical subject, the predicate derived from composing the passive morpheme with a base predicate is identical to the latter except that its logical subject is suppressed.

When the passive morpheme in (33) composes with a complete predicate such as *read*, represented in (30), we obtain a derived predicate in which the logical subject of the base predicate is suppressed. The derived predicate contains all the information specified in the two component morphemes, as shown in (34).

(34) read+*pass*: V_1 $\left[\ \text{PRED} \ \text{`read} \ \langle \ [\text{P-A}]_{②} \ [\text{P-P}] \ \rangle\text{'} \ \right]_1$

---

[24]I use the term "suppression," as in Grimshaw 1988, 1990, Bresnan and Kanerva 1989, Alsina 1992a, etc., although I do not indend it to mean that the suppressed argument cannot be syntactically expressed, as seems to be the intention in those works. A suppressed argument can be expressed, as we shall see.

Since the a-structure constrains the grammatical functions associated
with it, and this a-structure is different from the corresponding active
a-structure in (30), it follows that it licenses a different assignment of
grammatical functions. We can see this in (35), which gives the syntactic structures corresponding to the passive example (32). As the logical
subject of the predicate in (34) is suppressed, it cannot be accessed by
f-structure internal principles, and therefore it is ignored by the FMT
principles. Consequently, it cannot be mapped onto a direct function
and, as it is not required to map onto any grammatical function, may
be left without a grammatical function assignment, as it is in (35a).
The P-P argument is mapped onto a direct ([obl −]) function by principle (27), and, in order to satisfy the Subject Condition (5), this direct
function has to be the subject, as the structure would otherwise lack
a subject. Also, as shown in the f-structure (35a), Coherence (28) is
satisfied because there is no direct function that is not licensed by a
mapping principle: the only direct function in the matrix f-structure is
the subject, which is licensed by principle (27).

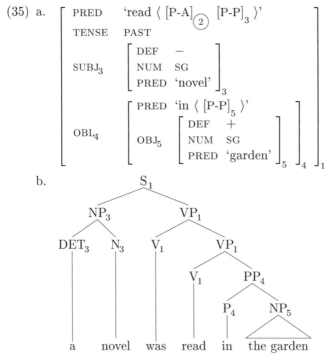

As we see in (35b), the c-structure of a passive sentence differs
from that of an active sentence (see (19b)). Since the f-structure (35a)

does not license an object associated with the matrix predicate, the c-structure cannot contain an NP sister of the verb, because this constituent would have to map onto an object by the principles of function-category association (13) and (14), which would result in an unlicensed grammatical function. Thus, we see that the syntactic representation of a passive sentence in the present theory does not involve an empty category corresponding to the object of the active sentence. Thus, for example, although *read* has an object in its active form, as shown in (19), its passive counterpart does not take an object at any level of representation, as we see in the f-structure in (35a) and the c-structure in (35b). What the object of an active sentence and the subject of the corresponding passive have in common is not expressed by assigning them the same phrase structure representation (as some theories assume), but by assigning them the same representation at the level of a-structure. The same argument maps onto an object in the active and onto the subject in the passive. This alternation is the result of applying the same set of principles to two minimally different a-structures: an active a-structure, such as (30), and a passive a-structure, such as (34), which only differ in that the logical subject is suppressed in one case (the passive) but not in the other.[25]

2.3.3   The Passive Oblique

The passive example (32) illustrates one of the possible assignments of grammatical functions to a passive a-structure: that in which the suppressed logical subject maps onto no grammatical function and therefore has no overt realization. In such cases, the unexpressed logical subject receives a generic or arbitrary interpretation, possibly as a consequence of a process that assigns such an interpretation to unexpressed arguments in general. Alternatively, as is well-known, the logical subject of a passive can be expressed as an oblique *by*-phrase, as in (36).

(36)   A novel was read by the girls in the garden.

The reason why it is possible to include the passive oblique in such an example is that obliques, unlike direct functions, are not licensed by the principles of the FMT, but can be used whenever their particular

---

[25] In addition to the difference in grammatical function assignment, active and passive structures differ in the morphology of the predicate. In English, the passive morpheme is the past participle. Since the past participle is a nontensed form of the verb, it follows that, in order for a passive verb form to be used as the main predicate of a clause, it must be accompanied by an appropriate auxiliary, namely, some form of *be*. This auxiliary verb and the passive verb form contribute their f-structure information to the same f-structure, in a manner similar to what will be proposed for syntactically discontinous complex predicates in chapter 6.

requirements are met in the clause. Although the logical subject of the passivized predicate is suppressed and, therefore, cannot be mapped by the FMT onto a direct function, nothing prevents it from being expressed by means of an *indirect* function. The preposition *by*, which introduces the passive oblique in English, establishes a correspondence between a c-structure category (the preposition) and an f-structure category (the logical subject). We can think of the lexical entry of *by*, given in (37), as a rule that licenses the passive oblique (similar to Jackendoff's (1990) *adjunct rules*). Therefore, this rule is not an f-structure internal principle, because it specifies some information about the c-structure realization of an argument, and, so, it can access a suppressed argument.

(37)   *Passive Oblique:*

$$\text{by:} \qquad P_1 \qquad \begin{bmatrix} \text{PRED} & \text{'X} \langle\, [\;]_1 \dots \rangle \text{'} \\ \text{GF} & [\, \text{PRED} \; \text{'by} \langle\, [\text{P-P}] \rangle \text{'}\,]_1 \end{bmatrix}$$

In this lexical entry it is unnecessary to specify that the grammatical function that maps onto the PP headed by *by* and onto the logical subject is an oblique. This is a result of the principles of function-category association, in particular, (14b), which requires argument-taking prepositions to correspond to an oblique function.

Notice that the structure in (37) does not require that the logical subject that is put into correspondence with the *by*-phrase be suppressed. This follows from the fact that there is no well-formed structure in which this argument is not suppressed and the passive *by*-phrase is used. If the logical subject were not suppressed, it would be mapped by one of the mapping principles (26)–(27) onto a direct function, normally a subject. If the passive oblique were used, the logical subject would also map onto an oblique. Thus, the logical subject would be coindexed with an f-structure that would be the value of both a direct function and an oblique. Such a structure is ruled out because, as will be argued in section 2.4, if two grammatical functions take the same f-structure as their value, one of the two must be nonthematic (i.e., not licensed by a mapping principle) and, if they are both in-clause functions, neither of them can be oblique. Consequently, the passive oblique can only be used with a passivized predicate, a predicate whose logical subject cannot be assigned a syntactic function by the FMT principles.

The systematic optionality of the passive oblique, illustrated in (32) vs. (36), is inherent in its being an oblique. Since there is no mapping principle that requires a particular argument to map onto an oblique, arguments that are expressed as obliques can (generally) be omitted. (Recall that obligatory obliques, a rather rare category, must be assumed to be marked with a lexical specification making them obligatory.) Since obliques are not subject to Coherence, they are not required to map onto an argument of the predicate: they may be adjuncts. Obliques can be used when their specific licensing conditions, such as (37), or semantic constraints are satisfied, but (generally) need not be used. The (schematic) f-structure of a sentence like (36), with a passive oblique, is given in (38).

(38)

$$
\begin{bmatrix}
\text{PRED} & \text{'read} \langle [\text{P-A}]_{\textcircled{2}} \ [\text{P-P}]_3 \rangle\text{'} \\
\text{TENSE} & \text{PAST} \\
\text{SUBJ}_3 & [(\text{a novel})]_3 \\
\text{OBL}_4 & \begin{bmatrix} \text{PRED} & \text{'in} \langle [\text{P-P}]_5 \rangle\text{'} \\ \text{OBJ}_5 & [(\text{the garden})]_5 \end{bmatrix}_4 \\
\text{OBL}_2 & \begin{bmatrix} \text{PRED} & \text{'by} \langle [\text{P-P}]_6 \rangle\text{'} \\ \text{OBJ}_6 & [(\text{the girls})]_6 \end{bmatrix}_2
\end{bmatrix}_1
$$

As in the f-structure in (35) of a passive sentence without a *by*-phrase, the logical subject cannot be licensed by the FMT, and the only other argument of the predicate is licensed by principle (27) as a direct function and further specified as the subject. In (38), in addition, an oblique is used which is licensed by the passive oblique rule (37); by this rule it is mapped onto the logical subject, constituting an oblique expression of the logical subject. This accounts for the fact that a passive sentence with a *by*-phrase, such as (36), is synonymous (ignoring differences in quantifier scope) with the corresponding active sentence (1): in both cases, the logical subject has an overt expression. Whereas in the active case it is expressed as a direct function licensed by an f-structure internal principle, in the passive case it is expressed as an indirect function licensed by a rule that directly relates an argument to its c-structure realization.

2.3.4 Obliques

Observe that, in this theory, it is unnecessary to introduce the category of *argument-adjuncts* proposed in Grimshaw 1990, distinct from both arguments and adjuncts, in order to account for the properties of the passive oblique. According to Grimshaw 1990, the passive oblique is like an adjunct in being optional, and like an argument in contributing information about a position in the a-structure.[26] Furthermore, the

---

[26]Notice that the term "argument" is used in this sentence as in Grimshaw 1990 to designate a c-structure constituent that is "theta-marked" by the predicate, that is, that corresponds to an argument role in the a-structure of the predicate.

assumption that the passive oblique is a kind of adjunct is forced in Grimshaw 1990 by the interpretation that suppression has in that theory: if a suppressed argument is one that cannot be syntactically satisfied, it follows that the passive oblique cannot be an argument because the argument it would satisfy is suppressed. Given the interpretation of suppression in the present theory (inaccessibility to f-structure internal operations), the possibility that a suppressed argument is syntactically satisfied is not excluded. If it is syntactically satisfied, it is realized as an oblique: this oblique is, therefore, the expression of the suppressed argument. The notion of logical subject supports the conclusion that the passive oblique is the expression of an argument, since the logical subject corresponds either to a grammatical subject in an active sentence, or to the passive oblique. Finally, the fact that the passive oblique is optional does not warrant assuming that it is an adjunct (albeit of a special kind), since, in the present theory, this property simply follows from its being an oblique.

In this theory, the notions of argument and adjunct are complementary and represented and defined at a-structure in conjunction with semantic structure. Both arguments and adjuncts are semantic participants and, hence, have a representation at semantic structure. Arguments are semantic participants also represented at a-structure, whereas adjuncts are not represented at a-structure. Given this complementarity in the definition of argument and adjunct, there is no room for the notion of "argument-adjunct." (What would be something that is and isn't represented at a-structure?) "Oblique," on the other hand, is a notion defined at f-structure: it is a type of syntactic function. Given the FMT, whereas direct functions can only correspond to arguments, obliques can correspond to either arguments (not licensed by the FMT principles) or adjuncts. There are, therefore, two kinds of obliques depending on the semantic participant they express: those that map onto arguments and those that map onto adjuncts.

The assumption that it is not just adjuncts that are optional, but obliques in general, seems to be contradicted by the existence of a few verbs that take obligatory obliques, of which the best-known example is *put*:

(39)   Mary put the book *(on the shelf).

As remarked in Jackendoff 1990:250, it is unlikely that a semantic account of the obligatoriness of oblique arguments such as those of *put* can be found: the oblique argument of *put*, *place*, and *set* is conceptually identical to that of *insert*, but is obligatory with the former verbs and optional with the latter. In the present theory, since optionality is a default property of obliques, the obligatoriness of these few cases has to be stipulated in the lexical entry of the relevant predicates. This treatment preserves the observation that adjuncts are always optional—since adjuncts are not part of the lexical entry of a predicate, it would not be possible to stipulate their obligatoriness—and the generalization that the vast majority of oblique arguments are optional, which is encoded as the default case in this theory. Examples of typical optional oblique arguments are given in (40) ((40a-b) based on Pollard and Sag 1987: 133–135), with (40c) representing the large class of locative arguments.

(40) a. Kim rented Apt. 3B (to Sandy).

  b. Kim complained (about the neighbors) (to the landlord).

  c. Kim fell/sat/was standing/... (on the mat).

While the optionality of these obliques represents the default situation in the present theory, it has to be stipulated in a theory such as Grimshaw's (1990), in which arguments, regardless of their morphosyntactic expression, are assumed to be obligatory.

Arguments such as those in (40) that are expressed as obliques are represented in the a-structure without a P-Role classification. Being indirect arguments (i.e., lacking a P-Role classification), they cannot be accessed by the mapping principles of the FMT, and so cannot be expressed as direct functions. As with the suppressed logical subject of passives, this accounts for the possibility of their being omitted and for the possibility of their being expressed by means of an oblique.

2.4 Nonargument Functions

The two preceding sections have been concerned with the principles that relate arguments to grammatical functions, or, conversely, that relate grammatical functions to arguments. However, there are various kinds of *nonargument* or *nonthematic* functions, about which the principles given so far have nothing to say. Intuitively, a nonargument function is a grammatical function that is not semantically selected by the predicate—the definition will be made more precise. In addition to adjuncts, which we have already briefly discussed, this includes (a) discourse functions (TOPIC or FOCUS), which correspond to fronted *wh*-phrases, topicalized constituents, etc., (b) raising functions (for example, the subject of *seem* taking an infinitival complement), and (c) expletive functions (such as existential and presentational *there*). The assumption that the information at a-structure is semantically based entails that expletive functions, which are semantically empty, should have no representation at a-structure. Likewise, raising functions bear no semantic relation to the raising verb and therefore should not be part of its a-structure. As for discourse functions, since any grammatical function can bear an additional discourse function, this possibility should not stipulated in the lexical entries of predicates. Consequently, we need a different set of principles from those already presented in order to account for nonargument functions.

I will first outline an account of discourse functions and their relations to in-clause grammatical functions such as subject, object, etc., in 2.4.1. This proposal will be necessarily sketchy, since there are many complexities involved in long distance dependencies (or "*wh*-movement") that cannot be adequately addressed in the present study, whose main topic— argument structure—is a very different one. In 2.4.2, I will present an analysis of raising functions, which has much in common with the treatment of discourse functions. And, finally, I will propose an analysis of expletive functions in 2.4.3.

2.4.1 Discourse Functions

Following standard assumptions in LFG, I will assume that long distance dependencies, or *wh*-movement in traditional transformational terminology, involve the assignment of a discourse function DF (such as TOPIC or FOCUS) to a constituent that also satisfies an in-clause function (such as SUBJ or OBJ). In a sentence such as (41), the fronted phrase *what* would be analyzed as bearing the discourse function FOCUS and, at the same time, the in-clause function OBJ.

(41)   What did the girls read in the garden?

The *wh*-phrase in this example is interpreted as the theme or internal argument of *read*; the internal argument of *read* in an active clause such as this is expected to be expressed as the object. Thus, we can say that the phrase *what* in (41) satisfies the object requirement of *read* and therefore corresponds to its internal argument. However, an object is normally expressed as a constituent immediately following the verb. What is it that allows the object in (41) to be expressed in the initial position of the sentence?

We can assume that *what* appears in a c-structure position that licenses the mapping of this constituent to a discourse function DF. A function-category association principle such as the following will ensure that a constituent C that is the sister of S will map onto a discourse function.

(42)   *C-structure Encoding of Discourse Functions*:

$$C_1, S_2 \longrightarrow \left[\begin{array}{c} DF \quad [\ ]_1 \end{array} \right]_2$$

Let us also assume that every semantically full grammatical expression must be integrated in the semantic representation of the sentence and interpreted as either an argument or an adjunct of some clause. This is possible if every meaningful expression is assigned an in-clause grammatical function such as SUBJ, OBJ or OBL. Then, every meaningful in-clause grammatical function is interpreted as an argument or an adjunct of the clause it is part of. In the case of discourse functions, this integration in the semantics of the sentence comes about by having the f-structure value of the discourse function be also the value of an in-clause grammatical function. Existing theories within LFG have proposed different mechanisms to achieve this result.[27] In the present theory, no specific mechanism is needed to achieve this: nothing we have said so far prevents the f-structure value of one grammatical function to be the value of another grammatical function. We shall see that the possibility of two (or more) grammatical functions taking the same f-structure as their value has to be severely restricted. For the moment, let us assume that this option exists at least when one of the grammatical functions involved is a discourse function and that no special principle need be invoked in order to license this option.

Let us consider what the syntactic structures corresponding to example (41) would be. Its c-structure, shown in (43a), has an initial NP in the position that maps onto a DF according to principle (42). In addition, it also includes the special verbal position for auxiliaries preceding the rest of the clause excluding the fronted constituent. Notice also that the c-structure does not include an object position, that is, a constituent following the verb that maps onto an object function. As for the f-structure, in (43b), its PRED value, or a-structure, is that of the active form of *read*, and consequently it licenses the same grammatical functions as in the f-structure given in (31) corresponding to sentence (1) without any DF. The grammatical functions licensed are the subject, mapped onto the external argument, and the object, mapped onto the internal argument. An additional oblique is included, which does not map onto any argument, but corresponds to an adjunct. In (43b), there is also a DF, which is licensed by principle (42). The f-structure that the

---

[27]See, for example, Kaplan and Bresnan 1982, Zaenen 1983, and Kaplan and Zaenen 1989, in which different equations or annotations on the c-structure are required in order to obtain the sharing of structure between the discourse function and the in-clause function. In some theories, an empty category is assumed to occupy the c-structure position of the in-clause function (for example, Kaplan and Bresnan 1982, Zaenen 1983, Bresnan 1994b); in other theories, there is no empty category in the c-structure corresponding to the in-clause function (for example, Kaplan and Zaenen 1989, Bresnan 1994a, 1994c). I will not discuss the issue of the empty category, although I will assume there is no empty category.

DF takes as its value is the same as the f-structure that the OBJ takes as its value. There is no c-structure constituent that is licensed to map onto an object function by any function-category association principle, and yet the f-structure requires an object. This requirement is satisfied by having the value of the discourse function be also the value of the object.

(43) a.

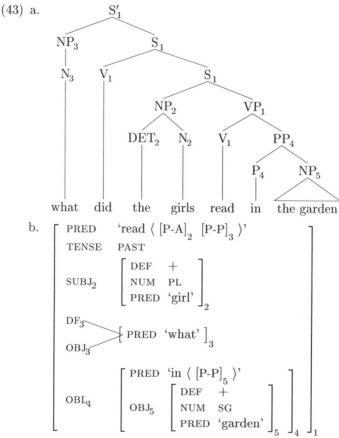

b.

$$\begin{bmatrix} \text{PRED} & \text{'read} \langle [\text{P-A}]_2 \ [\text{P-P}]_3 \rangle' \\ \text{TENSE} & \text{PAST} \\ \text{SUBJ}_2 & \begin{bmatrix} \text{DEF} & + \\ \text{NUM} & \text{PL} \\ \text{PRED} & \text{'girl'} \end{bmatrix}_2 \\ \begin{matrix} \text{DF}_3 \\ \text{OBJ}_3 \end{matrix} & \begin{bmatrix} \text{PRED 'what'} \end{bmatrix}_3 \\ \text{OBL}_4 & \begin{bmatrix} \text{PRED} & \text{'in} \langle [\text{P-P}]_5 \rangle' \\ \text{OBJ}_5 & \begin{bmatrix} \text{DEF} & + \\ \text{NUM} & \text{SG} \\ \text{PRED} & \text{'garden'} \end{bmatrix}_5 \end{bmatrix}_4 \end{bmatrix}_1$$

This representation expresses the claim that one single c-structure constituent, *what* in (43a), maps onto two different grammatical functions, the DF and the OBJ in (43b). This one-to-many mapping nevertheless preserves the Uniqueness of F-Structures (9), which does not allow a given c-structure node to correspond to more than one f-structure. The NP *what* in (43a) corresponds only to the f-structure with index 3 in (43b). (If the f-structure representation in (43b) contained more than one f-structure with index 3, it would be ill-formed.) Yet, this single f-structure, with index 3, is the value of two different grammatical functions.[28]

As mentioned above, no special principle has to be proposed to allow the sharing of structure represented in (43b): it is possible because nothing prevents assigning the same index to the value of two grammatical functions (as long as all existing principles are satisfied). In this particular example, an object function is licensed by the FMT mapped onto the internal argument of the predicate. Let us assume that this argument and, therefore, the f-structure it corresponds to have index 3. In the same f-structure (43b), a discourse function DF is licensed by the function-category association principle (42), given the associated c-structure (43a). Let us assume that this DF takes as its value an f-structure with index 3. By the Uniqueness of F-Structures (9), the f-structure value of the object and that of the DF must be the same. (Notice that, if the c-structure contained no constituent sister of S, no DF would be licensed, and thus either the object would have to be expressed in the c-structure position where objects are licensed, following the verb, or the structure would be ungrammatical as it would include no object or an object without any value.)

Having shown that it is, in principle, possible for any two grammatical functions in a structure to have the same value, it is clear that this possibility has to be restricted. While this sharing of structure may take place when one of the grammatical functions involved is a discourse function, it may not when both grammatical functions map onto different semantic roles (whether arguments or adjuncts). Thus, for example, sentence (44) cannot be interpreted as having *Mary* (that is, its f-structure representation) filling both the object function of *told* and the object of *seen*.

(44)   *I told Mary that John had seen.

In other words, this sentence cannot be interpreted as: "I told Mary that John had seen her" with *her=Mary*. In addition, even when one of the grammatical functions involved in structure sharing is a discourse

---

[28]The standard notation in LFG to indicate sharing of structure for two grammatical functions is a curved line joining the f-structure represented as the value of one of the grammatical functions to the empty position corresponding to the value of the other grammatical function involved. In the present implementation, the proposal that each grammatical function attribute has the same index as its value serves to indicate sharing of structure: the fact that two grammatical function attributes have the same index means that they have the same f-structure value. In addition, for perspicuity, I signal this sharing of structure by means of connecting lines. What is important to realize is that, whatever the notation (curved lines or identity of indices), the substance expressed is the same.

function, there is an asymmetry in the relative structural positions that the discourse function and the coindexed in-clause function may occupy. So, whereas the topic *Mary* may appear in the matrix clause coindexed with the object of the matrix clause, as in (45a), or with the object of the embedded clause, as in (45b), or it may appear in the embedded clause coindexed with the object of the embedded clause, as in (45c), it cannot appear in the embedded clause coindexed with the object of the matrix clause, as in (45d).

(45) a.   Mary (DF_1), I told (OBJ_1) [that John had seen Bill].

　　 b.   Mary (DF_1), I told Bill [that John had seen (OBJ_1)].

　　 c.   I told Bill [that, Mary (DF_1), John had seen (OBJ_1)].

　　 d.   *I told (OBJ_1) [that, Mary (DF_1), John had seen Bill].

From this we can conclude that two grammatical functions may have the same value provided one of them is (a) *nonthematic*, which accounts for the ungrammaticality of sentences like (44), and (b) structurally *superior* to the other (see definition in (52)), which rules out sentences like (45d). So, we can state the relevant constraint on structure sharing as follows, with the notion of "nonthematic" defined in (47).

(46)   *Constraint on Sharing of F-Structures*:

　　　 If any two GFs have the same value, one of them is nonthematic and superior to the other.

(47)   *Nonthematic*: A nonthematic function is one that is not licensed by its mapping to a-structure or to semantic structure.

The definition of "nonthematic" includes discourse functions, which, unlike semantically contentful in-clause functions, are licensed independently of their mapping to a particular argument or adjunct. Meaningful in-clause functions (subject, object, and oblique) are allowed only if they map onto an argument or an adjunct.

　　A complete theory of long distance dependencies should provide an account of many facts that are beyond the scope of the present study, such as island constraints, subject/nonsubject asymmetries, etc. The treatment of discourse functions given here is sufficient for present purposes and is a convenient starting point for the analysis of other nonargument functions, namely, raising functions and expletive functions.

2.4.2   Raising Functions

Whereas long distance dependencies involve a structure sharing relation between a discourse function and an in-clause function, raising constructions involve a structure sharing relation between two in-clause functions. Importantly, these two in-clause functions belong to two different clauses. Raising verbs take an infinitival complement whose subject is satisfied by a grammatical function of the matrix raising verb; I refer to this grammatical function as the *raising function*. The raising function can be the subject or the object of the raising verb, as in (48a) and (48b), respectively.

(48) a. John appears to enjoy the book.

b. I believe John to enjoy the book.

It is an established claim that the raising function, the phrase *John* in (48), behaves like a grammatical function of the raising verb: its subject in sentences like (48a), and its object in sentences like (48b). Nevertheless, it is not an argument of the raising verb.[29] The verb *appear* takes only one argument, semantically a proposition, which, in (48a), is expressed as the VP *to enjoy the book*; therefore, *John* is not an argument of *appear*, but it is an argument of the VP complement. The verb *believe* takes two arguments: the entity that experiences a belief and the thing believed, which is a proposition. In (48b), the c-structure constituent corresponding to the believer is the NP *I* and the constituent that maps onto the propositional argument is the VP *to enjoy the book*. Once again, *John* is not an argument of *believe*, but it is an argument of *to enjoy the book*.

In sum, the raising function is a grammatical function of the raising verb (*appear* in (48a) and *believe* in (48b)), but not an argument of that verb; it is only an argument (if at all) of the predicate of the infinitival complement of the raising verb. The phrase that appears in a position that allows it to map onto a grammatical function of the raising verb also licenses (i.e., maps onto the f-structure value of) the subject of the infinitival complement. Thus, *John* in (48a) is at the same time the subject of the clause whose predicate is *appear* and the subject of the embedded clause, whose predicate is *enjoy*; likewise, in (48b) it is the object of the main clause, with predicate *believe*, and the subject of the embedded clause.

The main problem that needs to be addressed, in the present study, is how and why a clause contains a grammatical function that doesn't bear any semantic relation to the predicate of the clause. This grammatical function, the raising function, is a direct function, either a subject or

---

[29]Given the assumption made here that a-structure information is semantically based, it follows that an argument at a-structure is a semantic argument; therefore, by this assumption, if a syntactic constituent is not a semantic argument, it cannot be an a-structure argument. The claim that something is not a semantic argument entails that it is not an a-structure argument.

an object. The FMT, through the principle of Coherence (28), requires every direct function to be licensed by a mapping principle. In order for a function to be licensed by a mapping principle, it must appear in the same f-structure as the PRED that includes the argument that maps onto it. (This follows from the way the mapping principles are formulated.) Apparently, then, the raising function would not satisfy Coherence. The mapping principles, (26) and (27), can be viewed as licensing not only a grammatical function attribute, but also the f-structure that this attribute takes as its value. Thus, in raising constructions like (48), the subject function of the infinitival complement, as well as its f-structure value, is licensed by a mapping principle. Since the raising function takes the same value as the complement's subject, the value of the raising function **is** licensed by Coherence. Then, the only thing that remains to be licensed is the grammatical function attribute of the raising function. We shall consider now what needs to be assumed in order to explain this aspect of raising constructions.

I assume, following, among others, Brame (1976), Bresnan (1976, 1978, 1982a), and Pollard and Sag (1987, 1993), that the propositional argument of raising verbs maps onto a VP sister of the raising verb. (See Pollard and Sag 1993:133ff for arguments in favor of this hypothesis.) A VP is a category that is assumed not to contain a constituent that maps onto the subject of the f-structure correlate of the VP. Loosely speaking, the subject of the VP must be found outside the VP. The VP *to enjoy the book* maps onto an f-structure that must include a subject function, not only because every f-structure with propositional content must include a subject, in satisfaction of the Subject Condition (5), but because the verb *enjoy* takes an argument that must be expressed as the subject. Thus, the only way to satisfy the requirement for a subject is for a constituent external to the VP to provide the f-structure value of the subject of the VP complement. This can be done in the same way as a constituent that is assigned a discourse function can license (i.e., map onto the f-structure value of) an in-clause function, seen in 2.4.1. The only difference is that, in raising, both grammatical functions in a structure sharing relation are in-clause functions.

Let us consider first constructions in which the raising function is the subject, such as (48a). As stated earlier, the raising verb *appear* is a predicate with only one argument, which is reflected in its lexical entry, as follows:

(49)   appear: V_1 $[$ PRED 'appear $\langle$ [P-P] $\rangle$' $]_1$

Since semantically the single argument of this verb is a proposition, it must be expressed either as a tensed clause (as in *It seems that Jack is sick*), or as a tenseless clause, i.e., a VP, which is the structure we are interested in here. The paired f-structure and c-structure of sentence (48a) are given in (50).

(50) a.

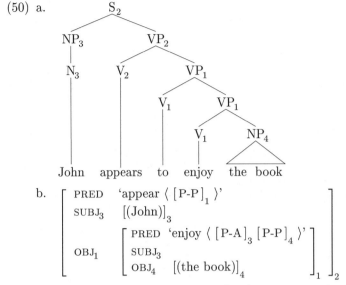

b.

$$
\begin{bmatrix}
\text{PRED} & \text{'appear} \langle\, [\text{P-P}]_1\, \rangle\text{'} \\
\text{SUBJ}_3 & [(\text{John})]_3 \\
\text{OBJ}_1 & \begin{bmatrix}
\text{PRED} & \text{'enjoy} \langle\, [\text{P-A}]_3\, [\text{P-P}]_4\, \rangle\text{'} \\
\text{SUBJ}_3 & \\
\text{OBJ}_4 & [(\text{the book})]_4
\end{bmatrix}_1
\end{bmatrix}_2
$$

The VP sister of the verb *appears* in (50a) maps onto the f-structure that is the value of the object of this verb.[30] Within this embedded or subsidiary f-structure, with index 1 in (50b), the predicate *enjoy* and its associated grammatical functions are represented. Since *enjoy* takes an external and an internal argument, the former maps onto the subject and the latter onto the object. The object of *enjoy* is satisfied in (50a) by the NP *the book*, which is contained in the c-structure correlate of the f-structure that includes the object. However, the subject of this verb is not satisfied by any constituent contained in the c-structure

---

[30]Standard LFG theories assign the syntactic function XCOMP, instead of OBJ, to the VP complement of such verbs. However, distinguishing predicative complements (phrases lacking a subject) from nonpredicative complements by means of a distinction in terms of syntactic function attributes (XCOMP vs. OBJ) is a redundancy: such complements have to be distinguished, independently of their syntactic function, in terms of their conceptual category (see Jackendoff 1990) by whether they are a *Proposition* or a *Thing*. Thus, if the distinction between XCOMP and OBJ correlates perfectly with the distinction between *Proposition* and *Thing*, it is sufficient (and therefore necessary) to make only the latter distinction, which appears to be irreducible, and to assume that a syntactic function OBJ may correspond to either of those conceptual categories, with subsequent syntactic differences. The standard LFG labels XCOMP and COMP distinguish between propositional complements with a controlled subject and those without one, a distinction that is presumably derivable from c-structure differences: XP vs. S.

correlate of f-structure that includes the subject. It is satisfied by the NP *John*, which also satisfies the subject of the matrix verb *appears* in conformity with the function-category association principles. Notice that, in (50b), the f-structure indexed 3, which maps onto the NP *John*, is the value of the SUBJ of the f-structure indexed 2 and of the SUBJ of the subsidiary f-structure indexed 1. The notation used here to indicate this sharing of value is the index on the grammatical function attribute: since every grammatical function attribute has the same index as its value, the correspondence between attribute and value is established by means of the indices. As there is only one f-structure indexed 3 in (50b), it doesn't matter where this f-structure is physically represented, because the pairing with the attributes of which it is a value is represented by means of coindexation. So, for example, the information conveyed in (50b), where the f-structure indexed 3 appears on paper to the right of the SUBJ of the matrix clause, is identical to the information conveyed in (51), where the same f-structure appears instead to the right of the SUBJ of the f-structure indexed 1. (This, again, is identical in substance to the standard LFG notational device of a curved line joining the values of two grammatical functions, with the shared f-structure represented in only one position.)

(51)
$$\begin{bmatrix} \text{PRED} & \text{`appear} \langle\, [\text{P-P}]_1 \,\rangle\text{'} \\ \text{SUBJ}_3 & \\ \text{OBJ}_1 & \begin{bmatrix} \text{PRED} & \text{`enjoy} \langle\, [\text{P-A}]_3\, [\text{P-P}]_4 \,\rangle\text{'} \\ \text{SUBJ}_3 & [(\text{John})]_3 \\ \text{OBJ}_4 & [(\text{the book})]_4 \end{bmatrix}_1 \end{bmatrix}_2$$

In a structure like (50) we have two apparent anomalies to explain: (a) why the f-structure indexed 1 includes a subject if the c-structure nodes indexed 1 contain no constituent that licenses that subject, and (b) why the f-structure indexed 2 contains a subject that does not map onto an argument of the PRED and therefore appears to violate Coherence. The first apparent anomaly is explained in the same way that an in-clause function may be satisfied not by a constituent in the canonical subject, object, or oblique position, but by a constituent that is required to map onto a discourse function DF (see 2.4.1). This is possible because the DF and the in-clause function have the same value. Notice that the only condition imposed on the sharing of values by two grammatical functions, given in (46), is that one of them must be nonthematic and superior to the other. Discourse functions are not the only nonthematic functions; raising functions are another type of nonthematic functions. A raising function is nonthematic according to (47), because it is not

licensed as an argument or an adjunct of its clause.[31] When considering the structure sharing involved in raising constructions, it becomes
important to define the notion "superior" precisely, as in (52).

(52) GF G is superior to GF F iff G f-commands F and, for every GF
      Q f-commanded by G whose f-structure value includes that of F,
      either

      a. Q does not f-command G, or

      b. Q is not higher than G in the GF hierarchy.

By the definition of "include" given in footnote 7, the f-structure value
of Q is either that of F or it contains F. The relation of f-command,
defined in (53) (from Bresnan 1982a:334), is identical to the more familiar relation of c-command, but the part-whole (or dominance) relations
that it refers to are those of the f-structure, instead of being those of
the c-structure. (Instead of using the term *f-command*, one could talk
of c-command applying at f-structure, as in K. P. Mohanan 1983.)

(53) *F-command*: GF α f-commands GF β iff the value of α does not
      contain β and every f-structure that contains α contains β.

The hierarchy of grammatical functions, based on similar hierarchies
proposed by Perlmutter and Postal 1974, Keenan and Comrie 1977, and
Pollard and Sag 1987, Sag 1987, among others, specifies that subject is
higher than object, and object is higher than oblique, thus:

(54) GF *Hierarchy*: SUBJ > OBJ > OBL

Given constraint (46), the raising function, which is nonthematic,
must be superior to the grammatical function it shares its value with.
The subject of the matrix f-structure in (50b) is superior to the subject
contained in the f-structure of the object, because the matrix subject
f-commands the matrix object, and, although the f-command relation is
mutual, the matrix object is not higher than the matrix subject in the
GF hierarchy. Therefore, as the matrix subject, which is nonthematic,
is superior to the subject of the embedded f-structure, the two GFs can
take the same value satisfying constraint (46). Thus, once we define
the notion "superior" precisely, which is part of this constraint, nothing

---

[31]The requirement of nonthematicity of one of the grammatical functions that have
the same value entails that the relation between the controller and the controllee in
"equi" control constructions is not treated as an instance of value sharing, unlike
raising, because the controller (of verbs like *promise*, *want*, *persuade*, *ask*, etc.) is
an argument. I follow Pollard and Sag (1991, 1993), among others, in treating the
controller-controllee relation in "equi" control as an anaphoric relation, an instance
of the antecedent-pronoun relation where the pronoun is phonologically null.

specific to raising constructions needs to be said in order to explain the first apparent anomaly.

In order to explain the second apparent anomaly, we need to understand the f-structure licensing conditions on nonthematic in-clause functions. Observe that, if the raising function in (50) were absent, the structures would be ill-formed because the matrix f-structure, with index 2, would lack a subject and therefore would violate the Subject Condition (5). (In addition, the structures would also violate the Part-Whole Parallelism (11) if the NP *John* did not map onto any GF of the matrix f-structure, or, if this NP were absent, the subject argument of the subsidiary f-structure, indexed 1, would not be satisfied.) Let us assume then that a nonthematic in-clause function is licensed if it satisfies a general principle, in this case, the Subject Condition. Thus, in the f-structure representation in (50b) (or (51)), the grammatical function attribute SUBJ contained in the f-structure indexed 2 is not licensed by Coherence (28), because it does not map onto an argument of the PRED, but it is licensed by the Subject Condition (5), because this principle requires a subject in every clause. Observe that the value of this grammatical function does satisfy Coherence, because, in the f-structure indexed 1, it is licensed by a mapping principle, the External Argument Mapping Principle (26).

Having given this analysis of raising constructions, it is easy to see that the raising function is licensed if it is the subject. But what happens when it is the object, as in (48b)? It is clear that nonthematic expressions are not licensed only in the subject function. For example, there are idioms that include a nonthematic (and nonreferential) object NP, such as *kick the bucket*. It seems inevitable to assume that, for such cases, the lexical entry of the idiom will have to specify that it is a predicate and that it takes a grammatical function object that does not map onto an argument of the predicate, but maps onto the NP *the bucket*. This leads us to conclude that nonthematic functions may also be licensed through a lexical stipulation, such as the one requiring a specific object in the idiom *kick the bucket*. For a raising verb such as *believe*, all we need to assume is that, in addition to its two arguments, the believer and the proposition believed, the verb takes a grammatical function GF (optionally), as shown in its lexical entry in (55).

(55)   believe: V_1 $\begin{bmatrix} \text{PRED 'believe} \langle\, [\text{P-A}]\,[\text{P-P}]\,\rangle\text{'} \\ (\text{GF}) \end{bmatrix}_1$

It is unnecessary and inappropriate to specify the grammatical function label of the nonthematic function (GF) in (55) for several reasons. First, if we assume a principle such as (56), there cannot be raising to oblique or raising out of an oblique. It follows that the GF in (54) cannot be an oblique function.

(56)   If in-clause functions F and G have the same value, both F and G and any GF Q that includes G and is f-commanded by F must be [obl −], i.e., direct.

Raising always involves the subject of the embedded clause and a subject is a direct function, and the nonthematic function with which it is coindexed must also be a direct function. This principle seems necessary in order to account for the claim that there is only raising to subject and to object, but not to oblique. (This seems to be a generally accepted claim, although analyses involving raising to oblique have been proposed by Joseph (1979) and by McCloskey (1984) for Greek and Irish respectively.) Second, the nonthematic function of raising verbs like *believe* is an object in the active form, but a subject in the passive form; so, we cannot stipulate whether it is one or the other. Third, whether it is a subject or an object follows from independent principles, as we shall see. In sum, all we need to assume is that raising verbs like *believe* are special in that they license a grammatical function that is not linked to an argument of their a-structure. The way this licensing is formally represented is by including an unspecified grammatical function (GF) in their lexical entry.

The paired f-structure and c-structure of the sentence (48b) with a raising object are shown in (57). The f-structure indexed 4 in (57b) is the value of both the object of the matrix clause (the f-structure indexed 2) and of the subject of the embedded clause (the f-structure indexed 1). This structure sharing of two grammatical functions is notated by the identity of indices between the attributes and the f-structure that is their common value. It comes about as a result of free assignment of indices to f-structures and to their associated c-structure and a-structure categories, subject to well-formedness conditions. The relevant well-formedness conditions are: the Uniqueness of F-Structures (9), which rules out two f-structures with the same index, and the constraint (46), which requires one of the two grammatical functions with the same value to be nonthematic and superior to the other. Both conditions are satisfied in (57b) as there is only one f-structure with index 4, although it is the value of two grammatical functions, and one of the two grammatical functions involved in structure sharing (the object of the matrix clause) is nonthematic and is superior to the other one. (In (57b), OBJ_4 is superior to $SUBJ_4$, according to (52), because OBJ_1, whose f-structure contains $SUBJ_4$ and its value, is in a mutual f-command relation with OBJ_4, but is not higher than it in the hierarchy of grammatical functions, since both

(57) a.

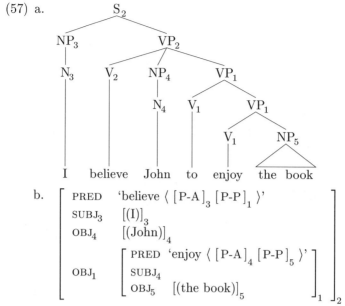

I believe John to enjoy the book

b.
$$
\begin{bmatrix}
\text{PRED} & \text{'believe} \langle\, [\text{P-A}]_3\ [\text{P-P}]_1\,\rangle\text{'} \\
\text{SUBJ}_3 & [(\text{I})]_3 \\
\text{OBJ}_4 & [(\text{John})]_4 \\
\text{OBJ}_1 & \begin{bmatrix} \text{PRED} & \text{'enjoy} \langle\, [\text{P-A}]_4\ [\text{P-P}]_5\,\rangle\text{'} \\ \text{SUBJ}_4 \\ \text{OBJ}_5 & [(\text{the book})]_5 \end{bmatrix}_1
\end{bmatrix}_2
$$

are objects.) The f-structure indexed 4 is licensed by Coherence in the subsidiary f-structure as the value of the subject; this attribute is also licensed by Coherence, as well as by the Subject Condition. However, the attribute of the raising function, namely, the object of the matrix clause, is not licensed either by Coherence or by the Subject Condition; it is licensed by the lexical entry of the verb *believe*, given in (55), which allows a grammatical function not independently licensed.

Why is this grammatical function an object in (57), given that (55) does not specify what type of grammatical function it should be? The existence of constraint (56) disallowing structure sharing when one of the two in-clause GFs involved is [obl +] excludes an oblique as a raising function, as noted above. This restricts the options to subject and object. The PRED feature of the matrix clause includes an external argument: by the External Argument Mapping Principle (26), this argument must map onto the subject function. By the Subject Condition (5), which rules out an f-structure with two subjects, the raising function cannot also be a subject. It must therefore be an object. On the other hand, it is well-known that raising verbs like *believe* can be passivized with the result that, in the passive construction, the raising function is the subject instead of an object. So, the passive counterpart of (48b) is (58a), whose skeletal f-structure is given in (58b):

(58) a. John is believed to enjoy the book.

b.
$$
\begin{bmatrix}
\text{PRED} & \text{'believe} \langle\, [\text{P-A}]_{\textcircled{3}}\ [\text{P-P}]_1 \,\rangle\text{'} \\
\text{SUBJ}_4 & [(\text{John})]_4 \\
\text{OBJ}_1 &
\begin{bmatrix}
\text{PRED} & \text{'enjoy} \langle\, [\text{P-A}]_4\ [\text{P-P}]_5 \,\rangle\text{'} \\
\text{SUBJ}_4 \\
\text{OBJ}_5 & [(\text{the book})]_5
\end{bmatrix}_1
\end{bmatrix}_2
$$

As the external argument of *believe* is suppressed in (58) by the passive morphology, it cannot be expressed as a direct function. Something else needs to fill the subject function. The internal (propositional) argument of *believe*, expressed as a VP, cannot fill this function because it would lack a subject. With the VP as the subject, the nonthematic function of *believe* would have to be an object, in order to satisfy the Subject Condition. But then the nonthematic object would not be superior to the subject of the subject's f-structure and the two would not be able to have the same value, given the requirement in (46). (Notice that, whereas a subject and an object of the same f-structure are in a mutual f-command relation, the object is not superior to the subject, because the subject is higher than the object in the GF hierarchy.) Also, as the subject of the VP subject cannot be coindexed with the matrix nonthematic object, the latter fails to satisfy Coherence. Thus, we explain the ungrammaticality of **To enjoy the book was believed John.* So, only the nonthematic function licensed in the lexical entry of *believe* and by the Subject Condition qualifies as a possible subject of the passive form of raising *believe*, as indicated in (58).

The main conclusion that emerges from the analysis of raising constructions is that Coherence as stated in (28) must be revised in order to allow direct functions that are nonthematic, while still restricting their distribution. Coherence should be revised as follows:

(59)   *Coherence (revised)*:

    a.   An f-structure value of a direct function[32] must be licensed by an FMT mapping principle, either (26) or (27); and

    b.   a direct function must be licensed either (i) by a mapping principle (26)–(27), (ii) by a general principle such as the Subject Condition (5), or (iii) by a lexical stipulation.

---

[32]Condition (59a) might have to be restricted to semantically contentful f-structures, in order to allow certain idiomatic and expletive functions whose f-structures have no mapping to semantics. However, as we shall see in 2.4.3, the examples of expletive functions examined here do take f-structure values with semantic content, for which this restriction is therefore unnecessary.

In the examples of raising that we have examined, the f-structure value of the raising function is licensed by a mapping principle as the value of the subject of the embedded clause; the subject of the embedded clause is also licensed by the same mapping principle; and the raising function is licensed either by the Subject Condition, when it is a subject, or by a lexical stipulation, when it is an object. Thus, very little needs to be specified in lexical entries of predicates in order to account for the appearance of nonthematic functions. In particular, the PRED value, namely, the a-structure, as the syntactic representation of lexical semantic information, remains free of semantically unmotivated elements such as nonarguments. Nonthematic functions are only represented in the f-structure (not in the a-structure) and their appearance need only be licensed in the lexical entry of the predicate when it is not licensed by a general principle. Even when a lexical stipulation is needed, as with *believe*, the type of grammatical function that is licensed is left unspecified, as it is determined by general principles.

2.4.3 Expletive Functions

Expletive functions can be defined as grammatical functions licensed by semantically empty categories. In addition to idiomatic phrases, which will not be discussed here, there are two types of expletive functions in English that can be identified by their overt expression: *there*, as in example (60a), and *it*, as in (60b).

(60) a. There stood a man by the window.

b. It seemed that Mary had a chance to win.

I will have very little to say here about expletive *it*, except that it is required by its lexical entry to be coindexed with an argument with propositional content. Notice that expletive *it* always cooccurs with a clausal complement, such as a *that* sentence. In what follows I will restrict myself to the analysis of expletive *there*.

In determining the lexical entry of expletive *there*, we have to take into account the lack of referential meaning of this word, which entails not only that it has no semantic representation, but also that it does not satisfy any argument of the predicate. In example (60a), the predicate *stand* takes one or two arguments, a theme and, possibly, a locative: the former is satisfied by the NP *the man* and the latter by the PP *by the window*; there is no argument left that can correspond to *there*. In addition, we have to take into account the fact that *there* seems to have no lexically specified features relevant for agreement (number, person, and gender). In sentences with expletive *there*, as in (61), the agreement features on the verb depend on the NP following the verb, even though *there* is generally assumed to occupy the subject position.

(61) a. There was/*were a dog in the street.

  b. There were/*was two dogs in the street.

The standard analysis of this puzzling phenomenon is to assume that, contrary to appearances, the verb in (61) conforms to the general principle of subject-verb agreement. In order to make this principle explain the facts, it is assumed that the subject *there* forms a "chain" with the NP following the verb, the object, to the effect that the subject and the object share the same features relevant for agreement. Thus, *there* acquires the number specification of the object and, when the verb agrees with the subject *there*, it indirectly agrees with the object. This analysis, in addition to positing the lexical entry of expletive *there*, has to posit a mechanism for forming a "chain" between *there* and the object that has no independent motivation.

The alternative that I am going to propose posits no such ad hoc mechanism. Given the preceding discussion, it seems reasonable to assume that expletive *there* has only a c-structure representation in its lexical entry. As shown in the lexical entry in (62), expletive *there* has no f-structure information.

(62)   there: N

The absence of a PRED feature in this lexical entry indicates the lack of semantic content of the word.[33] The lack of any inherent agreement features is represented by the absence of number, person, and gender specification in (62). An important consequence of the representation in (62), which is crucial in the subsequent analysis, is that, since the c-structure information of *there* is not specified to be linked to any f-structure, it can map onto any f-structure, provided all relevant principles are satisfied, and, in fact, it must map onto some f-structure in order to satisfy the requirement in (8) that every c-structure node must map onto f-structure.

In order to give the representation of a sentence such as (61a), we need to provide the lexical entries of the verb forms *was* and *were*, which specify subject agreement information. Restricting our attention to third person subjects, these lexical entries are as shown in (63).

---

[33]Previous treatments of nonsemantic expressions in LFG posit the feature FORM in their f-structure representation. The reason for this is unclear to me. If what is being expressed is the null semantic content of the expression, the absence of the feature PRED should suffice. Introducing a specification of form, as the FORM feature, is an undesirable intrusion of c-structure information into the f-structure.

(63) a. was: V_1

$$
\begin{bmatrix}
\text{PRED} & \text{`be} \langle\, [\text{P-P}]\ [\ ]\, \rangle\text{'} \\
\text{TENSE} & \text{PAST} \\
\text{SUBJ} & \begin{bmatrix} \text{PERS} & 3 \\ \text{NUM} & \text{SG} \end{bmatrix}
\end{bmatrix}_1
$$

    b. were: V_1

$$
\begin{bmatrix}
\text{PRED} & \text{`be} \langle\, [\text{P-P}]\ [\ ]\, \rangle\text{'} \\
\text{TENSE} & \text{PAST} \\
\text{SUBJ} & \begin{bmatrix} \text{PERS} & 3 \\ \text{NUM} & \text{PL} \end{bmatrix}
\end{bmatrix}_1
$$

If the c-structure expression that maps onto the subject is a third person singular NP, the appropriate verb form to use is *was*, in (63a), as the subject information it specifies is compatible (unifiable) with that of the NP. In such a case, the verb form *were*, in (63b), cannot be used, as it specifies information (plural number) of the subject that is inconsistent with the information specified by the NP that maps onto the subject (singular number). The problem with sentences like (61), with an expletive *there* as the subject, is that this expression does not specify any number or person information, and yet the sentences are well-formed with one of the two verb forms in (63), but not with the other one.

The explanation comes about as a result of not specifying any f-structure information in the lexical entry of *there*, which allows its c-structure representation to be coindexed with the f-structure of the object. In sentence (61a), whose paired c-structure and f-structure are given in (64), the NP *there* appears in a c-structure position that is required to map onto the subject, and the NP *the dog* is required to map onto an object function. Notice that the two NPs have the same index, which means they map onto the same f-structure. Therefore, this f-structure is at the same time the value of the object and the value of the subject, as indicated in (64b). Once again we find a structure in which two different grammatical functions take the same f-structure as their value. Here, the two grammatical functions in question are the subject, licensed by *there*, and the object, licensed by *a dog*. The f-structure they take as their value is provided exlusively by the lexical items that form the NP *a dog*, since *there* specifies no f-structure information. The f-structure information specified by the NP *a dog*, including third person singular, is information about both the subject and the object, as indicated by representing these two grammatical functions as taking the same value in (64b). Therefore, the appropriate verb form to use is *was*, which is specified to take a third person singular subject; using *were* instead, would yield a featural inconsistency, as it is specified to take a third person plural subject.

(64) a.

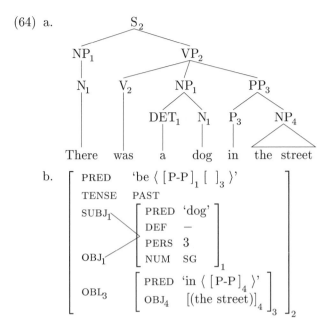

b.
$$\left[\begin{array}{ll} \text{PRED} & \text{'be} \langle [\text{P-P}]_1 \, [\;]_3 \rangle\text{'} \\ \text{TENSE} & \text{PAST} \\ \text{SUBJ}_1 & \left[\begin{array}{ll} \text{PRED} & \text{'dog'} \\ \text{DEF} & - \\ \text{PERS} & 3 \\ \text{NUM} & \text{SG} \end{array}\right]_1 \\ \text{OBJ}_1 & \\ \text{OBL}_3 & \left[\begin{array}{ll} \text{PRED} & \text{'in} \langle [\text{P-P}]_4 \rangle\text{'} \\ \text{OBJ}_4 & [(\text{the street})]_4 \end{array}\right]_3 \end{array}\right]_2$$

This structure sharing satisfies the licensing principles required independently of this construction. One of the two grammatical functions involved, the subject, is nonthematic and superior to the other one, the object. When two grammatical functions are involved in structure sharing, only one of them can be licensed by mapping to an argument (i.e., thematic). The other one must be nonthematic. Either the subject or the object can be licensed by the Internal Argument Mapping Principle (27) by mapping to the internal argument of the predicate. If the object is chosen as the thematic function, it is licensed by a mapping principle, satisfying the revised Coherence (59b). The subject, then, as a nonthematic function, is not licensed by a mapping principle, but is licensed by satisfying the Subject Condition (5), which is an alternative way of satisfying Coherence. If the subject were assumed to be thematic, it would be licensed by the mapping principle, but then the object would have to be nonthematic: as it would not be licensed by a mapping principle, it would have to be licensed either by a general principle or by a lexical stipulation. However, there is neither a general principle that licenses nonthematic objects nor an appropriate lexical stipulation with this effect in any of the lexical items involved. Thus, a structure like (64b) is well-formed only if the subject is assumed to be nonthematic.

The reason why expletive *there* can only appear in the subject position, or, to be more precise, in a position that licenses the subject function, is that it is a *last resort* element: it is only used in structures that would otherwise be ill-formed. (65a) is grammatical because *there* licenses the subject function, whereas (65b) is ungrammatical because there is no c-structure constituent that licenses the subject function, which is necessary to satisfy the Subject Condition (5). (66a) is grammatical as a structure with a subject and no object. The ungrammaticality of (66b) is due to the last resort status of expletive *there*: since the sentence is well-formed without *there*, because the subject is independently licensed by the NP *a dog*, the use of *there* is precluded.

(65) a. There was a dog in the street.

   b. *Was a dog in the street.

(66) a. A dog was in the street.

   b. *A dog was there in the street.

It follows from this that expletive *there* appears only and obligatorily in structures that would otherwise lack a subject, and it appears in a position that licenses the subject.[34] This means that *there* appears not only in the c-structure subject position, as in the examples examined, but also in any other position that is required to license the subject, for example, as the object of a raising verb like *believe*. Consider the following example:

(67)   I believe there to be a dog in the street.

Here, *there* appears in the position that licenses the nonthematic object of *believe*. This is necessary in order to license the subject of the infinitival complement. At the level of f-structure, the object of *believe*, the subject of *be*, and the object of *be* take all the same value, as shown in the simplified f-structure in (68) corresponding to (67).

---

[34]We have to assume that grammatical functions require a c-structure licensing, as well as the f-structure licensing expressed by Coherence (59). C-structure licensing sanctions a GF that either (a) is required by the c-to-f-structure mapping principles (13), which refer to the subject/nonsubject distinction, or (42), which introduces discourse functions, or (b) is coindexed with a GF outside its nucleus (where nucleus is defined as the set of in-clause functions associated with a PRED). This explains why (65b) is ungrammatical: the subject, which the sentence needs in order to satisfy the Subject Condition, cannot be licensed by coindexation with the object, because the object is not outside its nucleus; since there is no constituent in a position that requires the presence of a subject through the application of principle (13a), the subject is not licensed. In contrast, sentence (65a) is grammatical because its subject is licensed by the presence of the NP *there* in a position that calls for the application of principle (13a).

(68)

$$\begin{bmatrix} \text{PRED} & \text{'believe} \langle\, [\text{P-A}]_6\ [\text{P-P}]_2\,\rangle\text{'} \\ \text{SUBJ}_6 & [(\text{I})]_6 \\ \text{OBJ}_1 & \\ \text{OBJ}_2 & \begin{bmatrix} \text{PRED} & \text{'be} \langle\, [\text{P-P}]_1\ [\ ]_3\,\rangle\text{'} \\ \text{SUBJ}_1 & \\ & [(\text{a dog})]_1 \\ \text{OBJ}_1 & \\ \text{OBL}_3 & [(\text{in the street})]_3 \end{bmatrix}_2 \end{bmatrix}_7$$

Notice that the adequacy of this analysis of expletive *there* argues against the widespread theoretical assumption (expressed by principles such as Function-Argument Biuniqueness of earlier LFG) that requires expressed arguments and grammatical functions to be in a one-to-one correspondence. In f-structures such as (64b) and (68) there is one argument corresponding to two GFs of the same nucleus.

2.5 Summary

In this chapter we have presented the theoretical framework that is adopted in the remainder of this study. The fundamental idea is that the syntactic information of any linguistic object is factored into different levels of structure that describe different aspects of that object. The phonologically relevant arrangement of syntactic elements, the c-structure, is represented as a standard phrase structure tree. The representation of grammatical relations, the f-structure, is formalized as a feature structure, in which every attribute takes a unique value and values can themselves be feature structures. The syntactically relevant aspects of predicate argument relations, the a-structure, are represented as a list of elements whose properties are partially derivable from semantic characterizations.

A large part of this chapter is devoted to developing theories for linking the three levels of structure. A linguistic object is well-formed if and only if it has a well-formed a-structure, f-structure, and c-structure and these three structures satisfy the mapping principles relating them. Therefore, the mapping theories are as important as the structures that these theories relate in accounting for syntactic phenomena. C-structure nodes are assumed to map onto f-structures; every f-structure is either the matrix f-structure (not contained in any other f-structure) or the value of a grammatical function. Constraints are imposed on this mapping depending on the c-structure configuration involved and on the grammatical function involved. Arguments are also assumed to map onto f-structures, and the mapping theory also imposes constraints on the association between a particular type of argument and a particular type of grammatical function. An important idea about these mapping theories is that the mapping to f-structure is unique: there can never be more that one f-structure corresponding to any c-structure node or a-structure argument. Although c-structure nodes may be associated with arguments, this association arises through the mediation of the f-structure: whenever there is a c-structure node that maps onto an argument, there is a unique f-structure that maps onto both. Thus, we can say that the f-structure is an interface level between c-structure, the level that interfaces with the phonological component, and a-structure, the level that interfaces with lexical semantics. The association between a c-structure node and an argument is the result of satisfying both the function-category association theory, relating c-structure nodes and f-structures, and the Functional Mapping Theory (FMT), which relates arguments and f-structures.

A salient feature of the theory presented here is that the syntactic subcategorization of a lexical item is represented as its a-structure, which is largely invariant for the different uses of the lexical item. The particular grammatical functions associated with this lexical item in any specific instance are represented only in the f-structure of the sentence and they are not prespecified in the lexical entry of the lexical item in question. The a-structure determines, through the application of the FMT, the grammatical functions associated with the predicate. If an a-structure undergoes a change, possibly as a result of a morphological process, the grammatical functions that it selects are predictably different from those selected by the same a-structure in which the change in question has not taken place. The different arrays of grammatical functions selected by the active and the passive forms of the same predicate, and the consequent alternation in grammatical functions of the arguments involved, are the result of applying the same set of mapping principles to two different (but almost identical) a-structures. There is no change in the assignment of grammatical functions to arguments either in the lexicon or in the syntax: in the lexicon, because there are no grammatical functions specified; in the syntax, because syntactic representations are static (i.e., there are no structure changing, only structure building, rules).

The array of grammatical functions of an f-structure depends for the most part on the a-structure of the predicate: the number and type of grammatical functions is determined by the number and type of arguments, as a result of the FMT. However, there are some grammatical functions whose presence in an f-structure does not depend directly on the a-structure, because such grammatical functions are nonthematic: they exist in addition to the grammatical functions that are licensed by mapping to a-structure. In some cases, these grammatical functions are not part of the basic clause structure, but they correspond to an additional layer of information that expresses discourse notions: they are the discourse functions licensed by phrases in sentence initial position in questions, relative clauses, etc. In other cases, they are part of the basic clause structure, as with raising and expletive functions. I have proposed principles for predicting and constraining the appearance of such grammatical functions. Significantly, the presence of such grammatical functions can be predicted in most cases without having to be stipulated in the lexical entry of the governing predicate. Thus, we can maintain the claim that syntactic subcategorization is predictable on the basis of argument structure, in which only semantic arguments are represented.

3

The Romance Reflexive Clitic

The Romance reflexive clitic has been the object of very different analyses in current linguistic theory. It is clear that the reflexive clitic, *es* in the Catalan example (1a), indicates that two argument roles of the predicate, the "defender" and the "defendee" in this example, are interpreted as having the same referent, as in the English translation (1b).

(1) a. La directora es defensa.
    the director RF defends

     b. The director defends herself.

Many researchers assume that the reflexive clitic in (1a), like the English reflexive *herself* in (1b), is the expression of an argument role, so that the same argument roles are syntactically realized in both sentences and are realized as the same syntactic categories. An alternative view proposes that the reflexive clitic differs significantly from the English reflexive in that it is not itself the syntactic expression of any argument role, but rather signals the suppression or cancellation of one of the argument roles of the predicate so that only one is actually expressed. These are the two prevalent approaches to the analysis of the Romance reflexive clitic in current theories. In this chapter, after outlining these two approaches, I will present the relevant facts of the Romance reflexive clitic showing that they cannot be accounted for by either of those approaches because, given the assumptions made in those theories, they constitute a paradox.

3.1 Two Current Approaches

There are several competing approaches to the analysis of the Romance reflexivized construction.[1] I will consider two of them here, which enjoy

---

[1] I use the term *reflexivized construction* to refer to a structure with the reflexive clitic and with a reflexive or reciprocal interpretation. The reflexive clitic has many uses that are not associated with a reflexive or reciprocal semantics (see, for example,

a great deal of acceptance. The first one assumes that the reflexive clitic binds an empty category in object position, like a pronominal clitic, either through movement or chain formation, or by agreement, and that the clitic (or the empty category bound by it) is an anaphor and, as such, must be bound by the subject. Such an analysis is explicitly argued for in Rizzi 1986b, Moore 1991, and Fontana and Moore 1992, and is adopted without discussion in most work within the GB framework (for example, Guéron 1985:57, Riemsdijk and Williams 1986:251, Belletti 1990:107, etc.). I refer to it as the *pronominal approach*, because the syntactic structure it assigns to a reflexivized construction like (1a), schematically shown in (2a), is essentially the same it assigns to the corresponding sentence with a pronominal object clitic, (2b).

(2) *Pronominal approach:*

a. La directora es defensa $\overset{\text{NP}}{\underset{e}{|}}$ b. La directora el   defensa.

   the director RF defends —   the director him ACC defends

                                'The director defends him.'

Under this approach, the reflexive clitic *es* in (2a) and the pronominal clitic *el* in (2b) are assumed to fulfil a similar role in the syntactic structure: they are both coindexed with, or bind, an empty category in object position. We can say that they are both the overt expression of the object function, either because they are the object, which has cliticized to the verb leaving a trace in object position, as in Rizzi 1986b, or because they are verbal morphology that licenses a phonologically null object, as in Moore 1991. The two types of clitics differ in the usual way that anaphors and pronominals are assumed to differ according to the Binding Theory of Chomsky (1981, 1986): whereas the reflexive clitic must be bound by the subject, the pronominal clitic cannot be.

The second approach assumes that the reflexive clitic is a morpheme that signals an operation on the argument structure by which an internal argument of a predicate is bound to its external argument and the latter is suppressed, as in Grimshaw 1990 and S. Rosen 1989, following an idea in Marantz 1984, and developing Grimshaw's (1982) proposal that it is a valence reducing morpheme.[2] The suppression of the external argument entails that the subject position is generated empty, allowing the internal

---

Grimshaw 1982), and a reflexive or reciprocal meaning can be conveyed by means other than the reflexive clitic (by means of independent anaphors, such as *se stesso* in Italian, *si mateix* in Catalan, etc.). This chapter is concerned primarily with reflexivized constructions in the sense intended here.

[2]The assumption that the reflexive clitic involves valence reduction is also adopted in the work of Sanfilippo 1990 and others within the frameworks of Categorial Unification Grammar and Head-driven Phrase Structure Grammar, but it is generalized

argument, generated in object position, to move to subject position, as schematized in (3a), as with unaccusatives and passives. I thus refer to this analysis as the *unaccusative approach*: it assumes that a reflexivized construction, such as (3a), has essentially the same syntactic analysis as the corresponding passive construction, shown in (3b).

(3)   *Unaccusative approach:*

a. La directora es defensa `NP` b. La directora serà   defensada.
                             `e`   'The director will be defended.'

the director RF defends —

In this approach, the reflexive clitic has the same syntactic effect as the passive morpheme: they both absorb the external θ-role (or, equivalently, suppress the external argument), which causes the subject position to be empty at d-structure. Thus, in both the reflexivized (3a) and the passive (3b), the only argument role that is syntactically realized is the internal argument, as a d-structure object. Owing possibly to Burzio's Generalization (Burzio 1986), these structures, which do not assign an external θ-role, cannot assign accusative Case either: in order for the object to receive Case, then, it must move to subject position, in both structures.

These two approaches differ in two important ways:

1. The unaccusative approach assumes that the reflexive clitic is a marker of *valence reduction*, whereas the pronominal approach does not assume any change in the valence of the verb due to the reflexive clitic. In other words, the unaccusative approach assumes that a reflexivized construction such as (3a), based on a dyadic predicate, is intransitive, just like the corresponding passive (3b); the pronominal approach analyzes it as a transitive construction, just as if there were a full NP in object position instead of the reflexive clitic.

2. The pronominal approach analyzes the subject of a reflexivized construction in the same way as the subject of the corresponding nonreflexivized construction, namely, as an *external argument* in an example like (2a). The unaccusative approach, according to which the reflexive clitic signals the suppression of the external argument, proposes that the subject of a reflexivized construction is an *internal argument*.

---

to nonreflexive clitics as well. It is unclear how such an approach would explain the differences between the two types of clitics.

These differences of analysis predict important empirical differences, which we will test in the following sections. Section 3.2 presents evidence relevant to determining whether the reflexive clitic is a valence reducing morpheme. In section 3.3, we examine evidence that supports the claim that verbs with the reflexive clitic pattern with unaccusative verbs and require their subject to be analyzed as an internal argument. The facts presented in section 3.4, in contrast, show that verbs with the reflexive clitic are unlike unaccusative verbs and that their subject should be analyzed as an external argument. These three sections will show that, although both approaches can account for some of the facts of the Romance reflexivized construction, neither of them can account for the whole range of facts.

The evidence to be discussed will also throw light on another area of difference between the two approaches: whether the reflexive clitic is a syntactic anaphor or not. An approach, such as the pronominal approach, which assumes that the reflexive clitic of (1a) and the English reflexive of (1b) only differ in their morphological properties (the clitic surfaces attached to the verb) is committed to analyzing the reflexive clitic as a syntactic anaphor, i.e., as an NP that must be bound to an antecedent in the relevant minimal domain defined by the binding theory. For an approach that analyzes the reflexive clitic as signalling a binding relation at the level of argument structure, there is no a priori reason to assume that it is also a syntactic anaphor. Nevertheless, S. Rosen 1989, following a suggestion in Grimshaw 1990, proposes to treat the reflexive clitic as a syntactic anaphor (although not as a syntactic argument). Thus, whereas evidence showing that it is a syntactic anaphor would be consistent with both approaches, evidence showing that the reflexive clitic cannot be a syntactic anaphor would be inconsistent with the pronominal approach and only consistent with an analysis of the reflexive clitic as signalling binding at argument structure.

There are other possibilities in addition to these two alternative approaches. The unaccusative approach is characterized by analyzing the reflexive clitic as a marker that signals suppression of one of the argument roles that are in a binding relation (as a means to achieve valence reduction). However, one could just as easily conceive a theory in which the suppressed argument is the bound internal argument, instead of the external argument. Such a theory could be termed an *unergative approach*, since reflexive cliticization would derive unergative verbs from dyadic predicates such as *defend*: intransitive verbs whose subject is an external argument. It is unclear to me whether any analysis of the Romance reflexivized construction has been proposed that would qualify as an unergative approach. In any case, the subsequent three sections will also reveal problems for such an approach. Finally, an analysis that defies classification into any of the categories just outlined has been proposed within the framework of RG: the *multiattachment* analysis, developed by Perlmutter (1978b, 1989) and C. Rosen (1988). This analysis will be discussed in chapter 4.

3.2   Valence Reduction

The evidence in this section shows that the reflexive clitic signals valence reduction, or, in other words, that reflexivized constructions have one less grammatical function than their nonreflexivized counterparts. This was first argued by Grimshaw 1982 for French, building on Kayne 1975, with evidence involving *NP extraposition* and *case marking in causative constructions*. Additional evidence supporting the same conclusion can be found in *nominalizations* and in *past participle agreement with a clitic* in Catalan. In what follows, the data will be drawn from Catalan whenever possible, except where a particular phenomenon is attested in another of the Romance languages and not in Catalan.

3.2.1   NP Extraposition

NP extraposition in French is a construction with the nonargument subject *il* and an NP immediately following the verb. Extraposition constructions such as (4a) always alternate with constructions in which that NP appears in the subject position such as (4b), from Grimshaw 1982: 112, citing Martin 1970:377. (Among other constraints on NP extraposition, there is a definiteness restriction: as shown in Martin 1970:379–380, the extraposed NP must be indefinite. But see Legendre 1990b:fn. 7 for some qualifications on this restriction.)

(4) a.   Il passe un train toutes les heures.

    b.   Un train passe toutes les heures.

        'A train goes by every hour.'

Evidence from subject-verb agreement, word order (Grimshaw 1982: 113), and the partitive *en* clitic (Legendre 1990b:91–94) shows that the postverbal NP in extraposition constructions such as (4a) is not a (surface) subject, but an object. The phenomenon of NP extraposition cannot be so clearly documented in Catalan or any of the other Romance languages that have subject "pro-drop": as languages that allow phonologically null subjects also seem to allow inversion of their subject and lack overt expletive subjects (see Perlmutter 1971), it is difficult to tell whether in such a language a postverbal NP agreeing with the verb is a subject in postverbal position or truly an object. Since the evidence for NP extraposition is most clearly illustrated in French, I will draw it from this language.

NP extraposition is possible with intransitive verbs, as illustrated in (4), but completely impossible with transitive verbs, as we see in (5), from Kayne 1975:379.

(5) a. Trois mille hommes ont dénoncé la décision.

    b. *Il a dénoncé la décision trois mille hommes.

    c. *Il a dénoncé trois mille hommes la décision.

    'Three thousand men denounced the decision.'

The preceding evidence can be taken to show that a logical subject, such as *un train* in (4) and *trois mille hommes* in (5), cannot be expressed as an object if the construction includes another object unmarked for morphological case. Since (5) does include such an object, *la décision*, the appearance of the logical subject as an object is precluded. This prohibition holds whether the object is expressed as a full NP, as in (5), or as a pronominal object clitic, such as *l'* in (6), from Kayne 1975:379. However, a dyadic verb with a reflexive clitic does allow NP extraposition, as in (7), from Kayne 1975:381.

(6)   *Il l'a dénoncé trois mille hommes.
    'Three thousand men denounced it.'

(7)   Il s'est dénoncé trois mille hommes ce mois-ci.
    'Three thousand men denounced themselves this month.'

The contrast between (4) and (5)–(6) indicates that NP extraposition is restricted to intransitive verbs (i.e., verbs whose nonextraposed form does not take an accusative object). The fact that transitive verbs with a reflexive clitic can appear in this construction indicates that the reflexive clitic intransitivizes the verb. NP extraposition is possible in (7) because there is no accusative object cooccurring with the logical subject expressed as an object; in other words, the nonextraposed counterpart of (7) (*Trois mille hommes se sont dénoncés ce mois-ci*) does not include an accusative object. This evidence is highly problematic for the pronominal approach because, by analyzing reflexive clitics as object clitics, it cannot account for the grammaticality of (7), in contrast with (5) and particularly with (6).

3.2.2 Case Marking in Causative Constructions

Grimshaw 1982 shows that, in French, reflexivized dyadic verbs in causative constructions are treated like intransitive verbs regarding the morphological case of the causee. This is also true for Catalan. When the predicate embedded in a causative construction is intransitive, the causee is morphologically unmarked for case (accusative); when the embedded predicate is transitive, the causee is marked with dative case. This contrast is illustrated in (8a) and (8b) respectively.

(8) a. { L'   /*Li }   he   fet   ballar.
        him ACC/ him DAT I have made dance

    'I made him dance.'

    b. {*L'   / Li }   he   fet   rentar la cortina.
        him ACC/ him DAT I have made wash   the curtain

    'I made him wash the curtain.'

When a dyadic verb such as *rentar* of example (8b) is reflexivized and embedded in the causative construction, the causee is expressed as an accusative object, as in (9), just as if the embedded verb were intransitive.[3]

(9)   { L'   /*Li }   he   fet   rentar(-se).
        him ACC/ him DAT I have made wash   RF

    'I made him wash himself.'

Catalan differs from French in allowing even nonreflexive clitics to appear attached to the embedded verb in causative constructions. (In French, reflexive clitics, but not pronominal object clitics, can appear attached to the embedded verb.) When the object of the embedded verb in (8b) is cliticized to this verb, as in (10), the causee remains a dative object.

(10)   {*L'   / Li }   he   fet   rentar-la.
        him ACC/ him DAT I have made wash   it ACC

    'I made him wash it.'

The contrast in the morphological case of the causee in (9) and (10) is impossible to explain if reflexive clitics are assumed to be pronouns (or to bind an empty pronoun in object position), just like nonreflexive clitics.[4]

The omissibility of the reflexive clitic in the embedded verb of causative constructions, illustrated in (9), can be explained by appeal-

---

[3] The presence of the reflexive clitic in the embedded predicate of causative constructions is not obligatory. Its absence is the preferred option in many cases, and the sole option in some dialects. In this respect, Catalan resembles Italian, which tends to omit the reflexive clitic in these constructions, rather than French or Spanish, which generally require it.

[4] A reviewer observes that, in many dialects of Catalan, including the normative standard, example (10) would be unacceptable, as the entire clitic string must remain together, either with the top predicate, as in (ia) or with the lower predicate, as in (ib), but cannot be split, as in it in (10).

ing to one of the characteristic properties of the reflexive clitic: the fact that it reduces the valence of the verb it attaches to. In causative constructions, valence reduction of the embedded predicate may occur independently of the presence of a reflexive clitic. As will be shown in section 4.2.2, the causee, unless it is an internal argument, is freely omissible. Thus, in causative constructions, one of the characteristic functions of the reflexive clitic—valence reduction—is redundant, which may account for why it is optional only in these cases. In the pronominal approach, the optionality of the reflexive clitic in cases like (9) is not easily explained.

The evidence from case marking in causative constructions argues for the valence reducing effect of the reflexive clitic. If the assignment of dative case to the causee depends on there being an accusative object in the structure, the causee of a reflexivized predicate will fail to be assigned dative case if reflexivization has the effect of not licensing the accusative object that would otherwise cooccur with the causee.

(i) a. L'hi   he   fet   rentar.
     him/her-it I have made wash

     'I made him/her wash it.'

   b.   He fet rentar-l'hi.

I find this observation very surprising. (ia) is certainly acceptable, as an alternative to (10), but (ib), though acceptable, cannot have the same meaning as (ia) and (10): it can only mean 'I have got it washed for him/her'/'I made someone wash it for him/her'. It is a well-known fact (probably true of all the Romance languages) that the causee cannot cliticize onto the embedded verb, as would be required in order for (ib) to have the same meaning as (ia). Furthermore, in some cases, clitic splitting seems to be the only option available. Consider example (iia); in order to avoid clitic splitting, we would get sentence (iib), which is either unacceptable or means something different from (iia). (See Moore 1990, for similar facts in Spanish.)

(ii) a. Li   he   fet   tornar-me el   llibre.
     him/her DAT I have made return me the book

     'I made her return the book to me.'

   b.   *Me li he fet tornar el llibre.

However, the contrast that (9) and (10) illustrate can also be shown expressing the causee as an NP instead of as a clitic, as we can see in (iii). (The reason for expressing the causee as a clitic in those examples is that the difference between dative and accusative case is best manifested in third person pronominal clitics.)

(iii) a. He   fet   rentar(-se) (*a) la noia.
     I have made wash   RF   to the girl

     'I made the girl wash herself.'

   b.   He   fet   rentar-la   *(a) la noia.
     I have made wash   it ACC   to the girl

     'I made the girl wash it.'

3.2.3 Nominalizations

The infinitival form of verbs in Catalan can be nominalized, as shown in (11).

(11) a. El caminar pausat de l'abadessa marcava el ritme de
 the walk INF calm of the abbess marked the rhythm of

 la processó.
 the procession

 'The calm pace of the abbess marked the rhythm of the procession.'

 b. Tota la nit he sentit el plorar insistent d'un infant.
 all night I have heard the cry INF insistent of an infant

 'All night long I heard the insistent crying of an infant.'

There is evidence that infinitives such as those in (11) are fully nominal, and are not like verbal gerunds in English. Zucchi 1993 notes for Italian that NPs headed by a nominalized infinitive are distinguished from NPs headed by an infinitival VP in that only the former can take postnominal adjectives and a prepositional phrase expressing the logical subject, whereas the latter can take adverbial modifiers and direct objects, but no expression of the logical subject. Being NPs, both constructions take determiners and prenominal adjectives. Essentially the same facts hold in Catalan: the infinitives in (11) are fully nominal because they take postnominal adjectives (*pausat* in (11a) and *insistent* in (11b)) and a *de*-phrase expressing the logical subject (*de l'abadessa* in (11a) and *d'un infant* in (11b)), neither of which can occur with infinitival VPs.

Whereas intransitive verbs can be nominalized in their infinitive form, as the examples in (11) demonstrate, transitive verbs cannot, as we see in (12) (also noted by Zucchi 1993 for Italian).

(12) a. *El sàtir observava amagat el despullar les nimfes
 the satyr observed hidden the undress INF the nymphs

 sorollós del centaure.
 noisy of the centaur

 'Hidden, the satyr was observing the noisy undressing of the nymphs by the centaur.'

 b. *Aquell criticar els actors despietat pel director va
 that criticize INF the actors merciless by the director PAST

 minar la moral de la companyia.
 weaken the morale of the company

 'That merciless criticizing of the actors by the director weakened the company's morale.'

    c. *El mirar   la presa fix de l' animal anunciava una
       the look INF the prey fixed of the animal announced a

    lluita a mort.
    fight to death

    'The fixed looking at the prey of the animal announced a fight
    to the death.'

The presence of an object NP following the infinitive (such as *les nimfes*
in (12a)) is only consistent with the VP analysis of the structure headed
by the infinitive, but this analysis is inconsistent with the postnominal adjective and the *de*-phrase expression of the logical subject (for
example, *sorollós* and *del centaure* respectively in (12a)). In order for
(12) to contain grammatical instances of infinitival VPs, the postnominal adjective would have to be replaced by the corresponding adverbial
form and the expression of the logical subject would have to be omitted; so, for example, the infinitival phrase in (12a) could be rendered
as the verbal construction *el despullar les nimfes sorollosament*. The
expression of any argument other than the logical subject of the infinitive is inconsistent with the analysis of the infinitive as a noun; unlike
English nominalizations, which allow the object of the corresponding
verbal construction to be introduced by a preposition (see Grimshaw
1990), nominalized infinitives in Romance do not allow this possibility.[5]
In conclusion, a transitive verb, with an obligatory object, cannot be
nominalized in Romance, because its object argument is obligatory but
cannot be expressed in the nominalized form.

    In contrast with the transitive verbs in (12), their reflexivized coun-
terparts can be nominalized, as shown in (13).[6]

---

[5] In this respect, nominalized infinitives differ from other nominalizations in Romance. In Catalan, nominalizations such as *demostració* 'demonstration', *captura*
'capture', *descobriment* 'discovery', etc., allow arguments other than their logical
subject to be expressed introduced by prepositions such as *de* 'of', much like their
English counterparts (see Picallo 1991). In contrast, nominalized infinitives do not:
the infinitives in (12) remain ungrammatical when their "object" argument is expressed as a *de*-phrase and their logical subject is unexpressed or introduced by a
per part de phrase, as in (i), corresponding to (12a).

    (i)   *El despullar   de les nimfes   sorollós (per part   del centaure)
           the undress INF of the nymphs noisy   on the part of the centaur

The tests given in Picallo 1991 to distinguish event/process from result nominals
seem to indicate that nominalized infinitives in Catalan are unambiguously result
nominals.

[6] Zucchi 1993 also observes that the reflexive clitic in Italian differs from NP objects
in being able to appear in infinitival NPs, citing Grimshaw and Selkirk 1976 and Salvi
1983 as previous works where this fact is observed. He also takes this as evidence
that reflexive clitics are not the expression of an argument.

(13) a. El sàtir observava amagat el despullar-se sorollós de les
the satyr observed hidden the undress INF-RF noisy of the

nimfes.
nymphs

'Hidden, the satyr was observing the noisy undressing of the
nymphs.'

b. Aquell criticar-se despietat entre els actors va minar
that criticize INF-RF merciless among the actors PAST weaken

la moral de la companyia.
the morale of the company

'That merciless mutual criticism among the actors weakened
the company's morale.'

c. El mirar-se fix dels dos animals anunciava una lluita
the look INF-RF fixed of the two animals announced a fight

a mort.
to death

'The fixed looking at each other of the two animals announced
a fight to the death.'

The adjective following the infinitive in (13a-c), as well as the *de*-phrase
expressing its logical subject in (13a) and (13c), indicates that they are
instances of nominalized infinitives. Thus, while having an object NP in
the infinitival phrase in (12) makes it impossible to analyze the infinitive
as a noun, replacing this object NP by a reflexive clitic, as in (13), makes
this analysis possible. This follows directly from the assumption that the
reflexive clitic is not the expression of an object: the prohibition against
nominalizing infinitives taking an object would not apply in (13), since
the presence of the reflexive clitic indicates that the structure lacks the
object that it otherwise requires.

However, one might try to argue that the contrast between (12) and
(13) is not due to the absence of an object in the infinitival phrase in the
latter set of examples, but to the assumption that the object is morphologically incorporated in the verb, in which case one might stipulate that
the prohibition against nominalizing infinitives taking an object is sus-
pended. If the contrast between (12) and (13) were due to a difference in
the morphological realization of the object (full NP in the former, clitic
or affix in the latter), we would predict that pronominal object clitics
should behave exactly like the reflexive clitic in allowing nominalization
of the infinitive, since both kinds of clitics have the same morphological
status. The fact is, however, that, when we replace the object NP of
(12) by a pronominal object clitic, the nominalization of the infinitive

is still unacceptable, as we see in (14).[7] Such examples are clearly un-grammatical when compared with nominalized infinitives with reflexive clitics, such as those in (13), which are perfectly acceptable, but they are not as offensive as examples of nominalized infinitives with object NPs, such as those in (12). I represent the "mitigated ungrammaticality" of the following examples with the symbol "?*".

(14) a.?*La Maria esperava el despullar-la   impetuós del seu
        Maria   awaited the undress INF-her ACC impetuous of her

     amant.
     lover

   b.?*El mestre sempre acabava lamentant aquell criticar-nos
      the teacher always finished regretting that   criticize INF-us

     despietat a   què   es llançava.
     merciless into which he would plunge

   c.?*La llebre va   intuir el mirar-la   fix   del caçador.
      the hare PAST sense the look INF-it ACC fixed of the hunter

The unacceptability of these examples is due to the status of pronominal clitics, unlike reflexive clitics, as the expression of an argument of the predicate. As noted earlier, nominalized infinitives allow no expression of an argument other than that of the logical subject, as a *de*-phrase. The pronominal clitics in these example correspond to other arguments of the predicates, rendering the nominalization of the infinitive ungrammatical. The presence of postnominal adjectives in (14) requires the nominal analysis of the infinitive. The slightly improved status of (14) compared to (12) might be due to the morphological combination of the infinitive and the clitic: if these two elements combine in the lexicon, and category changing operations such as nominalization can only take place in the lexicon (as assumed in most versions of the "Lexicalist Hypothesis" since Chomsky 1970), it follows that nominalization can take as its input the item consisting of an infinitive and a clitic, although it cannot take as input the sequence of an infinitive and an object NP, which is not a lexical item. Nevertheless, if the nominalized structure contains an element, such as a pronominal clitic, that fulfils a grammatical function, the structure will be ruled out for the reasons stated above.

   The preceding evidence shows that reflexive clitics, unlike pronom-inal clitics, cannot be the expression of a grammatical function. The

---

[7]Nominalized infinitives with pronominal object clitics in Italian are marked as ungrammatical by Zucchi 1993, as in (i):

   (i)   *il   credergli   di Piero
          the believe(inf) him(cl) of Piero

prohibition against nominalizing infinitives taking an object correctly accounts for the ungrammaticality of (12), with full NP objects, and of (14), with pronominal object clitics. The reason why this prohibition does not also rule out (13), with reflexive clitics, is that reflexive clitics are not the expression of an object. Instead, reflexive clitics signal valence reduction: by attaching a reflexive clitic to a monotransitive verb, we derive an intransitive verb. A monotransitive verb may be nominalized only if it is combined with the reflexive clitic, because the derived form is intransitive, and intransitivity is a prerequisite for nominalization of infinitives in Romance.

It is important to note that it is impossible, within a restrictive theory of grammar, to posit a structure for examples such as (13) in which the nominalized infinitive would have a subject. One might think of analyzing the PP expression of the logical subject in those examples as the subject of the infinitive: this would be highly problematic for many reasons, but especially because these PPs are completely optional. In (11a), for example, a felicitous alternative to the PP may be a relative clause, as in (15a); in cases like (11b) and (11c), the PP can be omitted without any loss of acceptability, as in (15b) and (15c).

(15) a. El sàtir observava amagat el despullar-se sorollós amb
       the satyr observed hidden the undress INF-RF noisy   with

       què es divertien les nimfes.
       which RF amused   the nymphs

       'Hidden, the satyr was observing the noisy undressing with
       which the nymphs amused themselves.'

    b. Aquell criticar-se   despietat va   minar la moral de
       that   criticize INF-RF merciless PAST weaken the morale of

       la companyia.
       the company

       'That merciless mutual criticism weakened the company's
       morale.'

    c. El mirar-se   fix   anunciava una lluita a mort.
       the look INF-RF fixed announced a   fight to death

       'The fixed looking at each other announced a fight to the death.'

There is no syntactic constituent in these examples that can plausibly be analyzed as the subject of the nominalized infinitive. Positing a phonologically null category such as PRO as the subject of the NP headed by the nominalized infinitive does not seem to be an option: if we assume, as in Grimshaw 1990, that the external argument of the verbal base in a nominalization is suppressed, this argument cannot be realized as the subject of the nominalized verb. Consequently, there is no syntactic subject of nominalized verbs that can be the antecedent of the reflexive clitic.

Therefore, the evidence from nominalizations argues not only against the assumption that the reflexive clitic is the expression of an argument, but also against the assumption that it is a syntactic anaphor. Both of these assumptions are characteristic of the pronominal approach. The unaccusative approach explicitly rejects the former of these assumptions, and, although it is indeterminate with respect to the latter, Grimshaw 1990 and S. Rosen 1989 propose that the reflexive clitic may be a syntactic anaphor. Being a syntactic anaphor, even though not the expression of an argument, it would have to be bound by a c-commanding antecedent, which can only be a subject. The grammaticality of nominalized infinitives with a reflexive clitic, which, as shown in (15), lack a subject, indicates that the reflexive clitic is not a syntactic anaphor as it need not be bound by a c-commanding antecedent.

Given that the reflexive clitic in examples like (13) and (15) is responsible for the reflexive or reciprocal interpretation of the nominalized infinitives, just as it is responsible for this interpretation in all other reflexivized constructions, it is obviously desirable to have a unique analysis for the reflexive clitic whenever it carries the reflexive or reciprocal interpretation. Hence, the analysis of the reflexive clitic required by nominalizations, namely, as a valence reducing morpheme and not a syntactic anaphor, is the right one not only when it is necessary (as in nominalizations), but also in structures where other analyses appear possible.

3.2.4   Past Participle Agreement

A past participle in Catalan, when occurring with the perfective auxiliary, *haver* 'have', is generally morphologically unmarked for gender and number, phonologically identical to the masculine singular form. However, there is one situation in which the past participle may be overtly marked for these features: when the accusative object of the clause, if there is one, is expressed as a third person clitic, the past participle optionally agrees with that object in gender and number.[8] Thus, the accusative object of *defensat* 'defended', which is expressed as an object NP in (16a) and therefore does not trigger agreement on the participle, may be encoded by means of a pronominal clitic, as in (16b), (option-

---

[8]There is considerable dialectal and interspeaker variation with respect to past participle agreement. The dialect described here corresponds the standard spoken in Barcelona. In some dialects (Insular and Southern Catalan), the starred forms in (16a) and (17a) might be acceptable.

ally) triggering agreement on the participle. The same phenomenon can be observed in (17) with the participle *vist* 'seen'.

(16) a. La directora ha $\left\{ \begin{array}{l} \text{defensat} \\ \text{*defensada} \end{array} \right\}$ la proposta.

'The director has defended (M.S)/(*F.S) the proposal.'

  b. La directora l' ha defensada.
the director it (F.S) has defended (F.S)

'The director has defended it.'

(17) a. Hem $\left\{ \begin{array}{l} \text{vist} \\ \text{*vistes} \end{array} \right\}$ les ballerines.

'We have seen (M.S)/(*F.P) the ballerinas.'

  b. Les hem vistes.
them (F.P) we have seen (F.P)

'We have seen them.'

If, instead of a third person nonreflexive clitic, as in (16b) and (17b), we use a third person reflexive clitic, the participle remains in the morphologically unmarked (masculine singular) form, as in (18) and (19).

(18) La directora s' ha $\left\{ \begin{array}{l} \text{defensat.} \\ \text{*defensada.} \end{array} \right\}$
the director (F.S) RF has defended (M.S)/(*F.S)

'The director defended herself.'

(19) Les ballarines s' han $\left\{ \begin{array}{l} \text{vist.} \\ \text{*vistes.} \end{array} \right\}$
the ballerinas (F.S) RF have seen (M.S)/(*F.P)

'The ballerinas have seen themselves/each other.'

The contrast between reflexive and nonreflexive clitics in their ability to trigger agreement on the participle of perfective compound forms, illustrated in (16b)–(17b) vs. (18)–(19), is unexpected under the pronominal approach, according to which both kinds of clitics are the morphological expression (or licensor) of an argument represented in object position. If a third person object clitic may trigger agreement on the past participle, as examples (16b)–(17b) show, only a stipulation would account for the failure of the cliticized reflexive "object" in (18)–(19) to trigger agreement on the past participle.

However, if the reflexive clitic is assumed not to be an object, but a morpheme that detransitivizes the verb, as in the unaccusative approach, the contrast between (16b)–(17b) and (18)–(19) is fully expected. The rule that allows a past participle in a perfective clause to agree with its third person object clitic licenses the agreeing forms in (16b)–(17b) because the clitics in these examples are nonreflexive, and therefore object clitics. On the other hand, it does not license the agreeing forms in (18)–(19) because the reflexive clitic is not an object clitic.[9] If reflexivized constructions such as (18)–(19) are analyzed as intransitive sentences, there is no object clitic that may trigger agreement. In this respect, they do no differ from basic intransitive predicates (without a reflexive clitic), whose past participle in a perfective form must appear in the unmarked (masculine singular) form, as in (20):

(20) a. La directora ha $\left\{ \begin{array}{l} \text{arribat.} \\ \text{*arribada.} \end{array} \right\}$

       'The director (F.S) has arrived (M.S)/(*F.S).'

   b. Les ballarines han $\left\{ \begin{array}{l} \text{caigut.} \\ \text{*caigudes.} \end{array} \right\}$

       'The ballerinas (F.P) have fallen (M.S)/(*F.P).'

Catalan is unique among the Romance languages in providing this kind of evidence for the valence-reducing nature of the reflexive clitic. There are other Romance languages, such as French and Italian, in which the presence of an object clitic in a perfective compound form causes the past participle to agree with the object. However, in these languages, the reflexive clitic appears to behave like object clitics in also triggering

---

[9]One might be tempted to speculate that the reason why the reflexive clitic fails to trigger past participle agreement in examples like (18)–(19) is not that it is not an object (or the morphological expression or licensor of an object), but that it lacks the agreement features that are overtly distinguished in nonreflexive third person clitics in Catalan and other Romance languages. Whereas nonreflexive third person accusative clitics distinguish masculine vs. feminine and singular vs. plural, the reflexive third person clitic does not make gender or number distinctions. However, the failure to make overt gender and number distinctions cannot be the reason why the third person reflexive clitic does not trigger past participle agreement: the partitive object clitic *en*, in spite of being invariant for gender and number, does trigger past participle agreement, just like its definite counterparts, as the following examples demonstrate. The antecedent of *en* in (i) is a feminine singular NP, such as *proposta*, and in (ii) a feminine plural NP such as *ballarines*.

  (i)   La directora no n' ha defensada   cap.
        the director not EN has defended (F.S) any

       'The director has not defended any.'

  (ii)   N' hem   vistes   algunes.
        EN we have seen (F.P) some (F.P)

       'We have seen some of them.'

Since the object clitic *en* triggers past participle agreement, even though it does not manifest gender and number distinctions, the failure of the reflexive clitic to trigger past participle agreement cannot be attributed to its being nondistinct for the various gender and number categories.

agreement: not only do the French and Italian equivalents of (16b)–(17b) include an agreeing past participle, but so do the equivalents of the reflexivized (18)–(19). Interestingly, in these languages, but not in Catalan, there is a difference in the choice of perfective auxiliary between the former and the latter examples, as we shall see in section 3.3.1, transitive nonreflexivized verbs selecting *avere* (It.)/*avoir* (Fr.) and their reflexivized counterparts selecting *essere* (It.)/*être* (Fr.). The use of *essere*/*être* as a perfective auxiliary occurs independently of the presence of a reflexive clitic, as this is the auxiliary choice for a large class of predicates including those of the French or Italian equivalent of (20). In these cases, where auxiliary *essere*/*être* is chosen, the past participle agrees with the subject. Thus, in the French or Italian counterparts of (18)–(19), where the past participle is not in the invariant masculine singular form, the past participle agrees with the subject, and not with the object, since the reflexive clitic signals the absence of the object that the verb would otherwise require.

3.2.5 Conclusion

The four types of evidence discussed in this section—NP extraposition in French, case marking in causative constructions, nominalizations, and past participle agreement—are sensitive to the distinction between transitive and intransitive verbs. In all four cases, the reflexivized form of a monotransitive verb behaves like an intransitive verb, and not like the same verb without the reflexive clitic. The reflexive clitic, thus, reduces the valence of the verb it attaches to, turning a monotransitive verb into an intransitive one.

In addition, the fact that nominalizations can be based on reflexivized infinitives argues against analyzing the reflexive clitic as a syntactic anaphor because its binding requirements would not be met: the evidence presented in 3.2.3 indicates that nominalized infinitives lack a subject; therefore, there would be no possible antecedent for the reflexive clitic in a nominalized infinitive. A similar argument could be based on NP extraposition: in examples like (7), repeated here as (21), involving the reflexive clitic, a violation of the Binding Theory would ensue.

(21)   Il s'est dénoncé trois mille hommes ce mois-ci.
         'Three thousand men denounced themselves this month.'

Since the postverbal NP in this construction (*trois mille hommes* in (21)) is an object, if it is assumed to be coindexed with the reflexive clitic, the reflexive clitic, whether adjoined to the verb, as in Rizzi 1986b, or located in INFL, as in S. Rosen 1989, c-commands its antecedent, in violation of principle C of the Binding Theory (see Rizzi 1986b:87). The fact that

NP extraposition is grammatical with reflexivized verbs shows that the reflexive clitic cannot be analyzed as a syntactic anaphor. Causative constructions also provide support for this conclusion, as will be argued in chapter 7.

3.3 Reflexivized Verbs are Unaccusatives

The preceding section has shown that the reflexivized form of a mono-transitive verb behaves like an intransitive verb, but it has not told us whether it behaves like an unergative or an unaccusative (the two major classes of intransitive verbs proposed by Perlmutter 1978a). We shall now consider evidence that indicates that it behaves like an unaccusative, or, in other words, that the subject of a reflexivized construction such as (1) is the expression of an internal argument, as proposed in the unaccusative approach. This evidence includes: the facts of auxiliary selection in Italian, the behavior of reflexivized verbs in causative constructions, and the formation of participial constructions also in Italian.

3.3.1 Auxiliary Selection

One of the clearest ways in which a reflexivized verb behaves like an unaccusative is with respect to auxiliary selection in languages like Italian (and, to some extent, in French). (Catalan, like Spanish and Portuguese, has one single perfective auxiliary, and so has no auxiliary alternation to distinguish between unaccusatives and unergatives.) The facts of auxiliary selection in Italian have been extensively investigated by Perlmutter (1978b, 1989), C. Rosen (1988), and Burzio (1986). In Italian, among intransitive verbs, unaccusatives select the perfect auxiliary *essere*, (22a), while unergatives select *avere*, (22b). Among dyadic predicates, nonreflexive transitive verbs, such as those in (23), take *avere* in the perfective forms, like unergatives, whereas their reflexivized counterparts in (24) take *essere* like unaccusatives (examples based on Grimshaw 1990:156).

(22) a. Gianni è arrivato.
  'Gianni has arrived.'

  b. Gianni ha camminato.
  'Gianni has walked.'

(23) a. Gianni ha veduto un gatto.
  'Gianni has seen a cat.'

  b. Gianni mi ha comprato un auto.
  'Gianni has bought me a car.'

(24) a. Gianni si è veduto.
  'Gianni has seen himself.'

b.   Gianni si è comprato un auto.
     'Gianni has bought himself a car.'

This suggests that the reflexive morphology turns a transitive verb into an unaccusative, such as *arrivare* in (22a), rather than into an unergative, such as *camminare* 'walk' in (22b). Thus, the unaccusative approach makes the right prediction regarding auxiliary selection with reflexivized verbs, whereas the pronominal approach and the unergative approach cannot account for this evidence in a simple way.

3.3.2   Causatives of Reflexivized Verbs

As has been observed by Zubizarreta 1985 and Burzio 1986, among others, when a transitive or an unergative verb appears as the embedded predicate of a causative construction, the causee (i.e., the logical subject of the embedded predicate) can be omitted with a human arbitrary interpretation. The logical subject of the transitive *obrir* 'open' is omitted in the causative construction (25a), as is the logical subject of the unergative *treballar* 'work' in (25b). On the other hand, unaccusative predicates resist the omission of their logical subjects when embedded in causative constructions, as illustrated in (26).

(25) a.   El mestre   ha   fet   obrir el llibre.
          the teacher has made open the book

          'The teacher had the book opened.'

     b.   El mestre   ha   fet   treballar molt aquest curs.
          'The teacher has made people work a lot this   term.'

(26) a.   *El fum   farà   sortir   de la casa.
          'The smoke will make people come out of the house.'

     b.   *He   fet   caure tot el matí   per divertir-me.
          'I have made people fall   all morning to amuse myself.'

This is not to say that the causee of an unaccusative verb cannot ever be omitted. Rizzi 1986a observes that accusative objects in Romance can be omitted with a human arbitrary interpretation *only* with a generic time reference. From this it follows that the causee of unaccusative verbs in causative constructions, which is expressed as an accusative object, may be omitted given this generic time reference.[10] Controlling for time reference, there is a contrast between transitive verbs and unergatives,

---

[10]Examples like (i) show that the omission of the causee of unaccusative verbs may occur when licensed by the generic time reference characteristic of null accusative objects in Romance.

(i) a.   A l'estiu, la calor fa   sortir   al   carrer.
         'In summer, the heat makes people come out into the street.'

on the one hand, and unaccusatives, on the other, with respect to the omissibility of the causee, as shown in (25) and (26).

Reflexivized verb forms behave like unaccusatives in disallowing the omission of their logical subject when they appear embedded in a causative construction. (Here too it is necessary to control for time reference, as a generic time reference would allow the causee to be omitted.) As we see in (27), omitting the causee of a reflexivized embedded predicate in a causative construction creates ungrammaticality.[11]

(27) a. Encara no he   fet   disfressar(?-se) *(els actors).
       yet   not I have made disguise   RF   the actors

   'I haven't yet made (the actors) get disguised.'

  b. Farem   posar(?-se) un barret *(a la Maria).
     we will make put   RF a   hat   to Maria

   'We will make (Maria) put on a hat.'

The impossibility of omitting the causee of reflexivized verbs, as in (27), shows that reflexivized verbs behave like unaccusatives, and argues for analyzing the grammatical function that corresponds to the bound argument roles as the expression of an internal argument.

3.3.3 Participial Constructions in Italian

It has been noted (for example, by Perlmutter (1978b, 1989), Burzio (1986), and C. Rosen (1988)) that only verbs that take an "underlying object"—an initial 2 in RG, or a d-structure object in GB—can form a participle that heads a phrase functioning as an adjectival or adverbial modifier. The same generalization holds for Catalan, and probably for Romance in general. However, whereas Italian allows participial forms to take verbal clitics, including reflexive clitics, Catalan (like Spanish and

---

   b. Aquestes preguntes són per fer   caure.
       'These questions are for making people fall (err).'

It is reasonable to assume that the omission of the causee in (i) and in (25) are two different phenomena: whereas it is conditioned by the generic time reference in (i), it is not in (25).

[11] The presence of the reflexive clitic attached to the embedded verb in the causative construction in Catalan, although not ungrammatical, is often disfavored. (See 3.2.2 for a proposal to explain the omission of the reflexive clitic in this construction.) When the reflexive clitic is absent, the sentence is ambiguous between the interpretation in which the object (*els actors* in (27a), and *a la Maria* in (27b)) is the expression of the bound arguments and that in which it is the expression of only an internal argument, with an unexpressed logical subject. We are only interested in the bound argument (or reflexivized) interpretation here.

French) does not.[12] For this reason, the evidence concerning participial constructions will be drawn entirely from Italian.

The participle always agrees in gender and number with an internal argument—the initial 2 of RG and the d-structure object of GB. In the adjectival use of the participial phrase, this argument is unexpressed and controlled by (or coreferential with) the constituent that the adjective phrase is predicated of. In the adverbial use, that argument is either expressed as an NP following the participle (in which case the construction is sometimes referred to as a *participial absolute*) or it is unexpressed and controlled by an argument of the matrix clause. For simplicity, I will concentrate on participial absolutes. Since the construction requires an internal argument for the participle to agree with, and only transitive and unaccusative verbs have internal arguments, it follows that only these verbs can appear in participial absolutes. While a participial absolute can be based on a transitive verb, as in (28a), only its internal argument(s) may be expressed; expressing also its external argument, as in (28b), renders the construction ungrammatical (examples from C. Rosen 1988:60).

(28) a. Tagliati gli olmi, il paese pareva un deserto.
      cut   the elms the town seemed a desert

     'With the elms cut down, the town looked like a desert.'

   b. *Tagliati quei mascalzoni gli olmi, ...
      cut   those scoundrels the elms

     'After those scoundrels had cut down the elms, ...'

---

[12]The Italian forms consisting of a participle and a clitic, be it a nonreflexive clitic, as in *conosciute**ne*** 'known-NE', or *salutata**la*** 'greeted-her', or a reflexive clitic, as in *criticata**si*** 'criticised-self', (from Belletti 1990:104, 107) have no grammatical counterpart in Catalan: *conegudes-**ne**, *saludada-**la**, *criticada**'s**. Catalan is therefore unsuitable for testing whether reflexivized verbs can appear in participial constructions or not: if a participial form cannot take a clitic, and the reflexive (or reciprocal) interpretation is licensed by the reflexive clitic, it follows that a participial form should not have that interpretation. This appears to be correct: (i) shows that participial phrases in Catalan based on dyadic predicates that can be used reflexively elsewhere do not have a reflexive or reciprocal interpretation.

(i) a. Defensada la directora de les seves acusacions, ...
     defended the director of her   accusations

    'Once the director had been defended of her accusations, ...'
    *'Once the director had defended herself of her accusations, ...'

  b. La directora, defensada de les seves acusacions, ...
     the director defended of her   accusations

    'The director, having been defended of her accusations, ...'
    *'The director, having defended herself of her accusations, ...'

As for intransitive verbs, unaccusatives can appear in participial absolutes, as in (29a), but not unergatives, as in (29b) (examples from Belletti 1990:89), since only the former have an internal argument. When we consider reflexivized verbs, we see that they pattern with unaccusatives in allowing the formation of participial absolutes, as examples (30) (from C. Rosen 1990b:422) illustrate.

(29) a. Arrivata Maria, Gianni tirò un sospiro di sollievo.
    arrived Maria, Gianni was relieved

   b. *Telefonato Gianni, Maria andò all'appuntamento.
    telephoned Gianni, Maria went to the appointment

(30) a. Munitisi i contadini di bastoni e zappe, ...
    'The villagers having armed themselves with sticks and hoes, ...'

   b. Rintanatosi Don Enzo tra le amate antiche carte, ...
    'Don Enzo having shut himself away among his beloved manuscripts, ...'

The noun phrase that follows the participle and agrees with it in (30) must be an internal argument; otherwise it would not be able to appear in that position. The ability of reflexivized dyadic predicates to appear in participial absolutes, as in (30), can only be explained by assuming the valence reducing property of the reflexive clitic. If the reflexive clitic *si* in *muniti***si** in (30a) were like the pronominal object clitics *ci* 'us', *la* 'her', *mi* 'me', etc., in being the expression of an object of the verb, we would expect (30a) to be ungrammatical, just as (31) is (from C. Rosen 1988:70), where the object clitic *ci* replaces the reflexive clitic.

(31)   *Munitici i Frabiani di bastoni, ...
    'The Frabians having armed us with cudgels, ...'

(31) is ungrammatical because the participle is not agreeing with its internal argument (since the internal argument is the clitic), and because it is followed by an NP (*i Frabiani*) that is not its internal argument. Thus, in order to explain the grammaticality of (30), we have to assume that the reflexive clitic has the effect of turning a dyadic predicate into an intransitive verb whose subject is the expression of an internal argument.

3.3.4   Summary

This section has shown that reflexivized verbs behave like unaccusatives with respect to auxiliary selection in Italian, with respect to the omissibility of the causee in causative constructions, and with respect to their ability to form participial absolutes in Italian, and differ in all these respects from their nonreflexivized counterparts, from unergatives and from transitive verbs in general. This suggests that the syntactic constituent that corresponds to the argument roles bound by the reflexive clitic is the expression of an internal argument.

3.4 Reflexivized Verbs are not Unaccusatives

The fact that reflexivized verbs behave in several important ways like unaccusative verbs, as shown in the previous section, may suggest that they are, like unaccusatives in general, predicates that lack an expressed external argument. This is the assumption made in the unaccusative approach to reflexivized verbs of Grimshaw 1990, S. Rosen 1989, and Van Valin 1990, among others. As we shall see now, this analysis is inconsistent with a whole set of facts that distinguish internal from external arguments. Since, according to this analysis, reflexivized verbs lack an overt external argument, and the grammatical function that corresponds to the two bound argument roles is the expression only of an internal argument, it predicts that this grammatical function should behave strictly like the internal argument of a transitive verb.[13] In particular, this means it should exhibit properties that internal arguments are assumed to display, namely, being able to appear as a bare plural or mass NP following the verb, and triggering *en*-cliticization; if, as claimed, it is not the logical subject of the verb, it should not be modified by an adjective phrase that is predicated of the logical subject; and it should only be expressed as the grammatical subject when it corresponds to the accusative object in the nonreflexivized form, as with passives of ditransitive verbs. The following evidence shows all of these predictions to be false, and requires assuming that the grammatical function that corresponds to the two bound argument roles of a reflexivized predicate is its logical subject.

---

[13] The literature contains several purported diagnostics of the distinction between external and internal arguments and, therefore, between unaccusatives and unergatives, some of which have turned out to be not as reliable as initially thought. For example, Jaeggli (1986b) proposed that, in the Romance languages with subject pro-drop, a phonologically null third person plural subject could have an arbitrary interpretation only if it was an external argument. Nevertheless, as noted by a reviewer, appropriate examples can be constructed with unaccusative verbs where the subject is a null third person pronominal that can have an arbitrary interpretation. Since the subject of an unaccusative by definition is not an external argument, the purported diagnostic does not stand up. The evidence presented here to distinguish between external and internal arguments seems fairly reliable, but doubts have been raised about some of these diagnostics (see 3.4.1 and 3.4.2).

3.4.1 Bare Plural/Mass NP

One of the diagnostics of unaccusativity in Romance is whether the sole nominal argument of a verb may be expressed as a bare plural or mass noun, as observed in Belletti 1988:29 for Italian, with references given to Torrego 1984 and Lois 1986 for Spanish. The two arguments of transitive verbs contrast with respect to their ability to be expressed as a bare indefinite noun: the object can be so expressed, as shown in (32), but not the subject, as we see in (33).

(32) a. Aquest mecànic arregla motos.
   'This   mechanic fixes   motorbikes.'

   b. Hem   vist gent pels carrers.
   'We have seen people in the streets.'

(33) a. *Mecànics   arreglen el teu cotxe.
   'Mechanics fix   your car.'

   b. *Gent els   ha vistos, aquests errors.
   people them ACC has seen   these   mistakes

   'These mistakes, people will see them.'

Whereas a bare indefinite NP, such as *motos* in (32a) and *gent* in (32b), can appear in the object position, immediately following the verb, it cannot appear in the canonical subject position, preceding the verb, as with the NPs *mecànics* in (33a) and *gent* in (33b). One could argue, however, that the contrast between (32) and (33) does not illustrate a difference between the subject and the object grammatical functions, but between the preverbal and the postverbal NP positions. Could it be that the correct generalization is that bare indefinite NPs are not allowed in the preverbal (subject) position? (This generalization is proposed by Solà 1992:272 not only for Catalan, but more generally for the Romance null subject languages.) This restriction is correct, as the ungrammaticality of (33) indicates. But, given the observation that subject pro-drop languages like Catalan allow the subject to appear in postverbal (post-VP) position, this restriction leads us to expect sentences like (33) to become grammatical once their bare indefinite NP subject is placed in a postverbal position. The expectation is not borne out, as (34) illustrates.

(34) a. *Arreglen mecànics el teu cotxe. /*... el teu cotxe mecànics.
   fix   mechanics your car   ... your car   mechanics

   'Mechanics fix your car.'

   b. *Aquests errors,   els   ha vistos gent.
   these   mistakes them ACC has seen   people

   'These mistakes, people have seen them.'

The ungrammaticality of (34), with bare indefinite NPs as *postverbal* subjects, indicates that the generalization that accounts for both (33) and (34) is that bare indefinite NPs are not allowed as subjects (whether preverbal or postverbal) in Catalan and similar languages.

This generalization appears to hold not only with transitive verbs, as in the previous examples, but also with intransitive verbs. The single nominal argument of intransitive verbs cannot be expressed as a bare indefinite NP in preverbal subject position, as we see in (35) and (36) (example (35a) from Solà 1992:272).

(35) a. *Rocs   cauen de   la muntanya.
        'Stones fall   from the mountain.'

     b. *Nens   han passat pel   carrer.
        'Children have passed along the street.'

(36) a. *Durant les vacances, nens   treballen.
        'During the holidays, children work.'

     b. *Gent   ha   caminat per la muntanya.
        'People have walked on the mountain.'

However, intransitive verbs split into two classes when we consider the ability of the single argument of these verbs to appear as a bare indefinite NP in postverbal position. Verbs such as those in (35) allow their logical subject to be expressed as a bare indefinite NP following the verb, as in (37), but those exemplified in (36) do not, as we see in (38).

(37) a. Cauen rocs   de   la muntanya.
        fall   stones from the mountain

        'Stones fall from the mountain.'

     b. Ha   passat gent   pel   carrer.
        have passed people along the street

        'People have passed along the street.'

(38) a. *Durant les vacances, treballen nens.
        during the holidays   work   children

        'During the holidays, children work.'

     b. *Ha   caminat gent   per   la muntanya.
        have walked   people through the mountain

        'People have walked on the mountain.'

If we want to maintain the generalization argued on the basis of transitive verbs that bare indefinite NPs are not allowed as subjects (whether preverbal or postverbal) in Catalan, we are forced to conclude that the bare indefinite NP immediately following the verb in (37) is not a subject. Notice that this NP appears in the canonical object position, immediately following the verb, and that objects of transitive verbs can be expressed as bare indefinite NPs, as illustrated in (32). If we make a distinction within intransitive verbs between unaccusatives, such as those in (37), and unergatives, such as those in (38), we can explain the contrast in (37) vs. (38). If the logical subject (the single nominal argument) of unaccusative verbs is such that it can be expressed as an object, we can assume that it is expressed as an object in (37), and therefore these examples do not violate the restriction against bare indefinite NP subjects. If the logical subject of unergative verbs is like the logical subject of transitive verbs in that it cannot (normally) be expressed as an object, then the bare indefinite NP in (38) is a subject, which violates the prohibition against bare indefinite NP subjects.[14]

---

[14]There are potential complications with this unaccusative diagnostic. First, there are verbs whose classification as unaccusative or unergative is unclear or variable (*variable behavior verbs* of Levin and Rappaport Hovav 1995). This would explain an example such as (i), proposed by a reviewer to illustrate that unergatives also allow their single nominal argument to appear as a postverbal bare indefinite NP.

(i)   Quan pul·lula gent   per   la   muntanya, ...
        when wander people about the mountain

        'When people wander about the mountain, ... '

Second, the diagnostic works best when the bare indefinite NP consists only of a noun, unmodified and unquantified. The presence of a modifier in an NP suffices to make an otherwise ungrammatical structure grammatical. The following examples, suggested by the same reviewer, show that a bare indefinite NP can be the postverbal subject of transitive and unergative verbs *provided* it includes a modifier:

(ii)   a.   Aquí hi toquen música simfònica orquestres *(de tot el   món).
            here HI play   music symphonic orchestras   of all the world

            'Here, orchestras (from all over the world) play symphonic music.'

       b.   Als   jocs   olímpics hi participen atletes *(de qualitat).
            in the games Olympic HI participate athletes   of quality

            '(Quality) athletes compete in the Olympic games.'

In fact, this observation should not be restricted to postverbal subjects. Changing the subject in (ii) to preverbal position, in (iii), does not affect the grammaticality judgments. The sentences are ungrammatical if the subject (preverbal or postverbal) consists only of a bare indefinite and unmodified noun, such as *orquestres* in (iia) and (iiia) or *atletes* in (iib) and (iiib); they are gramatical if the subject includes the modifier in parentheses.

(iii) a.   Orquestres *(de tot el   món) toquen música simfònica a la   sala.
            orchestras   of all the world play   music symphonic in the hall

            'Orchestras (from all over the world) play symphonic music in the hall.'

       b.   Atletes *(de qualitat) participen als   jocs   olímpics.
            athletes of quality   participate in the games Olympic

            '(Quality) athletes compete in the Olympic games.'

Given this evidence that distinguishes unaccusatives from unergative and transitive verbs, we can consider reflexivized predicates to see with which of the two groups of verbs they pattern. What we find is that the sole direct function of reflexivized predicates cannot be expressed as a bare plural or mass noun, as shown in (39).

(39) a. *Es renten nens   al safareig.
         RF wash   children in the wash house

   'Children are washing themselves in the wash house.'

   b. *S' ha mirat   gent   pels   carrers.
         RF has looked at people in the streets

   'People have looked at each other in the streets.'

These two sentences are grammatical in a nonreflexive/nonreciprocal reading, irrelevant here, as impersonal passives: (39a) could mean 'Children are washed in the wash house', and (39b) could mean 'People have been watched in the street'. Crucially, with a reflexive or reciprocal interpretation, the grammatical function that corresponds to the bound argument roles cannot be expressed as a bare plural or mass noun, exactly like the external argument of transitive and unergative verbs, and unlike the internal argument of transitive and unaccusative verbs.

3.4.2 *En*-Cliticization

A well-known phenomenon in some Romance languages such as French, Italian, and Catalan is that indefinite objects that are unmarked for morphological case can be expressed by means of the pronominal clitic *en* (*ne* in Italian), while the quantifier, if there is one, and optional modifiers remain in object position. (See Kayne 1975 for French, Perlmutter 1978b, C. Rosen 1988, Burzio 1986, and Belletti and Rizzi 1981 for Italian, and Picallo 1984, 1990 for Catalan.) Since internal arguments can generally be expressed as objects, transitive and unaccusative verbs allow their internal argument to trigger *en*-cliticization, as shown in (40) and (41) respectively.

(40) a. Aquest mecànic n' arregla moltes (de motos).
         this   mechanic EN fixes   many of motorbikes

   'This mechanic fixes many (motorbikes).'

   b. No n' he   vist (de gent).
         not EN I have seen of people

   'I haven't seen any (people).'

Such examples indicate that the notion of bare indefinite NP relevant here should be understood to exclude NPs with modifiers.

(41) a. En surten   alguns del   soterrani.
        EN come out some   of the basement

'Some are coming out of the basement.'

     b. N' ha   passat poca pel   carrer.
        EN have passed little along the street

'Not many have passed along the street.'

External arguments, on the other hand, which are generally not expressed as objects, cannot trigger *en*-cliticization. For this reason, the external argument of a transitive verb or of an unergative verb cannot be expressed by means of the clitic *en*, as shown in (42) and (43).[15] Similarly, (44) illustrates that the syntactic expression of the bound arguments of a reflexivized predicate cannot trigger *en*-cliticization.

(42) a. *N' arregla un   el teu cotxe.
        EN fix   one your   car

'One of them is fixing your car.'

     b. *Què en veuen alguns?
        what EN see   some

'What do some of them see?'

(43) a. *En treballen molts.
        EN work   many

'Many of them are working.'

     b. *N' han   caminat tres.
        EN have walked   three

'Three of them have walked.'

---

[15] Serious doubts have been raised about the validity of *en*-cliticization as an unaccusative diagnostic, according to Levin and Rappaport Hovav 1995, citing Lonzi 1985, who reports that *ne*-cliticization in Italian is found not only with unaccusative verbs, but also with verbs that are independently classified as unergatives. Enric Vallduví (p.c.) claims that the same is true in Catalan. It is unclear how to evaluate these claims. On the one hand, for me and other Catalan speakers consulted, there is a definite difference in acceptability between unaccusatives and unergatives with respect to *en*-cliticization. On the other hand, it is likely that unaccusativity is not the only factor that determines the availability of *en*-cliticization with intransitive verbs. Lonzi (1985) points out that unergative verbs in Italian permit *ne*-cliticization, but only when they are found in a simple tense, that is, not when they take the perfective auxiliary. (This contrast is not found with unaccusative verbs.) If this contrast within unergative verbs between forms with the perfective auxiliary and forms without the auxiliary turns out to be robust and reliable, it would indicate that the aspectual properties of the clause would be an additional factor constraining the syntactic realization of the arguments. I leave the issue open to further research.

(44) a. *Se 'n renten dos al safareig.
     RF EN wash two in the wash house

    'Two are washing themselves in the wash house.'

  b. *Se 'n mira   molta pels   carrers.
     RF EN look at many in the streets

    'Many look at each other in the streets.'

This shows that reflexive verbs behave unlike unaccusatives and like unergatives in disallowing *en*-cliticization. This fact has also been observed for Italian: Perlmutter 1983, C. Rosen 1988:94, and Grimshaw 1990:184. In particular, Perlmutter 1983:154–156 notes that, while sentence (45a) is ambiguous for most speakers between the impersonal (or reflexive) passive interpretation (i) and the reflexive/reciprocal interpretation (ii), sentence (45b) with the clitic *ne* (equivalent to Catalan *en*) only has the passive interpretation (i).

(45) a.   Si sono denunciate molte persone.
    (i)   'Many people were denounced.'
    (ii)   'Many people denounced themselves.'

    b.   Se ne sono denunciate molte.
    (i)   'Many (of them) were denounced.'
    (ii)   *'Many (of them) denounced themselves.'

My judgments about the corresponding facts in Catalan agree with Perlmutter's observations: sentences (44a-b) are not grammatical with the reflexive/reciprocal interpretation given, but are grammatical with a passive interpretation. Sentence (44a) can only be interpreted as 'Two (of them) are being washed in the wash house', and (44b) as 'Many (of them) are being looked at in the streets'. While the syntactic expression of an internal argument in a passive construction can trigger *en*-cliticization, the grammatical function corresponding to the bound argument roles of a reflexive construction cannot, suggesting that it is the expression of the external argument.

3.4.3 Modifiers of the Logical Subject

Transitive verbs can generally take predicative adjective phrases that modify either the subject or the object. Semantic factors determine whether the adjective phrase may be predicated of one grammatical function or the other. (See, for example, Jackendoff 1990:200–207 on "depictive predication," and also Bresnan 1982a:323 and Rothstein 1983.) Let us consider here cases in which only the subject is a possible target of predication by the AP. (In the following examples, coindexation between an NP and an agreeing adjective signals a predication relation.)

(46) a. En Ferran$_i$ ajudava la Gertrudis$_j$ $\left\{\begin{array}{l}(^*\text{contenta}_j).\\(\text{content}_i).\end{array}\right\}$

     'Ferran$_i$ helped   Gertrudis$_j$ (happy$_{i/*j}$).'

  b. En Ferran$_i$ castiga   els nens$_j$ $\left\{\begin{array}{l}(^*\text{avergonyits}_j).\\(\text{implacable}_i).\end{array}\right\}$

     'Ferran$_i$ punishes the boys$_j$ (ashamed$_{*j}$/implacable$_i$).'

Only the subject in these examples can be the target of predication by the adjective phrase. However, being a grammatical subject is not a sufficient condition to guarantee a well-formed predication relation with these verbs. The corresponding passive forms in (47) show this:

(47) a. La Gertrudis$_j$ serà ajudada $\left\{\begin{array}{l}(^*\text{contenta}_j)\\(^*\text{content}_i)\end{array}\right\}$(per en Ferran$_i$).

     'Gertrudis$_j$ will be helped   (happy$_{*i/*j}$) (by Ferran$_i$).'

  b. Els nens$_j$ eren castigats $\left\{\begin{array}{l}(^*\text{avergonyits}_j)\\(^*\text{implacable}_i)\end{array}\right\}$ (per en F$_i$).

     'The boys$_j$ were punished (ashamed$_{*j}$/implacable$_{*i}$) (by F$_i$).'

Neither the grammatical subject of these passive examples, nor the suppressed logical subject, whether unexpressed or expressed as an oblique, can be modified by the adjective phrase. The argument that corresponds to the object in (46) cannot be the target of predication, whether it is an object, as in (46), or a subject, as in (47); the argument that corresponds to the subject in (46) can be the target of predication in (46), but not in (47), where it is not a subject (or an object). The conclusion is that the verbs in (46)–(47) allow an adjective phrase to be predicated only of their logical subject expressed as a direct function.[16]

If, as proposed by Grimshaw (1990) and others, reflexivized verbs had a suppressed logical subject (that is, a logical subject that cannot be syntactically expressed), the reflexivized forms of sentences like (46) would be predicted not to allow an adjective phrase modifying the subject, which, like the subject of the passive forms in (47), is analyzed as

---

[16]More generally, we can say that only direct functions (subjects and objects, but not obliques) can control the unexpressed subject of a predicative phrase. Given this general condition, it follows that the logical subject of passive examples like (47) cannot be the target of predication, because it is not expressed as a direct function and only as such can it control the subject of the predicative phrase. Notice that this is an argument against the analysis of passive proposed in Jaeggli 1986a, Baker 1988a, and Baker, Johnson, and Roberts 1989, according to which the external θ-role is assigned in passive forms just as in active forms, although it is assigned to an affix in passives, rather than to a full NP. It is, thus, inexplicable why the constituent to which this θ-role is assigned should be a possible target of predication in the active form, but not in the passive form.

being only the expression of an internal argument. This prediction is not correct, as shown by the grammaticality of (48):

(48) a. [En Ferran i   la Gertrudis]$_i$ s' ajudaven (contents$_i$).
  [Ferran   and Gertrudis]$_i$ RF helped   happy$_i$

  'Ferran and Gertrudis helped each other (happily).'

  b. Els nens$_i$ es castiguen (implacables$_i$).
  the boys$_i$ RF punish   implacable$_i$

  'The boys punish themselves/each other (implacably).'

Given the conclusions that the verbs in (46) only allow an adjective phrase to be predicated of the logical subject, and that the suppressed logical subject, as in (47), cannot be the target of predication by the adjective phrase, it follows that the logical subject is not suppressed in (48) but expressed as the subject. Therefore, since the logical subject of these verbs is an external argument, it is clear that the syntactic function that corresponds to the bound arguments in reflexivized constructions may be the expression of the external argument.[17]

3.4.4 Subject Selection with Ditransitives

A theory such as that of Grimshaw 1990 in which reflexivization suppresses the external argument, just as in passives, with subject selection being the result of movement of an internal argument from object position to subject position, predicts that subject selection should be the same with reflexivized as with passivized verbs. This appears to be true with monotransitive verbs: the single internal argument of the verb

---

[17] A similar argument can be constructed to show that the bound internal argument of a reflexivized verb is not suppressed either. Certain verbs, like *trobar* 'find', can take an AP predicated of the object of the verb in the nonreflexivized form, but not of the subject, as illustrated in (ia), which indicates that it is the internal argument that is the target of predication. The fact that, in the reflexivized form in (ib), the adjective phrase is predicated of the subject shows that the internal argument of the reflexivized form cannot be suppressed, since suppressed arguments cannot be targets of predication, as shown in (47), but must be expressed as the subject.

(i) a. En Ferran$_i$ ha trobat la Gertrudis$_j$ envellida$_{j}$/envellit$_{*i}$.
  'Ferran$_i$ found   Gertrudis$_j$ aged$_{j/*i}$.'

  b. En Ferran$_i$ s' ha trobat envellit$_i$.
  Ferran   RF has found aged

  'Ferran found himself aged.'

This is evidence against the unergative approach, which assumes that the argument corresponding to the object of a monotransitive verb is suppressed in its reflexivized form.

is the subject, both in the reflexivized form, (49a) (=(1)), and in the passive form, (49b).[18]

(49) a. La directora es defensa.
          the director RF defends

          'The director defends herself.'

      b. La directora serà   defensada.
          'The director will be defended.'

However, with ditransitive verbs, where there are two internal arguments, subject selection in passive forms differs markedly from subject selection in reflexivized forms. Subject choice in passives is restricted to that internal argument that is expressed as an accusative object in the active form. The active form of *donar* 'give', in (50), has two objects: one, *a la Maria*, is thematically a goal (or recipient) and is morphologically marked with dative case, expressed here by the preposition *a*; the other one, *el resultat*, is thematically a theme and is morphologically unmarked for case (or accusative). Only the theme argument can be the passive subject, as in (51a); never the goal, as in (51b).

(50)   El mestre   ha donat el resultat a la Maria.
          'The teacher has given the result to Maria.'

(51) a. El resultat ha estat donat a la Maria.
          'The result has been given to Maria.'

      b. *La Maria ha   estat donada el resultat.
          'Maria   has been given   the result.'

When a reflexivized form is based on a verb like *donar*, there are two possible outcomes depending on which of the two internal arguments, the theme or the goal, is bound to the logical subject. The hypothesis that reflexivization entails the suppression of the external argument predicts

---

[18]This does not hold with the few verbs whose single internal argument is specified to take dative case, such as *parlar* 'speak' or *mentir* 'lie'. The dative object of the active nonreflexivized form in (ia) corresponds to the subject in the reflexivized form, (ib), but the verb lacks a passive form, (ic). (See section 5.1 for evidence that *a la Gertrudis* in (ia) is an object, rather han an oblique, and that the preposition *a* is the dative case marker.)

(i) a. En Ferran ha mentit a la Gertrudis.
         'Ferran   has lied   to Gertrudis.'

     b. En Ferran i   la Gertrudis s' han mentit.
         Ferran   and Gertrudis   RF have lied

         'Ferran and Gertrudis have lied to each other.'

     c. *La Gertrudis ha estat mentida.
         'Gertrudis   has been lied to.'

that the reflexivized form of *donar* should behave exactly like the passive form of this verb: only the theme argument should be the subject, and never the goal, regardless of which is the bound argument. The reality is different: the theme argument is the subject of the reflexivized verb only when it is bound to the logical subject, as in (52), but not when it is the goal that is bound to the logical subject, as we see in (53). (Example (53b) is grammatical in an irrelevant reading as an impersonal passive.)

(52) El mestre s' ha donat a la Maria.
      the teacher RF has given to Maria

  a. 'The teacher has given himself to Maria.'

  b. *'Maria has given herself the teacher.'

(53) a. El mestre s' ha donat el resultat.
         the teacher RF has given the result

  b. *El resultat s' ha donat al mestre.
      the result   RF has given to the teacher

      'The teacher has given himself the result.'

If the external argument were suppressed in these reflexivized forms, we would expect only the theme to be the subject, as in the passive forms in (51). Given the fact that either the goal or the theme can be bound to the logical subject, we would predict that sentence (52) should have the two interpretations indicated depending on whether the theme or the goal is the bound argument. Likewise, we would expect sentence (53a) to be ungrammatical in a parallel fashion to what happens with the passive form (51b), where the goal is the subject; and we would expect (53b) to be grammatical. However, (52) has only the interpretation (52a), in which the theme is bound to the logical subject, and (53a) is grammatical and (53b) ungrammatical with the interpretation indicated. The right generalization is that, with reflexivized verbs, the bound internal argument is always encoded as the grammatical subject, and this result is explained straightforwardly if the external argument is also encoded as the grammatical subject, as the analysis to be presented in chapter 4 proposes.

3.5   The Paradox

The following points summarize the facts discussed so far about reflexivized verbs in Romance.

  (a) The evidence in section 3.2 shows that the reflexive clitic is a valence reducing morpheme, is not the expression of an argument, and is not a syntactic anaphor.

(b) The evidence in section 3.3 shows that the syntactic constituent that corresponds to the two bound roles of a reflexivized predicate is the expression of an internal argument.

(c) The evidence in 3.4 requires assuming that this same syntactic constituent is the expression of the external argument of the reflexivized verb.

This poses a paradox for many theoretical approaches to the interface between argument structure and syntax. The widely held assumptions that each syntactic constituent may correspond to at most one argument role of a predicate and that the notions of internal and external argument are represented (in a distinct way) in the phrase structure are inconsistent with the conclusions drawn in this chapter, namely, that a single syntactic constituent in reflexivized constructions corresponds to two different argument roles of a predicate and that it may be at the same time an internal argument and an external argument.

The following chapter shows how the theory presented in chapter 2 provides a way to explain the facts of reflexivized constructions without creating a paradox. The seemingly contradictory points noted above are reconciled in a theory that allows two (bound) argument roles to be expressed as one and the same syntactic function, instead of two, and that does not define the notions of external and internal arguments in phrase structure terms, so that a single syntactic function may be the expression of both an internal and an external argument.

4

Solving the Paradox

The paradox noted at the end of chpater 3 arises as a result of the assumptions that regulate the correspondence of arguments and grammatical functions in many current theories: principles such as the Theta-Criterion in GB (Chomsky 1981, 1982) and Function-Argument Biuniqueness in classic LFG (Bresnan 1980) stipulate that a given grammatical function may be the expression of at most one θ-role or argument role of a predicate. It is because of the restriction imposed by such principles that none of the theories that assume these principles can account for the whole range of facts of reflexivized constructions in Romance. In different ways, the two approaches presented in section 3.1 conform to this restriction: the pronominal approach, by having two grammatical functions in a reflexivized construction each being the expression of one of the bound arguments, and the unaccusative approach, by having only one of the bound arguments expressed as a grammatical function. Thus, the pronominal approach fails to account for the valence reducing properties of the reflexive clitic (see 3.2) and for the unaccusative behavior of reflexivized verbs (see 3.3), whereas the unaccusative approach fails to capture the unergative behavior of reflexivized verbs (see 3.4).

The analysis that I will propose in this chapter shares with the unaccusative approach the assumption that the reflexive clitic is not the expression of an argument role of the predicate but signals an operation on its argument structure, and shares with the pronominal approach the assumption that both bound argument roles are syntactically expressed in a reflexivized construction, but differs from both approaches in assuming that the two bound argument roles are expressed as a single syntactic function. These three assumptions are necessary in order to explain the facts of reflexivized constructions in Romance and fit naturally in the theoretical framework proposed here.

4.1 A-Structure Binding

I propose to analyze the Romance reflexive clitic as a morpheme whose lexical entry specifies an a-structure operation, like the passive morpheme presented in 2.3.2. A reflexivized predicate expresses a relation between two arguments both of which correspond to the same semantic participant. The predicate information of the Romance reflexive clitic specifies co-linking of two arguments of a predicate, as indicated in (1). Because of this, the two co-linked arguments map onto the same grammatical function (as will be shown below) and therefore correspond to a single semantic participant. I refer to this phenomenon as *a-structure binding*.[1]

(1) *A-Structure Binding*: $\left[\text{PRED 'P*} \langle \ [\ ]_1 \cdots [\ ]_1 \cdots \rangle \text{'} \right]$

The coindexation of two arguments in (1) entails that the two arguments involved have the same mapping to grammatical functions and to semantic structure.[2] The a-structure binding morpheme represented in (1) is an incomplete predicate, and can thus compose with any predicate, as long as its requirements are satisfied. All that is indicated in the a-structure of this morpheme is that two of its arguments, one of them the logical subject, must have the same linking index.

---

[1] In addition to the information specified in (1), reflexive clitics in Romance specify person and number information. First and second person clitics are alternatively pronominal (fulfilling an object function) and a-structure binding. The third person clitic *es/se*, which is unspecified for number, lacks the pronominal function, being unambiguously an a-structure binding morpheme; for this reason, this clitic is normally used to illustrate the phenomenon of a-structure binding.

[2] Although I am not concerned with the semantic representation of reflexivized constructions (the a-structure is not a semantic representation, even though it is constrained by it), this proposal is intended to be valid whether the reflexivized construction has a reflexive or a reciprocal interpretation. The idea that two arguments in a reflexivized construction correspond to the same semantic participant may be more obvious when it has a reflexive interpretation than when it has a reciprocal intepretation. However, this is true for both types of interpretations, as we can see in the following characterization of the distinction between the two:

  (i)   Given a relation R between arguments A and B, where A and B designate the same entity E, and there is an x that is an element of E and there is a y that is an element of E such that x is in the relation R with y, the relation is reflexive if $x = y$, and the relation is reciprocal if $x \neq y$.

There is much more that can be said about these two types of relations, particularly about the reciprocal relation (see Higginbotham 1980, Heim, Lasnik, and May 1991, Dalrymple, Mchombo, and Peters 1994, among others). What is important to note is that what distinguishes the reflexive from the reciprocal relation has no representation in the a-structure or in the syntax in general in structures where they are both conveyed by the reflexive clitic.

However, the fact that lexical entries do not normally specify any-thing about the indices of arguments does not mean that two arguments of a predicate may freely have their indices identified. In other words, identity of indices does not arise spontaneously, as by a random assign-ment of indices to arguments, which could result in two arguments with the same index: it must be lexically specified, by means of an a-structure binding morpheme, such as (1), or by some other means. This may fol-low from a basic fact about semantic structures observed in Sells 1991: 156, "namely that multiplace relations are (linguistically) specified as a default to involve distinct individuals." The following Japanese ex-ample, from Sells 1991:156, shows that, although it contains no overt expression corresponding to any of the three arguments involved, each argument is interpreted as referring to a different individual.

(2)   Syookaisita.
        introduce-PAST   'He introduced him to him.'

One of the consequences of this fact will be that, unless required to be identical (by an a-structure binding morpheme, for example), the arguments of a predicate must have distinct indices.

Two observations need to be made about the arguments that can be accessed by a predicate such as (1). First, recall that one of the consequences of the distinction between direct and indirect arguments proposed in 2.2.2 is that only direct arguments (those with a P-Role classification) can be accessed by principles and operations that refer to a-structure. This means that a-structure binding always involves ar-guments with a P-Role classification (P-A or P-P), which captures the observation that arguments that cannot be expressed as direct functions cannot participate in a-structure binding, because they are represented without a Proto-Role classification. (See 5.1.3, especially examples (5.7) and (5.8)–(5.9), for the correlation between expressibility as a direct function and accessibility to a-structure binding.) Second, the two ar-guments accessed by a-structure binding must be co-arguments, that is, arguments of the same minimal predicate.[3] The co-argument condition

---

[3]This co-argument condition on a-structure binding might follow from a *locality* constraint on a-structure operations, such as the following proposed by Isoda (1991): "a suffix that is associated with an operation on the a-structure can affect only the arguments in the outermost a-structure at the time of the application of the operation." This condition is proposed to account for several phenomena in Japanese, such as the failure to passivize complex predicates involving the aspectual verb *kake* 'be about to'. Such a condition appears to have the desired effect for a-structure binding: if the two bound arguments must be in the outermost a-structure of the base predicate, it follows that they must be co-arguments. However, certain facts presented in Hyman and Mchombo 1992 involving the reciprocal morpheme (an a-

on a-structure binding is needed when this operation applies to a complex predicate such as a causative: since the two bound arguments must be co-arguments, it will follow that an argument of the outer a-structure, such as the causer, cannot be bound (directly) to an argument of the base predicate. (An apparent problem with this condition in causatives is discussed in 6.3.3.)

As the a-structure binding morpheme is an incomplete predicate, it must compose with a complete predicate to yield a derived complete predicate. As an illustration, let us take the Catalan verb *defensar* 'defend', of example (3.1). In its lexical entry, shown in (3a), it has a PRED value with two arguments: an external and an internal argument. When this predicate composes with the reflexive clitic *es/se*, whose PRED value is shown in (1), the derived form has the combined information of the two morphemes involved: the two arguments of *defensar* are now specified with the same index, as shown in (3b).[4]

(3) a. defensar: V_1 $\left[\, \text{PRED 'defend} \langle\, [\text{P-A}]\, [\text{P-P}]\, \rangle\text{'}\,\right]_1$

     b. defensar-se: V_1 $\left[\, \text{PRED 'defend} \langle\, [\text{P-A}]_2\, [\text{P-P}]_2\, \rangle\text{'}\,\right]_1$

Let us now consider what syntactic functions will have to be associated with the PRED value in (3b) to yield a well-formed f-structure. One might suppose that, as the reflexivized verb form *defensar-se* in (3b), like its base form in (3a), has two arguments, neither of which is marked as unavailable for syntactic expression, it should take two syntactic functions, one for each of its arguments. If we take the nonreflexivized *defensar* of (3a) and apply the principles of the FMT to it, we will obtain an f-structure with a subject corresponding to the external argument and with an object corresponding to the internal argument, represented schematically in (4a). This adequately represents a sentence such as (4b) (=(1.1)) involving the base form given in (3a).

(4) a. $\left[\begin{array}{ll} \text{PRED} & \text{'defend} \langle\, [\text{P-A}]_2\, [\text{P-P}]_3\, \rangle\text{'} \\ \text{SUBJ}_2 & [\ ]_2 \\ \text{OBJ}_3 & [\ ]_3 \end{array}\right]_1$

     b. La directora defensa l'estudiant.
        'The director defends the student.'

---

structure binding morpheme) and causatives in Chicheŵa appear to contradict this strict locality condition, although the co-argument condition on a-structure binding always holds.

[4]The predicators included in a-structures, such as *defend* in (3), are given in English for convenience, but are not intended to denote the corresponding English verbs but a (possibly language independent) semantic representation.

The External Argument Mapping Principle (2.26) maps the external argument, the P-A argument in (4a), onto the subject function, and the Internal Argument Mapping Principle (2.27) maps the P-P, or internal, argument onto a direct function, which is further specified as an object (nonsubject). The f-structure in (4a) satisfies the well-formedness conditions on f-structures, in particular, the Subject Condition (2.5) and Coherence (2.59). However, if we should replace the PRED value in (4a) by that of the reflexivized form in (3b), merely changing the indices, we would obtain the f-structure shown in (5):

(5) $*\begin{bmatrix} \text{PRED} & \text{'defend} \langle \ [\text{P-A}]_2 \ \ [\text{P-P}]_2 \ \rangle\text{'} \\ \text{SUBJ}_2 & [\ \ ]_2 \\ \text{OBJ}_2 & [\ \ ]_2 \end{bmatrix}_1$

However, this f-structure is ill-formed because it fails to satisfy the principle of Uniqueness of F-Structures (2.9), which requires each f-structure to have a unique index. This principle constrains the correspondence between the f-structure and other levels of representation by requiring the mapping of other levels of structure (c-structure and a-structure) to f-structure to be unique. In other words, there can only be one f-structure corresponding to any element at c- or a-structure. This requirement is violated in (5) because there are two f-structures, the two f-structures indexed 2, mapping onto each of the arguments in the a-structure or PRED value. Thus, in order to avoid a violation of principle (2.9), there can only be one f-structure indexed 2 (which may be the value of two grammatical functions), as shown in (6).

(6) $*\begin{bmatrix} \text{PRED} & \text{'defend} \langle \ [\text{P-A}]_2 \ \ [\text{P-P}]_2 \ \rangle\text{'} \\ \begin{matrix}\text{SUBJ}_2 \\ \text{OBJ}_2\end{matrix} \Big\rangle [\ \ ]_2 & \end{bmatrix}_1$

This structure is still ill-formed. The reason now is that, since there are two grammatical functions with the same value, the structure should satisfy the Constraint on Sharing of F-Structures (2.46), which specifies that one of any two grammatical functions with the same value should be nonthematic and superior to the other one. In this case, this means that the subject, which is the superior GF of the two with the same value in (6) (see (2.52) for the definition of "superior"), should be nonthematic. But the subject here is not nonthematic because it is licensed by its mapping to the external argument: the subject is required by the External Argument Mapping Principle (2.26); since the a-structure contains an external argument that is not suppressed, there must be a subject coindexed with it. (An f-structure with the sharing of GF values shown in (6) will be argued to be well-formed corresponding to a different a-structure, as in 4.2.3.)

Thus, the two bound arguments in the a-structure in (3b) must map onto one single f-structure, which rules out (5), and this f-structure must be the value of one single grammatical function, which rules out (6). This grammatical function must be a subject, in order to satisfy the External Argument Mapping Principle (2.26), and a direct function, in order to satisfy the Internal Argument Mapping Principle (2.27). Since the a-structure contains an internal and an external argument, both mapping principles apply and must be satisfied. As a subject is a direct function, having the two bound arguments map onto a subject satisfies the two mapping principles, as well as all the well-formedness conditions, including the Subject Condition (2.5). So, the f-structure that corresponds to the reflexivized a-structure in (3b) is as shown in (7).

$$(7) \quad \begin{bmatrix} \text{PRED} & \text{'defend} \langle \; [\text{P-A}]_2 \; [\text{P-P}]_2 \; \rangle \text{'} \\ \text{SUBJ}_2 & [\quad]_2 \end{bmatrix}_1$$

In this way we obtain a representation in which two arguments map onto one single grammatical function, a situation that is disallowed by most current syntactic theories.

The paradox noted at the end of chapter 3 is solved within the theory adopted here. The assumption that the syntactic constituent that corresponds to the bound argument roles of a reflexivized verb (the subject in (3.1)) is indeed at the same time an external argument and an internal argument is not an inconsistency if the distinction between external and internal argument is not assumed to be represented in phrase structure terms, as it is in most versions of GB. If, instead, this distinction is represented at the level of a-structure, and the information at a-structure is accessible to principles of syntax, it is not necessary to replicate that distinction at any other level. Thus, the a-structure notions of external argument and internal argument need not have unique representations in the phrase structure or any other syntactic structure. We know whether a certain syntactic constituent is the expression of an external argument or of an internal argument, not by the position it occupies in the phrase structure (such as d-structure in GB), but by its correspondence to a-structure.

In addition, by not prohibiting a many-to-one correspondence between arguments in the a-structure and syntactic functions (which is explicitly disallowed in many theories), we predict the possibility of a single syntactic function corresponding to two different arguments. This possibility is restricted to instances in which the two arguments involved are lexically (or morphologically) specified to have the same index. Unless lexically specified to the contrary, arguments are assumed, as a default, to have different indices and therefore, a different mapping to f-structure and to semantic structure, given that indices are the notation used here to signal mapping between elements at different levels of representation. When two arguments have the same index, they must map onto the same f-structure, satisfying the Uniqueness of F-Structures (2.9), and this f-structure may be the value of a single syntactic function in order to satisfy the Constraint on Sharing of F-Structures (2.46).

In this way, the subject of a reflexivized construction such as (3.1) is at the same time the external argument and the internal argument of the predicate, as indicated in (7). The fact that two argument roles correspond to one single syntactic function provides the key to understanding all the properties of the reflexivized construction in Romance discussed in chapter 3, as we shall see now.

4.2 Explaining the Facts

The fact that reflexivized verbs behave as if they had one less object than their nonreflexivized forms, the fact that they behave like unaccusatives with respect to certain properties and the fact that they behave like unergatives or transitives with respect to other properties follow from the analysis of the Romance reflexive clitic as an a-structure binding morpheme.[5] No additional assumptions specific to reflexivized verbs need be made in order to explain their behavior.

4.2.1 Valence Reduction

Comparing the syntactic functions associated with an underived dyadic predicate, in (4a), with those associated with the reflexivized form of the same predicate, in (7), we immediately see that the former is transitive (it has a subject and an object), whereas the latter is intransitive (it has only a subject). This analysis, therefore, captures the valence reducing effect of the reflexive clitic argued for in section 3.2; it correctly predicts that any phenomenon that distinguishes transitive from intran-

---

[5]The idea of a-structure binding is motivated independently of the Romance reflexive clitic. Alsina 1993 proposes that the reciprocal affix in Bantu, with special reference to Chicheŵa, should be analyzed as an a-structure binding morpheme, just like the Romance reflexive clitic. See evidence in Alsina 1993 that this is the right analysis for the Bantu reciprocal affix. Unlike the Romance reflexive clitic, the Bantu reciprocal affix lacks the reflexive interpretation. Given what binding at a-structure means (mapping two arguments not only to a single f-structure, but also to a single semantic structure), it is expected that structures involving a-structure binding should have reflexive or reciprocal interpretations.

sitive verbs will treat the reflexivized form of a dyadic predicate unlike its underived counterpart, but like an intransitive verb.

NP Extraposition NP extraposition in French (discussed in 3.2.1) is a clear example of such a phenomenon: if a verb takes a direct (or accusative) object in its nonextraposed form, it cannot appear in the extraposition construction; otherwise, it can. The proposed analysis of the reflexive clitic predicts that the reflexivized form of a dyadic predicate should be able to appear in the extraposed form, as is the case, since, in the nonextraposed form, it does not take an object.[6]

Case Marking in Causative Constructions An object causee is realized as an accusative object if the structure contains no other accusative object, and is realized as a dative object if it does, as shown in (3.8). (See chapter 5 for a formal account of case assignment.) Thus, if a reflexivized predicate embedded in the causative construction licenses one single direct function (the expression of the two bound argument roles), this direct function will be realized as an accusative object (see (3.9)), since there is no other accusative object. The a-structure binding analysis predicts that a predicate with two bound arguments behaves like a predicate with one single argument with respect to this phenomenon.

Nominalizations Nominalizations of infinitive forms in Romance are constrained by a condition that prohibits the expression of any argument of the nominalized predicate except that of its logical subject. If a predicate takes two arguments that must be expressed as different syntactic functions, the resulting nominalization is ill-formed, since only one of the syntactic functions corresponds to the logical subject. Therefore, transitive verbs (unless they allow unspecified object deletion, in which case they are intransitive) cannot be nominalized (as in (3.12)). The reason why the reflexivized form of a dyadic predicate can be nominalized (see (3.13)) is that it is intransitive: as shown in (7), such a predicate only licenses one syntactic function, which corresponds to the logical subject. The argument that is expressed as an object in the transitive form of the verb in (4a) is expressed as the subject in its reflexivized form. Since there is no syntactic function that does not correspond to a logical subject, the form can be nominalized.

---

[6]The observation that the postverbal NP in the extraposition construction is an object, and that this NP may be an external argument (since Legendre 1990b shows that NP extraposition is possible with unergatives, as well as with unaccusatives) would require modifying the mapping principles to allow an external argument to map onto an object under certain conditions. This is not allowed by principle (2.26). This principle would have to be modified (for French, at least) so that the feature [subj +] would not be obligatorily assigned to the external argument only in case the structure contains no other argument mapped onto a (nondative) direct function.

Optional Past Participle Agreement The evidence presented in 3.2.4 shows that the past participle of a perfective compound form may agree in gender and number with its third person accusative object if the latter is encoded as a verbal clitic. The fact that a reflexive clitic may not trigger agreement on the participle, as in examples (3.18)–(3.19), contrasting with nonreflexive clitics, as in (3.16b)–(3.17b), follows from the assumption that the reflexive clitic does not bear an object function, but is the marker of an a-structure operation. Let us assume that the lexical entry of the past participle morpheme in Catalan is associated with a constraint stating that a past participle may bear gender and number features provided they are those of a third person pronominal accusative object. We can formalize this as follows:

(8)
$$
\begin{bmatrix}
V_2 \\
\text{MORPH} = \text{PART} \\
\begin{bmatrix} \text{GEND} & \alpha \\ \text{NUM} & \beta \end{bmatrix}_1
\end{bmatrix}
\longrightarrow
\begin{bmatrix}
\text{OBJ} & \begin{bmatrix} \text{PRED} & \text{'pro'} \\ \text{CASE} & \text{acc} \\ \text{PERS} & 3 \end{bmatrix}_1
\end{bmatrix}_2
$$

According to this principle, the gender and number features specified by a verb form with participial morphology are the features of an object specified as pronominal, accusative, and third person. Feminine gender is marked with the morpheme /-a/ and plural number is marked with the morpheme /-z/; the absence of these morphemes signals the opposite member of the gender and number features, namely, masculine and singular respectively. (Section 5.2.1 argues for treating masculine and singular as the unmarked values of binary gender and number features, and for treating accusative as the unmarked value of a binary case feature.)

Since pronominal objects in Catalan are always encoded as verbal clitics (see section 5.1), the information in (8) has the effect of allowing object agreement on a past participle only when the agreeing object is encoded as an accusative object clitic. A transitive sentence such as (3.16b) or (3.17b) includes an object, which is expressed as a pronominal clitic; therefore, past participial agreement is possible. In contrast, the reflexivized counterpart of such a sentence, (3.18) or (3.19), lacks an object altogether; therefore, there is no object for the past participle to agree with, as is the case with basic intransitive sentences.

4.2.2 The Unaccusative Behavior

If an unaccusative predicate is defined as one whose subject is an internal argument, it is clear that reflexivized verbs, given the a-structure binding analysis of the reflexive clitic, are unaccusative predicates: as indicated in (7), the subject maps onto an internal (or P-P) argument (although it also maps onto the external argument). This feature of the analysis is crucial for explaining the facts discussed in section 3.3.

Auxiliary Selection in Italian The generalization governing auxiliary selection in Italian has been stated as: "verbs with external arguments take *have*, and those without external arguments take *be*," in Grimshaw 1990:156 following Hoekstra 1984 (see also S. Rosen 1989). If this were the case, the present analysis would not account for why reflexivized verbs select *be* (*essere*) in Italian, because these verbs do have an external argument, which is expressed as the subject (see (7)). But there is an alternative way of stating auxiliary selection in Italian that does not refer to the presence or absence of an external argument and thus allows some verbs with an external argument, such as reflexivized verbs, to select *esssere*.

Auxiliary selection in Italian depends, first, on whether the subject is an argument or not, and, second, if it is an argument, what kind of argument it is. *Essere* is selected with what we might call the marked choice of subject, namely, a subject that is not an argument or is an internal argument.[7] In constructions with nonargument subjects, *essere* is the auxliary used. This situation arises in raising constructions, where the subject is not an argument of the raising verb but of the embedded clause, as in (9a) (from Burzio 1986:139), and in impersonal constructions, where the subject is a phonologically null expletive, as in (9b) (from Burzio 1986:313).[8]

---

[7]This is somewhat similar to the proposal by Van Valin (1990), following Centineo (1986), according to which *avere* is selected if the subject is an unmarked actor, with *essere* being the elsewhere case. The notion of actor in Van Valin 1990 is generally equivalent to the notion of external argument used here. An unmarked actor is an actor that is the highest-ranking argument in the actor-undergoer hierarchy (approximately equivalent to the thematic hierarchy assumed here) and nothing else. An actor that is both an agent and a theme, for example, as in Van Valin's analysis of the motion accomplishment verb *andare* 'go', would not be an unmarked actor and would not allow the auxiliary *avere* to be selected. The problem with this view of auxiliary selection, in which *essere* is the elsewhere auxiliary, is that it seems to predict that this is the auxiliary most likely to be retained if, through linguistic change, one of the two auxiliaries were to be lost. The diachronic facts of Romance languages like Catalan and Spanish that have retained the cognate of *avere* as the sole perfective auxiliary favors the analysis proposed here, in which *avere* is the elsewhere auxiliary. It seems reasonable to assume that the more general form should replace the more specific one in linguistic change.

[8]The clitic *si* in (9b), although homophonous with the reflexive clitic, cannot be analyzed as an a-structure binding morpheme, as it lacks the reflexive or reciprocal interpretation that characterizes this operation. Instead, it should be analyzed more like the passive morpheme, specifying the suppression of the logical subject. Thus, if the logical subject and sole argument of the predicate in (9b) is unexpressed, and

(9) a. Maria è   sembrata risolvere il problema.
   'Maria is (has) seemed   to solve the problem.'

   b. Si è telefonato.
      SI is telephoned   (='Someone has telephoned.')

The case in which the subject is an internal argument arises clearly with unaccusative verbs, as in example (3.22a), repeated here as (10).

(10)   Gianni è arrivato.
        'Gianni has arrived.'

Here the subject is nothing but an internal argument, and therefore *essere* is required as the perfective auxiliary, given that *essere* is chosen with subjects that are internal arguments.

A formalized account of auxiliary selection rests on the assumption that the two auxiliaries have a different set of lexical specifications that will cause one to be selected over the other depending on the context. I will assume that the lexical entry of *avere* contains a proper subset of the information specified in the lexical entry of *essere*. The principle that a more highly specified form is used instead of a less specified form whenever the former can be used (Andrews' (1990) Morphological Blocking Principle, similar to the Elsewhere Condition of Kiparsky (1973, 1983), and others) will ensure that *essere* is used whenever possible, leaving *avere* as a default. Thus, we can represent the lexical entry of these two verbs as shown in (11).

(11) a. essere: V_1
$$
\begin{bmatrix}
\text{ASP} & \text{perf} \\
\text{SUBJ}_2 & \\
\text{PRED} & \begin{Bmatrix} \neg\text{'X} \langle \ldots [\ ]_2 \ldots \rangle\text{'} \\ \text{'X} \langle \ldots [\text{P-P}]_2 \ldots \rangle\text{'} \end{Bmatrix}
\end{bmatrix}_1
$$

   b. avere: V_1 $\begin{bmatrix} \text{ASP} & \text{perf} \end{bmatrix}_1$

The aspectual information of the two perfective auxiliaries is the same (the first line of (11a) and (11b)), but they differ in that *essere* specifies more information about the context in which it can be used: it specifies that its subject must map onto an internal argument or no argument at all. Given the principle that a more general form can only be used when the more specific form can't be used, it follows that *avere* cannot be used in either of these contexts: by exclusion, it can only be used when the subject is an argument, but not an internal argument.

The constraint in the lexical entry of *essere*, in (11a), that its subject may be an internal argument accounts not only for the situation with

---

interpreted as an unspecified human, it follows that the subject, which is presumed to exist in order to satisfy the Subject Condition, is a nonargument.

unaccusatives, but also with reflexivized predicates. In both cases, the subject maps onto an internal argument of the predicate, which rules out the use of *avere*.[9] With a reflexivized predicate, such as those in (3.24), repeated here as (12), the subject is an internal argument, although it is also an external argument, as shown in the f-structure of a reflexived predicate in (7).

(12) a. Gianni si è veduto.
         'Gianni has seen himself.'

    b. Gianni si è comprato un auto.
        'Gianni has bought himself a car.'

The two arguments of *veduto* 'seen', the external argument and the internal argument, are coindexed, as required by the reflexive clitic, and therefore map onto the same grammatical function, namely, the subject. Thus, the subject of (12a) (and the same applies to (12b)) is an internal argument, as well as an external argument. The fact that it is an internal argument requires the use of auxiliary *essere* and excludes the use of *avere*.

Causatives of reflexivized verbs The observation that reflexivized verbs pattern with unaccusatives in not allowing the omission of the causee when embedded in a causative construction follows from the proposal that the grammatical function that expresses the causee in these cases, unlike what happens with ordinary transitives and unergatives, is the expression of an internal argument. Let us assume that the causative verb *fer* (in Catalan) is, or can be, a predicate that takes an external argument (the causer) as its sole argument and must combine with another predicate, which expresses the caused event of the causative complex predicate.[10] The predicate information of the causative verb is represented in (13).

(13)   *fer*: $\big[$ PRED 'cause $\langle$ [P-A] P* $\langle$ ... $\rangle$ $\rangle$' $\big]$

When this predicate composes with a dyadic predicate such as 'open' or an unergative one such as 'work', we obtain the complex a-structures

---

[9]The internal argument of an unaccusative verb may license the subject function, giving a noninverted construction, or the object function, giving an inverted construction. In the latter case, as will be argued in 4.2.3, we assume there is a nonthematic subject whose f-structure value is that of the object. Thus, in either case, the subject of an unaccusative verb maps onto (is coindexed with) an internal argument.

[10]An alternative representation will be proposed for the Romance causative predicate in chapter 6.

shown in (14a) and (14b) respectively (corresponding to (3.25a-b)), with their associated syntactic functions.[11]

(14) a.
$$\left[\text{PRED 'cause} \langle\, [\text{P-A}]_1 \quad \text{open} \langle\, [\text{P-A}]_2 [\text{P-P}]_3 \,\rangle\rangle' \atop \qquad\quad \text{SUBJ}_1 \qquad\qquad\qquad\quad \text{OBJ}_3 \right]$$

b.
$$\left[\text{PRED 'cause} \langle\, [\text{P-A}]_1 \quad \text{work} \langle\, [\text{P-A}]_2 \,\rangle\rangle' \atop \qquad\quad \text{SUBJ}_1 \right]$$

In both (14a) and (14b), the External Argument Mapping Principle (2.26) maps the external argument—defined as the P-A argument of the least embedded a-structure—onto the subject function. In (14a), in addition, the Internal Argument Mapping Principle (2.27) maps the internal (or P-P) argument onto a direct function, which, because there already is a subject, must be an object. Neither of the mapping principles refers to the logical subject of the embedded predicate, which is a P-A argument, but is not the external argument of the complex a-structure. Therefore, this argument (the causee) is not mapped onto any grammatical function and is unexpressed. (It may optionally, in some cases, be expressed by means of an oblique *per*-phrase.)

Compare this situation with what we obtain when the causative predicate in (13) composes with an unaccusative predicate such as 'come out' or with a reflexivized predicate such as 'disguise-self'. The derived a-structures and associated syntactic functions, in (15a) and (15b), correspond to examples (3.26a) and (3.27a) respectively.

(15) a.
$$\left[\text{PRED 'cause} \langle\, [\text{P-A}]_1 \quad \text{come out} \langle\, [\text{P-P}]_2 \,\rangle\rangle' \atop \qquad\quad \text{SUBJ}_1 \qquad\qquad\qquad\quad \text{OBJ}_2 \right]$$

b.
$$\left[\text{PRED 'cause} \langle\, [\text{P-A}]_1 \quad \text{disguise-self} \langle\, [\text{P-A}]_2 [\text{P-P}]_2 \,\rangle\rangle' \atop \qquad\quad \text{SUBJ}_1 \qquad\qquad\qquad\qquad\quad \text{OBJ}_2 \right]$$

Because the sole argument of an unaccusative predicate such as the embedded predicate in (15a) is an internal argument, it is mapped onto a direct function by the Internal Argument Mapping Principle (2.27); this direct function is an object in a structure already containing a subject. This contrasts with the sole argument of the unergative predicate in

---

[11] In the following representations the linking relation between arguments and functions is notated not only by means of indices, but also by connecting lines. The values of grammatical functions are not indicated.

(14b), which fails to be licensed by either of the mapping principles and may be unexpressed. In the case of the causative based on the reflexivized predicate, in (15b), neither mapping principle refers to the logical subject of the embedded predicate, because it is a P-A argument but not an external argument, as in (14); however, because it is bound to (coindexed with) the internal argument of the same predicate and this argument is required to map onto an object by principle (2.27), it maps onto an object, the same object. Since a-structure binding is sharing of indices of two arguments, and mapping is sharing of indices of an argument and a function, it follows that a bound argument maps onto the same function as the argument it is bound to. Thus, the causee of a reflexivized verb is obligatorily expressed, like the causee of unaccusatives and unlike the causee of transitives and unergatives.

Participial Constructions in Italian A necessary condition for the formation of participial absolutes (and other participial constructions) in Italian is that the predicate of the participial form includes an internal argument unmarked for dative case. The grammatical function that maps onto this argument agrees in gender and number with the participle. It thus follows that participial absolutes may be based on either unaccusative predicates or dyadic predicates, with the function that maps onto the internal argument triggering agreement on the verb. It also follows that unergative predicates cannot appear in participial absolutes, since they lack an internal argument. In addition, given the a-structure binding analysis of the reflexive clitic, we predict that reflexivized verbs should be able to appear in participial absolutes, because, like the transitive verbs from which they are derived and like basic unaccusative verbs, they have an internal argument that maps onto a direct function.

A formal analysis of the participial forms requires positing the following information as part of the lexical entry of the participial morpheme:

(16)
$$
\begin{array}{c}
\text{V} \\
\text{MORPH} = \text{PART} \\
\begin{bmatrix} \text{GEND} & \alpha \\ \text{NUM} & \beta \end{bmatrix}_1
\end{array}
\longrightarrow
\begin{bmatrix} \text{PRED} & \text{`X} \langle \ldots [\text{P-P}]_1 \ldots \rangle\text{'} \end{bmatrix}
$$

Thus, the participial morphology specifies the agreement features of a grammatical function that corresponds to an internal argument. The specific number and gender features are carried by the appropriate morphological formative (-*o*, -*a*, -*i* or -*e* in Italian). The grammatical function that agrees with the participle is unspecified in (16), since it can either be a subject or an object in Italian.[12] When the participle is based on an unaccusative or an underived transitive verb, the predicate includes the requisite internal argument that the participial verb form must agree with, giving well-formed structures such as (3.28a) and (3.29a). The constraint in (16) is satisfied also when the participle is based on a reflexivized predicate, as shown in (3.30); such a predicate contains an internal argument, as required, even though this argument shares its index with another argument, possibly the external argument.

4.2.3 The Unergative/Transitive Behavior

If unergative and transitive verbs are characterized as taking an external argument as their subject, it follows that reflexivized verbs may be unergative or transitive (depending on whether they are based on a dyadic or a triadic predicate). By the a-structure binding analysis of the reflexive clitic, a reflexivized verb is one whose external argument (if it has one) maps onto the subject, as indicated in (7). This aspect of the analysis accounts for the phenomena noted in section 3.4 that group reflexivized verbs with unergatives and transitives.

Bare Plural/Mass NP It can be argued that, in Romance, subjects cannot be licensed by bare NPs.[13] The failure of the subject function to be licensed by a bare NP entails that an argument that must be expressed as a subject cannot be expressed as a bare NP. I will assume that this is because bare NPs in Romance have a nonspecific interpretation and

---

[12]I cannot give a full account of the syntax of participial constructions in Italian, but, on the basis of Belletti 1990, one can conclude that the agreeing nominal in a participial construction based on an unaccusative should be analyzed as a subject, whereas the agreeing nominal in a participial construction based on a transitive verb should be analyzed, at least in some cases, as an object. For this reason, the lexical entry of the participial morphology cannot specify whether it agrees with a subject or with an object, since it can agree with either. It is probably necessary to specify in (16) that the agreeing nominal cannot be marked with dative case, because dative objects, which correspond to internal (or [P-P]) arguments, do not trigger agreement on participles in Romance.

[13]Belletti 1988:29 relates this observation to the assumption that a bare NP manifests partitive Case; on the assumption that partitive Case is a type of inherent Case and, as such, can be assigned only to objects, it follows that a bare NP must be an object. I would attribute this observation to a semantic incompatibility between subjects and bare NPs. If we assume that subjects must have specific (or generic) reference, at least in Romance, and a bare NP has a nonspecific interpretation (as it lacks the generic interpretation that bare plural NPs may have in English), it follows that a subject cannot be expressed as a bare NP. Therefore, a bare NP can only correspond to an object. The specificity requirement on subjects is probably a consequence of the subject's being an unmarked discourse topic, or a "weak indicator of topic," as in Dowty 1991:564: a nonspecific NP cannot refer to something whose reference has been established in the previous discourse.

there is a constraint on the relation between semantic structure and f-structure that requires a nonspecific expression to be encoded as a nonsubject function. We can formalize this constraint as follows:

(17) $[-\text{specific}]_1 \longrightarrow \left[\; [\text{subj } -] \; [\;]_1 \; \right]$

This principle is satisfied when the internal argument of a transitive verb maps onto an object that is expressed as a bare NP following the verb, as in an example like (18) (=(3.32a)).

(18)   Aquest mecànic   arregla motos.
         'This   mechanic fixes   motorbikes.'

Here the NP *motos*, because of its position within the VP, maps onto an object function; this function is licensed by the FMT, as it maps onto the internal argument of the predicate. The subject function maps onto the external argument of the predicate. Since the bare NP *motos* maps onto an object, a GF characterized by the feature [subj −], the structure satisfies principle (17).

This principle is also satisfied with unaccusative verbs, since their single argument, being an internal argument, may map onto an object and therefore may be expressed as a bare NP following the verb, as we see in example (19) (=(3.37a)).

(19)   Cauen   rocs   de   la   muntanya.
         fall-3 PL stones from the mountain

         'Stones fall from the mountain.'

The bare NP *rocs* is in a position where it can map onto an object function, given the c-to-f-structure mapping principles (2.13b) and (2.14a). Since the a-structure of the verb *cauen* includes an internal argument, this argument may license an object function, by the application of mapping principle (2.27). And so the bare, nonspecific, NP *rocs* maps onto an object (nonsubject) function, satisfying principle (17). However, things are a bit more complicated: doesn't an example like (19) have a subject, and, if so, what is it? We have two reasons to believe that there is a subject. On the one hand, the Subject Condition (2.5) requires every clause to have a subject; however, we could suspend this condition if there were evidence that there is no subject in sentences like (19). On the other hand, there is evidence that such sentences have a subject. The evidence is provided by subject verb agreement. In Catalan and more generally in Romance, verbs are assumed to agree in person and number with their subjects. What we find in inversion constructions like (19) is that the verb is not in an invariant form, agreeing perhaps with a phonologically null expletive subject, but varies in number agreeing with the postverbal NP, as the following examples illustrate.[14]

(20)   *Cau   rocs   de   la   muntanya.
          fall-3 SG stones from the mountain

       'Stones fall from the mountain.'

(21) a. Cau   aigua de   la   teulada.
         fall-3 SG water from the roof

       'Water is falling from the roof.'

    b. *Cauen aigua de   la   teulada.
         fall-3 PL water from the roof

When the postverbal NP argument of an unaccusative is plural, the verb must be in the plural from, as in (19), not in the singular, as in (20). When the postverbal NP is singular, the verb shows singular agreement, as in (21a), not plural agreement, as in (21b). Thus, this evidence suggests that the postverbal NP in these examples is the subject, but this conclusion appears to be inconsistent with the conclusion reached earlier that a bare NP, such as the postverbal NP in these examples, must be a nonsubject, namely, an object. This, of course, is only an inconsistency in a framework in which grammatical functions such as subject and object are defined in distinct ways, such that something cannot be both a subject and an object. In the present framework, this is no inconsistency, and, in fact, it is just what the theory predicts.

Take an example like (19). The predicate, *cauen*, has a single direct argument, an internal argument, which can map either onto a subject or onto an object, as required by (2.27). Since the predicate does not include an external argument, which would be required to map onto the subject, either of these mapping options for the internal argument are available. If it maps onto the subject, we have an ordinary intransitive construction, in which the single argument of the verb is the subject (and there is no other function); in this case, it cannot be a bare NP, because principle (17) would be violated. If it maps onto the object, we have an inversion construction, but how is the requirement of a subject satisfied? Recall that, according to Coherence (2.59), direct functions must be licensed in one of several ways: by a mapping principle (2.26)–(2.27), or by a general principle such as the Subject Condition (2.5). In an

---

[14]This is true of the dialect under description and, as far as I can tell, of the corresponding constructions in standard Spanish and Italian. However, some Catalan dialects (Northwestern Catalan) take an invariant verb form in such cases (Joan Solà, class lectures); these dialects would have to be analyzed as having a phonologically null expletive subject.

inversion construction, the object is licensed by mapping principle (2.27), and the subject is licensed because it satisfies the Subject Condition. And the most economical way for these two grammatical functions to have a value is for them to have the same value, as shown in the f-structure (22) corresponding to example (19).

(22)

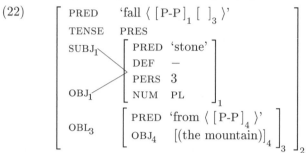

Notice that this is the same analysis as that proposed for English constructions with expletive *there* in 2.4.3. The main difference between English and Catalan is that English requires a constituent in the appropriate c-structure position to license a subject, whereas Catalan, like subject pro-drop languages in general, does not; in Catalan, as in most languages with rich subject verb agreement morphology, the subject agreement morphology is sufficient to license the subject function, whether thematic or expletive.[15]

Given a structure like (22), the constituent that maps onto the object, *rocs* in (19), also maps onto the subject. This explains why apparently the verb agrees with the object (i.e., the postverbal NP): because the subject and the object have the same value. Thus, we do not have to give up the Subject Condition, or the principle that verbs in Romance agree with their subjects. Since (22) is the f-structure of a sentence with an unaccusative verb like (19), we can explain why the logical subject of unaccusatives can be expressed as a bare NP. This structure can satisfy principle (17), because the nonspecific expression corresponding to this

---

[15]In order to understand why a sentence like (19) is grammatical, whereas one like (3.35a), repeated here as (i), is ungrammatical, we need to take into account c-structure licensing, discussed in chapter 2, fn. 34.

(i)   *Rocs   cauen de   la   muntanya.
        'Stones fall   from the mountain.'

In both examples, the subject function is licensed by the verbal morphology. In (19), the postverbal NP also licenses the object function, by application of (2.13b). In (i), the same NP appears preverbally and, therefore, can only license the subject, by application of (2.13a). Therefore, there cannot be an object in (i) because the object function fails to satisfy c-structure licensing. Since *rocs* would only map onto the subject in (i), as a nonspecific expression, it would not satisfy principle (17).

NP is encoded as a nonsubject, an object. The claim that it also maps onto the subject does not cause a violation of principle (17).

The reason why unergative verbs do not allow their logical subject to be expressed as a bare NP, as shown in examples like (3.38), is that it is an external argument and, therefore, must map onto the subject. Unlike the logical subject of unaccusatives, which is an internal argument, it lacks the option of mapping onto an object. Therefore, it cannot map onto a bare NP, as principle (17) would not be satisfied. Similarly with a reflexivized verb whose predicate contains a coindexed external and internal argument: even though it has an internal argument, it does not take an object corresponding to it, since this argument is bound to the external argument and two bound arguments must map onto the same grammatical function, in this case, the subject, because both mapping principles, (2.26) and (2.27), must be satisfied and the subject is the only function that can satisfy both principles. As the bound internal argument of a reflexivized verb is not mapped onto an object, but onto a subject, it follows that it cannot be expressed as a bare NP, as shown in (3.39). In this respect, then, a reflexivized verb does behave like an unergative, and unlike an unaccusative.

***En*-Cliticization** The assumption generally agreed on in various theoretical frameworks (see references in section 3.4.2) regarding the partitive clitic *en* (*ne* in Italian) is that it must correspond to an object. It follows, then, that an argument that may be expressed as an object may trigger *en*-cliticization, whereas an argument that may not be expressed as an object may not trigger *en*-cliticization. A direct function licensed only by the Internal Argument Mapping Principle (2.27) may be specified as an object and therefore be morphologically encoded as the clitic *en*. This is possible with unaccusative and transitive verbs, whose internal argument may map onto an object function. But it is not possible with unergative verbs, since their sole direct function is licensed by the External Argument Mapping Principle (2.26) and is therefore a subject. It is likewise not possible with a reflexivized verb such as that in (7): its sole direct function is licensed by the External Argument Mapping Principle (in addition to the Internal Argument Mapping Principle) and is therefore a subject. As a subject it cannot trigger *en*-cliticization.

Modifiers of the Logical Subject The fact that the subject of a reflexivized verb can be the target of predication by an adjective phrase that can only be predicated of the logical subject of that verb follows in the present theory from analyzing the subject of reflexivized verbs as the expression of the logical subject.

Subject Selection with Ditransitive Verbs Finally, the facts of reflexivized ditransitive verbs are an obvious consequence of the assumption that the bound logical subject of a reflexivized verb is overtly expressed: as an external argument, this argument cannot be anything but a subject. This captures the generalization noted by Zubizarreta (1987) and Grimshaw (1990) that, in reflexivized constructions, the subject is always "'coreferential' with the clitic anaphor" (Grimshaw 1990:157).

4.2.4   Conclusion

The a-structure binding analysis of the Romance reflexive clitic not only makes it possible to account for the facts of reflexivized constructions, but predicts that reflexivized predicates should behave the way they do. An immediate consequence of binding of two arguments at a-structure is that the two bound arguments will be encoded as one and the same syntactic function. The application of the FMT to a predicate with an external and an internal argument, such as 'defend' or 'see', requires there to be a subject mapped onto the former argument and an object mapped onto the latter, if there is no a-structure binding; if there is a-structure binding, the result is that there is only a subject mapped onto both arguments. Thus, any phenomenon that is sensitive to the presence or absence of an object, or a nonsubject function more generally, is predicted to treat the reflexivized form of such a predicate differently from the nonreflexivized form and to group it with basic intransitive predicates. This kind of phenomenon is presented in section 3.2 attesting to the valence-reducing effect of the reflexive clitic.

The assumption that the single syntactic function of a reflexivized dyadic predicate such as 'defend' corresponds at the same time to an external and to an internal argument predicts that such a predicate should behave in some ways like a monadic predicate whose single syntactic function corresponds to an external argument (i.e., an unergative predicate) and in other ways like a monadic predicate whose single syntactic function corresponds to an internal argument (i.e., an unaccusative predicate). Whether a reflexivized predicate behaves in one way or another with respect to a particular phenomenon depends on the phenomenon in question. Thus, if the phenomenon is sensitive to whether the single syntactic function of a predicate is the expression of an internal argument, then a reflexivized predicate behaves like an unaccusative predicate because the single syntactic function of both types of predicates corresponds to an internal argument. Section 3.3 documents this kind of phenomenon. On the other hand, if the phenomenon depends on whether that syntactic function is an object, or whether it corresponds to an external argument, then the reflexivized form of a predicate like 'defend' behaves like an unergative predicate: the single syntactic function of both types of predicates corresponds to an external argument; because of this it cannot be an object, but a subject. Such phenomena are discussed in section 3.4. In sum, the a-structure binding analysis of reflexivized constructions correctly predicts the syntactic behavior of these constructions.

4.3 Is Reference to the External Argument Needed?

The a-structure binding analysis of the Romance reflexive clitic proposed in this chapter requires that one of the arguments involved in the binding relation be the logical subject of the predicate. However, an assumption found in many theories that deal with reflexive clitics in Romance is that the notion of external argument (or the generally equivalent notion of d-structure subject) is involved in the licensing of the reflexive clitic. (Recall that the notion of external argument picks out a proper subset of logical subjects, according to the definitions given in chapter 2.) In Grimshaw 1990 and S. Rosen 1989, the external argument is explicitly referred to by the reflexive clitic, which suppresses it (or satisfies it by lexical binding, in Grimshaw's (1990:154) words). In Burzio 1986, it is stipulated that the reflexive clitic must be bound by a d-structure subject. In Rizzi 1986b, the properties of chain formation are proposed to capture the same facts. In Moore 1991 and Fontana and Moore 1992, the stipulation that the reflexive clitic (or the anaphor bound by it) must be bound by a subject, together with the chain formation algorithm, accomplishes the same result. The requirement that the external argument be involved in the licensing of the reflexive clitic is designed to rule out the occurrence of reflexive clitics with passives, raising verbs, and unaccusative verbs. In all three cases, the predicate is assumed to lack an external argument, either inherently or through suppression, making it unsuitable for licensing a reflexive clitic. Although there is nothing inherent in the present theory that would rule out making reference to the external argument in the statement of a-structure binding, in what follows I will show that this is not only unnecessary, as in the case of passive and raising verbs, but incorrect, as in the case of unaccusatives.

4.3.1 Passives

If we were to assume that clitics, both pronominal and reflexive, are the expression of an object of the sentence, which is what the pronominal approach assumes, it would be unexpected to find an asymmetrical distribution between pronominal and reflexive clitics. But this is what occurs in passive constructions. A passive sentence with a dative object, such as (23a), may have its dative object expressed as a pronominal clitic, as in (23b), but this dative object cannot be replaced by a reflexive clitic, as in (23c). The ungrammaticality of (23c) is not due to a general prohibition against clitics in passive forms, since (23b) contains a clitic, and it cannot be due to a semantic incompatibility of reciprocity or reflexivity with passive clauses, since the expected meaning of (23c) is conveyed by (23d), which contains a syntactic anaphor expressing reciprocity, instead of the reflexive clitic. (See chapter 7 on the difference between anaphoric binding and a-structure binding.)

(23) a. En Ferran i la Gertrudis han estat presentats a la directora.
          Ferran   and Gertrudis have been introduced to the director

          'Ferran and Gertrudis have been introduced to the director.'

    b. En Ferran i la Gertrudis li   han estat presentats.
        Ferran   and Gertrudis her DAT have been introduced

        'Ferran and Gertrudis have been introduced to her.'

    c. *En Ferran i la Gertrudis s' han estat presentats.
        Ferran   and Gertrudis RF have been introduced

        'Ferran and Gertrudis have been introduced to each other.'

    d. En F. i la G. han estat presentats l'un   a l'altre.
        F.   and G. have been introduced the one to the other

        'Ferran and Gertrudis have been introduced to each other.'

The analysis that both the reflexive and the passive morphology suppress the external argument, as in Grimshaw 1990 and S. Rosen 1989, predicts the ungrammaticality of (23c) on the assumption that once an argument is suppressed it is no longer available for subsequent argument structure operations. However, I have argued that a-structure binding (the operation performed by the reflexive clitic) does not involve suppression of any argument; therefore, it is necessary to provide a different account of the ungrammaticality of (23c), since one could imagine that the passive operation, suppressing the external argument, applies after a-structure binding.

   The explanation that I propose has to do with the order in which the two predicate composition operations involved (passive and a-structure binding) apply and what their effects are. The morphology that forms passive predicates in Romance is the participial morphology, which is clearly a morphological concatenation process that takes place in the lexicon, given the principles of the theory of Lexical Phonology and Morphology (Kiparsky 1982, 1983, 1985, K. P. Mohanan 1986, among

others): for example, the verb stem that carries the predicate information and the passive participial morpheme are inseparable; the resulting
morphological combination can further combine with other morphemes,
such as number and gender affixes (e.g., in (23), the participial form
presentat is concatenated with the plural affix *s*); the passive morphology determines placement of stress (cf. *presénta* 'presents' vs. *presentát*
'presented'); the participial (passive) morphology has idiosyncratically
conditioned allomorphs and suppletive forms (cf. *presentat* 'presented'
vs. *vist* 'seen', *fos* 'melted', etc.); etc. In contrast, the morphology that
produces a-structure binding in Romance is the reflexive clitic, which is
either not a lexical affix or is a lexical affix that concatenates at a much
later stratum of the lexicon than the passsive morpheme:[16] for example,
the reflexive clitic and the verb with which it undergoes predicate composition need not be adjacent to each other and often appear separated
(cf. *es presenta* 'he introduces himself' and *s'havia presentat* 'he had
introduced himself'); a verb and a reflexive clitic cannot further combine with any lexical affix, except with other clitics; the reflexive clitic
does not determine placement of stress;[17] the reflexive clitic has no idiosyncratically conditioned allomorphs or suppletive forms; nor does it
condition allomorphy of the verb form to which it attaches; etc. Because
of the different morphological nature of the two argument structure operations involved in Romance, the only way the two could cooccur would
be for a passive predicate to be formed first, and subsequently for a-
structure binding to apply to the passive predicate. However, given that
passive suppresses the logical subject of the predicate, and given the
assumption that suppression makes an argument unavailable for subsequent argument structure operations, it follows that a-structure binding
cannot apply to a passive predicate because it needs to access the logical
subject for binding, but the logical subject is suppressed and, therefore,
inaccessible in a passive form.

---

[16]There is evidence that verbal clitics, including the reflexive clitic, may combine in
the lexicon with their hosts. Nominalizations involving a (postverbal) reflexive clitic,
illustrated in 3.2 (e.g., *el despullar-se de les nimfes* 'the undressing of the nymphs'),
show that verbal clitics must be morphological affixes at least when suffixed to the
verb. See Miller (1991), who argues persuasively for treating verbal clitics, including
preverbal clitics, in French as morphological affixes. Assuming that verbal clitics are
in fact morphological affixes, they would belong to a later stratum of the lexicon than
affixes that condition stress placement, gender and number affixes, etc.

[17]In some dialects (Insular Catalan), clitics in enclitic position cause a stress shift
to the final vowel. My understanding is that this stress shift is different from the
regular lexical stress assignment rule, since the output of the latter undergoes vowel
reduction, but the output of the former does not.

Thus, we predict that, in Romance, because of the nature of the morphology involved, and because of the argument structure operations involved, passive and a-structure binding cannot cooccur in the same predicate. This correctly rules out the existence of passive forms with reflexive clitics, such as (23c). And this is possible without appealing to the notion of external argument. This analysis predicts that, in a language where the a-structure binding morpheme did not belong to a later stratum than the passive morpheme, it should be possible to form passive predicates out of predicates with a-structure binding. This prediction is correct and is documented in Bantu languages such as Kichaga, where a reciprocal verb stem, which contains an a-structure binding morpheme (the reciprocal affix), can be passivized, as shown in Bresnan and Moshi 1990. The Kichaga example (24a) (from Bresnan and Moshi 1990:153) contains an active reciprocal verb form; example (24b) (from Bresnan and Moshi 1990:156) is the corresponding passive form.

(24) a. Wà-chàkà wắ-ǐ-kòr̩-í-àn-à   shí-míì.
        2-Chaga   2 s-PR-burn-AP-RCP-FV 8-firebrand

        'The Chagas are burning each other with firebrands.'

    b. Shǐ-míǐ   sh-ǐ-kòr̩-í-àn-ò   (nà) wà-chàkà.
        8-firebrand 8 s-PR-burn-AP-RCP-PAS (by) 2-Chaga

        'Firebrands are being used by the Chagas to burn each other.'

Crucially, in passivized reciprocal forms such as that of (24b), the passive morpheme is affixed later than the reciprocal morpheme in the morphological derivation of the verb form, reflecting by the compositionality of word formation (the "mirror principle" of Baker 1985—see also Grimshaw 1986 and Di Sciullo and Williams 1987) that the base predicate composes with a-structure binding before composing with the passive morpheme.

A theory in which both passive and a-structure binding involve suppression of the external argument would wrongly predict the situation illustrated in (24b) not to arise: once the external argument had been suppressed by one of these operations, it would be unavailable for any subsequent operation. Likewise, Rizzi's (1986b) theory, adapted to the analysis of the Kichaga reciprocal morpheme, would predict the impossibility of a verb form containing both the reciprocal and the passive morphemes. Once the passive morpheme dethematizes the subject position, there no longer is a possible antecedent for the reciprocal morpheme, which is analyzed as an anaphor following Rizzi 1986b. Notice that the surface subject in (24b) (*shǐ-míǐ* 'firebrands') cannot be the antecedent of the putative reciprocal anaphor, which is interpreted as referring to *wà-chàkà* 'the Chagas'. Therefore, a structure like (24b) should be ungrammatical under this view. If one were to adopt the analysis of passive of Jaeggli 1986a, Baker 1988a, and Baker, Johnson, and Roberts 1989, according to which the passive morpheme is the external argument, the grammaticality of (24b) would be accounted for, under the assumption that the reciprocal morpheme is like the Romance reflexive clitic in being an anaphor, since this anaphor would have an antecedent even in the passive form. However, this account would then leave the ungrammaticality of the parallel Romance form unexplained. The passive form corresponding to the active (25a) is ungrammatical in Romance as shown in (25b).

(25) a. El president s' ha atorgat el premi.
        the president RF has awarded the prize

        'The president has awarded himself the prize.'

    b. *El premi s' ha estat atorgat pel president.
        the prize RF has been awarded by the president

        'The pize has been awarded by the president to himself.'

The Catalan example (25b) is parallel to the Kichaga example (24b), in that they both involve passive and a-structure binding (or anaphoric cliticization in Rizzi's terms). Rizzi's (1986b) theory, extended to the analysis of the Bantu reciprocal, cannot account for the contrast between these two examples, whether we adopt the analysis of the passive morpheme as an argument or not. The reason is because that theory does not take into account the different strata in which the morphology responsible for passive and a-structure binding takes place in Romance, on the one hand, and in Bantu, on the other. In the present approach, this is what accounts for the contrast between (24b) and (25b): in Bantu, a verb form that has undergone a-structure binding, signalled by the reciprocal morpheme, can further combine with the passive morpheme, (24b), whereas, in Romance, a verb form that has undergone a-structure binding, signalled by the reflexive clitic, has already exited the stratum of the grammar in which the passive morpheme can combine, accounting for the nonexistence of forms like (25b).

4.3.2 Raising Verbs

A second area in which the notion of external argument (or corresponding ones) is claimed to do some work in accounting for the distribution of the reflexive clitic is with raising constructions. Example (26a), based on Fontana and Moore 1992, illustrates that a raising verb cannot cooccur with a reflexive clitic, although it can cooccur with a nonreflexive clitic, as in (26b)

(26) a. *Els professors se semblen intel·ligents.
the professors RF seem intelligent

'The professors seem intelligent to themselves.'

b. Els professors li semblen intel·ligents.
the professors him DAT seem intelligent

'The professors seem intelligent to him.'

It is standardly assumed that the grammatical subject of a raising verb like *semblar* 'seem' is not an argument of the verb, but of the complement of this verb, the adjective phrase of (26). In addition to this complement, this verb takes an optional experiencer internal argument that is expressed as a dative clitic in (26b). The reason why a-structure binding cannot apply to a raising verb like this is that the two arguments that we might expect to be bound (the arguments corresponding to the subject and to the dative clitic in (26b)) are not arguments of the same predicate: they do not satisfy the co-argument condition on a-structure binding. (The sole arguments of a raising verb like *semblar*—the experiencer argument and the propositional argument—are of such different semantic types that they cannot be semantically identical or even coreferential.) Once again, reference to the external argument is unnecessary for a-structure binding.

4.3.3 Unaccusative Verbs

It has been suggested by Burzio (1986) that unaccusative verbs too disallow reflexive clitics. This claim, which has been taken to be an established fact by many researchers, seems to be based exclusively on the following two Italian examples ((27a) from Burzio 1986:398, and (27b) from Rizzi 1986b:73, where an example similar to (27a) is also cited):

(27) a. Maria e Giovanni $\left\{ \begin{array}{l} \text{*si} \\ \text{gli} \end{array} \right\}$ venivano spesso in mente.
Maria and Giovanni *RF/him DAT came often to mind

'Maria and Giovanni often came to *each other's/his mind.'

b. Il ladro e il poliziotto $\left\{ \begin{array}{l} \text{*si} \\ \text{mi} \end{array} \right\}$ sono caduti adosso.
the thief and the policeman *RF/me are fallen on top

'The thief and the policeman fell on top of *each other/me.'

In order to show that the ungrammaticality of these examples with the reflexive clitic is due to syntactic factors, rather than to semantic factors, Burzio 1986 and Rizzi 1986b give examples parallel to (27) in which the reciprocal expression *l'uno ... l'altro* is used, instead of a clitic, giving the interpretation that would be expected for (27) with the reflexive clitic, as in (28).

(28) a. Maria e Giovanni venivano spesso in mente l'uno all'altro.
'Maria and Giovanni often came to each other's mind.'

b. Il ladro e il poliziotto sono caduti l'uno adosso all'altro.
'The thief and the policeman fell on top of each other.'

While examples like (27) ranging from ungrammatical to marginal can be constructed also in Catalan, there are a great many examples of unaccusative verbs with reflexive clitics that are perfectly acceptable. Some examples follow. The verbs in (29) are all unaccusatives: *agradar* 'like' in (29a) (like Italian *piacere*, French *plaire*, and Spanish *gustar*) takes an experiencer expressed as a dative object in the nonreflexivized form and a theme argument; *anar* 'go' in (29b) and *estar* 'be', 'stand' in (29c) take a theme argument generally corresponding to their sole direct function, but, when followed by a locative phrase, may also take an experiencer or beneficiary argument expressed as a dative object in nonreflexivized clauses.

(29) a. En Ferran i   la Gertrudis s'   agraden molt.
Ferran   and Gertrudis   RF like   much

'Ferran and Gertrudis like each other very much.'

b. En Ferran i   la Gertrudis es van al darrere.
Ferran   and Gertrudis   RF go behind

'Ferran and Gertrudis go after each other.'

c. En Ferran i   la Gertrudis s'   estan al damunt tot el dia.
Ferran   and Gertrudis   RF are on top   all the day

'Ferran and Gertrudis are on top of each other all day long.'

It has been noted by Burzio (1986:429) and Rizzi (1986b:74) that examples such as these, particularly such as (29a), do exist (in Italian), and their grammaticality is left unexplained.[18]

---

[18]C. Rosen (1988), who makes no claim about the supposed inability of unaccusative verbs to take reflexive clitics, gives the following example of a reflexivized construction in Italian:

(i)   I partecipanti alle   trattative   si sono venuti incontro.
the participants in-the negotiations RF are come   toward

'The participants in the negotiations met each other halfway.'

The first thing to observe regarding the question of whether unaccusatives can take reflexive clitics or not is that unaccusative verbs typically are monadic, in the sense that they have only one direct argument, i.e., only one argument with a P-Role classification. This property of most unaccusative verbs automatically excludes the possibility of combining them with a reflexive clitic, because this a-structure binding morpheme must access two arguments of the predicate but the predicate has only one argument that can be accessed by such an operation. However, those unaccusative verbs that are dyadic, such as *agradar* (and its Italian counterpart *piacere* 'like', which selects the perfect auxiliary *essere* showing unmistakably that it is unaccusative), combine with the reflexive clitic unproblematically, as indicated in (29a).

In order to allow a monadic unaccusative (or any other basically monadic predicate) to take two direct arguments, it must appear in some form of complex predicate where each component of the complex predicate contributes one direct argument. The possibility of binding the two arguments will depend on the structure of the resulting complex predicate. Consider the Italian example (28): whereas *venire* 'come' normally takes only one direct argument, *venire in mente* 'come to mind' takes an additional direct argument expressed as a dative object. This argument designates the possessor of the mind to which some remembrance comes. Given this, the a-structure representation of this complex predicate would be as follows:[19]

(30)

$$\text{come-to-mind:} \quad \text{`come} \; \langle \; [\text{P-P}] \; [\;\;]_1 \quad \text{have} \; \langle \; [\text{P-P}] \; [\;\;]_1 \; \rangle \rangle\text{'}$$

with th — loc over the first pair, goal over the second.

In this structure, *in mente* 'to mind' would correspond to the locative argument of 'come' and to the possessed argument of 'have', which are coindexed. The dative object of (28a) (*l'uno all'altro*) is the possessor, i.e., the goal argument of 'have' in (30). Notice that the two direct arguments of this complex a-structure do not satisfy the co-argument condition on a-structure binding: one is an argument of 'come' (the

---

Notice that the verb in this example is the unquestionable unaccusative *venire* 'come', the same verb used in (27a) by Burzio to illustrate the incompatibility of unaccusatives and reflexive clitics.

[19]This complex a-structure consists of the predicate 'come', which takes a theme and a locative argument, and of the predicate designating possession *'have'*, which takes a possessor (or goal) argument and a possessed argument. The possessed argument is coindexed with the locative argument of 'come', indicating that the goal argument is the possessor of the location. The possession predicate 'have' corresponds to Jackendoff's (1990) GO_Poss function.

theme) and the other is an argument of 'have' (the possessor). Therefore, we predict that a predicate such as (30) cannot combine with the reflexive clitic.

A minimal contrast that illustrates very clearly that unaccusativity is not a factor involved in the unacceptability of examples like (27) is found in the following two French examples of Burzio 1986:429, reportedly provided by Richard Kayne:

(31) a. Ils se sont venu[s] en aide.
          'They came to each other's help.'

      b. *Ils se sont venu[s] à l'esprit.
          'They came to each other's mind.'

Presumably, *venir* 'come' is an unaccusative in both (31a) and (31b) (both of which are grammatical with a nonreflexive clitic replacing the reflexive clitic and still select the perfect auxiliary *être*). Whereas *venir à l'esprit* of (31b) can be assumed to have the same complex a-structure given in (30) for the corresponding Italian form, *venir en aide* 'come to help' of (31a) would constitute a different kind of complex predicate in which both direct arguments involved would be arguments of the same predicate, such as the following:

(32)   exp   th
                               | |
      come-to-help: 'come-help $\langle$ [P-P] [P-P] $\rangle$'

Since the theme argument (the 'comer') and the experiencer (the argument that benefits from the help) are treated as arguments of the same predicate, they can both be accessed by an a-structure binding morpheme.

Although this proposal for accounting for the ungrammaticality of instances such as (27) and (31b) is somewhat speculative, it is clear from the grammaticality of examples such as (29) and (31a) that unaccusative predicates, which lack an external argument, can combine with the reflexive clitic.

4.3.4 Summary

I have shown that reference to the external argument for licensing the reflexive clitic is not only unnecessary, but inadequate. The evidence from passives shows that it is sufficient to require one of the arguments bound by the reflexive clitic to be a logical subject, and that it is necessary to take into account the properties of the morphology involved in these two a-structure operations. The evidence from raising is explained simply by the assumption that the two bound arguments must be co-arguments (i.e., arguments of the same predicate). The evidence from unaccusatives shows that the reflexive clitic does occur with many verbs that lack an external argument; the failure of the reflexive clitic to occur with certain unaccusatives that are part of a complex predicate is due, probably, to properties of the complex a-structures in which these unaccusatives are used, which would not satisfy the co-argument condition on a-structure binding.

4.4 Comparison with Other Theories

The analysis of the Romance reflexivized construction proposed in this chapter argues for introducing the notion of a-structure binding into linguistic theory. A-structure binding is an operation on the a-structure by which two argument roles are bound (i.e., coindexed, or co-linked) as a result of which the two bound argument roles map onto the same grammatical function, or, in other words, correspond to the same morphosyntactic expression. This entails valence reduction, because there is only one grammatical function, instead of two, corresponding to the two bound argument roles. It is important to note that the valence reducing effect of a-structure binding is not captured independently of the binding of the two arguments by stipulating that one of them is suppressed (as it is in other theories that analyze the reflexive clitic as an a-structure operation, such as Grimshaw 1990, and S. Rosen 1989), but follows solely from the binding of arguments. This is a positive result, for several reasons: (1) it eliminates a stipulation from the statement of this operation; (2) it predicts that valence reduction is an automatic consequence of a-structure binding and that therefore there should be no language in which a-structure binding does not have a valence reducing effect; (3) it reduces the number of possible grammars of natural languages, because there cannot be a-structure binding involving roles A and B with suppression of role A in language x and with suppression of role B in language y, since suppression is not an option in a-structure binding; and (4) it derives the right empirical results in the Romance languages, unlike what happens with theories that stipulate suppression of one of the bound argument roles. The assumption that there is one single grammatical function that expresses two different argument roles predicts that this grammatical function should display some properties attributable to one of the roles it expresses and other properties attributable to the other role it expresses. This is what explains the observation that reflexivized predicates in Romance display both unaccusative and unergative behavior.

The alternative analyses to reflexive cliticization in Romance considered so far fail to provide an adequate account of all of the facts, either because they stipulate suppression of one of the arguments involved, as is the case with the unaccusative (and the unergative) approach, or because they do not assume valence reduction, as is the case with the pronominal approach. However, there is another analysis not discussed so far that does not have the empirical shortcomings of those analyses—the *multiattachment* theory developed within RG by C. Rosen (1988) and Perlmutter (1978b, 1989) on the basis of reflexivized constructions in Italian. In this theory, a multiattachment arises when a single nominal bears two or more grammatical relations in the same stratum. Thus, in a clause with a predicate that subcategorizes for two initial grammatical relations—for example, a 1 or subject, and a 2 or direct object—each grammatical relation may be borne by different nominals, or they may both be borne by the same nominal. The latter option is an instance of multiattachment, which is illustrated in (33) in a relational network corresponding to example (3.1). In (33), the nominal *la directora* bears the grammatical relations 1 and 2 in the initial stratum (above the horizontal line), but only the grammatical relation 1 in the following, and final, stratum.

(33)

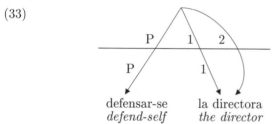

This approach is quite similar to the one proposed in this chapter: to the extent that initial grammatical relations (which are the ones that are normally multiattached in reflexive/reciprocal constructions) correspond to arguments in the a-structure in the present theory, we can say that multiattachment corresponds to coindexing of arguments in the present theory, and, like coindexed arguments, multiattached grammatical relations map onto one single nominal or morphosyntactic expression. This accounts for the fact that reflexivized constructions have one less nominal than their nonreflexivized counterparts. A nominal with multiattachment, because of its bearing two distinct grammatical relations at some stratum, may display properties characteristic of either of the grammatical relations involved. This makes it possible to account for both the unaccusative and the unergative or transitive properties of reflexivized constructions.

Like the present approach and unlike the alternative approaches discussed, the multiattachment analysis expresses the idea that two argument roles (encoded as initial grammatical relations in RG) correspond to one and the same morphosyntactic expression, which is essential in order to give a descriptively adequate account of the reflexivized construction.[20] Nevertheless, the multiattachment analysis requires two stipulations that have no counterpart in the present theory. In the first place, it has to stipulate that, although multiattachments are possible in principle, they cannot occur in the final stratum: a nominal can only bear one final grammatical relation. In the present theory, it is a necessary consequence of the principles that relate a-structure to f-structure that two coindexed arguments must map onto one single f-structure; whether this f-structure is the value of one or more grammatical functions does not have to be stipulated. In the second place, since multiattachments have to be resolved (=eliminated) by the final stratum, the multiattachment approach has to stipulate which of the two multiattached grammatical relations is cancelled.[21] Again, no such stipulation exists in the present theory, since the equivalent of multiattachment resolution is automatically achieved.

The present theory also resembles Jackendoff's (1990) in allowing a single syntactic function to bear more than one thematic role. Since each argument in the present theory bears (at least) one thematic role, when a-structure binding arises there is one syntactic function corresponding to two arguments, and, therefore, to at least two thematic roles. Jackendoff 1987, 1990 allows various conceptual constituents, or thematic roles, to be bound; all bound thematic roles are linked to one single syntactic constituent. To this extent the two theories are alike; however, they differ in the levels between which the many-to-one correspondence takes place. In the present theory, a many-to-one correspondence is allowed to take place in the linking of arguments at a-structure to syntactic functions (at f-structure), whereas in Jackendoff 1990 this linking is strictly one-to-one. Although Jackendoff (1990) does not posit a-structure as a level of representation formally distinct from the Lexical Conceptual Structure (LCS), the a-structure is derived from the LCS by A-marking "the *dominant* θ-role in a bound complex of θ-roles in the LCS

---

[20] It is difficult to know whether every specific property of the Romance reflexivized construction discussed in this study can be accounted for in the multiattachment approach, since not all of these properties have been addressed in the RG literature.
[21] The choice of which of the two multiattached grammatical relations to cancel cannot be arbitrary, subject to general principles, since that would yield wrong results. For example, when multiattachment involves a 1 and a 3, the cancelled relation must be the 3. If the 1 were allowed to be cancelled, a cooccurring 2 could be promoted to 1 by unaccusative advancement, would would be an undesirable consequence.

of a verb" (Jackendoff 1990:249) and ordering the A-marked constituent according to a thematic hierarchy (Jackendoff 1990:258). By assuming that various thematic roles can be bound and that each complex of bound thematic roles links to one single syntactic function, Jackendoff captures the claim that one single syntactic function may bear various thematic roles. However, this linking is mediated by a-structure, and it is in fact only in the interface between the LCS and the a-structure that a many-to-one correspondence arises; the correspondence between A-marked constituents (arguments at a-structure) and syntactic constituents is strictly one-to-one (see, for example, Jackendoff 1990:263). The intuition behind this is that, of the various thematic roles that a syntactic constituent may bear, there is only one that is linked to a syntactic position, in other words, that is relevant for syntax. What the theory presented in this chapter claims is that the many-to-one correspondence between thematic roles and syntactic functions may take place in the interface between arguments at a-structure and syntactic functions. (This theory is perfectly consistent with the assumption that a many-to-one correspondence may also take place in the interface between thematic roles in the LCS and arguments in the a-structure.) Crucially, when a-structure binding applies, as in reflexivized constructions in Romance, there are two arguments corresponding to one syntactic function, and, since both bound arguments are relevant for determining properties of the syntax, both should have argument status at a-structure.

5

Objects and Case Marking

In this chapter I will propose that one of the areas in which a-structure plays a role is in determining the morphological case feature of arguments. Whereas the preceding chapters have argued that the a-structure is the level of representation at which operations responsible for syntactic function alternations apply (such as passive and a-structure binding), we will see in this chapter that the principles that constrain the morphological case features that syntactic functions may bear refer to the level of a-structure. I will argue that, in the Romance languages, morphological case has the function of distinguishing among internal arguments in an a-structure that contains more than one.

Internal arguments are typically expressed as objects. Since an a-structure may contain more than one internal argument, it follows that a clause may include more than one object. This arises, for example, with ditransitive verbs, as in the following sentence:

(1)   El parlament   ha concedit l'indult   als generals.
       'The parliament has granted (the) pardon to the generals.'

The two objects in this sentence are *l'indult*, traditionally called a direct object, and *als generals*, traditionally called an indirect object. However, these two phrases are different both in appearance and in behavior, which raises doubts as to whether they should both be classified as objects. For example, whereas the direct object is generally an NP unmarked by a preposition, the indirect object, when expressed as a full phrase, rather than a pronominal clitic, is always a PP introduced by the preposition *a*, which in an example like (1) is coalesced with the definite article. In this respect, then, the indirect object resembles obliques, which are also marked by prepositions. And, like obliques, the indirect object tends to follow the direct object, when both are expressed as XPs in the VP. In addition, whereas the direct object corresponds to the subject of the corresponding passive form, as in (2a), the indirect object never does, as in (2b).

(2) a. L'indult ha estat concedit als generals   pel parlament.
'Pardon has been granted to the generals by the parliament.'

   b. *Als/Els generals han estat concedits l'indult pel
'The generals   have been granted   pardon by the

parlament.
parlament.'

With respect to the contrast illustrated in (2), indirect objects also resemble obliques, since the oblique of an active clause never alternates with the subject of the corresponding passive in Romance. Thus, one might be tempted to account for the differences between direct and indirect objects by assuming that the latter are obliques.

However, in what follows I will show, first, that, in spite of these differences with direct objects, indirect objects behave in most respects like direct objects, and unlike obliques. This justifies analyzing indirect objects as direct functions (the class of syntactic functions that includes subjects and objects). I will then argue that all that distinguishes direct from indirect objects is morphological case: indirect objects are objects marked with dative case, whereas direct objects are objects without dative case. All of the differences between these two types of objects follow from this morphological case difference. In many instances, the morphological case difference follows, in turn, from an a-structure asymmetry of the arguments involved. Thus, the asymmetry among arguments of a predicate at a-structure, determined by the thematic hierarchy, is ultimately responsible for capturing the difference between direct and indirect objects. Once the differing properties of these two types of objects are traced to an overt distinction (morphological case), which, in turn, is predictable on the basis of their representation at a-structure (and, in some cases, at conceptual structure), it becomes clear that we can dispense with positing ad hoc covert distinctions (in terms of "abstract Case" or grammatical relations) from which the overt distinction is claimed to derive.

5.1   Indirect Objects are Direct Functions

There are many properties of indirect objects that group them with direct objects, and also with subjects, and distinguish them from obliques, or indirect functions. Following are some of these properties.

1. Personal pronouns with an object function are obligatorily expressed as clitics, with optional doubling; this is true not only of direct objects, as shown in (3), but also of indirect objects, as shown in (4). Obliques containing personal pronouns, on the other hand, are only optionally expressed as clitics, *hi* or *en*, as in (5)–(6). (This is noted by Kayne (1975: 171) for French.) In addition, objects expressed as clitics, whether direct objects (3b) or indirect objects (4b), are optionally doubled by independent pronouns. (The presence of the doubling pronouns in (3b)–(4b) corresponds to contrastively stressed forms in English.) Obliques expressed as clitics, on the other hand, cannot be doubled by independent pronouns, as in (5b)–(6b); the presence of a full PP with an independent pronoun in these cases can only be interpreted as a right-dislocated structure.

(3) a. *La Maria coneix (a) mi.
     the Maria knows   me

   b. La Maria em coneix (a mi).
     the Maria me knows   me

     'Maria knows me/mé.'

(4) a. *La Maria va   donar el llibre a ell.
     the Maria PAST give   the book to him

   b. La Maria li   va   donar el llibre (a ell).
     the Maria him DAT PAST give   the book to him

     'Maria gave him/hím the book.'

(5) a. La Maria pensa en   tu.
     'Maria   thinks about you.'

   b. La Maria hi pensa (*(,) en tu).
     the Maria HI thinks about   you

(6) a. La Maria parlarà   d'   ell.
     'Maria   will speak about him.'

   b. La Maria en parlarà   (*(,) d' ell).
     the Maria EN will speak about   him

While the preceding examples show a contrast between objects (both direct and indirect objects) and obliques, we can generalize the statement of this contrast by referring also to the class of direct functions, which includes subjects and objects. Assuming that pronominal clitics are, in fact, part of the verbal morphology,[1] and given that subject agreement in finite forms is an obligatory part of the verbal morphology that

---

[1]This has been claimed by Miller (1991) for French, and there is evidence to make this assumption in Catalan. Recall from 3.2.1 that the combination of an infinitive and a reflexive clitic can be freely nominalized, which argues for treating verbal clitics as affixes.

can optionally function as a personal pronoun, it is possible to view the contrast in (3)–(4) vs. (5)–(6) as a contrast between direct and indirect functions: a direct function represented by a personal pronoun must be encoded in the verbal morphology.

2. Pronominal clitics representing an object, direct or indirect alike, express person and number distinctions. (In addition, third person direct object clitics also express gender distinctions. The direct object clitic *ho* is a special case: it is used to refer to unnamed things and to propositional and predicative complements; it is therefore a third person singular pronoun, but it is neither masculine nor feminine.) For example, replacing the object pronouns *mi* in (3b) and *ell* in (4b) by pronouns expressing other person and number values would require changing the object clitics to agree with these values. On the other hand, the oblique clitics *hi* and *en* of (5b) and (6b) are invariable for person, number and gender. The choice of one or the other depends on the preposition which introduces the oblique phrase. So, substituting the first person plural pronoun *nosaltres* for the second person singular *tu* in (5a), or for the third person masculine singular *ell* in (6a) would have no effect on the clitic forms, which would still be *hi* in (5b) and *en* in (6b).

Given the assumption that verbal subject agreement can have a pronominal function, and given that subject agreement morphology expresses person and number distinctions, we can restate the contrast just noted between objects and obliques as a contrast between direct and indirect functions: morphologically incorporated pronominal direct functions encode person and number distinctions, whereas indirect functions don't. This can perhaps be reduced to the fact that direct functions generally correspond to nominal categories, which express person and number distinctions, whereas obliques correspond to nonnominal categories, which do not express such distinctions.

3. The reflexive clitic, as an a-structure binding morpheme, binds a logical subject to another argument, which, if it weren't for the reflexive clitic, would appear expressed as an object, either direct or indirect. That argument can never correspond to an oblique in a nonreflexive construction. Thus, we can replace the object clitics in (3b)–(4b), direct and indirect respectively, by reflexive clitics, as in (7), but a reflexive clitic cannot replace the obliques of (5)–(6), as shown in (8a)–(9a) respectively, with the intended interpretation, which is only possible using the syntactic anaphor *si mateix* (or *ell mateix*, the preferred form for many speakers) and its gender and number variants, as in (8b)–(9b).

(7) a. La Maria es coneix.
the Maria RF knows

'Maria knows herself.'

b. La Maria es va   donar el llibre.
the Maria RF PAST give   the book

'Maria gave herself the book.'

(8) a. *La Maria es pensa.
the Maria RF thinks

b. La Maria pensa en   si   mateixa.
the Maria thinks about self same

'Maria thinks about herself.'

(9) a. *La Maria es parlarà.
the Maria RF will speak

b. La Maria parlarà   de   si   mateixa.
the Maria will speak about self same

'Maria will speak about herself.'

One could think of explaining the contrast between (7) and (8)–(9) by assuming that the reflexive clitic can only replace an NP, not a PP. However, as will be argued in 5.2.3, indirect objects, which can alternate with a reflexive clitic, are PPs, not NPs.

The contrast between (7) and (8a)–(9a) follows from the theory assumed so far. (A) An object function can only be assigned to an internal argument (an argument with the P-P classification), because direct functions (subjects and objects) must be licensed by a mapping principle, and the only principle that can license an object is the Internal Argument Mapping Principle (2.27). (B) An argument without a P-Role classification cannot be accessed by any principle that refers to the a-structure (such as mapping principles or operations on the a-structure). (C) Consequently, such an argument can only be expressed as an oblique, since obliques are not licensed by mapping principles, and it cannot be involved in a-structure binding. (It follows from this that the oblique complement of examples like (8) and (9) should be analyzed as an indirect argument, that is, without a P-Role classification.) In contrast, an argument that can be expressed as an object can also be accessed by a-structure binding, and that is because it has a P-P classification. Thus, since the argument that corresponds to an indirect object can be involved in a-structure binding, as shown in (7b), it must be a P-P, or internal, argument. As an internal argument, by the Internal Argument

Mapping Principle, it must be expressed as a direct function, either a subject, as in (7b), or a nonsubject, as in (4b).

4. In Catalan, object clitics, direct or indirect alike, can be modified by the "floating" quantifiers *tot* 'all', or *cadascun* 'each', but oblique clitics cannot, as the contrast between (10) and (11) shows. This is noted by Perlmutter (1984:301–302) for Italian (see also Kayne (1975) for French).[2]

(10) a. La Maria els   coneix a tots.
         the Maria them ACC knows   all

         'Maria knows them all.'

    b. La Maria els hi   va   donar un llibre a cadascun.
        the Maria them DAT PAST give a book   to each

        'Maria gave them each a book.'

(11) a. *La Maria hi pensa en   tots.
          the Maria HI thinks about all

          'Maria thinks about all of them.'

    b. *La Maria en parlarà   de   cadascun.
        the Maria EN will speak about each

        'Maria will speak about each of them.'

The ability to launch a floating quantifier is shared also by subjects (e.g., *Els meus amics han vingut tots* 'My friends have all come', *Els meus amics han menjat cadascun una pizza* 'My friends have each eaten a pizza'). Once again, then, this is a property that distinguishes direct functions (subjects and objects, both dative and accusative) from indirect functions: only a direct function, when encoded in the verbal morphology, can be modified by a quantifier within the VP.

5. As observed by Suñer (1988:427) for Spanish, objects, both accusative and dative, contrast with obliques with respect to pronominal coreference: a pronominal object must be disjoint in reference with the subject of its clause, as in (12), while a pronominal oblique (i.e., a pronominal object of an oblique preposition) is free to refer to the subject of its clause, as in (13).

---

[2] According to a reviewer, oblique arguments sometimes marginally allow modification by floating quantifiers:

(i)   ?Hi ficarem   una dutxa en cada un.
         HI we'll put a   shower in each one

Whatever the explanation for this might be, it remains that direct and indirect object clitics can be modified by a floating quantifier without this marginal status.

(12) a. La Maria$_i$ la$_{*i/j}$ coneix a ella$_{*i/j}$.
      the Maria A F S knows   her

      'Maria knows her.'

   b. La Maria$_i$ li$_{*i/j}$ va donar un llibre a ella$_{*i/j}$.
      the Maria D S PS give   a book to her

      'Maria gave her a book.'

(13) a. La Maria$_i$ només pensa en   ella$_{i/j}$.
      the Maria only   thinks about her

      'Maria only thinks about her/herself.'

   b. La Maria$_i$ parlarà   d'   ella$_{i/j}$.
      the Maria will speak about her

      'Maria will speak about her/herself.'

If we assume that pronominals in Romance cannot find an antecedent within their nucleus,[3] we explain the contrast between objects and obliques with respect to disjoint reference. Whereas in (12) the pronoun *ella*, as an object of the verb, is in the same nucleus as the subject of the verb, and therefore cannot take it as its antecedent, in (13) it is an object of a preposition and not of the verb. The prepositions *en* in (13a) and *d'/de* in (13b), which introduce an oblique function, provide the PRED of the nucleus in which the pronoun fills a syntactic function. Therefore, the pronoun must be free in this nucleus, but can be bound to the subject of the verb since they are contained in different nuclei.[4]

6. A clear contrast between indirect object and oblique is reported in Demonte 1987 concerning quantifier binding: a possessive pronoun modifying the accusative object can be bound by a quantified dative object, (14a) (based on Demonte's ex. 6a), but not by a quantified oblique, (14b).

(14) a. Vaig donar el seu$_i$ dibuix preferit a cada alumne$_i$.
      'I gave   his   favorite drawing to every student.'

---

[3]This corresponds to the specification [−ncl] in the system of Kameyama (1984, 1985) and Bresnan, Halvorsen, and Maling (1985). A *nucleus* is the minimal f-structure containing a PRED and its associated syntactic functions.

[4]The notion of nucleus appealed to here is similar to the notion of *governing category* of Chomsky 1981:188 and *minimal governing category* (MGC) of Chomsky 1986: 169. However, a governing category is assumed to be only S, or NP with a subject; therefore, the notion of governing category does not distinguish between (12) and (13). Whether the pronoun is an object of the verb, as in (12), or the object of an oblique preposition, as in (13), the governing category is the whole S. If pronominals are required to be free in their governing category, the coindexing between the subject and the pronominal in (13) is wrongly predicted to be ungrammatical. This problem does not arise with the notion of nucleus adopted here.

b. *Vaig obtenir el seu$_i$ dibuix preferit   de   cada alumne$_i$.
   'I got   his   favorite drawing from every student.'

If we assume that the bound variable interpretation of a pronoun is possible only if it is f-commanded by its antecedent, the contrast in (14) follows immediately.[5] (14a) is grammatical because the possessive pronoun contained in the direct object is f-commanded by *cada alumne* 'every student', which is an object, as the preposition *a* merely specifies a case feature in the f-structure. (14b), in contrast, is ungrammatical because the possessive pronoun is not f-commanded by its antecedent, which is the object of the preposition *d'/de* and therefore is contained in an f-structure which does not contain the pronoun. (See Bresnan 1982a for similar observations.)

Notice that the grammaticality of (14a), in which the quantified indirect object binds the possessive pronoun of the direct object, matches the judgment assigned to English sentences like (15a), where the first object binds the possessor of the second object, rather than the judgment assigned to (15b), where the possessor of the object would be bound by a so-called *to*-dative (examples from Larson 1988:336 and 338).[6]

(15) a.   I gave every worker$_i$ his$_i$ paycheck.

     b.??I gave his$_i$ paycheck to every worker$_i$.

Therefore, the indirect object of (14a) behaves like the first object in the English double object construction, as in (15a), and unlike the oblique expression of the recipient of (15b).

7. Rigau (1988:505ff) notes that, when the resumptive pronoun strategy is used in relative clauses in Catalan (in a colloquial or nonliterary style), strong (or emphatic) pronouns cannot be used as resumptive pronouns functioning as subjects or objects, although they can when functioning as the objects of prepositional obliques. Sentences (16a-b), from Rigau 1988:ex. 7, show that a subject and a dative object respectively do not

---

[5] The *f-command* relation, defined in (2.53), but not c-command, brings out the contrast in (14): both sentences have the same c-structure—a verb followed by an NP followed by a PP. C-command cannot distinguish between these two sentences; f-command does, because, as we shall see, the dative preposition *a* does not have a PRED feature, whereas other prepositions, such as *d'/de*, do. An approach that relies only on phrase structure configuration to determine the binding possibilities of a pronoun by a quantifier is forced to assume that the dative *a* in (14a) is not a preposition, in order to allow the quantified indirect object to bind the pronoun in the direct object. This assumption is also necessary to explain the absence of a weak crossover effect, which is predicted to arise if the quantified indirect object does not c-command the NP containing the bound pronoun. However, the assumption that dative phrases are not PPs is highly problematic, as we shall see in the next section.

[6] Note, however, that not all speakers of English agree that there is such a clear contrast between (15a) and (15b) as that reported in Larson 1988.

allow a resumptive pronoun interpretation when expressed by a strong pronoun. Sentences (17a-b), on the other hand, contain strong pronouns acting as resumptive pronouns, functioning as objects of prepositions.

(16) a. Aquest és el   nen que no sabem   a quina escola va
        this   is the boy that we don't know to which school goes

        (*ell).
        he

     b. Aquest és el   nen que diuen   que li   van regalar un
        this   is the boy that they say that him they gave   a

        cavall (*a ell).
        horse   to him

(17) a. Aquest és el nen   que no podem sopar   sense   ell.
        this   is the boy that we cannot have dinner without him

     b. Aquest és el nen   que diuen   que parlarem   d'ell.
        this   is the boy that they say that we will talk about him

The relative pronoun can be seen as a topic that binds a pronoun with an in-clause function. As claimed by Bresnan and Mchombo (1987) for the object markers in Chicheŵa, this bound pronoun must be a topic-anaphoric pronoun, one that is coreferential with a discourse topic, rather than a contrastive pronoun. Object markers in Chicheŵa are always topic-anaphoric, whereas independent pronouns are only topic-anaphoric when an object marker or a reduced or contracted form of the pronoun is not available, and are otherwise contrastive. The same is true about Catalan, with object clitics having the topic-anaphoric function, like object markers in Chicheŵa. It was noted earlier that, in Catalan, the verbal morphology obligatorily doubles personal pronouns functioning as direct functions (by means of clitics or subject agreement); in this case, independent pronouns have a purely contrastive use, and cannot be topic-anaphoric. This explains why an independent pronoun as the subject, (16a), or as a dative object, (16b), cannot be anaphoric to the topic of the relative clause, whereas the morphologically incorporated pronoun (the subject agreement or the object clitic) does have this use. In contrast, an independent pronoun as the object of an oblique preposition, as in (17), can be topic-anaphoric, because it is not possible to encode the pronoun in the verbal morphology.[7] In this respect, then,

---

[7] In an example like (17b), it is possible to replace the whole oblique phrase d'ell by the oblique clitic en with a topic-anaphoric use, as in (i), but it is not possible to cliticize just the pronominal object of the preposition.

the dative object patterns once again with direct functions, rather than with obliques.

As shown in Rigau 1988, the same situation holds in Left Dislocation constructions and in constructions with pronouns functioning as bound variables: independent pronouns as direct functions cannot have a topic-anaphoric or bound variable use, whereas independent pronouns as objects of obliques can.

8. Like direct objects and subjects, indirect objects can be the target of secondary predication, whereas obliques cannot. Examples like (18), containing an adjective phrase immediately following the head noun of the object (direct object in (18a) and indirect object in (18b)) and agreeing with it in gender and number, have an ambiguous analysis where the AP is either part of the object NP or an independent constituent. Only in the latter case is the AP a secondary predicate taking the object as the target of predication.

(18) a. Volen   retratar   la Maria disfressada de vestal.
        'They want to portray   Maria disguised   as a vestal.'

   b. Volen   fer   un retrat a la Maria   disfressada de vestal.
      they want make a portrait to the Maria disguised   of vestal

      'They want to take a picture of Maria disguised as a vestal.'

The analysis can be disambiguated when the object is not expressed as a full NP in the VP, as through *wh*-extraction or pronominal cliticization. If the AP remains in the VP, it is a secondary predicate. This is the situation illustrated in (19), where the object is expressed as a pronominal clitic.

(19) a. La   volen   retratar   disfressada de vestal.
        her ACC they want to portray disguised   as a vestal

   b. Li   volen   fer   un retrat disfressada de vestal.
      her DAT they want to make a portrait disguised   as a vestal

Since the AP in these examples takes the object, expressed as a clitic, as the target of predication, which is signalled by the agreement on the adjective, it follows that an indirect object, as in example (19b), as well as a direct object, as in (19a), can be the target of secondary predication.[8]

(i)   Aquest és el nen   que diuen   que en parlarem   (*de).
       this   is the boy that they say that EN we will talk about

[8]I take this as counterevidence to the claim made by Bresnan (1982a:352) that the indirect object (in Spanish), which is analyzed as an oblique in that work, cannot be the target of secondary predication. While it is possible to give examples in which an indirect object cannot qualify as the target of secondary predication, similar ex-

In contrast with objects and subjects, obliques can be shown to be unacceptable targets of secondary predication. The contrast between active and passive sentences illustrated in (3.46) and (3.47) indicates that the logical subject can be the target of secondary predication in the active form, but not in the passive form: the crucial difference is that it is expressed as a subject (a direct function) in the active form, but as an oblique in the passive form. Similar evidence that obliques fail to qualify as targets of secondary predication and that this cannot be due to semantic factors can be provided comparing semantically similar pairs of verbs that differ in that one takes an oblique and the other takes an object corresponding to the same argument. A relevant example would be *recordar* vs. *recordar-se (de)*, illustrated in (20), the former taking a direct object and the latter taking an oblique complement introduced by the preposition *de*. Both verbs are translated as 'remember', although the transitive *recordar* may denote a greater degree of control on the part of the experiencer than the intransitive and inherently reflexive form *recordar-se*. This semantic difference seems to involve the experiencer, but not the theme, which is the object of remembrance. Even so, the fact that it is expressed as a direct function in one case and by means of an oblique in the other implies a contrast with respect to its ability to be the host of a secondary predication, as the contrast between (20b) and (20c) illustrates.

(20) a. $\left\{ \begin{array}{l} \text{Recordàvem} \\ \text{Ens recordàvem} \quad \text{de} \end{array} \right\}$ la Maria   disfressada de vestal.
    1 P   we remembered of   the Maria disguised   of vestal

   'We remembered Maria disguised as a vestal.'

   b. La   recordàvem   disfressada de vestal.
      her ACC we remembered disguised   of vestal

   'We remembered her disguised as a vestal.'

---

amples can be constructed in which a direct object is unacceptable as the target of secondary predication—see examples (3.46) in 3.4.3, which illustrate the latter situation. As noted in Jackendoff 1990:207, "object hosts [=targets of secondary predication] are highly restricted by a number of syntactic and semantic criteria." Therefore, the existence of examples in which a predication relation between an AP and an object, direct or indirect, does not hold cannot be taken as evidence that objects, direct or indirect, in general aren't possible targets of secondary predication. Bresnan's claim that indirect objects in Spanish cannot be targets of secondary predication is assumed to follow from their analysis as obliques, or semantically restricted grammatical functions, a conclusion that is also adopted in Zubizarreta 1985: 251. The assumption that indirect objects (in Spanish) are semantically restricted is adequately rebutted in Suñer 1988:429–430.

c. Ens en recordàvem   (*disfressada de vestal).
1 P   EN we remembered   disguised   of vestal

'We remembered her (disguised as a vestal).'

The minimal contrast between (20b) and (20c) shows that, as assumed by Bresnan (1982a), Zubizarreta (1985), and others, the possibility of predicating an adjective phrase of a grammatical function is indeed conditioned by whether this grammatical function is a direct or an oblique function (semantically restricted or not). Oblique functions cannot be the target of secondary predication, (20c), while direct functions can, (20b). Since indirect objects can be the target of secondary predication, as shown in (19b), we are led to the conclusion that, despite the misleading terminology, indirect objects are direct functions.

Summary Eight pieces of evidence converge to show that indirect objects belong in the class of direct functions (like subjects and direct objects), contrasting systematically with obliques: (1) doubling of independent personal pronouns in the verbal morphology, (2) expression of person and number distinctions in morphologically incorporated pronouns, (3) the ability to be bound at a-structure, (4) the ability to launch a floating quantifier, (5) disjoint reference of pronouns, (6) the ability to bind quantifiers, (7) the ability to function as resumptive pronouns and bound variables, and (8) the ability to be the target of secondary predication. The class of direct functions to which I claim the indirect object belongs is equivalent to the class of "terms" in RG, to the class of arguments θ-marked directly by the verb or one of its projections in GB, and to the class of grammatically linked arguments in Kiparsky's (1987) Direct Linking Theory.

5.2   Morphological Case

Since the indirect object is a direct function and it is not a subject, it is characterized by the features [obl −] (direct) and [subj −] (nonsubject); that is, it is an object. In this respect, then, an indirect object is nondistinct from a direct object. In this section, I will argue that what distinguishes these two types of objects is a difference in morphological case: Catalan (and other Romance languages) has a binary case opposition, which can be formalized as the feature [DAT(IVE) ±]. All and only direct functions are specified for this feature, so that an indirect object is a dative object (i.e., an object that takes the positive value for this feature) and a direct object is a nondative object (i.e., an object that takes the negative value for this feature). (From now on, I use the terminology "dative object" and "nondative object," instead of the traditional indirect and direct object, for consistency with these assumptions.) First, I will argue that $[\text{DAT} +]$ (dative) is the marked member of the case opposition, then I will discuss the morphological realization of case, and finally I will argue for the PP analysis of dative phrases.

5.2.1 Dative: The Marked Case Value

There are four ways in which dative is marked, whereas nondative (or accusative) is unmarked. In the first place, when an object is expressed as a noun phrase, it is marked with the preposition *a* if it is dative, but it is generally unmarked (a simple NP) if it is nondative. This has been illustrated in many examples in the preceding sections. This is an instance of "zero expression of the unmarked category," according to Greenberg (1966:26): if a syntactic distinction is expressed by the presence of overt morphology for one of the categories vs. the absence of overt morphology for the other category, the former is the marked category, and the latter is the unmarked category.[9]

In the second place, among third person pronominal clitics, which distinguish the two case values overtly, dative case is morphologically marked, while accusative is not. The chart in (21) gives the forms of third person dative and accusative clitics. As some of the clitics have alternative forms that are phonologically conditioned, the citation form is given in boldface. The dative plural clitic is consistently *(e)ls hi* in the dialect reported here (Barcelona), although the literary norm prescribes *els*.

(21)

	ACCUSATIVE		DATIVE
	MASC.	FEM.	
SINGULAR	**el**, 'l, l', lo	**la**, l'	**li**
PLURAL	**els**, 'ls, los	**les**	**els hi**, 'ls hi (literary: **els**, 'ls, los)

If we examine these clitics, we can analyze them morphologically in such a way that each phonological segment corresponds to an abstract feature (as in Viaplana 1980), as follows:

(22)   3 PERSON: l
       FEMININE: a
         PLURAL: z
        DATIVE: i

---

[9]It should be pointed out that the preposition *a* is also used for certain animate nondative objects: in some dialects, only with pronouns; in other dialects, more generally. I will not be concerned with *a* as a marker of animacy in objects.

The third person morpheme /l/ can combine with zero or more of the other morphemes in (22) to yield the various forms in (21). The feminine and plural morphemes /a/ and /z/ respectively are the markers of feminine gender and plural number found elsewhere in the language. The other member of each opposition, masculine and singular respectively, is morphologically unmarked. For example, adjectives generally make the gender distinction by having an unmarked form for the masculine and a form marked with /a/ for the feminine: *verd* (masc.) vs. *verda* (fem.) 'green', *clar* (masc.) vs. *clara* (fem.) 'clear', etc. Likewise, with the number distinction, singular is characterized by the absence of plural marking. We can conclude that masculine and singular are the unmarked values of the gender and number oppositions. Thus, when the third person clitic morpheme combines with no other morpheme, it has the unmarked features of gender and number: it is masculine and singular. (The underlying representation of this form, /l/, is realized either with an epenthetic vowel before it, *el*, or after it, *lo*, or without an epenthetic vowel, *l'*, *'l*, depending on the phonological environment—see Wheeler 1979.) A similar conclusion can be drawn with respect to the case distinction. Only dative case is overtly marked on (third person) clitics: *li* in the singular, and *els hi* in the plural (see, for example, Lunn and DeCesaris 1981). (In spite of the orthography, *els hi* is, morphologically, third person /l/, plural /z/, and dative /i/; the initial vowel is inserted in the appropriate phonological environment.) The accusative clitics lack case morphology. Thus, as with NPs, the presence vs. absence of case morphology characterizes dative as the marked category and nondative as the unmarked category.[10]

In the third place, the fact that the gender distinction is overtly expressed in the third person accusative clitics (for example, masc. *el* vs. fem. *la*), but not in the corresponding dative clitics (for example, masc./fem. *li*) is consistent with the assumption that dative is the marked member of the case opposition: it follows from Greenberg's (1966:27) observation that morphological syncretism occurs in forms that express a marked category, rather than in those that express an unmarked category. If gender syncretism should occur at all in the pronominal clitic system, Greenberg's universal predicts that it should occur in forms that express dative, the marked category of the case

---

[10]The clitic system of some varieties of Spanish allows a similar morphological decomposition to that proposed for Catalan clitics: *l* would be the third person morpheme, *o* the masculine gender morpheme, *a* the feminine gender morpheme, *s* the plural morpheme, and *e* the dative case morpheme. Thus, in Spanish too, there is an overt marker for dative case in the clitic system, but there is no overt marker for accusative case; the gender morphemes occur where case is unmarked.

opposition, rather than in those that express nondative, the unmarked category.

Finally, nondative can be considered the default case specification for objects, while dative is used normally only in the presence of a nondative internal argument. Except for a small number of verbs whose sole internal argument is marked with dative case, dative objects only occur in clauses that contain another internal argument, which can be either an object or a subject. This is clearly the situation with triadic verbs like *donar* 'give', where the recipient is a dative object while the other internal argument, the theme, is the accusative object in an active form. This is also the situation with experiencer verbs like *agradar* 'like', where the experiencer is a dative object whereas the other internal argument, the theme or stimulus, alternates between subject and object. The default status of nondative (or accusative) and the marked status of the dative are most obvious when we consider the morphological marking on the object causee: it is dative whenever the causative complex argument structure contains an accusative object; otherwise, it is accusative (see chapter 6).

This evidence suggests that the morphological case system of Catalan (and other Romance languages) can be analyzed as consisting of a binary opposition between dative and nondative, in which dative is the marked member of the opposition and nondative the unmarked member. I propose to formalize this opposition by means of the binary case feature [DAT $\pm$], where dative case is represented by the positive value and nondative by the negative value. In addition, I argue that it is unnecessary in languages like Catalan to further distinguish between nominative and accusative case. While some theories (such as the GB Case Theory) may need to posit an abstract distinction between subjects and objects in terms of case (nominative vs. accusative), such a case distinction is unmotivated in the present theory, where the feature [subj $\pm$] constitutive of syntactic functions distinguishes subjects from objects. Whatever morphosyntactic properties distinguish subjects from objects can be seen to be a correlate, not of an abstract case distinction, but of an abstract distinction in terms of syntactic functions. Notice that subjects and objects are distinguished by means other than morphological case in Romance: 1) as an NP, an object is internal to the VP, while a subject is usually external to the VP;[11] 2) a subject triggers person/number agreement on the verb, while an object does not; 3) an object may be expressed by means of a pronominal clitic, while a

---

[11]It is possible that a subject in postverbal or clause-final position might have to be analyzed as being VP-internal. I leave this possibility open.

subject may not (at least, in the so-called "subject pro-drop" varieties of Romance); etc.

5.2.2 Overt Realization of Case

I have argued that Catalan (and Romance in general) has a binary case opposition, formalized by the feature $[\text{DAT} \pm]$ of direct functions, in which only the positively specified feature, dative, has an overt realization. It follows that there are pieces of the morphology that can be identified as being bearers of the feature value $[\text{DAT} +]$, but none that can be uniquely identified as bearers of the feature value $[\text{DAT} -]$.

In the case of pronominal object clitics, the case distinction is only overtly marked in third person forms. First and second person object clitics, both singular and plural, do not make an overt distinction between dative and nondative. These clitics can be analyzed as being lexically specified with a choice of values for the case feature: either $[\text{DAT} -]$ or $[\text{DAT} +]$. The choice of one or the other of these specifications will allow the clitic to satisfy the case requirement imposed on the f-structure by the predicate (see 5.3). In third person object clitics the dative/nondative opposition is expressed by the presence or absence of the segment /i/ (in the dialect of Catalan being described), found in the dative clitics [li] and [əlzi], but not in the nondative clitics [əl], [lə], [əls], etc. We can assume that the segment or morpheme /i/ carries the marked case specification $[\text{DAT} +]$, which, added to the third person clitic morpheme /l/, yields a third person dative clitic. Thus, the clitic *li* has the lexical specifications indicated in (23) (ignoring the feature $[\text{PRED} \ \text{'pro'}]$, which is optional).

(23)   *li*: $\begin{bmatrix} \text{PERS} & 3 \\ \text{NUM} & \text{SG} \\ \text{DAT} & + \end{bmatrix}$

However, the clitic morpheme /l/ cannot be assumed to be always unspecified for case. Since the unmarked feature value $[\text{DAT} -]$ is characterized by the absence of specific case morphology, we can analyze the morpheme /l/ as being lexically specified with the optional feature value $[\text{DAT} -]$. This will allow the clitic *el*, without any case morphology, to fulfil a nondative object function.

When a dative object is realized as an XP, as opposed to a pronominal clitic, the piece of c-structure that bears the feature $[\text{DAT} +]$ is the preposition *a*. The dative preposition *a*, unlike other prepositions including the locative and other uses of the preposition *a*, has no semantic content and imposes no semantic restriction on the NP it introduces.

Therefore, that preposition has no PRED value, but it does specify a case feature value, as shown in its lexical entry, represented in (24).

(24) a: P_1 $\left[\,\text{DAT} \,+\,\right]_1$

As a preposition, the dative a heads a PP and takes an NP as its structural sister. Since it does not specify any f-structure feature except for case, the remaining specifications associated with the PP, including the PRED value, are specified in the lexical entries of the words that make up the NP sister of the preposition.[12] So, a dative phrase in Romance always has the following (underspecified) representation at c- and f-structure.

(25)

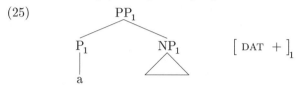

As the P head of this PP is lexically specified with the feature $\left[\,\text{DAT} \,+\,\right]$, the object function associated with this node will be a dative object, an object whose case attribute DAT has a positive value.

In order for the dative preposition a to determine the case feature of the XP that contains it, the NP it introduces must be unspecified for case; otherwise, there would be a feature conflict. In a language in which nouns do not inflect for case, it seems natural to assume that they are lexically unspecified for case, and that the case feature of their syntactic function is determined exclusively by the presence or absence of the case marker, for example, the dative a. Its presence determines dative case, as we have seen. However, its absence would appear to determine no case feature whatsoever. Since, as I have argued, all direct functions must have a specification for the feature $\left[\,\text{DAT} \,\pm\,\right]$, it is necessary to provide a way for NPs to have the default specification $\left[\,\text{DAT} \,-\,\right]$. This can be done by assuming that all nouns are optionally specified with this default case feature. If this case specification is chosen from the lexical entry of a noun, the NP that it projects will be able to map onto a syntactic function required to be $\left[\,\text{DAT} \,-\,\right]$. If no case specification is chosen for a noun, the NP that it projects will be compatible with the dative preposition a yielding a phrase that maps onto a syntactic function constrained to be $\left[\,\text{DAT} \,+\,\right]$. As we shall see in section 5.3, what constrains direct functions to have one case specification or the other is

---

[12]Thus, while the dative preposition is the *categorial* head of its PP, since it determines the syntactic category of its phrase, the NP is its *functional* head, since it contributes the PRED value of the f-structure that corresponds to the PP. (See Simpson 1983 and Alsina 1995 for these terms.)

the Case Assignment Convention (43): this principle does not "give" a case specification to a grammatical function that otherwise would not have one, but rather checks that each direct function has the right case feature.

5.2.3   The Dative Object as a PP

From the preceding discussion, it is clear that I am assuming that a dative phrase in Romance is a PP. This is in contradiction with the conclusion drawn by Suñer (1988:427–431) that the dative object in Spanish is an NP. However, the arguments presented by this author for the NP status of the dative object are, in the present theory, arguments for its status as a direct function.[13] Once syntactic function is factored apart from syntactic category, there is no need to assume that a direct function is encoded as an NP. There is evidence concerning its internal structure and its distribution that the dative object is a PP.

In order to claim that a dative object is an NP, like other direct functions, one would have to assume that the dative preposition *a* is not a preposition, but a nominal particle, like a determiner. However, appositions provide evidence that the dative *a* behaves like other prepositions, and unlike genuine nominal particles such as determiners. An NP in Romance may contain an apposition modifying the head noun, and this apposition is itself an NP, which may, therefore, include a determiner. If the dative object were an NP we would expect an apposition contained in it to include, at least optionally, the dative particle; this is not possible, as shown in (26a), where the determiner, but not the dative *a*, can

---

[13]Suñer 1988 shows that dative objects differ from oblique PPs with respect to the Binding Theory, in being semantically unrestricted, and in allowing a conjunction of dative phrases to antecede a relative clause. In LFG, the binding properties of pronominals and anaphors are stated at the level of f-structure (see Dalrymple 1993), which encodes distinctions in terms of syntactic functions, not in terms of syntactic categories; therefore, if dative objects differ from obliques with respect to binding properties, their syntactic categories are irrelevant: what matters is that they have different syntactic functions. The semantic unrestrictedness of dative objects follows from the assumption that the dative preposition *a* has no semantic content, unlike other prepositions, but is merely a case marker; this property of that preposition is not reflected in the c-structure, but in the f-structure and semantic structure. The ability of conjoined dative phrases to antecede a relative clause, unlike what happens with obliques, is also a consequence of the assumption that the dative preposition has no semantic content: since the dative preposition does not express a relation, the whole dative PP is of the same semantic type as an NP, that is, a Thing ontological category in Jackendoff's (1990) terms; if APs, relative clauses, and semantically similar modifiers modify constituents of type Thing, the dative PP qualifies as such, just like an NP. So, there is, in fact, no need to assume that the dative phrase is an NP, as long as the different grammatical properties of syntactic constituents are adequately factored apart, as they are in LFG.

be part of the apposition of a dative object. In this respect, this particle behaves like undisputed prepositions such as *de* in (26b). (In these cases, repeating the particle/preposition is only possible as a correction or afterthought.)

(26) a. He enviat   els llibres a la Maria, (*a) la meva amiga.
         'I have sent the books to   Maria, (*to) my   friend.'

    b. He rebut   els llibres de la Maria, (*de) la meva amiga.
         'I have received the books from Maria, (*from) my   friend.'

If the Romance dative case marker were a nominal particle, we would expect to find case concord. In Latin, where nominal categories inflect for case, as well as for gender and number, the head noun of an apposition must agree in case (and, if possible, also in number and gender) with the NP it modifies. Thus, the appositive head noun of a dative NP must also be dative, as the following Latin example illustrates:

(27) Bellum intulit Dario,   regi   /*rex   /*regem Persarum.
      war ACC waged Darius DAT king DAT k. NOM k. ACC Persians GEN

      'He waged war with Darius, king of the Persians.'

If the apposition of an NP must be an NP, the assumption that the dative *a* is a preposition accounts for why it does not occur in an apposition, as example (26a) shows, although nothing prevents dative case from being specified in an apposition, as long as the case morphology is a nominal affix, as in Latin.

In addition, the dative *a* can introduce a coordinate NP. In this respect, too, this particle parallels the behavior of undisputed prepositions in allowing two conjoined NPs to follow them, as the Catalan examples (28a) and (28b) illustrate for the dative *a* and for the preposition *de* respectively.[14]

(28) a. He enviat   els llibres a la Maria i   la Teresa.
         'I have sent the books to   Maria and   Teresa.'

    b. He rebut   els llibres de la Maria i   la Teresa.
         'I have received the books from Maria and   Teresa.'

(28a) shows that two conjoined dative objects can share the same dative case-marker. Once again this follows from the assumption that this case-marker is a preposition. The NP that it introduces, like that of any preposition, can be a coordinate NP, in which case the case feature of that preposition distributes into each of the conjuncts, as in the theory

---

[14]This has also been observed by Demonte (1987:150) and Suñer (1988:430) for Spanish. In contrast, according to Vergnaud (1974) and Jaeggli (1982), French requires the dative *à* to be repeated for every conjunct.

of coordination proposed by Bresnan, Kaplan, and Peterson (1986), and by Kaplan and Maxwell (1988).

Not only is the internal structure of a dative object like that of a PP; so is its distribution. The unmarked order of an accusative and a dative object is like the unmarked order of an NP and an oblique PP: the former precedes the latter. If we reverse the normal order of the two objects in (26a) (ignoring the apposition), we get a marginal to ungrammatical result, very much like what happens when we reverse the normal order of the accusative object and the oblique PP in (26b), as we see in (29a) and (29b) respectively.

(29) a.?*He enviat   a la Maria els llibres.
       'I have sent to   Maria the books.'

    b.?*He rebut   de   la Maria els llibres.
       'I have received from   Maria the books.'

These word order facts follow from assuming that there is a linear precedence principle in Romance that requires NPs to precede any other type of XP. Analyzing the dative object as a PP, we see that this principle is violated in (29a), just as it is in (29b).

One could claim that the word order contrast between (26) and (29) follows from Case Theory of GB, which has an adjacency requirement on the assignment of structural Case: since it is assumed that only the accusative object receives structural Case in both (26a) and (26b), it must be adjacent to the verb in the unmarked case, and, therefore, will precede any other constituent, whether it is an inherently Case-marked NP like the dative object or a Caseless constituent like a PP. However, it is possible to show that, in languages where objects that are analyzed as inherently Case-marked are not realized as PPs, it is still necessary to posit a word order principle that places NPs, regardless of Case, before PPs. This will show that dative phrases in Romance cannot be analyzed as NPs, since that would predict that they should always precede (other) PPs, contrary to fact.

Chicheŵa is a language that has been analyzed by Baker (1988a, 1988b) as having both structurally and inherently Case-marked objects, although they are not distinguished by any overt case morphology. As predicted by the Case-theoretic assumptions, the structurally Case-marked NP precedes not only an inherently Case-marked NP, but also a PP, which is Caseless. But Case Theory makes no prediction about the relative order of an inherently Case-marked NP and a PP. It turns out that the unmarked order is for the inherently Case-marked NP to precede the PP. Example (30a), based on Baker 1988b:ex. 61b, represents the unmarked order, where the NP *chīngwe* 'rope' precedes the PP *ndí*

fisi 'by the hyena', while the reverse order of these constituents, shown
in (30b), is unacceptable. (The sole surface object of this construction is
assigned inherent Case, because it is a passive construction, and passive
morphology has the effect of depriving the verb of its ability to assign
structural Case.)

(30) a. Mpēni u-na-dúl-ír-idw-á   chīngwe ndí fisi.
      3 knife 3 S-PS-cut-AP-PAS-FV 7 rope   by 1a hyena

      'The knife was used by the hyena to cut the rope.'

   b.?*Mpēni u-na-dúl-ír-idw-á   ndí fisi   chīngwe.
      3 knife 3 S-PS-cut-AP-PAS-FV by 1a hyena 7 rope

The contrast between (30a) and (30b) shows that, independently of
Case-theoretic assumptions, NPs precede PPs. This fact suggests that,
if the dative object in Romance were analyzed as an inherently Case-
marked NP, we should expect it to precede oblique PPs. However, what
we find is that it is freely ordered with PPs, as illustrated in (31), just
as oblique PPs are freely ordered with each other, as we see in (32).

(31) a. He   parlat a la Maria dels teus   problemes.
      'I have spoken to Maria   about your problems.'

   b. He   parlat dels teus   problemes a la Maria.
      'I have spoken about your problems   to Maria.'

(32) a. Aquest llibre ha arribat de l'Argentina per a la Maria.
      'This   book has arrived from Argentina for   Maria.'

   b. Aquest llibre ha arribat per a la Maria de l'Argentina.
      'This   book has arrived for   Maria   from Argentina.'

These examples show that the Romance dative object does not behave like an inherently Case-marked object in Bantu or like a (nondative)
NP object in Romance: it is not constrained to precede PPs, but may
either follow or precede PPs in the unmarked order. In sum, the distribution of dative objects in Romance supports their analysis as PPs,
given that they are subject to the same ordering constraints as oblique
PPs.

5.3   Case Assignment

It is quite standard to assume that dative case in Romance is "inherently" determined by the predicate, which is generally interpreted to
mean that there are semantic generalizations governing the assignment
of dative case, although they are normally left unstated. I will show
in this section that, while a semantically based principle of dative case
assignment is necessary, it cannot account for all of the instances in

which dative case is assigned. In addition, it is necessary to assume that the assignment of dative case is also determined by properties of the a-structure. This will allow us to formulate a general case assignment convention for Romance, which will be illustrated for a variety of predicates, including reflexivized predicates. Finally, while case assignment is stated independently of the assignment of syntactic functions to arguments, the two are shown to interact by the absence of dative subjects in Romance.

5.3.1 Two Competing Generalizations

For the moment, let us make the traditional assumption that the assignment of dative case is sensitive to the semantics exclusively. Such a semantically based principle of dative case assignment would be stated as follows:

(33) *Semantically Based Principle of Dative Case Asignment:*

A direct function mapped onto an argument (other than the external argument) that is semantically a goal (or recipient) must bear the case feature [DAT +].

This principle correctly predicts the assignment of dative case for a large class of predicates, including all ditransitives expressing transfer of possession, such as *donar* 'give'. Consider the a-structure with associated thematic role labels of this predicate, in (34). Principle (33) assigns dative case to the syntactic function that maps onto the goal argument.

(34)

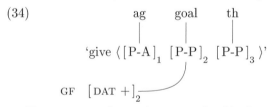

However, an alternative way of achieving the same result for this predicate would be to assume that dative case is not assigned on the basis of the semantics, but on the basis of the a-structure, as stated in the following principle:

(35) *A-Structure Based Principle of Dative Case Assignment:*

A direct function mapped onto the more prominent of two arguments (other than the external argument) must bear the case feature [DAT +].

Given the a-structure in (34), principle (35) would assign dative case to the same syntactic function as principle (33): since the goal argument is the more prominent of two arguments, excluding the external argument in the a-structure in (34), principle (35) would also assign dative case to the function that corresponds to that argument. Thus, the same function in (34) is assigned dative case by both principles. Although the two proposed principles of dative case assignment, (33) and (35), have the same effect with ditransitive verbs, we will see that they have differing consequences with other types of verbs. I will argue that dative case assignment in Romance cannot be reduced to either of these two principles, and that both must be assumed to coexist. In fact, they will be collapsed as one single principle of case assignment in (43).

The requirement that the grammatical function that is assigned dative case not be the expression of the external argument is necessary for both principles of dative case assignment. Evidence that an external argument is never assigned dative case comes from verbs like *rebre* 'receive', which has an argument that is both a recipient and the more prominent of two arguments; however, it is not assigned dative case. The reason is that this argument is the external argument and, as such, is exempt from being assigned dative case. Further evidence comes from reflexivized verbs, as we shall see shortly. The condition that exempts external arguments from being assigned dative case may be derivable from a universal property of external arguments: if, as Grimshaw (1990: 37–38) suggests, external arguments can never be assigned quirky case, and assuming that dative case would qualify as quirky case, then it would follow that external arguments would be blocked from being assigned dative case. I leave the possibility of deriving this condition along these lines to further exploration.

The semantically based principle of dative case assignment (33) has to be assumed to operate in all those verbs whose sole internal argument is expressed as a dative object. Since there is no other less prominent argument, the alternative principle (35) would not predict the assignment of dative case to that argument. Examples of verbs whose sole internal argument is expressed as a dative object are given in (36a). (36b-c) illustrate verbs that take a dative object irrespective of whether a thematically less prominent argument is overtly expressed or not.[15]

---

[15] Not all speakers of Catalan would agree with the use of dative in all of the examples in (36), which corresponds to the more conservative standard dialect. Many speakers use some of the verbs in (36a) consistently with a nondative object; this is particularly the case with *telefonar* (but not with the other examples). The verbs in (36b-c), especially *pegar*, are treated by many speakers as verbs that take a dative object only in the presence of a nondative object.

(36) a. En Ferran li   ha telefonat / parlat / mentit/ escopit.
        Ferran   him DAT has telephoned/ spoken/ lied   / spat

        'Ferran has telephoned him, spoken/lied to him, spat at him.'

     b. En Ferran li   ha escrit (una carta).
        Ferran   him DAT has written a letter

        'Ferran has written him (a letter).'

     c. En Ferran li   ha pegat (una cleca).
        Ferran   him DAT has hit   a clout

        'Ferran has hit him/has given him a clout.'

The argument that is expressed as a dative object in (36) can be characterized semantically as a goal or recipient, interpreting this notion to include the receiver of words or messages. It is clear that only the semantically based principle of dative case assignment (33) can account for these examples, whereas the hierarchically based principle (35) cannot: in (36a), there is no grammatical function corresponding to an argument less prominent than the one expressed as a dative object, and in (36b-c), the presence or absence of that grammatical function does not affect the case marking on the remaining object. Further evidence that dative case can be semantically determined comes from the fact that different meanings associated with a verb may determine a different case value on the object: an example of this is the verb *cridar*, which selects a dative or a nondative object depending on its meaning, as we see in (37). In (37a), the object is the receiver of loud auditory stimuli, but that is not necessarily the case in (37b).

(37) a. En Ferran li   crida.   b. ... el   crida.
        Ferran   him DAT shouts   him ACC calls

        'Ferran shouts at him.'   '... calls him.'

However, when we consider predicates that do not include recipient arguments, the pattern of facts can no longer be accounted for by the semantically based principle (33), but are instead predicted by the hierarchically based principle (35). In the first place, there are verbs with an optionally expressed object that are unlike those illustrated in (36b-c) in that the dative object of the ditransitive form corresponds to a nondative object in the monotransitive form, as we see in (38)–(39).

(38) a. Li   ensenyen llatí.   b. L'   ensenyen.
        him DAT they teach Latin   him ACC they teach

        'They teach him Latin.'   'They teach him.'

(39) a. Li   serveixen te.   b. El   serveixen.
       him DAT they serve tea   him ACC they serve
       'They serve him tea.'   'They serve him.'

Given that the object clitic in these examples expresses the same thematic relation to the predicate whether it is a dative object, as in (38a)–(39a), or an accusative object, as in (38b)–(39b), the case alternation does not reflect a semantic difference, as it does in (37), but a purely syntactic difference: whether the object cooccurs with a nondative object or not. This case alternation is predicted by the hierarchically based principle (35): assuming that the dative object in (38a)–(39a) corresponds to an argument hierarchically more prominent than that of the nondative object, the former argument will only map onto a dative object when the latter argument is assigned a grammatical function.[16]

In the second place, there are thematic paraphrases where an argument alternates between a dative and a nondative expression without changing its thematic status: the alternation is always conditioned by the presence or absence of a nondative object. A relevant example is given in (18), repeated here as (40): the presence of the object *un retrat* 'a portrait' in (40b) forces the thematically more prominent object to be marked with dative case; when the predicate, *retratar* 'portray' in (40a), incorporates semantically the content of that object, the sole object of the construction is not marked with dative case.

(40) a. Volen   retratar   la Maria disfressada de vestal.
       'They want to portray   Maria disguised   as a vestal.'

     b. Volen   fer   un retrat a la Maria   disfressada de vestal.
         they want make a portrait to the Maria disguised   of vestal

         'They want to take a picture of Maria disguised as a vestal.'

Further illustration of this point can be made with the pairs of synonymous (or near synonymous) expressions *fer nosa* (lit. 'make nuisance') and *molestar* 'annoy', shown in (41), and *fer por* (lit. 'make fear') and *espantar* 'frighten', shown in (42). (These examples are representative of a large class of verbs, which take an accusative object, and their verb-object paraphrases, which take a thematically identical or similar dative object: for example, *petonejar* 'kiss (repeatedly)' and

---

[16]It is not particularly relevant for the hierarchically based principle of dative case assignment to decide which specific thematic role each argument bears, as long as the right prominence relations are established. However, we can assume that the objects of *ensenyar* 'teach' are thematically an experiencer (the learner) and a theme (the thing taught), and that the objects of *servir* 'serve' are thematically a beneficiary (the person who is helped) and a theme (the object served). Thus, the thematic hierarchy (2.20) determines the required ranking.

fer petons (lit. 'make kisses') 'kiss', *bufetejar* 'slap (repeatedly)' and *pegar bufetades* (lit. 'hit slaps') 'slap', *espellar* 'skin' and *treure la pell* 'remove the skin', etc.)

(41) a. Aquesta música li   fa   nosa.
        this   music   him DAT makes nuisance

    b. Aquesta música el   molesta.
        this   music   him ACC annoys

      'This music annoys him.'

(42) a. Els llamps   li   fan   por.
        lightning flashes him DAT make fear

    b. Els llamps   l'   espanten.
        lightning flashes him ACC frighten

      'Lightning frightens him.'

The argument expressed as an object clitic in these examples is, according to standard assumptions, an experiencer. The fact that it is a dative object in (41a)–(42a) and an accusative object in (41b)–(42b) cannot be plausibly argued to reflect any semantic difference, as the two pairs of sentences are synonymous. What is obviously conditioning the case difference in the object that expresses the experiencer is the presence or absence of another object. *Nosa* in (41a) and *por* in (42a) are objects unmarked for case (nondative objects); since they are thematically lower than the experiencer (presumably, themes), the experiencer is required to map onto a syntactic function marked as dative, according to the hierarchically based principle of case assignment. In (41b) and (42b), on the other hand, there is one single syntactic function not mapped onto the external argument (the object that expresses the experiencer), and so the hierarchically based principle cannot require it to be marked as dative; since that syntactic function is not the expression of a recipient, it cannot be dative either according to the semantically based principle.

Further evidence for the hierarchically based principle of case assignment comes from the case alternation in causative constructions, which will be illustrated in chapter 6.

5.3.2   Case Assignment Convention

Having established that both the semantically based and the hierarchically based generalizations governing the assignment of dative case are necessary in Catalan, I will propose that case assignment in Catalan (and more generally in Romance) can be reduced to a principle of dative case assignment (sensitive to the semantics and to the a-structure), together with a default specification. This principle assigns the marked value [DAT +], while the unmarked value [DAT −] is supplied by default wherever the marked specification is not assigned. The case assignment convention can be stated as follows:

(43) *Case Assignment Convention*:

a. A direct function (one that has the feature [obl −]) must take the marked feature value [DAT +] if it is mapped onto an argument that is either thematically a goal or more prominent than another argument expressed as a nondative function and if it is not the expression of the external argument.

b. All other direct functions take the default feature value [DAT −].

This convention can be seen as requiring a particular case value in the f-structure of a syntactic function: it is a constraint that the c-structure has to satisfy by including the appropriate case morphology.[17] On the assumption that all and only direct functions have a value for the feature DAT and that the marked specification [DAT +] can only appear where licensed by principle (43a), all direct functions not required to have the marked value will take on the default specification [DAT −], by (43b).

Let us consider the application of this convention to specific examples. It is illustrated with the triadic predicate *donar* 'give' in (44). The three arguments of this predicate are mapped onto direct functions, following the FMT: the External Argument Mapping Principle (2.26) requires the external argument (the agent argument in (44)) to map onto the subject function; the other two arguments, both internal (or [P-P]) arguments, are required to map onto direct functions by the Internal Argument Mapping Principle (2.27); both of these direct functions are further specified as objects (nonsubjects) in order to satisfy the Subject Condition (2.5), since the structure already contains a subject. The function that maps onto the external argument (the agent) is excluded from consideration for the assignment of dative case. Of the two other functions, the one that maps onto the recipient or goal argument is assigned dative case, because it meets both requirements of principle (43a): it is the expression of a goal and it is the hierarchically more prominent of two direct functions. Both the external argument and the lower internal argument (the theme) are assigned the default case specification.

---

[17]The result is like a *constraining equation* in classic LFG (see Kaplan and Bresnan 1982:207–209): the Case Assignment Convention (43) specifies that the attribute DAT of a certain syntactic function is constrained to take the value +, if (43a) applies, or −, if (43b) applies. A constraining equation imposes a requirement that must be met. Convention (43) is a well-formedness condition on f-structures that imposes a requirement that must be satisfied. A similar approach to case assignment is taken in T. Mohanan 1994 and in Butt and King 1991.

(Here, as elsewhere, lines connecting different pieces of structure are included only for visual clarity; they are not part of the formal notation used for this purpose.)

(44) *donar*:

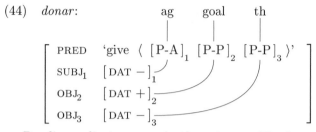

Dyadic predicates come in three types. The largest class is made up of verbs like *obrir* 'open', which have an external argument and one internal argument: they escape the application of principle (43a), because, once the external argument is excluded, there is only one direct function that is not the expression of a goal argument; hence, both arguments map onto functions with the default case specification. A small class of dyadic predicates consists of verbs like *mentir* 'lie (to)', with an external argument and an internal argument that is thematically a goal; because of its thematic role, the function that corresponds to this internal argument is required by principle (43a) to have the dative case specification, while the external argument is specified by default as nondative. The last, rather numerous class of dyadic predicates, consists of verbs like *agradar* 'like', which have two internal arguments. These verbs are subject to principle (43a) because both of their arguments map onto direct functions and neither of them is an external argument, as (45) illustrates.

(45) *agradar*:

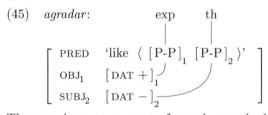

The experiencer argument of *agradar*, as the higher of the two internal arguments, is assigned the marked case feature [DAT +], whereas the lower argument receives the default case specification. This class of verbs includes, in addition to "psych"-verbs or experiencer verbs like *agradar*, *escaure* 'suit', *doldre* 'regret', *saber greu* 'regret', 'feel bad about', *picar* 'itch', etc., many unaccusatives used with an argument that is interpreted as the experiencer of the event and in many cases as the possessor of the theme or patient argument, as with *passar* 'happen', *caure* 'fall', *créixer* 'grow', *sortir* 'come out', *desaparèixer* 'disappear', etc. The following examples illustrate the use of these verbs with experiencer arguments.

(46) a. A la Maria sempre li   passen desgràcies sense
       to the Maria always her DAT happen misfortunes without

       adonar-se'n.
       realizing it

       'Misfortunes always happen to Maria without her realizing it.'

   b. Tot corrent   li   han caigut els pantalons.
      while running him DAT have fallen the trousers

      'His trousers fell off while he was running.'

Unaccusative predicates such as *passar* 'happen' and *caure* 'fall' have the theme or patient argument as their logical subject when this is their sole internal argument. However, when they are used with an additional experiencer argument, this is their logical subject, as shown in (46) by the ability of this argument to control the unexpressed subject of the adverbial clauses.

Monadic predicates always escape the application of principle (43a), and have their sole direct function specified with the default case feature. The sole argument of unergatives, as an external argument, is excluded from receiving dative case. The sole argument of unaccusatives doesn't meet the conditions for being assigned dative case, as it is not a goal and there isn't another, hierarchically lower, argument mapped onto a direct function. So, the sole direct function of monadic predicates necessarily receives the default [DAT −] feature.

5.3.3   Case and Reflexivized Predicates

Let us consider the situation with reflexivized verbs, predicates that have undergone a-structure binding. With dyadic predicates, simple transitive base verbs such as *veure* 'see' or *obrir* 'open', the binding relation holds between the external argument and the single other direct argument (an internal argument). As the two bound arguments map onto the same syntactic function, which is the sole direct function of the structure and, in addition, is mapped onto the external argument, principle (43a) cannot apply. Apparent complications arise when the verb is a triadic predicate such as *donar*, which has a choice of two internal arguments for the external argument to be bound to. As shown in the following examples, dative case is not assigned in the structure in

which the goal is the bound argument, (47a), although it is assigned in
the structure in which the theme is the bound argument, (47b).

(47) a. Els diputats s' han donat un augment de sou.
         the deputies RF have given an increase of salary

         'The deputies have given themselves a salary increase.'

     b. La cantant es dóna al seu públic.
         the singer   RF gives to her audience

         'The singer gives herself to her audience.'

The fact that dative case fails to be assigned in a structure like (47a)
might appear to be unexpected, given the assumption that the verb has
two expressed internal arguments and therefore would seem to satisfy the
requirement for the application of principle (43a). However, observe how
case assignment treats the reflexivized structure in (48) corresponding
to (47a):

(48) *donar-se*:

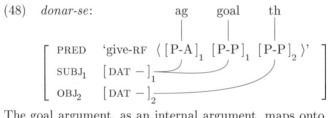

The goal argument, as an internal argument, maps onto a direct function, and there is another function that maps onto a less prominent
argument (the theme), which might suggest that the more prominent
argument should receive dative case. However, the function that maps
onto the goal also maps onto the external argument, and, hence, is excluded from the scope of principle (43a). Dative case cannot be assigned
to a function that maps onto the external argument, even though it may
also map onto an internal argument. Thus, the two functions in a structure such as (48) are treated by the case assignment convention in the
same way as the two functions that correspond to a dyadic predicate
like *obrir*: both are assigned the default case specification [DAT −].

   In a-structure binding constructions in which the external argument
is bound to the lower of two internal arguments, as in example (47b),
the sole object of the construction is assigned dative case, going against
the informal generalization that dative case is only assigned to the thematically higher of two objects. There is, of course, no violation of
the case assignment convention of Romance, as shown in the simplified
f-structure (49) corresponding to sentence (47b).

(49)   *donar-se*:

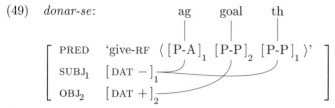

As the goal argument maps onto a direct function and there is another function that maps onto an argument hierarchically lower than the goal (the theme), the former function must be marked with dative case according to (43). The fact that the function that maps onto the theme is the subject, rather than an object, does not affect case assignment. Notice that the case features assigned to the functions of the reflexivized predicate in (49) are the same as those assigned to the functions of an experiencer predicate like *agradar* shown in (45), although such a predicate lacks an external argument altogether. (Naturally, the two predicates differ in many other ways that follow from the difference in the argument structures.)

We have seen that the distribution of case in Romance is predictable by means of a principle that assigns the marked case specification to a syntactic function on the basis of the semantics of the argument and of its a-structure prominence in relation to another syntactic function, together with the assumption that the unmarked case specification is filled in as the default. The correct pattern of facts is predicted with underived predicates as well as with predicates that have undergone a-structure binding.

5.3.4   No Dative Subjects in Romance

The foregoing discussion of case assignment has not paid much attention to the grammatical function (subject or object) to which a particular case feature is assigned. Since both dative and nondative are case specifications of direct functions, it would follow that both subjects and objects could take either case specification. However, the fact is that in Catalan (and Romance in general) a subject can never be marked with dative case. I assume this follows from a constraint in the grammar of Romance applying at the level of f-structure that rules out subjects with the marked case specification [DAT +], as represented in (50).

(50)   *Nondative Subject Constraint*:

$$*[\,[\text{subj} +]\ [\text{DAT} +]\,]$$

Taking this principle to mean that subjects must be nondative (in Romance), it will follow that any direct function constrained to bear the

[DAT +] specification by principle (43a) will not be able to be specified as the subject, because it would then violate the Nondative Subject Constraint. Therefore, a syntactic function that is assigned dative case in Romance can only be an object.

This constraint may appear to be redundant with the condition in (43) that prevents the assignment of dative case to functions mapped onto the external argument. However, both constraints are needed, and neither can be reduced to the other. On the one hand, the failure to assign dative case to a function mapped onto an external argument seems to have a much greater cross-linguistic generality: according to Grimshaw (1990), following Zaenen, Maling, and Thráinsson (1985), even languages such as Icelandic that allow dative subjects do not allow external arguments expressed as dative subjects. On the other hand, even constructions without an external argument in Romance do not allow dative subjects. Constraint (50) has a vacuous effect in structures with an (unsuppressed) external argument: since an external argument must map onto the subject function by the External Argument Mapping Principle (2.26) and cannot be assigned dative case by (43), it follows that, independently of the Nondative Subject Constraint, it is a nondative subject and that a cooccurring dative expression cannot be the subject, by the Subject Condition (2.5), but must be an object. The effect of this constraint, however, is visible in structures without an (unsuppressed) external argument and with a dative argument: passivized ditransitives and experiencer verbs such as *agradar*.

Consider first the passive form of the ditransitive *donar*: its external argument is suppressed, as required by the passive morphology, and its internal arguments are associated with direct (nonoblique) functions, as required by the Internal Argument Mapping Principle (2.27). In addition, the direct function that maps onto the hierarchically more prominent of the nonexternal arguments is marked with dative case, according to (43), and the other function is assigned the default case feature. These minimal requirements are illustrated in (51).

(51) *donar*-PAS:

$$
\begin{array}{ccc}
& \text{ag} & \text{goal} & \text{th} \\
& | & | & | \\
\end{array}
$$

$$
\left[
\begin{array}{ll}
\text{PRED} & \text{`give-PAS } \langle\ [\text{P-A}]_{\textcircled{1}}\ [\text{P-P}]_2\ [\text{P-P}]_3\ \rangle\text{'} \\
[\text{obl} -]_2 & [\text{DAT} +]_2 \\
[\text{obl} -]_3 & [\text{DAT} -]_3
\end{array}
\right]
$$

In this underspecified f-structure, the syntactic function attributes are unspecified for the feature [subj ±]. One of the two direct functions in (51) has to be specified as the subject in order to satisfy the Subject Condition, while the other function will be specified as an object (nonsubject).[18] As there are two direct functions that can be specified as [subj +] or [subj −], there would seem to be two alternative ways to fully specify the functions in (51). However, only one of these options is grammatical:

(52) a. *$\left[\begin{array}{cc} \left[\begin{array}{c} \text{subj} + \\ \text{obl} - \end{array}\right] & [\text{DAT} +] \\[2ex] \left[\begin{array}{c} \text{subj} - \\ \text{obl} - \end{array}\right] & [\text{DAT} -] \end{array}\right]$ b. $\left[\begin{array}{cc} \left[\begin{array}{c} \text{subj} - \\ \text{obl} - \end{array}\right] & [\text{DAT} +] \\[2ex] \left[\begin{array}{c} \text{subj} + \\ \text{obl} - \end{array}\right] & [\text{DAT} -] \end{array}\right]$

The structure in (52a) is ruled out by the Nondative Subject Constraint (50): it contains a subject with the marked case feature [DAT +]. The structure in (52b), on the other hand, is well-formed because its subject has the unmarked case feature [DAT −]. Thus, we account for the puzzle noted earlier that, although dative objects are objects, that is, direct functions, they cannot alternate with the subject function. The passive form of a ditransitive predicate in Romance only allows the argument that in the active form is unmarked for case (i.e., accusative) to surface as the subject, never the argument that takes dative case (see example (2)).[19]

---

[18]It should also be possible for both direct functions to be specified as objects, provided there is a nonthematic subject. However, given the analysis of null nonthematic subjects proposed in 4.2.3, one of these two objects would share its f-structure value with the nonthematic subject. Thus, in order for constraint (50) to be satisfied in such a structure, the object whose value is shared with the subject could only be the nondative object.

[19]Not all languages with dative objects disallow dative subjects or the alternation of a dative object of an active form with the (nondative) subject of the passive. This is the situation in Romance because both the Case Assignment Convention (43) and the Nondative Subject Constraint (50) must be satisfied independently of each other. Now, suppose that one of the two principles were allowed to override the other, treating the latter as a default. If the Nondative Subject Constraint were a default, we would have a language where subjects would normally be nondative (nominative), but could be dative when required by a principle such as (43); this type of language is represented by Icelandic, where, according to Zaenen, Maling and Thráinsson 1985, an argument is assigned dative case, or other marked cases such as genitive, irrespective of whether it is realized as a subject or as an object. On the other hand, if the Case Assignment Convention is a default, we have a type of language in which subjects are always nondative (nominative), and in which a dative object alternates with the nominative subject in active/passive pairs, as has been illustrated for ancient Greek in Feldman 1978 and O'Neill 1990, among others. Thus, the way principles (43) and (50) interact with each other predicts the existence of three types of languages, represented by Romance, Icelandic, and ancient Greek. I am overlooking certain complications that may arise in languages with more complex case systems, such as Icelandic and ancient Greek. In Icelandic, for example, where a distinction between nominative and accusative case is needed, the principles that assign these case features must account, among other things, for the fact that an

Experiencer predicates like *agradar* are predicted to behave exactly like the passive form of ditransitive predicates like *donar* with respect to subject selection. Their argument structures contain only two internal arguments, the more prominent one of which is assigned dative case, as illustrated in (45). Although both arguments map onto direct functions, by the Internal Argument Mapping Principle, and are potential candidates for the subject function, the function specified with dative case is prevented by constraint (50) from being the subject. Hence, only the theme or stimulus argument of experiencer predicates qualifies as a possible subject.

Although the dative argument of experiencer predicates is a logical subject, there is evidence that it is not a grammatical (or surface) subject. The fact that this argument is marked with dative case, rather than nondative (or nominative), which otherwise characterizes subjects, the failure to trigger subject agreement on the verb, and the failure to be "pro-dropped" with a definite interpretation make it unlike ordinary subjects. More compelling evidence for the nonsubject status of this argument is the fact that it cannot be controlled in "equi" type constructions and nonfinite adverbial clauses and cannot undergo raising; in contrast, the nondative (theme) argument does have these properties (see Alsina 1993:chapter 6).

5.4   Implications

In this chapter I have presented an account of case and syntactic functions in Romance that rests on the assumption that the role of case is (at least) to distinguish among potential objects. When a structure has two direct functions in addition to the external argument, it is necessary to make a distinction among them in order to identify their thematic roles, and morphological case is widely used cross-linguistically as a means to make this distinction. The external argument is the default subject—whenever there is an available external argument, it is expressed as the subject—and the subject is sufficiently distinct from the other direct functions, even without a case distinction. So, a case distinction between subjects and nonsubjects is much less necessary than a case distinction among nonsubjects. Thus, the Romance case system is reduced to a dative/nondative opposition with only the dative case feature overtly expressed, and dative case is assigned to a direct function that does not map onto the external argument and is the expression of

argument that is expressed as an accusative object in an active form is assigned nominative case in the passive form even though it may also be an object. See Zaenen, Maling, and Thráinsson 1985, Smith 1992, and Van Valin 1991 for accounts of case assignment in Icelandic.

either a goal (or recipient) argument or an argument hierarchically more prominent than another argument also expressed as a direct function. This proposal treats the assignment of dative case as predictable in the vast majority of cases (the assignment of dative case to a goal being subject to some idiosyncrasies), which, to my knowledge, has not been previously achieved. A single dative case assignment principle and a default convention predict the case patterns of all predicates in Romance: ditransitives, monotransitives, unergatives, unaccusatives, dative experiencer predicates, reflexivized verbs, passive forms, and, as we shall see in chapter 6, causatives. The crucial elements that make this possible are a sufficiently articulated argument structure, which represents prominence relations among arguments and a distinction between external and nonexternal arguments, and a minimal theory of syntactic functions that treats direct functions as a natural class.

A widespread approach to the treatment of multiple object constructions in languages like Romance has been to posit various abstract grammatical categories (generally assumed to be universal) that correlate with, or are manifested as, the observable morphological case distinctions. Those abstract categories are, for example, the Case-theoretic "structural" and "inherent" Case in GB, and the grammatical relations "2" (direct object) and "3" (indirect object) in RG.[20] The present approach has shown that it is possible, and therefore desirable, to dispense with these abstract distinctions. Both the Case-theoretic and the relational approaches assume that determining which argument is expressed as a dative object is largely unpredictable from independent features of the grammar and thus has to be stipulated, and that the distinctive properties of objects depend on the abstract categories assumed, rather than on the morphological case distinction. This chapter has shown that the case frame of predicates can be predicted, and that in the majority of instances it is predictable on the basis of the a-structure. Since the assignment of dative case (and, by complementarity, nondative case) is *structurally* based, there is no motivation, aside for theory internal reasons, for assigning dative case to the abstract category of inherent Case, rather than structural Case. In addition, this chapter has shown that all of the distinctive properties of dative and nondative objects follow

---

[20]The syntactic functions OBJ (unrestricted object) and OBJ$_\theta$ (restricted object) of many versions of LFG have a similar consideration in analyses such as Ackerman 1992:22, where OBJ is the nondative object and OBJ$_\theta$ is the dative object. Since an alternative treatment is possible where the distinction between these two syntactic functions does not correlate with the case distinction (and, in fact, plays no role in the grammar of the language), I will not discuss the status of the OBJ/OBJ$_\theta$ distinction, which is not assumed in the present work.

naturally from the morphological case difference and from the way morphological case is expressed, making additional theoretical distinctions unnecessary.

6

Causatives

The Romance causative construction poses problems for certain conceptions of syntactic theory because it consists of two θ-role assigning verbs that behave in many ways like one single verb. Verbs seem to project different syntactic structures when used as base verbs in the causative construction and when used as independent verbs. As an example, compare the syntactic realization of the single argument of a verb like *treballar* 'work' when used as an independent verb, in (1a), and when used as the base verb in the causative construction, in (1b).

(1) a. El nen   treballa molt.
      'The boy works   very much.'

    b. Fas   treballar molt el nen.
      you make work   much the boy

      'You make the boy work very much.'

The logical subject of *treballar* is realized as a grammatical subject in (1a), but is realized as an object in the causative construction (1b). Thus, the same argument is realized as a subject in one case and as an object in the other.

For theories that adopt the GB hypothesis that each lexical item projects a uniform syntactic structure represented at d-structure, this situation is difficult to resolve. There are two alternatives: (a) either the two verbs in the causative construction are assumed to be in fact one single compound verb, which would then be a lexical item distinct from the verb that appears as its base verb, so that the syntactic structures that they project would be expected to be different, or (b) the base verb projects the same syntactic structure as it does as an independent verb, so that the subject/object alternation of its logical subject in structures like (1) is not a real alternation, but merely an apparent one. The treatment of the two verbs of the causative construction as one single lexical

185

item, which has been proposed by Zubizarreta (1985) and Di Sciullo and Williams (1987), among others, is faced with the difficulty that the putative lexical item does not behave as such with respect to coordination, separability, and the ability to undergo lexical derivations, as shown in Alsina 1993, 1995. The second treatment, which has a long tradition in generative grammar, including among its proponents Marantz (1984), Aoun (1985), Burzio (1986), Baker (1988a), S. Rosen (1989), Di Sciullo and Rosen (1990), Li (1990), Moore (1991), etc., requires assuming that the base verb projects its syntactic structure in a clausal complement of the causative verb, in which its logical subject (if an external argument) is realized as a subject. The problem with this approach is that the putative clausal complement does not behave as clausal complements are expected to behave and the putative subject of this complement does not have the properties that would be expected from its proposed syntactic representation, as shown in Alsina 1992b, 1993. Therefore, we are led to the conclusion that the two verbs in the causative construction are independent lexical items and that the base verb projects a different syntactic structure from that projected by the corresponding independent verb.

In the present approach, the syntactic function alternation of the logical subject of the base verb illustrated in (1) will follow from the assumption that the causative verb and the base verb undergo predicate composition yielding one single, complex, a-structure. Section 6.1 derives the syntactic expression of the arguments of causative constructions from the proposed a-structure of the causative complex predicate, including the dative/accusative case alternation of the object causee and the object/oblique alternation of the causee. The salient c-structure features of causative constructions are discussed in section 6.2. We next address the question of the subjecthood of the causee: while many current theories propose that the causee is a syntactic subject, the available evidence argues strongly against this claim, as will be shown in 6.3. However, the evidence presented in 6.4 supports the assumption that, although syntactically a nonsubject, the causee is a logical subject, a notion represented at a-structure. Section 6.5 brings out the main conclusions that can be drawn from causative constructions regarding the role of a-structure.

6.1   The A-Structure and F-Structure of Causatives

One of the most salient features of the Romance causative construction is what we can refer to as its *monoclausality*: it behaves in many ways as if it consisted of one single clause in the syntax. Perhaps the clearest indication of this monoclausality is the fact that the two predicates involved in the causative construction, the causative verb and the base verb (for example, *fas* 'you make' and *treballar* 'work' respectively in sentence (1b)), behave as one single predicate with respect to case assignment. As we shall see in 6.1.2, the case feature of the object causee depends on the transitivity of the base verb. If the causative construction were analyzed as a control structure, in which the object causee is an object of the matrix causative verb that controls the unexpressed subject of the base verb, as has been proposed in Bordelois 1988, this morphological case alternation would be very difficult to explain. Further evidence for the monoclausality of causative constructions is provided by the ability of these constructions to passivize in some of the Romance languages.[1] Thus, in Catalan, an active causative construction such as (2a) has the passive form in (2b), whose subject corresponds to the object of the active form.

(2) a. L'alcalde ha fet enderrocar el pont per un especialista.
    the mayor has made demolish the bridge by a specialist

    'The mayor had the bridge demolished by a specialist.'

   b. El pont ha estat fet enderrocar per un especialista.
    the bridge has been made demolish by a specialist

    'The bridge has been caused to be demolished by a specialist.'

---

[1] Whereas causative constructions do not passivize in French and Spanish (see, for example, Kayne 1975, Aissen 1979, but see also Zubizarreta 1985:285, where it is claimed that causatives with a base unergative verb in French can passivize), they do in Italian (see Burzio 1986) and Catalan. Passivization of causative constructions is nevertheless more restricted in Catalan than it is in Italian, since only causatives based on transitive and unaccusative predicates can passivize in Catalan provided the internal argument of the base verb surfaces as the passive subject. The logical subject of transitive and unergative base verbs in causative constructions in Catalan cannot be expressed as passive subjects (as it is not an internal argument of the base verb), unlike what happens in Italian (see Burzio 1986:232). Thus, the causative construction in (1b) does not have a grammatical passive form, as shown in (i), contrasting with what is reported for French in Zubizarreta 1985:285. In contrast with this example, (ii) shows that a causative whose base verb is an unaccusative can passivize. Notice that the passive subject is an internal argument of the base verb in (ii), as in (2b), but not in (i).

(i)   *El nen ha estat fet treballar molt.
      the boy has been made work much

(ii) Els conills van ser fets sortir del cau.
      'The rabbits PAST be made to come out of the burrow.'

I will not attempt to explain contrasts such as (i) vs. (ii) or the differences among the Romance languages in their ability to passivize causative constructions. (See Zubizarreta 1985 and S. Rosen 1989, among others, for some proposals.)

Passivization is a clause-bound phenomenon: when a verb is passivized, only one of its arguments (if any) may appear as the passive subject, never an argument of a clausal complement of the passivized verb. Since we find an argument of the base verb as the passive subject in (2b), we are led to assume that the causative verb and the base verb form one single clause. Impersonal passivization, by means of the clitic *es* (equivalent to *si* in Italian and *se* in Spanish), provides similar evidence for the monoclausality of causative constructions. Further evidence is provided by floating quantifiers, to be discussed in 6.3.2, and reflexive cliticization (a-structure binding), to be discussed in 6.3.4.

In the remainder of this section we shall see how the present theory proposes to account for the monoclausal structure of causative constructions in Romance, and how the alternative syntactic expressions of the causee follow from this proposal.

6.1.1 A Complex Predicate

In the present approach, the monoclausality of causatives is accounted for by assuming that the two verbs involved in the causative construction undergo predicate composition yielding one single predicate (or PRED in the f-structure). A crucial element in this is the assumption that the causative predicate is an incomplete predicate, like the a-structure binding morpheme; because it is an incomplete predicate, it must undergo predicate composition with another predicate. The infinitive verb form that follows the causative verb provides the predicate that the causative predicate composes with.

I will assume, following Alsina's (1992a) proposal regarding the a-structure of causatives in Chicheŵa, that the causative predicate in Romance may express not only a relation in which a participant (the causer) causes an event, but also a relation in which the causer affects (or acts upon) a participant of the caused event. Since this participant is acted upon by the causer, it can be said to be an argument of the causative predicate (and to bear a thematic role, such as patient, to this predicate), in addition to being an argument of the caused event. Thus, the a-structure representation of the causative predicate just described is as shown in (3).

(3) 'cause $\langle$ [P-A] [P-P]$_1$ P* $\langle$ ... [ ]$_1$ ... $\rangle$ $\rangle$'

The causer or agent role of the causative predicate is represented here as the P-A argument. The argument that the causer acts upon is represented as the P-P argument. The predicate that the causative predicate must combine with is represented in (3) by the symbol P^*, which denotes an unspecified predicator, and its underspecified a-structure. The binding relation, represented by coindexing, between this argument and an argument of the embedded predicate indicates that the two bound arguments are the same semantic participant. As we shall see, the argument that the internal (or P-P) argument of the causative predicate is bound to may be the logical subject of the embedded predicate, but may also be an argument distinct from the logical subject.

When the causative predicate in (3) composes with a predicate such as that of *treballar* of example (1), we obtain the complex predicate shown in (4) in which *treballar* provides the embedded predicate and its single argument is coindexed with the internal argument of the causative predicate.

(4) 'cause $\langle$ [P-A] [P-P]$_1$ work $\langle$ [P-A]$_1$ $\rangle$ $\rangle$'

The mapping of arguments to syntatic functions that corresponds to this predicate is given in (5). The P-A argument of the causative predicate qualifies as the external argument of the structure, as it is the P-A argument of the least embedded a-structure, and thus maps onto the subject by the External Argument Mapping Principle (2.26). The P-P argument maps onto a direct function according to the Internal Argument Mapping Principle (2.27); this direct function is further specified as an object in compliance with the Subject Condition (2.5). The P-A argument of the embedded predicate is not constrained by either of the mapping principles, since it is not an internal (i.e., P-P) argument or the external argument (as it is not the P-A argument of the least embedded a-structure). Nevertheless, this argument, because it is bound to another argument, maps onto the same syntactic function as the argument it is bound to, namely, the object.

(5) $$\begin{bmatrix} \text{PRED} & \text{'cause } \langle \, [\text{P-A}]_2 \, [\text{P-P}]_1 \text{ work } \langle \, [\text{P-A}]_1 \, \rangle \, \rangle \text{'} \\ \text{SUBJ}_2 & [\ ]_2 \\ \text{OBJ}_1 & [\ ]_1 \end{bmatrix}$$

What is important to point out here is that, whereas the single argument of the embedded predicate in (5) maps onto a subject when its predicate is not composed with any other predicate as it then qualifies as the external argument, the same argument maps onto an object in the causative construction. This is because, in the causative complex predicate, the logical subject of the embedded predicate is not an external argument and is bound to an argument constrained to map onto an object function. In this way we account for the subject/object alternation of the logical subject illustrated in (1).

6.1.2 Morphological Case Alternation

A well-known fact about causatives in Romance is that the object causee exhibits a morphological case alternation that depends on the transitivity of the embedded predicate. If the embedded predicate is intransitive, the causee is a nondative (accusative) object, as in (1b); if the embedded predicate is transitive, the causee is a dative object. The transitive verb *llegir* 'read', which is illustrated in (6a) as an independent predicate taking a subject and an object, has the causee expressed as a dative object when it is the embedded predicate of a causative construction, as shown in (6b).

(6) a. El nen   llegeix   un poema.
      'The boy is reading a poem.'

    b. El mestre fa   llegir un poema al nen.
      the teacher makes read a poem   to-the boy

      'The teacher is making the boy read a poem.'

The claim that the causee in (1b) is a nondative object and that the causee in (6b) is a dative object is clearly evidenced when these objects are expressed as pronominal clitics, as in (7a) and (7b) respectively.

(7) a. { El   /*Li }   fas   treballar molt.
         him ACC/ him DAT you make work   much

      'You make him work very much.'

    b. El mestre {*el   / li }   fa   llegir un poema.
      the teacher   him ACC/ him DAT makes read a poema

      'The teacher is making him read a poem.'

The case marking alternation of the causee illustrated in (7) is accounted for in the present theory without making any assumption about case marking specific to causative constructions. The Case Assignment Convention (5.43), repeated in (8) for convenience, accounts for this alternation.

(8) *Case Assignment Convention*:

    a. A direct function (one that has the feature [obl −]) must take the marked feature value [DAT +] if it is mapped onto an argument that is either thematically a goal or more prominent than another argument expressed as a nondative function and if it is not the expression of the external argument.

    b. All other direct functions take the default feature value [DAT −].

Consider the structure in (5) corresponding to a causative construction such as (1b) or (7a) based on an intransitive verb. Applying the Case

Assignment Convention (8) to that structure we obtain the structure in (9) specified for the case feature. The function that maps onto the external argument (the subject) is exempt from the assignment of dative case, and is assigned the default nondative. The object (the causee), being neither a goal nor the thematically more prominent of two direct functions, is not assigned dative case, but also the default specification.

$$(9) \quad \begin{bmatrix} \text{PRED} & \text{'cause} \langle\, [\text{P-A}]_2\, [\text{P-P}]_1\ \text{work} \langle\, [\text{P-A}]_1\,\rangle\,\rangle\text{'} \\ \text{SUBJ}_2 & [\text{DAT} -]_2 \\ \text{OBJ}_1 & [\text{DAT} -]_1 \end{bmatrix}$$

In contrast with this structure, the a-structure that results from composing the causative predicate (3) with the transitive predicate *llegir*, in which the logical subject of the latter is bound to the internal argument of the former, licenses the f-structure in (10), which meets the context for the assignment of dative case.

$$(10) \quad \begin{bmatrix} \text{PRED} & \text{'cause} \langle\, [\text{P-A}]_3\, [\text{P-P}]_2\ \text{read} \langle\, [\text{P-A}]_2\, [\text{P-P}]_1\,\rangle\,\rangle\text{'} \\ \text{SUBJ}_3 & [\text{DAT} -]_3 \\ \text{OBJ}_2 & [\text{DAT} +]_2 \\ \text{OBJ}_1 & [\text{DAT} -]_1 \end{bmatrix}$$

As in (9), the external argument of the structure (the causer) maps onto the subject and the internal argument of the causative predicate maps onto an object; and the logical subject of the embedded predicate, which is bound to this internal argument, maps onto the same syntactic function as its bound argument. This structure contains an additional internal argument that is not present in (9), the internal argument of the base predicate; as an internal (P-P) argument it maps onto a direct function, which must be an object since it cooccurs with a subject. The Case Assignment Convention (8) requires the case features specified in (10). The function that maps onto the causee is assigned dative case, because it satisfies the condition in (8a) of being the thematically more prominent of two direct functions (and not the expression of the external argument). The remaining two syntactic functions in (10) cannot be assigned dative case: the subject, because it is the expression of the external argument, and the object that maps onto the internal argument of the base predicate, because it is neither a goal nor the hierarchically more prominent of two direct functions. Consequently, they are assigned the default nondative specification according to (8b). The crucial element here is that, since both arguments of the embedded predicate map onto direct functions, the one that is more prominent in the a-structure, the object that maps onto the causee, is assigned dative case.

Causatives based on ditransitive verbs such as *donar* 'give' do not differ from those based on monotransitive verbs in the case feature assigned to the object causee. The complex a-structure derived from composing the causative predicate with a ditransitive predicate is identical to that given in (10) except that the base predicate contains an additional internal argument. It doesn't matter that one of the two internal arguments of the base predicate is assigned dative case (possibly because it satisfies both the thematic condition and the relative prominence condition of (8a)). The logical subject of the base predicate, which, as in (10), maps onto an object function because it is bound to the internal argument of the causative predicate, satisfies the relative prominence condition, as it is more prominent than another argument mapped onto a nondative function, and therefore is assigned dative case. Thus, a causative construction based on the ditransitive *enviar* 'send', whose use as an independent verb is illustrated in (11a), contains two dative functions, as we see in (11b): one corresponding to the causee, expressed here as the clitic *li*, and one corresponding to the goal argument of the base verb, expressed here as the dative PP.

(11) a. En Ferran ha enviat una postal a la Gertrudis.
       'Ferran   has sent   a postcard to Gertrudis.'

    b. Li   he   fet   enviar una postal a la Gertrudis.
      him DAT I have made send   a postcard to Gertrudis

      'I made him send a postcard to Gertrudis.'

While there are interesting restrictions on the placement of the two dative objects involved in causative constructions such as (11b),[2] what is important to note here is that the object causee is a dative object,

---

[2]For example, the two dative objects do not normally appear as full phrases in the VP. Thus, (ia), with the two dative PPs in the VP, is marginal to unacceptable; (ib), however, suggested by a reviewer, is considerably more acceptable.

(i) a. ?*He   fet   enviar una postal a la Gertrudis a en Ferran.
      I have made send   a postcard to Gertrudis   to Ferran

      'I made Ferran send a postcard to Gertrudis.'
      'I made Gertrudis send a postcard to Ferran.'

   b. Els capellans sovint fan   donar diners als   pobres als seus feligresos.
     the priests   often make give   money to the poor to their parishoners.

     'Priests often make their parishoners give money to the poor.'

I will not speculate here as to what may account for the difference in acceptability between (ia) and (ib). It is clear that it is generally acceptable for the causee to be expressed as a dative clitic attached to the matrix verb, cooccurring with another dative argument in the clause, as in (11b). It is also acceptable for one of the two

as predicted by the proposed a-structure and by the Case Assignment Convention.

In sum, once we assume that causative constructions in Romance have one single complex a-structure in which the causative verb provides the outer a-structure and the infinitive verb provides the embedded a-structure, the morphological case features of their syntactic functions are predicted by the independently motivated Case Assignment Convention (8) (=(5.43)). No principle specific to causative constructions is needed to explain the case patterns, in particular, the case alternation of the causee. This case alternation is conditioned by the presence or absence of a syntactic function thematically less prominent than the causee. The claim that this case alternation is not conditioned by semantic factors is supported by the facts of causatives based on verbs with an optional internal argument, such as *cantar* 'sing'. Although the logical subject of such verbs is semantically unchanged by having this internal argument syntactically expressed or not, its case feature does depend on this, as we see in (12).

(12) a. L'   he   fet   cantar.
        him ACC I have made sing

    'I made him sing.'

   b. Li   he   fet   cantar l'himne   grec.
      him DAT I have made sing   the anthem Greek

    'I made him sing the Greek anthem.'

The fact that the object causee is obligatorily nondative in (12a) and dative in (12b) cannot be argued to follow from any semantic difference between the two sentences. This case difference follows from the fact that (12b) includes a nondative object that is analyzed as being thematically less prominent than the causee, which is absent from (12a).

6.1.3 Object/Oblique Alternation

Although the case alternation on the object causee is purely conditioned by syntactic factors, as indicated by (12), there is yet another syntactic alternation in the expression of the causee, which does reflect semantic differences. Many base transitive verbs in causative constructions allow

---

dative objects, preferentially the causee, to be expressed as a displaced constituent, as in (ii).

(ii)   A qui has   fet   enviar una postal a la Gertrudis?
         'Whom have you made send   a postcard to Gertrudis?'

Similar facts are reported for French in Kayne 1975:290. See Miller 1991 for an explanation for this kind of facts in French causatives.

the causee not only to be expressed as a dative object, but also to be omitted or expressed as an oblique *per*-phrase, as shown in (13).

(13) a. L'alcalde ha fet   enderrocar el   pont   (per un
        the mayor has made demolish   the bridge by a

        especialista).
        specialist

        'The mayor had the bridge demolished (by a specialist).'

    b. Faré   endreçar   la classe   (pels   meus alumnes).
       I will make put in order the classroom by-the my   students

       'I will have the classroom put in order (by my students).'

I propose that the difference between having the oblique causee or the object causee reflects a difference in the a-structure.[3] Recall that the internal (patient) argument of the causative predicate (3) may be bound to the logical subject of the embedded predicate, which is the situation I have illustrated up to now, but need not be bound to that argument. Suppose that, instead, it is bound to an internal argument of the embedded predicate distinct from the logical subject. With an embedded predicate such as *enderrocar* 'demolish' of example (13a), the resulting a-structure would be as shown in the PRED value of (14).

(14)
$$
\begin{bmatrix}
\text{PRED} & \text{'cause} \ \langle \ [\text{P-A}]_3 [\text{P-P}]_2 \ \text{demolish} \ \langle \ [\text{P-A}]_1 [\text{P-P}]_2 \ \rangle \ \rangle \text{'} \\
\text{SUBJ}_3 & [\text{DAT} -]_3 \\
\text{OBJ}_2 & [\text{DAT} -]_2
\end{bmatrix}
$$

Here, the internal argument of the causative predicate is not bound to the logical subject of the embedded predicate, but to another argument. Since the two bound arguments are internal arguments, they map onto an object, which satisfies their mapping requirements. The logical subject of the embedded predicate, being a P-A argument but not the external argument, and not being bound to an internal argument, is not licensed to map onto a direct function. It, thus, may remain unexpressed, which is the option illustrated in (14), where there is no syntactic function corresponding to the causee (with the index 1).

---

[3] Many studies of Romance causatives have proposed that the presence of the oblique causee is the result of passivizing the embedded predicate in the causative construction. The main argument in favor of this analysis, although others are presented by Kayne (1975), is that the oblique causee is identical in form to the passive oblique. However, this analysis has been persuasively argued against by Legendre (1990a), and I therefore reject it referring the reader to Legendre 1990a and C. Rosen 1990b: 439 for arguments and further references on the two sides of the debate.

An alternative to having the causee unexpressed, given the a-structure in (14), is for it to map onto an oblique, provided there is an oblique preposition (or case marker) whose requirements can be met in that structure. Since obliques, unlike direct functions, are not licensed by mapping principles, they can be used freely when their requirements are met, accounting for their optionality. The preposition *per* in Catalan (equivalent to Spanish *por*, French *par*, and Italian *da*) can introduce an oblique mapped onto (coindexed with) a causee, yielding the partially specified f-structure in (15).

(15)

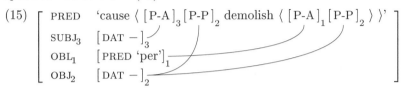

$$\begin{bmatrix} \text{PRED} & \text{'cause} \langle\, [\text{P-A}]_3\, [\text{P-P}]_2 \text{ demolish} \langle\, [\text{P-A}]_1\, [\text{P-P}]_2\, \rangle\, \rangle\text{'} \\ \text{SUBJ}_3 & [\text{DAT} -]_3 \\ \text{OBL}_1 & [\text{PRED 'per'}]_1 \\ \text{OBJ}_2 & [\text{DAT} -]_2 \end{bmatrix}$$

As we see comparing (14) and (15), the only difference between the structures is whether the *per* oblique is used or not. The structure in (15) corresponds to the sentences in (13) in which the optional oblique causee is used.

It has been known since Kayne 1975 that there is a difference in the interpretation of causatives with an oblique causee and those with an object causee. The following examples, based on Hyman and Zimmer's (1975) French exx. 32–33, contrast not only in the syntactic expression of the causee, but also in their semantics.

(16) a. He   fet   netejar els lavabos al   general.
     I have made clean   the toilets to the general

     'I made the general clean the toilets.'

   b. He   fet   netejar els lavabos pel   general.
     I have made clean   the toilets by the general

     'I had the toilets cleaned by the general.'

According to Hyman and Zimmer (1975), in (16a), "it is the case that I did something to the general, e.g., because I didn't like him, I made him do an undesirable task." On the other hand, in (16b), "the general is more incidental to the task. I wanted to get the toilets cleaned and it happened to be the general that I got to do it." Within the present theory, this semantic difference is expected: the syntactic difference between (16a) and (16b) follows from a difference in their a-structures, which, in turn, reflects a difference in the semantics. Compare the a-structures of these two sentences, in (17a) and (17b), corresponding to (16a) and (16b) respectively.

(17) a.

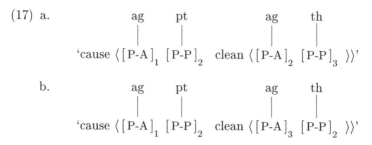

b.

(17a) corresponds to a sentence such as (16a), in which the causee (*el general*) is expressed as an object, marked with dative case. This occurs because the logical subject of the base predicate is semantically identified with the internal argument of the causative predicate, as in the structure shown in (10). As this internal argument is thematically a patient, it follows, then, that the causee is acted upon, or directly affected, by the causing event. In (17b), in contrast, which corresponds to a sentence like (16b), the causee is expressed (optionally) by means of an oblique, because it is not semantically identified with the internal argument of the causative predicate, as in the structures in (14) and (15). In this case, then, the causee is not interpreted as being directly affected by the causing event.

Since the same preposition is used to introduce the passive oblique and the oblique causee, one might suppose that this preposition introduces an oblique coindexed with a logical subject, which may be the logical subject of the least embedded a-structure, as in the passive case, or the logical subject of an embedded a-structure, which corresponds to a causee. However, it has been noticed by Hyman and Zimmer (1975), Bordelois (1988), and Guasti (1990), among others, that the argument expressed as a passive oblique may bear any thematic role (to be more precise, any thematic role borne by a logical subject), whereas an oblique causee is much more restricted semantically. According to these authors, the oblique causee, in contrast with the passive oblique, would only correspond to an agent. Thus, whereas a verb with an experiencer logical subject such as *veure* 'see' can appear in the passive form with a passive oblique, as in (18a), it cannot take an oblique causee in the causative construction, as shown in (18b), where the causee can only be expressed as a dative object.

(18) a. El problema, tal com és vist pel   director, ...
       'The problem, as   it is seen by the director, ...'

b. He   fet   veure el problema $\left\{\begin{array}{c}\text{al}\\ \text{*pel}\end{array}\right\}$ director.

I have made see   the problem to/*by the director

'I made the director see the problem.'

This evidence indicates that, whereas the logical subject expressed by the passive oblique is quite unselective as to its thematic role, and may be an experiencer, that is not the case with the logical subject expressed by an oblique causee, which may not correspond to an experiencer.

Although the requirement that the oblique causee be an agent accounts for the unacceptability of the oblique causee in many cases, such as (18b), it does not account for the full distribution of the oblique causee. Recall from 3.3.2 that both causatives based on transitive verbs and causatives based on unergative verbs allow the omission of the causee quite freely, contrasting with causatives based on unaccusatives, which do not. Example (3.25b), repeated here as (19), illustrates the ability of causatives with unergative base verbs to omit the causee.

(19)   El mestre   ha fet   treballar molt aquest curs.

'The teacher has made people work a lot this   term.'

The possibility of omitting the causee of a base unergative, as in (19), is argued here to be due to the existence in Catalan (and Romance more generally) of a causative predicate different from that given in (3) in that it lacks the internal argument that is bound to an argument of the embedded predicate. This alternative a-structure of the causative verb is given in (4.13) and repeated in (20).[4]

(20)   *fer*:   [PRED 'cause $\langle$ [P-A] P* $\langle$ ... $\rangle$ $\rangle$']

---

[4] The need to posit these two alternative a-structures for the causative verb is motivated not only by the ability of causatives based on unergatives to omit the causee, but also by the possibility of forming causatives based on verbs that lack an argument, such as "weather" verbs like *ploure* 'rain' and *nevar* 'snow', as in (i).

(i)   Si continues   cantant així, faràs   ploure.

if you continue singing thus you will make rain

'If you continue singing this way, you will make it rain.'

On the assumption that a predicate like *ploure* has no arguments, it would be impossible for the causative predicate (3) to compose with it, because the internal argument of (3) needs an argument of the embedded predicate to be bound to and it would not find one in *ploure*. Therefore, the well-formedness of a causative construction with this base predicate requires assuming the existence of an alternative causative predicate that lacks a patient internal argument. Even if we assumed that weather verbs have an argument (or quasi-argument), as has sometimes been proposed, it would be very implausible to assume that such an argument can designate the kind of semantic participant that can be acted upon (as a patient argument is) by the causative predicate. So, even under this assumption, the well-formedness of causatives based on weather verbs motivates the alternative causative predicate in (20).

When an unergative such as *treballar* 'work' of example (19) is the embedded predicate of a causative without the internal argument, the single argument of the embedded predicate is not bound to an internal argument. As the logical subject of an unergative predicate, it has the P-A classification, but, once this predicate is embedded in the causative complex predicate, its logical subject does not qualify as an external argument, because it is not the P-A argument of the most inclusive a-structure. Therefore, being neither an external argument, an internal argument, nor bound to one, it cannot be mapped onto a direct function. It may be unexpressed, as illustrated in (19). However, unexpectedly, since it is an agent, it cannot be expressed as an oblique *per*-phrase, as we see in (21).

(21)   *El mestre   ha fet   treballar molt pels   estudiants.
         the teacher has made work   much by-the students

        'The teacher made the students work a lot.'

The contrast beween this example and grammatical examples containing an oblique causee, such as (13) and (17b), suggests that the oblique expression of the causee is available only when the base verb takes another direct argument, in addition to the causee. Notice that, in (13) and (17b), the base predicate includes an internal (therefore, direct) argument in addition to its logical subject.

The reason for this contrast is to be sought in the explanation proposed in Pinkham 1974: the oblique causee can only be used when an argument of the embedded verb is affected by the event denoted by this verb. In other words, the oblique causee signals a relation in which the argument designated by the oblique affects another argument overtly expressed. Thus, (21) is ungrammatical because there is no syntactic constituent that designates an argument that may be affected by the logical subject of the embedded predicate. In contrast, in (13) and (17b) there is such a syntactic constituent, which makes it possible to use the oblique causee: a clear affect relation is encoded between the oblique causee and another overtly expressed argument of the same predicate. (See Alsina 1993 for further evidence favoring this account.) This explanation, therefore, reduces to the licensing conditions on the preposition

---

It should be noted, however, that the postulation of these two causative a-structures predicts a systematic ambiguity in causatives based on unaccusatives and on transitives whose causee is omitted or expressed as an oblique. In such cases, the internal argument of the base predicate can be analyzed either as being bound to the internal argument of the causative predicate (3) or not, if the causative predicate is (20), and, in either case, is expressed as the sole object of the construction. I am not able to provide strong evidence for this ambiguous analysis.

per, which can be represented as an "adjunct rule" of the type proposed in Jackendoff 1990 referring simultaneously to syntactic information and to lexical-conceptual information.

6.1.4   Summary

The assumption that the two predicates involved in a causative construction in Romance (the causative predicate and the base predicate) form a complex predicate, and therefore yield one single PRED value in an f-structure accounts for the monoclausality of this construction. Because we are dealing with one single, although complex, a-structure, the principles and operations that are sensitive to a-structure treat that a-structure as a unit. Thus, the FMT applies to it yielding one single array of associated syntactic functions, ensuring, for example, that it includes one and only one subject, as required by the Subject Condition. The Case Assignment Convention (8) also applies to it, as it does to any a-structure, assigning the case specifications [DAT +] and [DAT −] to direct functions.

Whereas a predicate, outside of the causative construction, typically has its logical subject expressed as a subject, its position when embedded in the causative a-structure, which includes another logical subject (in fact, an external argument), guarantees that its logical subject will not be expressed as the subject. The hypothesis that the causative predicate may include an internal argument (acted upon by the causer) that may be bound to the logical subject of the embedded predicate makes it possible for this argument to be expressed as an object, which it would not otherwise if it has the P-A classification. The morphological case specification of this object, as dative or nondative, is determined by the application of the Case Assignment Convention (8), sensitive to the a-structure representation. The assumption that the P-A logical subject of the embedded predicate in a causative a-structure need not be bound to the internal argument of the causative predicate (either because this argument is bound to another argument of the embedded predicate or because it is absent from the causative predicate altogether) accounts for the possibility of its being unexpressed or expressed by means of an oblique phrase. The fact that, of the causative structures in which the causee can be omitted, not all allow the oblique expression of the causee is accounted for by imposing a licensing condition on the preposition that introduces the oblique causee requiring there to be a semantic relation of affect between the causee and another direct argument of the predicate.

The ability of causative structures to passivize taking an argument of the embedded predicate as their subject, illustrated in (2), was presented at the beginning of section 6.1 as an indication of the monoclausality of causative constructions. Analyzing causative constructions as consisting of one single (complex) a-structure or PRED value accounts for their passivizability. The effect of passive morphology on this a-structure is the same as with a simple a-structure: it suppresses the logical subject of the structure.[5] Once the logical subject of the causative predicate is suppressed, it cannot be accessed by the mapping principles of the FMT and, therefore, cannot map onto a direct function (including the subject). The subject function may then map onto an argument other than the logical subject. Thus, the passivized causative example (2b) has the skeletal f-structure in (22), which is the passive counterpart of the f-structure in (15).

$$(22) \quad \begin{bmatrix} \text{PRED} & \text{'cause} \langle [\text{P-A}]_{\textcircled{3}} \ [\text{P-P}]_2 \ \text{demolish} \langle [\text{P-A}]_1 \ [\text{P-P}]_2 \rangle \rangle ' \\ \text{OBL}_1 & [\text{PRED 'per'}]_1 \\ \text{SUBJ}_2 & [\text{DAT} -]_2 \end{bmatrix}$$

The two internal (P-P) arguments in the a-structure, which are coindexed, are licensed to map onto a direct function by the Internal Argument Mapping Principle (2.27). This direct function is specified as the subject, satisfying the Subject Condition. In this way, the passivizability of causative constructions is a natural consequence of analyzing them as having a single PRED value.

6.2 The C-Structure of Causatives

The preceding section has argued for a specific representation of the a-structure and f-structure of causatives in Romance. In order to have a complete picture of the structure of Romance causatives, it is still necessary to provide their c-structure representation. A possibly surprising feature of the analysis of Romance causative constructions proposed here is that the two predicates that compose to yield the complex causative predicate are independent syntactic constituents; that is, they occupy different terminal nodes in the c-structure. This means that the composition of the two predicates involved takes place in the syntax, rather than in the lexicon, which is often assumed to be the component of grammar in which all operations on a-structure (or operations that affect the syntactic subcategorization of predicates) take place. In this section, I articulate a proposal to account for predicate composition in the syntax;

---

[5]Although causative a-structures, because they contain an embedded a-structure, have two logical subjects, only the logical subject of the least embedded a-structure (the causer in the case of causative constructions) is accessible to passivization. This would follow from a locality condition on a-structure operations such as that proposed by Isoda (1991), according to which only the least embedded a-structure in a complex a-structure is accessible to a-structure operations such as passivization.

within this proposal, the c-structure position of constituents in causative constructions is determined by independently motivated principles.

6.2.1   A Functionally Double-Headed C-Structure

On the basis of evidence from separability, coordination, and nominalizations, Alsina 1993, 1995 argues that the two predicates involved in a causative construction in Romance are independent syntactic constituents, X^0's. In what follows, I adopt the proposals of Alsina 1993, 1995 regarding predicate composition in the syntax. Given standard LFG assumptions, two lexical items can only specify a value for the same f-structure attribute if the two values unify. However, it is assumed that two PRED values cannot unify, which effectively means that only one X^0 specifying a PRED value may map onto a given f-structure. This raises a problem for a treatment of Romance causatives in which two distinct constituents contribute information to the same PRED feature.

I propose to solve this problem by assuming that, although PRED values cannot unify, there is an alternative mechanism for handling multiple PRED values, namely, predicate composition. Predicate composition in the syntax requires that, if a constituent M immediately dominates two constituents that map onto the same f-structure and are specified with a PRED value, the PRED value associated with M is the result of composing the PRED values of its two (co-linked) daughters. The composition of two PRED values is only well-formed if one of the two is *incomplete*, that is, it includes the symbol P^* (an unspecified predicator) and an underspecified a-structure, and if P^* is replaced by the predicator of the other PRED value whose a-structure must unify with the underspecified a-structure of the incomplete predicate. As a result, the composition of two complete predicates is ill-formed. If we further assume that the composition of a complete predicate with nothing is identical to the single composed predicate, predicate composition becomes the general mechanism by which predicate information is passed from a node to its co-linked mother.

As an illustration of an instance of predicate composition in the syntax, consider the portion of the c-structure of a causative construction in Catalan in which predicate composition takes place: the VP that immediately dominates the causative verb and the phrasal projection of the embedded verb, *llegir* 'read' in (23), corresponding to an example like (6b). The dotted lines in (23) indicate the PRED values associated with each node in the c-structure.

(23)

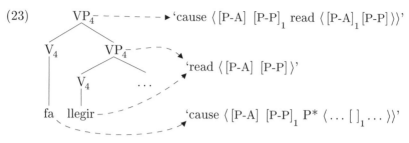

For the purpose of this illustration, only the PRED values are indicated, although the verbs involved may be specified for other f-structure features, such as TENSE and ASPECT. Only the structurally highest verb in a sequence of verbs that undergo predicate composition may bear tense and aspect features. This can be accounted for by including INFL in the c-structure (following Kroeger's (1993) proposals for introducing this category in an LFG theory) and assuming that only this category may bear those features. The verb that appears in INFL, necessarily the structurally highest one, will be the only one specified for these features.

The embedded VP in (23) has a single co-linked daughter, its head, and so it inherits the PRED value of its head unchanged. This VP, in turn, is co-linked with its mother VP, which is also co-linked with its X^0 head, the causative verb. As this higher VP is co-linked with its two daughter nodes, its PRED value is the result of composing the PRED values of its two daughters. As one of the PREDs is an incomplete predicate (the causative), the composition of the two PREDs is possible. So, we see that, once it is accepted that a mechanism other than unification, namely composition of predicates, is necessary for the flow of information in the syntax, it is possible to account for complex predicates formed in the syntax.

Alsina (1993, 1995) proposes that the defective nature of incomplete predicates has a reflex in their c-structure position. An incomplete predicate is a defective verb because it does not have a complete a-structure, and, because of this, it must combine in the c-structure with a constituent with which it undergoes a-structure composition to yield a complete predicate associated with the node immediately dominating them. Therefore, the X^0 specified as an incomplete predicate is always the sister of a phrase which is the projection of the predicate it composes with. Consequently a constituent of bar level greater than 0 cannot be specified as an incomplete predicate: if one of its daughters is specified as an incomplete predicate, predicate composition must have taken place yielding a complete predicate. Thus, the c-structure shown in (23) is well-formed because the VP dominating the incomplete predicate *fa* is associated with a complete predicate, that which results from composing the PREDs of its two co-linked daughters.

In addition, the restricted X′ theory proposed in 2.1.1 requires that a phrasal category (or XP) be the projection of no more than one X^0 or *lexical head*. (I use the term *head* to refer to the constituent whose categorial features (except for the phrasal/lexical distinction) are identical to those of its mother. Heads are always co-linked with their mothers—that is, they have the same mapping to f-structure. In addition, some non-heads can also be co-linked with their mothers, such as the phrases that undergo predicate composition in complex predicate constructions.) The c-structure in (23) satisfies this requirement since each of the two Vs involved is the lexical head of a different VP, and, consequently, although the higher VP has two co-linked daughters (the V *fa* and the VP headed by *llegir*), it has only one V as its lexical head. This restriction implies that a verb whose predicate is incomplete is always the c-structure sister of a co-linked VP. Complex predicates formed in the syntax consist of a PRED feature (and therefore an entire f-structure) that is determined by two different lexical heads. We can thus say that, as far as the f-structure is concerned, such complex predicates have two heads, i.e., are functionally double-headed.

The constraints just proposed for the c-structure position of incomplete predicates are particularly relevant when more than one incomplete predicate contributes to the PRED of the clause. This situation, involving multiple predicate composition, occurs quite commonly in Catalan (and Spanish, Italian, etc.) when we take into account so-called restructuring verbs, which, following S. Rosen (1989) and others, can be analyzed, at least optionally, as incomplete predicates (or light verbs). Each incomplete predicate is the lexical head of a VP and the sister of a co-linked VP. The PRED value of the mother VP is the result of composing the PRED values of its two functionally co-linked daughters. The composed PRED of the mother VP may in turn undergo further predicate composition with another incomplete predicate, which would be the sister of this VP. (See Alsina 1993, 1995, for an illustration of this.)

6.2.2 Word Order in Causative Constructions

Having established the dominance relations between the two predicates in a causative construction (or, more generally, among the various predicates in structures involving complex predicate formation in the syntax), we can turn to the linear precedence relations among constituents in this construction. The first thing to note is that, since the Romance languages are clearly head-initial languages, a general principle requiring an X^0 head to precede any sister category immediately accounts for the ordering of the two predicates of the causative construction. According to this principle, the causative verb (*fa* in (23)) precedes its sister VP; it therefore precedes any constituent contained in this VP, including the base verb (*llegir* in (23)). By the same principle, this base verb will precede all of its sister constituents.

Let us take an example like (6b), repeated here as (24) for convenience, in order to flesh out the c-structure in (23) with the constituents that correspond to the arguments of the a-structure associated with the higher VP. The c-structure representation of (24) is as shown in (25). The f-structure of this sentence, given in skeletal form in (10), is repeated in (25) (omitting the PRED value for space considerations), with indices specifying its correspondence with the c-structure.

(24)   El mestre   fa   llegir un poema al nen.
        the teacher makes read a poem   to-the boy

        'The teacher is making the boy read a poem.'

(25)

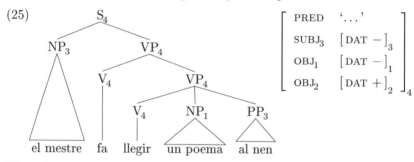

The subject NP, *el mestre*, is realized externally to the highest VP in (25). The two objects, the nondative object *un poema* and the dative object *al nen*, are realized internally to the most embedded VP. This c-structure asymmetry between subject and objects is accounted for by the principles of function-category association proposed in 2.1.3 for configurational languages. According to (2.13a), an XP sister of a VP that is co-linked with their mother maps onto the subject function, and, according to (2.13b), an XP sister of an X^0 major category maps onto a nonsubject function.[6] The ordering of the two objects in (25) is determined by the linear precedence principle proposed in 5.2.3: an NP

---

[6]This statement of the function-category association principle that captures the subject/nonsubject asymmetry, in (2.13), requires subjects to be realized externally to the highest VP in the clause, and objects, and other nonsubjects, to be realized internally to the most embedded VP. An XP sister of the causative verb in (25) could not be assigned any syntactic function since, as a sister of V (the causative verb), it would have to be a nonsubject, but, as a sister of the head VP headed by the base verb, it would have to be a subject. This featural inconsistency prevents the

precedes any sister XP of a different category. Since the nondative (or accusative) object is realized as an NP (*un poema* in (25)), whereas the dative object is realized as a PP (*al nen* in (25)), as argued in chapter 5, that linear precedence principle requires the nondative object to precede the dative object. Thus, the causee, because it is expressed as a dative object (at f-structure) and therefore a PP (at c-structure), follows the internal argument of the base predicate, which is mapped onto a nondative object (at f-structure) and an NP (at c-structure).

It is important to note that the linear ordering of constituents in a causative construction is not directly determined by their correspondence at a-structure, but by principles that refer exclusively to features of the c-structure. In other words, it is not because it is a causee (the logical subject of the base predicate) that the dative object in (25) follows the internal argument of the base predicate, but because of the c-structure realization of these arguments. The causee is assigned dative case by the Case Assignment Convention (8) because of the a-structure it appears in (see (10)), and the internal argument of the base predicate is assigned nondative case. The dative case feature is realized by the preposition *a* when the dative object is expressed as a full XP (as opposed to a clitic), as proposed in chapter 5. In contrast, the nondative case feature is the default specification of NPs. Consequently, the dative object is a PP and the nondative object is an NP. The linear precedence principle just mentioned requires this NP to precede the dative PP.

A consequence of this is that, in a structure in which the causee is not assigned dative case, but is assigned nondative case, it will be realized as an NP and will therefore appear preceding other nonsubject XPs in the structure. This happens whenever the base predicate in the causative construction does not take an argument mapped onto a nondative object in addition to the causee. In the absence of this object, the Case Assignment Convention will assign nondative case to the causee, which then corresponds to an NP.[7] Any cooccurring nonsubject argument (or

---

realization of GF-bearing constituents in this intermediate position in the c-structure of causative constructions.

[7] There are some complications having to do with the fact that, for certain speakers and dialects, nondative objects that are human and definite can be expressed as PPs introduced by the preposition *a* and are therefore indistinguishable from dative PPs. They are nevertheless still distinguished from dative objects when expressed as pronominal clitics. For such speakers, a sentence such as (26b) has the causee, at least optionally, expressed as a PP, as in (ia). Since PPs are assumed to be freely ordered with each other, we correctly predict that the arguments of (ia) can appear in the alternative order shown in (ib), provided the causee is expressed as a PP.

(i) a. Farem   parlar (a) l'avi   de   la guerra.
        we will make talk   to the grandfather about the war

adjunct) is expressed as a PP, whose preposition is semantically selected. The following are examples of causatives in which the causee is expressed as a nondative object, preceding other arguments of the base verb:

(26) a. He   fet   passar el ratolí   pel   forat.
     I have made pass   the mouse through-the hole

     'I made the mouse go through the hole.'

   b. Farem   parlar l'avi   de   la guerra.
     we will make talk   the grandfather about the war

     'We will make grandfather talk about the war.'

   c. Penso   fer   escriure en Joan a la policia.
     I intend make write   Joan   to the police

     'I intend to make Joan write to the police.'

---

   b. Farem   parlar de   la guerra *(a) l'avi.
     we will make talk   about the war   to the grandfather

     'We will make grandfather talk about the war.'

Similar examples, such as (ii), are presented by Villalba (1992:378), who claims that the NP/PP alternation that we observe in the causee is in fact an accusative/dative alternation and that it is exclusive to causative constructions. (Villalba 1992 also claims that the preposition *a* is obligatorily absent when the object causee is adjacent to the verb, as in (ia) and (iia); I disagree with this claim and thus include the option of having this preposition in these examples.) I believe both claims are incorrect. First, if this NP/PP alternation were really a case alternation, we would predict that the causee of examples such as (i) and (ii) should be expressible either as an accusative or a dative clitic, but in fact only the former option is grammatical, as shown in (iii). Second, this alternation occurs not only in causative constructions, involving the verb *fer*, but elsewhere as well, as we see in (iv).

 (ii) a. Farem   creure /confiar (a) la Maria en   l'atzar.
     we will make believe /rely   to   Maria in/on the chance

   b. Farem   creure /confiar en   l'atzar   *(a) la Maria.
     we will make believe /rely   in/on the chance   to   Maria

     'We will make Maria believe in/rely on chance.'

(iii) a. El   /*li   farem   parlar de   la guerra.
     him ACC / him DAT we will make talk   about the war

     'We will make him talk about the war.'

   b. La   /*li   farem   creure /confiar en   l'atzar.
     her ACC / her DAT we will make believe /rely   in/on the chance

     'We will make her believe in/rely on chance.'

(iv) a. Informarem   (a) la   directora de les dificultats.
     we will inform   to the director   of the difficulties

   b. Informarem   de les dificultats *(a) la   directora.
     we will inform   of the difficulties   to the director

     'We will inform the director of the difficulties.'

In these examples, the object causee precedes a constituent that corresponds to another argument of its predicate. The reason is that the object causee is an NP, whereas the cooccurring constituent is a PP, and an NP is required to linearly precede a sister PP.

This section has shown that, once principles are provided that allow predicate composition to take place in the syntax and constrain the c-structure position of the verbs that undergo predicate composition, the c-structure realization of the arguments of a causative construction is determined by general principles of function-category association and linear precedence constraints. Nothing specific to causative constructions need be assumed, except that the causative verb is an incomplete predicate, which, therefore, must undergo predicate composition with another predicate.

6.3   The Causee is not a Grammatical Subject

Many theories of causatives assume that at some level of syntactic analysis a causative construction of the Romance type is biclausal; that is, it consists of a matrix clause whose predicate is the causative verb and of an embedded clause whose predicate is the base verb. The main motivation for this syntactically biclausal analysis is the assumption that the arguments of a predicate are uniformly represented in the syntax, either in terms of phrase structure configurations, as in GB, or in terms of grammatical relations, as in RG. In order to maintain this assumption when dealing with causative constructions it is necessary to assume that the base verb assigns the same syntactic representation to its arguments in the causative construction as it does when functioning independently of the causative construction. Possibly the most striking consequence of the biclausal analysis of causative constructions is the assumption that the causee is syntactically represented as a subject, at least at the level of representation at which the structure is biclausal: if a verb selects an argument that is realized as a subject in noncausative constructions, the assumption of the uniformity of syntactic representation of arguments requires representing that argument as a subject also in causative constructions.

Thus, it is standard within GB and RG, at least, to analyze causative constructions of the Romance type as being biclausal, in the sense that the base verb syntactically projects its arguments within a domain distinct from that in which the causative verb projects its arguments and subordinate to this verb. The specific implementation of this biclausal analysis varies considerably in the various existing theories of causatives. Within GB the category of the complement of the causative verb in which the base verb projects its arguments has been assumed to be S, S' or CP (as in Rouveret and Vergnaud 1980, Marantz 1984, Aoun 1985, Burzio 1986, Baker 1988a, and Reed 1991), or a VP with a VP-internal subject (as in S. Rosen 1989, Di Sciullo and Rosen 1990, Li 1990, Moore 1991, and Villalba 1992), or a VP or V' with an external subject (as in Zagona 1982, and Di Sciullo and Williams 1987), or an S with a PP controller of the subject (as in Bordelois 1988).[8] Within RG, the classical approach of Perlmutter and Postal 1974 and Gibson and Raposo 1986 assumes that the base verb projects its arguments in a clause that bears the grammatical relation 2 to the causative verb at the initial stratum and, in a subsequent stratum, ceases to bear any grammatical relation, when its predicate acquires the grammatical relation "Union" (U) to the main clause; and the "multi-predicate clause" approach of Davies and Rosen 1988 assumes that the base verb projects its arguments as the sole predicate of the initial stratum and that the causative predicate is introduced at a later stratum.[9]

In contrast with the theories just mentioned, the present theory proposes a monoclausal analysis of causative constructions because it does not assume that the domain in which the base predicate projects its arguments onto the syntax is distinct from that in which the causative predicate projects its arguments or subordinate to it. Since the two predicates compose to yield one single complex predicate, the domain in which they project their arguments onto the syntax is the same: the f-structure that takes that complex predicate as its PRED value. A direct consequence of this monoclausality is that the causee is not a syntactic subject: as the complex a-structure of causatives contains an external argument, the causer, which is required to map onto the subject

---

[8]Zubizarreta 1985 is an exception within this tradition, since she assumes that causatives in Italian are monoclausal. Nevertheless, her analysis of French and Spanish causatives involves parallel structures one of which is biclausal with an S complement of the causative verb.

[9]Some of the theories mentioned claim to propose a "monoclausal" analysis of causatives because they assume that causative constructions include one single category considered to be definitional of a clause. Suppose the clause is represented as the phrase structure category S (or S' or CP), as in some GB approaches; then, if we assume that the causative verb takes a VP complement headed by the base verb (as in S. Rosen 1989, Moore 1991, and others), a causative construction will be analyzed as including only one of those categories definitional of the clause, and may be claimed to be monoclausal in this sense. Likewise, in RG, Davies and Rosen 1988 claim to propose a monoclausal analysis because they do not posit any stratum in which the two predicates head separate clauses. Nevertheless, none of these theories qualifies as monoclausal in the sense intended in the text, since they all posit a syntactic domain, be it a VP, be it the initial stratum, in which the base predicate of the causative construction projects its arguments independently of the causative predicate, just as if it were the single verb of the clause.

function by the External Argument Mapping Principle (2.26), and the Subject Condition (2.5) requires that there be no more than one subject in any f-structure, it follows that the causee cannot also be the subject. Therefore, the present theory does not analyze the causee as a syntactic subject.

Significantly, however, the present theory analyzes the causee as a logical subject: since the a-structure of the base predicate is embedded in the complex a-structure of causatives, the causee can still be defined as a logical subject, the logical subject of the embedded a-structure. When the notions of grammatical (or syntactic) subject and logical subject are clearly factored apart, as in the present theory, it becomes possible to identify certain properties as properties of grammatical subjects and certain others as properties of logical subjects. In this section I will argue that there is no basis for the generally accepted claim that the causee is a grammatical subject. In 6.3.1, I argue that none of the properties of the causee can be attributed to its being a grammatical subject. Furthermore, the assumption that the causee is a grammatical subject leads to wrong results: I show that the causee behaves unlike a subject with respect to floating quantifiers, in 6.3.2, and with respect to quantifier binding, in 6.3.3. Finally, in 6.3.4, I will discuss some facts involving reflexivized causatives, which have been taken to indicate the syntactic biclausality of causatives, and will argue that they follow from the complex a-structure of causatives and that they provide support for the assumption that the causative predicate may involve a (patient) internal argument bound to an argument of the base predicate.

6.3.1 Absence of Subjecthood Properties

Possibly the clearest indication that the causee is not a grammatical subject is provided by the observation that none of the properties relating to its formal expression depends on having this argument represented as a grammatical subject at some level of representation (such as d-structure in GB or the initial stratum in RG). The theory presented in this chapter has shown that it is possible to capture the morphosyntactic properties of the causee without making the assumption that it is a grammatical subject. Whereas other theories, such as those mentioned at the beginning of section 6.3, are capable of deriving the morphosyntactic expression of the causee from its (underlying) representation as a subject, none of its morphosyntactic properties depends on its being a subject. For example, the position of the causee in the phrase structure does not follow in any way from its being a subject, but rather from its being a nonsubject. It is because it is a nonsubject that it is realized in the way it is. As an oblique in (27a) (=(13a)), it is expressed as a PP introduced by the preposition *per* and, as such, it is constrained to follow the object NP. As a dative object in (27b) (=(24)), it is expressed as a PP introduced by the preposition *a* and is likewise constrained to follow the object NP. As a nondative object in (27c) (=(26a)), it is expressed as an object NP and constrained to precede any sister XP.

(27) a. L'alcalde ha fet   enderrocar el pont   per un especialista.
the mayor has made demolish   the bridge by a specialist

'The mayor had the bridge demolished by a specialist.'

b. El mestre   fa   llegir un poema al nen.
the teacher makes read a poem   to-the boy

'The teacher is making the boy read a poem.'

c. He   fet   passar el ratolí   pel   forat.
I have made pass   the mouse through-the hole

'I made the mouse go through the hole.'

Furthermore, when we consider the ability to encode the causee as a topic-anaphoric pronominal, we see that it cliticizes on the tensed verb form just like any object in a noncausative construction, with the form of the clitic depending on its morphological case feature, dative or nondative, as well as on person and number. Thus, the dative causee in (27b) cliticizes by means of the clitic *li*, as shown in (28a), just like the dative object of (28b), which is not a causee. Also, the nondative causee in (27c) cliticizes by means of the clitic *l(a)'*, as in (29a), as does the nondative object of the noncausative construction (29b).

(28) a. El mestre   li   fa   llegir un poema.
the teacher him DAT makes read a poem

'The teacher is making him read a poem.'

b. El mestre   li   escriu un poema.
the teacher him DAT writes a poem

'The teacher is writing him a poem.'

(29) a. L'   he   feta   passar pel   forat.
it ACC (F.S) I have made (F.S) pass   through-the hole

'I made it go through the hole.'

b. L'   he   treta   del   forat.
it ACC (F.S) I have removed (F.S) from-the hole

'I have removed it from the hole.'

Whereas the clitic *li* in (28a) corresponds to the causee, and thus to a grammatical subject according to certain theories, in (28b) it corresponds to a goal or recipient argument that is not a subject in any theory. The clitic *l'* corresponds to an argument in (29a) (the causee) that might be analyzed as a subject in some theories, and to an argument in (29b) that would not be analyzed as a subject in any theory. Notice that the nondative clitic in (29) triggers past participle agreement (with the past participles appearing in the feminine singular forms *feta* and *treta* instead of the unmarked *fet* and *tret* in (29a) and in (29b) respectively), an optional phenomenon in Catalan, which is restricted to pronominal objects, as discussed in 3.2.4. These examples show that the putative representation of the causee as a subject is irrelevant to its expression by means of a clitic; as far as cliticization is concerned, what matters is that the causee is represented as an object, dative or nondative as the case may be.

Villalba 1992 presents evidence that is argued to show that certain properties of the causee do depend on its being represented as a grammatical subject. I briefly discuss this evidence. (A) The putative subject-orientation and clause-boundedness of the reflexive clitic is taken to support the subjecthood of the causee, but, as argued here, the reflexive clitic expresses binding at the level of a-structure, where there is no grammatical subject, and, as shown in 6.3.4, the interaction of the reflexive clitic with causative constructions is best accounted for without assuming that the causee is a grammatical subject. (B) Idioms (with and without possessives) and phrases expressing inalienable possession: they can only be taken as evidence for the subjecthood of the causee if it can be shown that such phrases are subject-oriented. Idioms, whose meaning is partly unpredictable and therefore listed (in the lexicon), may signal a dependency between two arguments of a predicate; whether one of the arguments is a subject or not seems to be irrelevant. In the case of inalienable possession, it is clear that the possessor of an inalienable object may be a subject, as shown in (30a) (Villalba 1992: 349), but need not be a subject, as an example like (30b) indicates, with indices signalling the possession relation. It is therefore not surprising that a dative causee can also be the possessor in an inalienable possession relation, as shown in (30c) (Villalba 1992:350).

(30) a. La Maria$_i$ va ficar els nassos$_i$ a l' assumpte.
the Maria PAST put the noses in the business

'Maria stuck her nose into the business.'

b. La Maria va trencar el braç$_i$ a en Ferran$_i$.
the Maria PAST brake the arm to the Ferran

'Maria broke Ferran's arm.'

c. La Maria els$_i$ farà   ficar els nassos$_i$ a l'   assumpte.
the Maria them will make put   the noses   in the business

'Maria will make them stick their nose into the business.'

Just as there is no reason to assume that the dative object in (30b) is a grammatical subject, it is unnecessary to assume that the dative causee in (30c) is a grammatical subject in order to explain its ability to be the possessor in an inalienable possession relation. (C) Quantifier binding is claimed to reveal an asymmetry between the causee and the other arguments of the base verb that would support assuming that the former is a subject. However, as we will see in 6.3.3, there is no such asymmetry. (D) The fact that a causee can be the controller of obligatorily controlled clauses just as the subject of the same verb in a noncausative construction merely indicates that controller status is determined primarily on the basis of semantics, as argued convincingly by Pollard and Sag (1991), among others. Since both subjects and objects can be controllers given the appropriate semantic conditions, there is no need to assume that an object causee is a subject just because it has controller status. (E) A "subject"-oriented predicative complement is predicated of the causee, in a causative construction, whereas an "object"-oriented predicative complement cannot be predicated of the object causee. This is taken by Villalba (1992) to indicate that the causee is a subject. It can also be taken to indicate that the predication relation between a predicative complement of a verb and another argument of the same verb is lexically fixed at the level of argument structure or at a semantic level without specifying the syntactic realization of the arguments involved. In conclusion, none of these pieces of evidence require in any way the assumption that the causee is a syntactic subject.

Theories that posit a representation of the causee as a grammatical subject require a set of rules or principles (such as transformations of the phrase structure or grammatical relation changing rules) that will allow the causee to behave as a nonsubject, in essence obliterating the subject representation of the causee for the purpose of capturing its morphosyntactic expression. In the present theory, the syntactic representation of the causee need not be changed (from subject to nonsubject or otherwise), since the causee is directly represented as a nonsubject: an oblique or an object with the appropriate case feature.

If representing the causee as a subject had no negative consequences, even though it had no positive consequences either, one might still want to adhere to it in order to preserve some cherished theoretical assumption. However, the fact is that the subject representation of the causee does make undesired predictions. The relevant evidence is provided by "floating quantifiers" and "quantifier binding," as we shall see in the next two subsections.

6.3.2   The Causee and Floating Quantifiers

I will now show that, among full NPs, only subjects can launch a floating quatifier, such as *tot* 'all' or *cadascun* (also *cada un*) 'each', and that causees are unable to launch a floating quantifier.[10] The sentences in (31) show that a quantifier contained in the VP may be interpreted as quantifying over the subject, with which the quantifier agrees in gender and number in the case of *tot* (31a), and only in gender in the case of *cadascun* (31b).[11]

---

[10]These facts constitute evidence against the assumption that the causee is represented as a subject in the phrase structure and that this representation is preserved throughout the syntactic derivation (even if somewhat obscured by means of movements and/or principles of Case Theory), which is the standard assumption within GB. If a causee is a subject at all levels of syntactic representation, the generalization that a subject can launch a floating quantifier would be expected to extend to causees. This evidence is not problematic for RG approaches, as long as the relevant generalization is stated about *final subjects*.

[11]There is an asymmetry between *tot* and *cadascun* regarding their position in the clause. *Tot* is preferentially placed immediately following the verb, as in (31a); its position following another constituent in the VP is extremely marked, as in (ia). In contrast, *cadascun* is much less restricted in this sense, appearing either immediately following the verb, as in (31b), or following another constituent in the VP, as in (ib).

(i) a. ??Els nens han llegit el llibre tots.
       the boys have read the book all

     b.   Els nens han llegit un llibre cadascun.
          the boys have read a book   each one

On the other hand, *cadascun* imposes greater semantic restrictions than *tot*. *Cadascun* has a distributive interpretation requiring that the denotation of the VP be applied separately to each of the individuals that compose the denotation of the subject, whereas *tot* lacks this requirement. The distributive requirement of *cadascun* implies that each denotation of the VP applied to any given individual component of the subject is different from the denotation of the VP applied to any other individual component of the subject. This requires the presence of an NP in the VP that can be interpreted distributively, typically an indefinite or cardinal NP, the D(istributive)-NP of Safir and Stowell's 1988 analysis of English *each* and Tellier and Valois's 1993 analysis of French *chacun*. Thus, examples like (31b) and (ib) containing an indefinite or cardinal NP are well-formed because the VP may have a different denotation (i.e., the reading of a different book) for each individual to which it is applied. However, the D-NP need not be an indefinite or cardinal NP, contrary to what seems to be implied by Tellier and Valois 1993:577 regarding French *chacun*. Notice that in (ii) the presence of the participial adjective *assignat* 'assigned' modifying the definite NP *el llibre* 'the book' renders the sentence grammatical; the reason is that, whereas a simple definite NP like *el llibre* does not allow a distributive interpretation, the modified NP *el llibre assignat* can be interpreted distributively, since each boy may have been assigned a different book.

(31) a. Els nens han llegit tots el llibre.
        the boys have read all   the book

        'The boys have all read the book.'

    b. Els nens han llegit cadascun un llibre.
        the boys have read each one a book

        'The boys have each read a book.'

The evidence that grammatical (or surface) subjecthood is the relevant property for licensing a floating quantifier is provided by examples like (32) and (33). (32) shows that a dative object cannot license a floating quantifier, whether the floating quantifier is adjacent to the verb and preceding the nondative object, as in (32a), or whether it follows the nondative object and is adjacent to the dative object, as in (32b). (33) shows that, whereas a nondative object cannot license a floating quantifier (33a), the argument that corresponds to that object in a passive form can license a floating quantifier (33b), and that is because that argument is the subject of the passive form.[12]

(32) a. *He   donat $\left\{ \begin{matrix} \text{tots} \\ \text{cadascun} \end{matrix} \right\}$ una ploma als nens.

        I have given all/each one a pen   to-the boys

(ii)   Els nens han llegit cadascun el   llibre *(assignat).
        the boys have read each one the book   assigned

        'The boys have each read the assigned book.'

[12]The facts of French *chacun* discussed in Tellier and Valois 1993 are considerably different from the facts of *cadascun* in Catalan. In the first place, Tellier and Valois 1993 argue that at least some speakers allow *chacun* to be construed with the dative object; thus, French sentences similar to (32) with *chacun* would be grammatical. The Catalan informants consulted unanimously reject (32), and I find it difficult to imagine that anyone could accept it. In the second place, the evidence presented by Tellier and Valois 1993 in support of the claim that *chacun* forms a constituent with the D-NP when it immediately precedes or follows it cannot be replicated in Catalan. I will not discuss all the evidence they present, but I will only note that, in Catalan, when the D-NP is introduced by a preposition, *cadascun* cannot appear immediately preceding this NP, but can instead precede the preposition. Thus, example (ia), based on Tellier and Valois's 1993:ex. 7, with *cadascun* immediately preceding the NP object of the preposition *amb* 'with', is ungrammatical, whereas (ib), with *cadascun* preceding the whole PP is grammatical.

  (i) a. *Els estudiants han arribat amb cadascun un llibre.
        the students   have arrived with each   a   book

    b. Els estudiants han arribat cadascun amb un llibre.
        the students   have arrived each   with a   book

        'The students have arrived with a book each.'

Consequently, I will assume that the floating quantifier *cadascun*, just like floating *tot*, does not form a constituent with any NP.

b. *He   donat una ploma $\left\{ \begin{array}{l} \text{tots} \\ \text{cadascun} \end{array} \right\}$ als nens.

   I have given a pen   all/each one to-the boys

   'I have given all the boys a pen.'
   'I have given the boys a pen each.'

(33) a. *El president ha presentat cadascun els diputats a
        the president has introduced each one the deputies to

        un senador.
        a senator

        'The president introduced each of the deputies to a senator.'

    b. Els diputats van   ser presentats cadascun a un senador.
       the deputies PAST be introduced each one to a senator

       'The deputies were each introduced to a senator.'

Having established that the floating quantifiers under discussion
must be construed with a grammatical subject, we can now turn to
causative constructions. The first thing to observe is that the causer
can launch a floating quantifier, as we see in (34).[13]

(34) a. Les mestres fan   ballar $\left\{ \begin{array}{l} \text{totes} \\ \text{cadascuna} \end{array} \right\}$ un nen.

         the teachers make dance all/each one   a boy

         'The teachers all/each make a boy dance.'

    b. Les mestres fan   llegir $\left\{ \begin{array}{l} \text{totes} \\ \text{cadascuna} \end{array} \right\}$ un llibre als nens.

        the teachers make read all/each one a book   to-the boys

        'The teachers all/each make the boys read a book.'

---

[13]An example like (34a), with *cadascuna*, is evidence against extending to Catalan
the generalization in Reed 1991:325 that French *chacun* cannot modify an NP that
is a d-structure subject, or, in other words, cannot appear with a D-NP analyzed
as a d-structure subject or external argument. Since *ballar* 'dance' is an unergative verb, it is analyzed as taking an external argument, or d-structure subject, in
Reed's (1991) analysis. Therefore, according to this analysis, the causee in (34) is a
d-structure subject and should not be modified by *cadascun*, if Reed's generalization
were to apply in Catalan. Further evidence that a causee (analyzed as a d-structure
subject in standard GB approaches) can be the D-NP of a floating *cadascun* is provided by (i). (Note that Reed 1991:325 gives a French example comparable to (i) as
ungrammatical.)

(i)   Les mestres fan   netejar la pissarra   a un nen cadascuna.
       the teachers make clean   the blackboard to a boy each one

       'The teachers each make a boy clean the blackboard.'

The fact that the floating quantifier in (34) can be construed with the causer is unsurprising, since the causer is a subject under all existing analyses of causative constructions.[14] What is revealing about the structure of causatives is that a floating quantifier cannot be construed with the causee. This fact is illustrated in (35), with (35a) and (35b) showing alternative positions for the quantifiers.

(35) a. *La mestra   fa   llegir un llibre $\begin{Bmatrix} \text{tots} \\ \text{cadascun} \end{Bmatrix}$ als nens.
      the teacher makes read a book   all/each one to-the boys

   b. *La mestra   fa   llegir $\begin{Bmatrix} \text{tots} \\ \text{cadascun} \end{Bmatrix}$ un llibre als nens.
      the teacher makes read all/each one a book   to-the boys

      'The teacher makes the boys all read a book.'
      'The teacher makes the boys read a book each.'

A causee such as the logical subject of *llegir* in (35), *als nens*, is analyzed as the subject of this verb in many current theories, and, in most GB approaches, is analyzed as a subject at all levels of syntactic representation. However, although the logical subject of *llegir* can launch a floating quantifier when this verb is not embedded in the causative construction, as shown in (31), it cannot do so when the verb is embedded in the causative construction. If this argument is a grammatical subject in both cases, how can we account for the contrast between (31) and (35)? The answer that the current theory proposes is that the logical subject of *llegir* looks and behaves like a grammatical subject in noncausative constructions such as (31) because it is a grammatical subject, whereas it does not look or behave like a grammatical subject in causative constructions such as (35) because it is not a grammatical subject. The

---

[14]Nevertheless, examples such as (34) constitute evidence against the theory of floating quantifiers of Sportiche 1988, where it is argued that a (floating) quantifier forms a constituent with a following NP and that this NP may be empty due to NP movement. Assuming that subjects are generated in VP-internal position and that they may move to a position external to the VP in languages like French and English, Sportiche 1988 argues that floating quantifiers are just part of an NP left behind by NP movement and that they signal positions that the NP occupies at d-structure or in the mapping of d-structure to s-structure. Since it is standard in GB analyses of causatives to assume that the base verb is contained in a complement clause of the causative verb, examples like (34) are problematic for Sportiche's theory of floating quantifiers: they include a floating quantifier that is construed with the subject of the causative verb and yet appears between the base verb and one of its arguments, in other words, inside the putative complement clause of the causative verb. Clearly, one would not want to say that the subject of the causative verb is generated inside a complement of this verb.

contrast with respect to floating quantifiers is just a consequence of this difference.

To further illustrate the inability of a causee to launch a floating quantifier, consider the example in (36), where both the causer and the causee are plural expressions and therefore satisfy the requirement that the quantifier *cadascun* be construed with a plural expression. (Note that, in this example, the permissive causative verb *deixar* is used instead of the coercive causative verb *fer*, which I have used throughout in examples of causative constructions. Although the two verbs differ semantically, they have identical syntactic behavior and can be assumed to have the same representation at a-structure.)

(36)   Els metges ens deixen beure una cervesa cadascun.
           the doctors us let   drink a beer   each one

    a.   'Each of the doctors lets us drink a beer.'

    b.   *'The doctors let each of us drink a beer.'

Even though the interpretation (36b) is the pragmatically more plausible one (where several patients remark that they are only allowed by their doctors to drink one beer each), it is ungrammatical. The only grammatical interpretation is the pragmatically unusual one (36a) (where a group of patients remarks that each of their doctors lets them drink a beer, so that if they have three doctors they can drink three beers).[15]

6.3.3   The Causee and Quantifier Binding

Catalan exhibits a subject/object asymmetry with respect to quantifier binding: whereas a quantified subject may bind an anaphoric possessor of the object, a quantified object may not bind an anaphoric possessor of the subject. This asymmetry is illustrated in the following sets of sentences: the examples in (37) are grammatical, with a subject binder

---

[15]A sentence like (36) can be slightly modified so as to allow interpretation (36b) instead of interpretation (36a). Since the causee is expressed as an object clitic (*ens*) and object clitics can launch a floating quantifier, as noted in 5.1, it is possible to have a floating quantifier construed with the causee expressed as a clitic. But, in order for this to be possible, the floating quantifier must be introduced by the preposition *a* (the dative case marker in the case of a dative object), as in (ia). As we see in (ib), however, there is nothing peculiar to causees expressed as clitics regarding their ability to launch a floating quantifier: any object clitic can do that.

  (i)   a.   Els metges ens deixen beure una cervesa a   cadascun.
            the doctors us let   drink a beer   to each one

            'The doctors let each of us drink a beer.'

      b.   Els metges ens donen una cervesa a   cadascun.
            the doctors us give   a beer   to each one

            'The doctors give each of us a beer.'

and an anaphor in object position, and the examples in (38) are un-grammatical, with an object binder and an anaphor in subject position.

(37) a. Cada autor$_i$ ha defensat la seva$_i$ proposta.
    'Every author$_i$ has defended his$_i$ proposal.'

   b. Cada ponent$_i$ llegirà el seu$_i$ escrit.
    'Every lecturer$_i$ will read his$_i$ paper.'

   c. Cada arquitecte$_i$ acabarà de realitzar el seu$_i$ projecte.
    'Every architect$_i$ will finish carrying out his$_i$ project.'

(38) a. *El seu$_i$ autor defensa cada proposta$_i$.
    *'Its$_i$ author defends every proposal$_i$.'

   b. *El seu$_i$ detractor principal llegeix cada escrit$_i$.
    *'Its$_i$ main opponent reads every paper$_i$.'

   c. *El seu$_i$ arquitecte original acabarà de construir cada casa$_i$.
    *'Its$_i$ original architect will finish building every house$_i$.'

The preceding examples show that a subject and an object are in an asymmetrical relation with repect to quantifier binding. In contrast, objects are not in an asymmetrical relation to each other with respect to quantifier binding: either a quantified indirect object can bind an anaphoric possessor of the direct object, as in (39) ((39a)=(5.14a)), or a quantified direct object can bind an anaphoric possessor of the indirect object, as in (40).

(39) a. Vaig donar el seu$_i$ dibuix preferit a cada alumne$_i$.
    'I gave his$_i$ favorite drawing to every student$_i$.'

   b. Han ofert el seu$_i$ premi a cada finalista$_i$.
    'The have offered his$_i$ prize to every finalist$_i$.'

(40) a. Han tornat cada article$_i$ al seu$_i$ autor.
    'They have returned every article$_i$ to its$_i$ author.'

   b. Presentarem cada convidat$_i$ als seus$_i$ companys
    'We'll introduce every guest$_i$ to his$_i$ fellow guests

   de taula.
   at the table.'

   This shows that a quantified object (be it direct or indirect) cannot bind an anaphoric possessor of the subject, although it can bind an anaphoric possessor of another object (be it direct or indirect). Thus, if a causee is a syntactic subject, as assumed in many theories, it should not be able to contain a possessive anaphor bound by a quantified object. But if it is not a syntactic subject, as assumed here, it should be able to contain a possessive anaphor bound by an object. The facts confirm the latter assumption: the sentences in (41) show that a causee, expressed as an indirect object, may contain a possessive anaphor bound by a quantified object.

(41) a. Farem   defensar cada proposta$_i$ al seu$_i$ autor.
        we will make defend   every proposal$_i$ to its$_i$ author

      'We will have every proposal defended by its author.'

    b. Farem   llegir cada escrit$_i$ al seu$_i$ detractor principal.
        we will make read   every paper$_i$ to its$_i$ opponent main

      'We will have every paper read by its main opponent.'

    c. Farem   acabar de construir cada casa$_i$ al seu$_i$
        we will make finish   of build   every house$_i$ to its$_i$

      arquitecte original.
      architect   original

      'We will have every house completed by its original architect.'

Compare these causative examples with the corresponding examples in (38), where the base predicates of (41) are used in noncausative structures. The logical subject of these predicates cannot contain a possessive anaphor bound by its object in (38), but it can in (41). Thus, a theory that claims that the logical subject of these predicates is a syntactic subject whether the predicate is the single predicate of the clause, as in (38), or the base predicate of a causative complex predicate, as in (41), makes the wrong prediction with respect to quantifier binding: it incorrectly claims that sentences like (41) should be ungrammatical, given the assumption that a quantified object cannot bind a possessive anaphor in the subject position. The fact is that the logical subject of the base predicate in a causative construction, in other words, the causee, behaves like the (indirect) object of sentences like (40) in being able to contain a possessive anaphor bound by an object of the same predicate. A theory, such as the present one, that rejects the claim that the causees in (41) are grammatical subjects and, instead, analyzes them as dative objects correctly predicts that they should behave syntactically like the dative objects of (40) and unlike the grammatical subjects of (38).

Naturally, this theory also predicts that a quantified dative object causee should be able to bind a possessor of the direct object, as illustrated in example (42), from Villalba 1992:360.[16] This fact does not

---

[16] Crucially, Villalba 1992 claims that there is an asymmetry between the causee and the other arguments of the base verb in a causative construction in that a quantified causee may bind another argument of the base verb, but not vice versa. This claim

require assuming that the causee is a subject, since it merely reveals a property of dative objects in general, as shown in (39).

(42)   Vaig fer   castigar el seu$_i$ professor a cada alumne$_i$.
        I PAST make punish his   teacher to each student

        'I made every student punish his teacher.'

The evidence presented here indicates that the properties of dative causees with respect to quantifier binding are the properties of dative objects in general, and it constitutes a strong argument against the assumption that causees are grammatical subjects, since this assumption leads to incorrect predictions.

6.3.4 Reflexivized Causatives

The facts of reflexivized causatives in Romance have sometimes been taken as evidence for the syntactic biclausality of causative constructions and for the representation of the causee as a grammatical subject when it is expressed as an object, as opposed to an oblique. I will argue that these facts are an indication of the complex a-structure representation of causative constructions and that they do not warrant assuming that this complexity is replicated at any other level of syntactic representation.

When the reflexive clitic is attached to the causative verb signalling a binding relation between the logical subject of the causative predicate (the causer) and an argument of the embedded predicate other than its logical subject, the causee cannot be expressed as an object, as in (43a), but must be either omitted or expressed as an oblique, as in (43b).

(43) a. *En Ferran es farà   pentinar a la Maria.
       Ferran   RF will make comb to   Maria

    b. En Ferran es farà   pentinar (per la Maria).
       Ferran   RF will make comb by   Maria

       'Ferran will have himself combed (by Maria).'

This fact has sometimes been taken as evidence that the causee is syntactically a subject when expressed as an object, although not when expressed as an oblique, and that the reflexive clitic is an argument and a syntactic anaphor that must be bound by a subject in a minimal domain,

---

is at odds with the data in (41), which are deemed acceptable by all the Catalan speakers consulted. Villalba 1992:352 marks example (i) as ungrammatical, where the quantified direct object binds the dative causee. I do not see any difference in acceptability between this example and (42).

(i)   Vaig fer   castigar cada alumne$_i$ al seu$_i$ professor.
       I PAST make punish each student to his teacher

     'I made every student be punished by his teacher.'

such as Chomsky's (1986) "Complete Functional Complex" (CFC) (=the phrase in which all the grammatical functions compatible with the head of the phrase are realized) (see S. Rosen 1989, and Moore 1991, among others). The reason why only the object causee, and not the oblique causee, is considered to be a grammatical subject is that a subject needs to be assigned Case in order to satisfy the Case Filter, and, in the causative construction, it is assigned Case by the verb, either dative or accusative, whereas an oblique PP does not need Case, and its NP object is Case-marked by the preposition. Since the causee (*a la Maria*) in (43a) is an object, it would be analyzed as a subject, and so the phrase headed by the embedded predicate *pentinar* would qualify as a CFC, ruling out the binding relation between the object of this verb and the matrix subject. In (43b), on the other hand, since the causee would not qualify as a subject, the whole sentence is the CFC in which the binding relation takes place.

Such an explanation, however, is not available in the present theory, since the reflexive clitic is argued not to be a syntactic anaphor (or the expression of an argument) and the causee is argued not to be a subject even in cases like (43a). The contrast in (43) follows from two assumptions made in the present theory: the requirement that the two arguments involved in a-structure binding be co-arguments (semantic arguments of the same predicate), and the presence of an internal (patient) argument of the causative predicate in (3) that must be bound to an argument of the embedded predicate. When the embedded predicate has a P-A argument as its logical subject, this argument (the causee) can only be expressed as a direct function when it is coindexed with the internal argument of the causative predicate; otherwise, being neither an external argument nor a P-P argument (nor bound to one), it is not licensed by either of the two mapping principles of the FMT and is therefore either unexpressed or expressed as an oblique. Consequently, a structure like (43a) is one in which the causee, a P-A argument, is coindexed with the patient of the causative predicate, which is necessary for the causee to be mapped onto an object. However, if the reflexive clitic signals coindexation between the causer and the internal argument of the embedded predicate, the co-argument condition on a-structure binding is violated, as shown in (44). Here the reflexive clitic would be signalling the coindexation of the logical subject of the causative predicate and the internal argument of the embedded predicate, but this binding relation is ill-formed because the two arguments involved are not co-arguments. This accounts for the ungrammaticality of a sentence like (43a), whose a-structure would be as shown in (44).

This implies that the only well-formed structure in which a causative

(44)

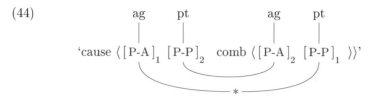

complex predicate undergoes a-structure binding is one that results in the binding of the two arguments of the causative predicate. If the internal argument of the causative predicate is bound to the internal argument of the embedded predicate, it is possible to coindex the two arguments of the causative predicate, with the result that the causer is coindexed with the internal argument of the embedded predicate.[17] This is legitimate, as shown in (45), because the coindexing triggered by the a-structure binding morpheme involves the two arguments of the most prominent argument structure, thus satisfying the co-argument condition on a-structure binding.

(45)
$$\text{ag} \quad \text{pt} \qquad \text{ag} \quad \text{pt}$$
$$\text{`cause} \langle [\text{P-A}]_1 \ [\text{P-P}]_1 \quad \text{comb} \langle [\text{P-A}]_2 \ [\text{P-P}]_1 \ \rangle \rangle \text{'}$$

The important thing to note is that, whereas the causee in (44), because of its being bound to the patient of the causative predicate, would be mapped onto a direct function, the causee in (45), which is not coindexed with any argument, fails to be licensed by either mapping principle of the FMT and is, therefore, unexpressed or expressed as an oblique. The well-formed structure in (45) corresponds to a grammatical sentence like (43b). Thus, we account for the fact that, in order for the reflexive clitic in Romance to bind the causer and an internal argument of the embedded predicate in causative constructions, the causee cannot be expressed as an object.

---

[17] An alternative structure would be one in which the patient of the causative predicate is coindexed with the causee (an option allowed in the formation of the causative complex predicate) and the causer is coindexed with the patient of the causative predicate (by a-structure binding), with the result that the causer is coindexed with the causee. However, such a structure is ungrammatical, although there is no general principle that would rule it out. This phenomenon is noted in Italian by C. Rosen (1988), who proposes the "Reflexive Causee Constraint" as an ad hoc condition to account for it. A similar constraint would have to be proposed in the present theory. The fact that this restriction does not follow from any general principle is, in fact, a desirable situation, given that, in a language like Chicheŵa, where the reciprocal morpheme signals a-structure binding, as argued in Alsina 1993, this morpheme can attach to causative verb forms co-linking the causer with the causee.

6.3.5 Summary

In sum, many theories of causative constructions of the Romance type assume that the causee (except of unaccusative verbs) is a grammatical subject and then have to account for why the causee does not have any morphosyntactic properties of grammatical subjects. In addition, those theories, particularly within the GB framework, that assume that the causee is a subject at all levels of syntactic structure are incapable of accounting for why the causee does not behave like a grammatical subject with respect to the possibiliy of launching a floating quantifier and the ability to contain an anaphoric possessor bound by an object. The facts examined in this section argue for analyzing the causee not as a grammatical subject of the base predicate, but as an object (or an oblique) of the causative complex predicate.

The present theory makes the claim that the arguments of a predicate have a representation that is invariant regardless of their morphosyntactic expression, but this representation should not be captured at the syntactic levels in which phrase structure or grammatical functions are represented, but at the level of argument structure. It is this level that captures the commonality between the grammatical subject of a non-causative sentence like (37a) and the same argument in the corresponding causative sentence, expressed in (41a) as an object, representing them both as logical subjects.

6.4 The Causee is a Logical Subject

It has been argued by Kiparsky (1987), T. Mohanan (1994), Joshi (1989, 1993), among others, that the notion of logical subject, is needed for the analysis of certain grammatical phenomena, such as binding phenomena. In what follows, I will propose that the properties of the causee in the Romance causative construction that have been attributed to its being represented as a grammatical subject are all accounted for in this theory by appealing to its representation as the most prominent argument in its a-structure, and I will show that referring to a putative representation of the causee as a syntactic subject is not only unnecessary, but inadequate for capturing those properties. The phenomena that I will focus on here, drawn from Catalan, are binding of a reflexive phrase that only allows logical subject antecedents and control of the unexpressed subject of certain adverbial clauses, which is sensitive to prominence at a-structure. Binding and control are similar phenomena in that both involve a referential dependency between an overt anaphor (in the case of binding) or a phonologically null pronominal or anaphor (in the case of control) and an antecedent (or controller).

6.4.1   A Logical Subject Reflexive

In Catalan, the reflexive phrase *per si sol* 'on one's/its own', 'by one's/its own accord', in which the adjective *sol* agrees in gender and number with the antecedent, can only take a logical subject as its antecedent, although not all logical subjects qualify as antecedents. (The Italian phrase *da sè*, discussed in Chierchia 1989, appears to be similar.) This reflexive phrase can take the subject of an active verb as its antecedent, (46a), but not its object, (46b). However, in the corresponding passive form (46c), neither the grammatical subject nor the passive oblique (the logical subject) qualifies as its antecedent.[18]

(46) a.   En Joan$_i$ va resoldre els problemes per si sol$_i$.
          'Joan   solved   the problems on his own.'

      b.   *En Joan va resoldre els problemes$_j$ per si sols$_j$.
          'Joan   solved   the problems on their own.'

      c.   *Els problemes$_j$ van ser resolts (per en Joan$_i$) $\left\{ \begin{array}{l} \text{per si sol}_i. \\ \text{per si sols}_j. \end{array} \right\}$
          'The problems were   solved   by Joan   on their/his own.'

The possibility that the choice of antecedents for this reflexive may be restricted thematically (for example, to an agent, as in (46a)) or to arguments represented as external arguments (or equivalent notions such as d-structure subject or initial 1) is ruled out when we consider the facts involving unaccusatives. The subject of an unaccusative verb like *sortir* 'go out' is not an agent, but a theme, and is not an external argument, but an internal argument (or, correspondingly, a d-structure object or an initial 2). Yet, it can function as the antecedent of this reflexive phrase, as evidenced in (47).

(47)   Els lladres$_j$ van sortir de la cova   per si sols$_j$.
          'The thieves went out of the cave on their own.'

Although the subjects of (47) and (46c) bear a similar (or the same) thematic relation to their predicates, and both are internal arguments, the subject of the (underived) unaccusative is a legitimate antecedent of *per si sol*, whereas the passive subject is not.

One feature that the legal antecedents of this reflexive in (46a) and (47) have in common is that they are the logical subjects of their respective predicates: the (agent) external argument of *resoldre*, whose a-structure is $\langle\,[\text{P-A}]\,[\text{P-P}]\,\rangle$, and the (theme) internal argument of *sortir*, whose a-structure is $\langle\,[\text{P-P}]\,\rangle$. But logical subjecthood is not a sufficient

---

[18]There are also semantic constraints on the use of this reflexive. For example, stative predicates such as *estimar* 'love', *saber* 'know', *tenir* 'have', etc., do not allow it. Not all Catalan dialects have *per si sol*: some use *ell sol* and its morphological variants.

condition for the antecedent of this reflexive, as this alone would predict that (46c) should be grammatical with the demoted logical subject as the antecedent. The missing condition is given to us by what is known to be the condition on the antecedent of the independent reflexive *si (mateix)*. As the equivalent *se stesso* in Italian (Rizzi 1986a:504, Belletti and Rizzi 1988:317), this general reflexive takes a direct function (i.e., subject or object) as its antecedent:

(48) a. Aquest psiquiatre$_i$ ha reconciliat en Joan$_j$ amb si mateix$_{i/j}$.
     'This psychiatrist$_i$ has reconciled Joan$_j$ with himself$_{i/j}$.'

    b. *Aquest psiquiatre parla dels   pacients$_i$ amb si mateixos$_i$.
     'This psychiatrist talks about the patients$_i$ with themselves$_i$.

The two direct functions in (48a), the subject and the object, are potential antecedents of the independent reflexive, whereas the oblique phrase *dels pacients* in (48b) is not. Assuming that the reflexive phrase *per si sol* is just a restricted form of the independent reflexive *si (mateix)*, the conditions on antecedents of the former should include those of the latter. Therefore, in addition to a logical subject, the antecedent of *per si sol* should also be a direct function: a logical subject expressed as a direct function. While the logical subjecthood condition accounts for why *els problemes* in (46b-c) cannot antecede this reflexive, the direct function condition accounts for why the logical subject *en Joan* in (46c) also fails as an antecedent: as the demoted subject of passives, it is not a direct function, but an oblique (an adjunct in Zubizarreta 1985, Jackendoff 1990, and others, and an argument-adjunct in Grimshaw 1988, 1990).

When we consider the situation in causative constructions, we find that the causee of an embedded dyadic predicate can be the antecedent of this reflexive phrase, provided it is a direct function, as in (49a). The alternative expression of the causee in such instances, as an oblique *per*-phrase, does not qualify as an antecedent, as in (49b). Neither does the theme of the embedded predicate in either case. Interestingly, the theme of the embedded predicate can be the antecedent of *per si sol* when this predicate is an unaccusative, as we see in (49c).[19]

---

[19]Some speakers, including a reviewer, do not accept sentences similar to (49c). I fail to see the problem, but I believe that using the permissive causative *deixar*, instead of the coercive causative used in (49c), helps eliminate possible semantic anomalies. The following sentences, with the permissive causative and unaccusative base verbs, seem perfectly natural to me taking the phrase *per si sol* referring to the causee.

(i) a. La policia no ha forçat els lladres a sortir, sinó que els$_i$ ha
    the police not has forced the thieves to go out but that them has

(49) a. En Joan ha fet   resoldre els problemes$_j$ a la Maria$_i$
      Joan   has made solve   the problems to   Maria

      per si sola$_i$ / *per si sols$_j$.
      on her own / *on their own

      'Joan made Maria solve the problems on her/*their own.'

    b. En Joan ha fet   resoldre els problemes$_j$ per la Maria$_i$
      Joan   has made solve   the problems by   Maria

      *per si sola$_i$ / *per si sols$_j$.
      on her own / *on their own

      'Joan got the problems solved by Maria on *her/*their own.'

    c. La gana   ha fet   sortir els lladres$_j$ de la cova per
      the hunger has made go out the thieves of the cave on

      si sols$_j$.
      their own

      'Hunger made the thieves go out of the cave on their own.'

The assumption that the causee is a logical subject, which may be syntactically realized as either a direct or an indirect function (cf. (49a) and (49b)) explains the pattern of facts shown in (49). In (49a-b), the logical subject of the embedded predicate is *la Maria*, which means that *els problemes* is not a logical subject and therefore not a possible antecedent of *per si sols*. Although *la Maria* is a logical subject in both (49a) and (49b), it is only a possible antecedent of this reflexive in the former because of the direct function condition on antecedents of reflexives in Romance: in (49a), it is a dative object, and, therefore, a direct function, but not in (49b), where it is an indirect function (an oblique). In (49c), which is a causative construction based on the unaccusative *sortir*, the logical subject of this predicate is *els lladres*, which, as a direct argument, can be the antecedent of the reflexive *per si sols*.

---

      deixat sortir per si sols$_i$.
      let   go out on their own

      'The police has not forced the thieves to come out, but has let them come out on their own.

    b. El govern   té tants   problemes que l' oposició es
      the government has so many problems that the opposition RF

      limitarà a deixar-lo$_i$ caure per si sol$_i$.
      will limit to let   it fall   on its own

      'The government has so many problems that the opposition will just let it fall on its own.'

Examples such as (49c), as well as (47), show that the relevant notion to define the possible antecedents of this reflexive is the notion of logical subject, rather than external argument (or d-structure subject, or initial 1): in these examples, the antecedent is the sole argument of an unaccusative, which, by definition, lacks an external argument, and, so, it is a logical subject, but not an external argument.

6.4.2 Control into Adverbial Clauses

The second area in which the notion of logical subject is pertinent is in determining the controller of the unexpressed subject of certain adverbial clauses. Studies in RG, particularly Legendre 1986, 1990b, have proposed properties that hold of grammatical constituents assumed to be subjects (or "1's"). I will argue that these properties hold of arguments that are maximally prominent, with prominence defined either at the level of a-structure or at the level of syntactic functions. Consequently, causees, as logical subjects and therefore maximally prominent in the a-structure, exhibit these properties. The adverbial clauses that I shall be considering (following Legendre's (1990b) work on French) are the gerund phrase, optionally preceded by *tot*, and the infinitival *sense*-phrase.[20] In the following examples, an italicized phrase is a possible controller of the subject of the adverbial clause, whereas a phrase followed by an asterisk (*) is not a possible controller.

Examples (50) show that the subject of an active transitive verb is a possible controller of both the gerund and the *sense*-phrase, while the object of such a verb is not:

(50) a. *Els policies*   han dispersat els manifestants* tot
      'The policemen have dispersed the demonstrators while

      cridant.
      shouting.'

   b. *En Pere* ha abraçat la Maria* sense dir   ni un mot.
      'Pere   has hugged Maria   without saying a word.'

Not only can an agent subject control the subject of these adverbial clauses, as in the preceding examples, but so can the theme/patient subject of unaccusative verbs, as shown in (51):

(51) a. *El bebè*   ha caigut tot provant de caminar.
      'The baby has fallen while trying to walk.'

---

[20]Although Legendre (1990b) also uses the temporal *avant/après* 'before/after' phrases to determine subjecthood properties, I have found the corresponding phrases in Catalan (*abans/després*) to have less restrictive conditions on their controller, as they sometimes admit nonsubjects. I will therefore not take them into account. The examples that follow are based on Legendre 1990b.

b. *En Pere* ha fugit sense   dir   ni un mot.
'Peter   has fled without saying a word.'

Interestingly, in passive clauses, there are two potential controllers of the adverbial clause. On the one hand, the demoted (or suppressed) logical subject is a possible controller, whether unexpressed, as in (52a), or expressed as an oblique *per*-phrase, as in (52c). And, on the other hand, the surface (or grammatical) subject is also a possible controller, as shown in (52a-b).

(52) a. *Els manifestants*   han estat dispersats tot cridant.   (*Ag*)
    'The demonstrators have been dispersed while shouting.'

b. *Els estrangers* han estat arrestats per la policia sense
    'The foreigners have been arrested by the police without

    saber   per què.
    knowing why.'

c. Els estrangers han estat arrestats per *la policia* sense
    'The foreigners have been arrested by the police without

    dir-los-hi   per què.
    telling them why.

(Both *els estrangers* and *la policia* are potential controllers in (52b-c), although the former is pragmatically a more plausible controller in (52b), and the latter in (52c).) What these passive examples show is that it is sufficient to be either a grammatical subject or a logical subject in order to be a controller of the subject of these adverbial clauses. Whereas in the active forms, in examples like (50) and (51), the same argument is both a grammatical and a logical subject, and so there is only one potential controller, in the passive forms the grammatical subject and the logical subject are two different arguments, accounting for the existence of two potential controllers.

One might wonder what the categories of logical subject and grammatical subject have in common, apart from conveniently sharing the label "subject." What they have in common is that they are the most prominent element within a certain dimension (as in T. Mohanan 1994). The logical subject is the most prominent argument in the a-structure, determined by the ordering among arguments imposed by the thematic hierarchy. The grammatical subject is the most prominent syntactic function in the hierarchy of syntactic functions (2.54), where the subject is higher than nonsubjects, and direct functions (subjects and objects) are higher than obliques. Given this, the condition on controllers of the subject of the adverbial clauses under inspection can be stated in a more concise, and, as we shall see, more precise, way than by referring to logical and grammatical subjects, as follows:

(53)   *Condition on Controllers:*

The subject of a gerund clause and of a *sense*-clause is controlled by *a maximally prominent argument* of the matrix clause.

On the assumption that prominence of arguments is determined either at a-structure or at f-structure, this condition may appear to be equivalent to saying that the controller is either the logical or the grammatical subject: the logical subject is the most prominent category in the a-structure, and the grammatical subject is the most prominent category among syntactic functions.[21] However, there is a difference: as the control relation is an anaphoric relation between two syntactic

---

[21]Notice that sentences that are identical as far as their syntactic functions are concerned may differ with respect to their a-structures in ways that are relevant to the control properties of the arguments involved. Legendre (1989) points out an interesting contrast between experiencer verbs and passive verbs in French that reveals that, whereas the dative object of the former (the experiencer) is a logical subject, the dative object of the latter (for example, the goal of *donner* 'give') is not. Thus, (i), from Legendre 1989:774, shows that either the subject (*Marie*), in (ia), or the dative object (*lui*), in (ib), of the experiencer verb *manquer* 'miss' can control the unexpressed subject of the gerund clause. In contrast, (ii), from Legendre 1989: 773, shows that the subject (*la jeune fille*), in (iia), but not the dative object (*à son oncle*), in (iib), of the passive of the ditransitive *confier* 'entrust' can control the unexpressed subject of the gerund clause. (The agreement features on the participial forms (*remis(e)* in (i) and *séduit(e)* in (ii)) depend on the controller and, thus, make the choice of controller unambiguous in these examples.)

(i) a.   S'étant remise à sortir, *Marie* lui manque terriblement.
'Having started (FEM) to go out again, he misses Mary terribly.'

   b.   S'étant remis à sortir, Marie *lui* manque terriblement.
'Having started (MASC) to go out again, he misses Mary terribly.'

(ii) a.   Ayant été séduite, *la jeune fille* fut confiée à son oncle.
'Having been seduced (FEM), the girl was entrusted to her uncle.'

   b.   *Ayant été séduit, la jeune fille fut confiée *à son oncle*.
'Having been seduced (MASC), the girl was entrusted to her uncle.'

The contrast follows in the present theory from the assumption that the dative object in (i), being more prominent at a-structure than the single other argument of the predicate, is maximally prominent at a-structure, a logical subject. On the other hand, the dative object in (ii), although, as a goal, more prominent at a-structure than the subject, which is a theme, is not maximally prominent at a-structure, because the agent argument, even if unexpressed, is the logical subject of the predicate. Thus, while the grammatical subject is a legitimate controller in both (ia) and (iia), because it is the most prominent argument at the level of syntactic functions, the dative object is only a legitimate controller in (ib), where it is a logical subject, but not in (iib), where it is not a logical subject and therefore not the most prominent argument at either of the two relevant levels. (The control condition on the gerund construction exemplified in (i) and (ii), following Legendre 1989, is more restrictive

constituents, whereby the unexpressed element picks its reference from another element in the sentence, the controller must have semantic content, in other words, it must be an argument or semantic participant. By referring to the most prominent *argument* we are excluding non-arguments (dummies or expletives) from consideration.[22] Therefore, in inversion or impersonal constructions, where the grammatical subject is a non-argument (*there* or *it* in English, *il* in French), the most prominent argument at the level of syntactic functions is not the grammatical subject, because it is not an argument; rather, the object, if there is one, is the most prominent argument at this level and will qualify as a controller. This is the situation that we find in impersonal passives in French, as reported by Legendre (1990b). In a passive sentence with a dummy (non-argument) subject, the logical subject, whether unspecified or overt, is a potential controller of the type of adverbial clauses under consideration. In addition, the object, the NP following the verb, is also a potential controller, as the following sentence (Legendre 1990b: ex. 88a) illustrates:[23]

(54) Il a été arrêté *plusieurs terroristes* en essayant de passer la frontière.
  'There were arrested several terrorists while trying to cross the border.'

In this example, the controller *plusieurs terroristes* is neither the logical

---

than that given in (53), in that the controller must additionally be a direct function, thus excluding obliques, such as the passive oblique.)

[22] However, Legendre 1990b:116 states that a dummy can be a controller, as evidenced by examples like (i), from Rouveret and Vergnaud 1980:148, where the unexpressed subject of the adverbial clause would be analyzed as an expletive subject and, according to Legendre (1990b), as controlled by the overt expletive subject *il* of the matrix clause.

  (i)   Ici *il* tombe rarement beaucoup de neige sans pleuvoir.
     'Here, it rarely snows much without raining.'

The problem with this analysis is that, if control is an anaphoric relation and an anaphoric relation is a relation between two referential expressions, control cannot be involved in an example like (i), since dummies are by definition not referential expressions. (Presumably the adverbial clause *sans pleuvoir* in (i) would be ungrammatical if the matrix clause did not include the dummy subject *il*, although the substantiating evidence is not given in Legendre 1990b.) What (i) indicates is that an overt expletive can license an unexpressed expletive. The problem does not disappear if we assume that the subject of a weather verb like *pleuvoir* 'rain' in (i) is an argument and, therefore, not an expletive, because *tomber* 'fall' in (i) is not a weather verb and its subject would have to be analyzed as an expletive.

[23] Following Legendre 1990b, I assume that this NP is an object, because it appears following the verb, it does not trigger agreement on the verb, and can trigger *en* pronominalization, as shown in Legendre 1990b:ex. 20b, which is a property of objects.

subject, which is an unexpressed agent, nor the grammatical subject, which is the non-argument *il*, but it is the most prominent argument at the level of syntactic functions. Therefore, by our condition (53), it qualifies as a controller of the unexpressed subject of the gerund clause.[24]

Having established that the control facts under considerations are best stated as in (53), without reference to any notion of subjecthood, we can now consider the situation in causatives. Causative constructions are composed of two predicates, each defining a distinct prominence domain at a-structure; so, we predict that there should be two potential controllers, as we see in the following examples:

(55) a. *En Pere els* ha fet   cantar tot ballant.
      Pere   them has made sing   while dancing

      'Pere has made them sing while dancing.'

  b. *En Pere els-hi* farà   saludar el professor* sense   cridar.
       Pere   them will make greet the professor without shouting

       'Pere will make them greet the professor without shouting.'

  c. *En Pere* els* farà   criticar (*pels seus col·legues*)
       Pere   them will make criticize by his   colleagues

       sense   dir   res   a la direcció.
       without saying anything to the management

       'Pere will have them criticized by his colleagues without telling the management anything.'

The causer, as the logical subject of the causative predicate and as the grammatical subject (the maximally prominent argument both at a-structure and among syntactic functions), is a potential controller of the adverbial clauses. In addition, the causee, as the logical subject of the embedded predicate (maximally prominent at a-structure), is also a potential controller, whether it is expressed as an object, as in (55a-b), or as an oblique or unexpressed, as in (55c). No other argument qualifies as a controller.

It is important to note that the causee need not be an agent or an external argument, as it might be analyzed in (55), in order to be a controller of an adverbial clause. When a causative has an unaccusative

---

[24]In Legendre's (1990b) account, the ability to control the subject of a clause such as the ones considered here, and the ability to antecede the reflexive *soi* are assumed to be properties of 1's (subjects) at any stratum. In order to account for the fact that *plusieurs terroristes* in (54) has these properties, Legendre (1990b) assumes that this argument, which is an initial 2 (object), advances to 1 and is subsequently demoted to chômeur by the entrance of the dummy subject. This derivation is motivated solely by the control and antecedence properties of that constituent.

verb as the embedded predicate, the causee cannot be analyzed as an agent or an external argument, but as a patient/theme and an internal argument. Even in such cases, control by the causee is possible:

(56) a. *En Pere* ha fet   venir *els nens*   tot cantant.
      Pere   has made come the children while singing

     'Pere has made the children come while singing.'

    b. *En Pere els*   ha fet   sortir sense   parlar.
       Pere   them has made go out without talking

     'Pere has made them go out without talking.'

Once again, the causee in these examples can control the adverbial clauses because it is the logical subject of the embedded predicate. The verbs *venir* 'come' and *sortir* 'go out' are clear examples of unaccusatives, as can be determined by several syntactic tests such as those given in 3.3 and 3.4. The single argument of these verbs would not be treated as a d-structure subject in GB, as an initial 1 in RG, or as an external argument in Grimshaw 1990, and yet, as (56) shows, it has the same control properties as the agent or putative external argument of *cantar* 'sing', *saludar* 'greet', and *criticar* 'criticize' in (55).

6.4.3 Conclusion

In sum, the evidence just discussed involving binding and control indicates that nothing whatsoever is gained by representing the causee (of those verbs that would be analyzed as taking an external argument) as a syntactic subject at any level of representation. The facts of unaccusative predicates in causative constructions show that the notion of grammatical subjecthood is irrelevant for characterizing these phenomena. Since unaccusatives are assumed not to have a d-structure subject or initial 1 (or an external argument), the logical subject of unaccusatives in causative constructions is not a grammatical subject at any level of representation. (It is generally assumed that there is no promotion or movement of the unaccusative argument to subject in causative constructions, for reasons that depend on the particular theory. In C. Rosen 1983, for example, the principle of "Downstairs Freeze" disallows advancements to 1 in the inner clause of causatives.) Therefore, the fact that the causee of unaccusatives has the binding and control properties that other subjectlike arguments have indicates that these properties cannot be assumed to be properties of grammatical subjects. The relevant notion that groups the causee of unaccusatives with the other arguments that exhibit those properties is a notion of maximal prominence, which can be defined at the level of a-structure. In short, the causee of unaccusatives is a logical subject, maximally prominent at a-structure. It is this characterization of causees that is necessary for capturing their "subjecthood" properties.

6.5   Conclusions

The assumption that causative constructions in Romance involve the formation of a complex predicate resulting from the composition of the causative predicate and an embedded predicate makes it possible to account in a simple way for the syntactic properties of these constructions. This complex predicate is formed at the level of a-structure and its correspondence to the other levels of syntactic representation (f- and c-structure) is predicted by independently required principles. A significant feature of the present approach is that it allows us to encode the lexical information of predicates that is relevant for their syntactic subcategorization in a uniform way at a level of representation that is formally distinct from the level in which the actual syntactic functions associated with a predicate are represented. Because the a-structure, whose role is to represent the lexical information of predicates that is relevant for their syntactic subcategorization, is autonomous from the other syntactic levels of representation, the notions or categories represented at a-structure need not have unique correspondences with notions or categories at other levels. Thus, the information that a certain argument of a verb is its logical subject is represented uniquely at a-structure; whether this argument is expressed as a grammatical subject or in some other way will depend on properties of the a-structure and of the f-structure to which this a-structure corresponds.

The study of causative constructions of the Romance type brings out very clearly the need to divorce a-structure information from information used to encode morphosyntactic properties (such as information about syntactic categories, morphological case, syntactic functions, linear precedence, etc.). The fact that the logical subject of a certain verb (for example, *llegir* 'read') is expressed as the grammatical subject of this verb in its *canonical* use (i.e., in an active, noncausativized sentence) has led to the assumption in many linguistic theories that it is always expressed as a grammatical subject. This achieves the desirable goal of reducing the lexical information of predicates pertaining to their syntactic subcategorization to a unique representation. However, the assumption that this unique representation that predicates carry from the lexicon into the syntax is encoded in the same vocabulary used for representing the actual morphosyntactic expressions of arguments has placed linguistic theories in the position of positing syntactic represen tations for which there is no empirical evidence. This is particularly clear in the case of the causative constructions studied in this chapter: the assumption just mentioned requires the causee (of a verb like *llegir*, for example) to be represented as a grammatical subject. However, not only is there no aspect of the morphosyntactic expression of this argument that reveals its representation as a grammatical subject (and therefore theories require an elaborate apparatus to obliterate or obscure this representation), but this representation may lead to incorrect predictions, as has been argued in 6.3.

The hypothesis that the a-structure is autonomous from other syntactic structures, in other words, that its vocabulary is formally different from that which is used to represent morphosyntactic expressions, allows nonisomorphic correspondences between the a-structure and the other levels with which it is related. This makes it possible to posit a unique representation for the lexical information of each predicate pertaining to its syntactic subcategorization, while at the same time not stating this information in terms that have a direct correspondence with morphosyntactic properties. Thus, the a-structure representation of a verb like *llegir* 'read', for example, allows us to define one of its arguments as its logical subject, regardless of whether it is expressed as a grammatical subject or not. When this verb functions as an independent (active) predicate, the principles of the FMT require its logical subject to be expressed as a grammatical subject. When the a-structure of this verb is embedded in the complex a-structure of causatives, the logical subject of the embedded a-structure retains its status as a logical subject, but, in this complex a-structure, the principles of the FMT do not license it as a grammatical subject, but as an object or an (optional) oblique (depending on the properties of the a-structure). Characterizing the causee as a logical subject, as in the present theory, predicts that the causee should display certain properties typical, but not exclusive, of grammatical subjects. Such are the binding and control properties discussed in 6.4, where it is argued that the a-structure definition of logical subject is necessary to account for the "subjecthood" properties of the causee, since it does not correspond to any other existing notion of subject.

In short, the analysis proposed here captures the monoclausality of causative constructions in Romance, which is most saliently manifested by the fact that the embedded verb does not have an argument that looks or behaves like a grammatical subject. This monoclausality follows from having the two component predicates undergo predicate composition, which results in one single (complex) predicate, formally represented as the PRED value for the whole sentence at f-structure. Since the a-structure that appears as a PRED value is the structure to which the FMT applies, it follows that there is one single array of syntactic functions associated with the complex a-structure of causatives, which entails, among other things, that there is one single subject, that the Case Assignment Convention applies to the complex a-structure of causatives and assigns dative or nondative case to the causee depending on this a-structure, etc. Given the assignment of syntactic functions to the complex a-structure of causatives, we predict the morphosyntactic (or c-structure) realization of arguments in causative constructions by general principles of function-category association.

7

Two Types of Binding

The theory of a-structure binding proposed in chapter 4 makes the assumption that the morpheme that contributes a reflexive or reciprocal interpretation to the Romance reflexivized construction is not the expression of any argument of the predicate. This analysis is clearly not the right one for other types of constructions that have a reflexive or reciprocal interpretation: for example, the English translations of the reflexivized constructions given in this work normally involve syntactic anaphors such as *himself, herself, each other*, etc., which should be analyzed as expressing an argument of a predicate. In this chapter, I will show how such anaphoric expressions differ from the phenomenon of a-structure binding, even though they can be used in constructions with the same semantic interpretations as those involving a-structure binding. I will first deal with syntactic anaphors in English, a language that lacks the phenomenon of a-structure binding. I will then consider the existence of syntactic anaphors in Catalan, which in many cases cooccur with the reflexive clitic giving rise to a "clitic doubling" situation. This poses a prima facie problem for the a-structure binding analysis; however, once a solution is proposed that is consistent with this analysis, several empirical consequences are correctly predicted that are extremely problematic for alternative conceptions of the Romance reflexive clitic. Finally, the possible readings that a reciprocal interpretation of a reflexivized construction gives rise to will be shown to follow from the a-structure binding analysis and to be inconsistent with an analysis of the reflexive clitic as a syntactic anaphor.

7.1 Syntactic Anaphors

The English reflexive and reciprocal expressions, such as *himself* or *each other*, cannot be analyzed as a-structure binding morphemes, but must be analyzed as NPs bearing a syntactic function that are referentially dependent on another nominal expression; I refer to such expressions as *syntactic anaphors*. An NP like *himself* is the expression of an argument distinct from the argument that it is referentially dependent on. (Referential dependency does not arise in a-structure binding because there is a single expression for the two bound arguments.) According to this, an example of a-structure binding such as (1a) (=(3.1a)) and its English translation in (1b), although synonymous, have very different syntactic representations, as shown in (2).

(1) a. La directora es defensa.

    b. The director defends herself.

(2a) and (2b) show the c- and f-structures of the Catalan example (1a) and of the English example (1b) respectively, leaving out features such as TENSE, DEF, NUM, etc.

(2) a.   C-structure   F-structure

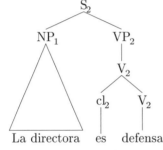

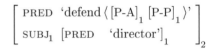

$$\left[\begin{array}{l} \text{PRED 'defend} \langle [\text{P-A}]_1 \ [\text{P-P}]_1 \rangle \text{'} \\ \text{SUBJ}_1 \ [\text{PRED} \quad \text{'director'}]_1 \end{array} \right]_2$$

    b.   C-structure   F-structure

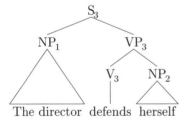

$$\left[\begin{array}{l} \text{PRED 'defend} \langle [\text{P-A}]_1 \ [\text{P-P}]_2 \rangle \text{'} \\ \text{SUBJ}_1 \ [\text{PRED} \quad \text{'director'}]_1 \\ \text{OBJ}_2 \ [\text{PRED} \quad \text{'pro'}]_2 \end{array} \right]_3$$

The Catalan example has one single syntactic function, a subject, as shown in (2a), which corresponds to the two coindexed arguments, this coindexation being determined by the presence of the reflexive clitic *es*. The English example has two syntactic functions, a subject and an object, as shown in (2b), each corresponding to a different argument in the argument structure. Why is it that constructions such as these that are syntactically so different can have the same interpretation? The fact that the two arguments of 'defend' have the same semantic content, and therefore the same referent, in (2a) is captured by analyzing the two arguments as having the same syntactic expression; the semantic content of this syntactic expression corresponds to both bound arguments of the predicate. This analysis is not available for the English example, (2b), where nevertheless the two arguments are interpreted as having the same referent. The relation holding between the subject and the object in the English example (1b)/(2b) is a relation of referential dependency, which is standardly assumed to hold between an anaphoric expression and its antecedent.

Let us assume that all referring expressions (including anaphoric expressions) have a semantic representation that includes a referential index. Part of the meaning of an NP such as *the director* is constant across the possible uses of this NP, but part of its meaning depends on the specific context in which it is used. This context-dependent part of the meaning of an NP is what I refer to as the *referential index*.[1] The referential index fixes the referent that an NP has in a given context of use. Anaphoric expressions such as pronouns and anaphors (reflexive and reciprocal expressions) have their referential index determined by the linguistic context. (In some cases, pronouns, but not anaphors, may have their referential index determined by the extralinguistic context, which would be the deictic use of pronouns.) The principles by which the referential index of anaphoric expressions is determined constitute the "binding theory." I will not adopt any specific version of the binding theory (see Dalrymple 1993 for an approach to anaphoric binding within LFG, or Pollard and Sag 1992, 1993 within Head-Driven Phrase Structure Grammar), but I will assume that the referential index of an anaphor must be token-identical to that of another expression (the antecedent) in a properly defined syntactic domain.

Now we are in a position to see why the two sentences in (1) can be synonymous, in spite of their syntactic differences shown in (2). A simplified semantic structure for (1a) and (1b) is shown in (3a) and (3b)

---

[1] This is similar to Kaplan's (1971 [1989]) proposal that there is an aspect of the meaning of various expressions that is constant across their various uses, which he calls "character," and an aspect of their meaning that depends on the specific context of use, which he calls "content." The idea that part of the meaning of a pronoun or anaphor is independent of the context in which it is used justifies assuming that its semantic structure (its semantic representation at s-structure) is not identical to the semantic structure of its antecedent, in other words, that they do not have a *shared* semantic structure. It could even be that the semantic structure of two (nonanaphoric) NPs in a clause happens to be the same, as in "Only John$_i$ likes John$_i$," but it is not shared structure: each NP has a distinct semantic structure, which happens to have the same representation.

respectively. Each semantic structure corresponding to a syntactic function includes, in addition to the attribute CM, for *compositional meaning*, representing the context-independent part of the meaning (using the terminology of Halvorsen 1983), the attribute R-IX, for *referential index*, which takes a letter (i, j, k, l, etc.) as its value, following standard practice. Each (semantically contentful) syntactic function has one unique semantic representation: from this it follows that (2a) and (2b), which consist of different syntactic functions, have different semantic representations. In (3a), we see that the two arguments have the same semantic representation, because of a-structure binding, and consequently both have the same referential index. In (3b), although each argument has a different semantic representation, the referential index of the two arguments is the same, as required by the binding theory.

(3) a.

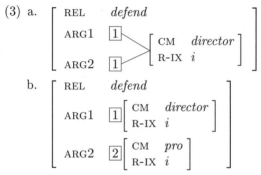

b.

Given that the referential indices associated with each of the arguments are identical in both (3a) and (3b), we account for the fact that the semantic interpretation of the two sentences may be the same.

There is an important semantic difference between constructions involving a-structure binding, signalled by a morpheme such as the Romance reflexive clitic, and constructions involving referential dependency, or anaphoric binding, signalled by a syntactic anaphor, which is noted in Sells, Zaenen and Zec 1987: clauses with an elliptical verb have a different range of interpretations depending on whether the predicate of the elliptical clause is provided by a clause involving a-structure binding or by a clause involving anaphoric binding. To illustrate this difference, we will consider comparative sentences in which the first, nonelliptical, clause contains a reflexive clitic in Catalan, (4), and a reflexive syntactic anaphor in English, (5).

(4)   La Maria es defensa millor que la Gertrudis.
        Mary   RF defends better than Gertrude

    a. 'Mary defends herself better than Gertrude (defends herself).'

    b. *'Mary$_i$ defends herself better than Gertrude (defends her$_i$).'

    c. *'Mary defends herself better than (she defends) Gertrude.'

(5)   Mary defends herself better than Gertrude.

    a. 'Mary defends herself better than Gertrude (defends herself).'

    b. 'Mary$_i$ defends herself better than Gertrude (defends her$_i$).'

    c. 'Mary defends herself better than (she defends) Gertrude.'

The single NP (*la Gertrudis*) of the elliptical clause in (4) can only be interpreted as the subject with the so-called sloppy reading of the reflexive, (4a), excluding both the strict reading of the reflexive, (4b), and the object interpretation of the NP, (4c). In contrast, the single NP of the elliptical clause in (5) has all three interpretations. The difference between an a-structure binding morpheme such as the Catalan reflexive clitic and a syntactic anaphor such as the English reflexive *herself* is responsible for this contrast.

Let us assume, following Sells, Zaenen and Zec 1987, that the f-structure that is constructed for the elliptical clause is a copy of the f-structure of the nonelliptical clause except for the information overtly provided in the elliptical clause. Thus, in example (4), the only information provided in the elliptical clause comes from the NP *la Gertrudis*: being a morphologically unmarked NP, it must be a direct function, either a subject or an object. The remainder of the f-structure, including the predicate information, is copied from the previous clause. Since this clause contains the reflexive clitic, its predicate incorporates a-structure binding. Thus, the relevant PRED value is like that of the f-structure in (2a). Since this PRED value, because of a-structure binding, only licenses one syntactic function (the subject), it follows that the single NP in the elliptical clause can only be interpreted as the subject, ruling out the object interpretation in (4c). Furthermore, this NP is the expression of both bound arguments of the predicate, so that it is impossible for them to have different referential indices, which rules out the strict reading of the reflexive in (4b). This leaves us with (4a) as the sole grammatical interpretation of example (4) involving a-structure binding.

As in (4), the only information provided by the elliptical clause in (5) comes from the NP *Gertrude*, which, as an unmarked NP, has to be a direct function.[2] Since the nonelliptical clause does not involve a-structure binding, the PRED value of this clause, which is copied into the elliptical

---

[2] Such an NP cannot correspond to an oblique, but can correspond to the object of a prepositional oblique, as in an example like 'Mary spends more money on herself than Gertrude', provided by Tom Wasow, in which 'Gertrude' can be interpreted as the object of the elliptical preposition 'on'. It is interesting to observe that, in Catalan and Romance in general, an NP cannot be interpreted as the object of an elliptical

clause, is like that of the f-structure in (2b). This PRED value, having two distinctly indexed arguments, licenses two direct functions—a subject and an object. This allows the single NP in the elliptical clause to be interpreted as the object, while the subject information is copied from the f-structure of the nonelliptical clause (provided by the NP *Mary*), accounting for (5c). That NP can also be interpreted as the subject, in which case the object information is copied from the nonelliptical clause. This allows two possibilities: as with any referring expression, the object may be copied from the nonelliptical clause along with its referential index, giving rise to the strict interpretation in (5b); alternatively, as this object is a syntactic anaphor (*herself*), its referential index may be determined in the f-structure of the elliptical clause, in which case it has to be identical to the subject's, since the subject is the only potential antecedent, giving the sloppy interpretation in (5a).

In sum, it is necessary to acknowledge the existence of two types of constructions that have a reflexive or reciprocal interpretation: those that involve a-structure binding and those that involve anaphoric expressions.[3] The two types of constructions differ at many levels of representation: in the c-structure and the f-structure, as seen in (2), and also in the semantic structure, as seen in (3). These differences have a clear reflex in the different interpretations associated with the two types of constructions, shown in (4)–(5).

7.2 The Reflexive Clitic as Clitic Double

Syntactic anaphors are found not only in languages that lack a-structure binding morphemes, as in English, but also in languages that have such morphemes. Among the Romance languages, in which I have proposed that the reflexive clitic functions as an a-structure binding morpheme, we can distinguish two situations: one in which a syntactic anaphor can be used instead of the reflexive clitic (and cannot be used alongside the reflexive clitic), represented by Italian, and another in which a syntactic anaphor can be used in addition to the reflexive clitic (and, in fact, must be used in addition to the reflexive clitic when the latter is appropriate), represented by Catalan and Spanish. The situation represented by Italian does not pose any problem for the current analysis:

---

preposition; perhaps this is related to the Romance prohibition against preposition stranding.

[3] Although this section has only exemplified constructions with a reflexive interpretation, the same contrast between a-structure binding and anaphoric binding can be made for constructions with a reciprocal interpretation. Recall that the Romance reflexive clitic allows both a reflexive and a reciprocal interpretation with essentially the same syntactic properties.

the reflexive NP *se stesso* 'himself' is a syntactic anaphor, and like its English counterpart fulfils a syntactic function, an object in an example like (6a), whereas the reflexive clitic *si* functions only as an a-structure binding morpheme and therefore does not bear a syntactic function, as in example (6b) (examples from C. Rosen 1988:139).

(6) a. Ugo ha difeso   se stesso.
'Ugo has defended himself.'

    b. Ugo si è difeso.
Ugo RF is defended   ('Ugo has defended himself.')

Difendere 'defend', as a dyadic predicate, takes a subject and an object in its basic (i.e., nonreflexivized) form, accounting for the possibility of having the object expressed by a syntactic anaphor referentially dependent on the subject, as in (6a). If this predicate combines with the reflexive clitic (the a-structure binding morpheme), it takes a subject as its sole grammatical function, as in (6b). This derived predicate cannot take an object, be it anaphoric or not. C. Rosen 1988:163–166 shows that the reflexive clitic in Italian cannot function as a clitic double even in contexts where pronominal clitics can. The choice of auxiliary in (6a-b) provides evidence that the reflexive form in (6a) is a syntactic anaphor, and not an a-structure binding morpheme, thus requiring *avere*, whereas (6b) involves a-structure binding and therefore requires *essere* (see 3.3.1 for auxiliary selection in Italian).

In Catalan, however, the reflexive syntactic anaphor *si mateix* 'himself' does cooccur with the reflexive clitic. This is illustrated in (7), where this syntactic anaphor is optionally used as an accusative or direct object in (7a), and as a dative or indirect object in (7b).[4]

(7) a. La Maria es pentina (a si mateixa).
Maria   RF combs   herself

       'Mary combs herself.'

    b. En Ferran no es permet cap luxe   (a si mateix).
Ferran   not RF allows any luxury himself

       'Ferdinand does not allow himself any luxury.'

If, according to the a-structure binding analysis proposed for the reflexive clitic in Catalan, the subject in (7) is the expression of both the external argument and an internal argument, how can this internal argument be also expressed as an object NP, as appears to be the case in

---

[4]The accusative object in (7a) is introduced by the preposition *a*, just like the dative object in (7b), because this preposition not only marks dative objects, but also introduces certain animate accusative objects in Catalan, in particular those that contain a pronoun.

(7)? Moore 1991 observes that Spanish also allows the reflexive clitic to function as a clitic double of the reflexive NP *si mismo* and presents this fact as an objection to analyzing the reflexive clitic as a valence reducing morpheme. Since the reflexive clitic seems to parallel the pronominal object clitics in having the optional doubling function, illustrated in (8) for Catalan, Moore 1991 argues for treating the two kinds of clitics in essentially the same way, although subject to different principles of the Binding Theory.

(8) a. La Maria el   pentina (a ell).
      Maria   him ACC combs   him

      'Mary combs him.'

   b. En Ferran no   em permet cap luxe   (a mi).
      Ferran   not me allows   any luxury   me

      'Ferdinand does not allow me any luxury.'

However, an analysis of the clitic doubling function of the reflexive clitic is available that is consistent with the a-structure binding analysis.

In LFG, object clitics in languages that allow optional clitic doubling, such as Catalan and Spanish, have alternative functions: they function either as pronouns or as agreement markers. In Catalan, object clitics are used as agreement markers when the agreeing object is dative or pronominal (see 5.1). When an object is pronominal, clitic doubling is obligatory (see examples in 5.1.1); dative objects, in addition, allow clitic doubling also when nonpronominal. A way of representing this alternative function of clitics is to indicate in their lexical entry that the [PRED 'pro'] specification is optional, as in the treatment of the Chicheŵa subject agreement marker by Bresnan and Mchombo 1987. This treatment would be the right one for dative object clitics; for accusative object clitics, that specification would have to be optionally a constraint, indicating that the clitic either functions as a pronoun or agrees with a pronoun. However, if, as argued here, reflexive clitics are not pronouns or anaphors, this treatment cannot extend to reflexive clitics.

In order to account for the alternative function of reflexive clitics, an optionality has to be posited in their lexical entries, which can be represented as in (9).

(9)   *Catalan Reflexive Clitics:*

$$\left[\text{PRED } \text{'P*} \langle \; [\;\;]_1 \cdots \; [\;\;]_2 \cdots \rangle \text{'} \right]$$

where either (a): $1 = 2$

        or   (b): $\boxed{1}\text{R-IX} = \boxed{2}\text{R-IX}$

According to this, a reflexive clitic may function either as an a-structure binding morpheme, when, according to option (a), the linking index (and therefore the semantic structure) of the two arguments involved is identical, or as a marker of coreference between the arguments involved, when, according to option (b), the referential index (R-IX) of the two arguments is required to be identical. These two functions of the reflexive clitic manifest the same basic property of the reflexive clitic, namely, signalling semantic identity between two arguments of a predicate, and they differ only in the level at which this identification is stated: at a-structure, for option (a), and at semantic structure (s-structure), for option (b). The empirical differences that will be shown to follow from these two uses constitute evidence for distinguishing argument structure from semantic structure.

The a-structure binding function of the reflexive clitic is the one that we have considered so far. The second option is the one that allows the reflexive clitic to cooccur with a syntactic anaphor. In fact, if option (b) is chosen, it must cooccur with a syntactic anaphor: within this option, there is no a-structure binding, and, therefore, both arguments involved must map onto distinct syntactic functions; given that coreference (identity of referential indices) is imposed between the two arguments, one of them must be expressed as an anaphor, which is the only type of expression that allows clause-bound coreference. Thus, we account for the fact that the reflexive clitic in Catalan (and Spanish) may cooccur with an object (coreferential with its logical subject) provided this object is a syntactic anaphor. An important prediction that follows from the present proposal is that a syntactic anaphor can only be doubled by the reflexive clitic if the argument that the syntactic anaphor expresses can be a-structure bound. Since the information of the reflexive clitic, stated in (9), refers to a-structure (whether the binding takes place at a-structure or s-structure), it can only refer to arguments accessible to a-structure operations, that is, arguments with a P-Role classification, or direct arguments (see section 2.2.2). Thus, whereas doubling occurs in examples like (7), where the syntactic anaphor is an object and, therefore, corresponds to a [P-P] argument, it is not possible in an example like (10), where the syntactic anaphor is an oblique and, as such, corresponds to an argument without a P-Role classification.

(10)   La Maria (*es) pensa en si mateixa.
        Mary   RF thinks in herself

        'Mary thinks about herself.'

Just as the reflexive clitic cannot function as an a-structure binding morpheme with the predicate of example (10), because one of the arguments involved lacks a P-Role classification (this example is still ungrammatical with the reflexive clitic when we omit the oblique PP), it cannot function as a clitic double for the oblique phrase.

An interesting consequence of this analysis is that the pair of sentences corresponding to the two options in (7a), with the syntactic anaphor, (11a), and without it, (11b), should differ not only in their c- and f-structures—for example, the former has an object that is absent in the latter—but also in the range of semantic interpretations that they are associated with.

(11) a. La Maria es defensa a si mateixa.

     b. La Maria es defensa.

        'Mary defends herself.'

The present theory predicts that example (11a), when it provides the predicate information of a construction with an elliptical verb, should allow the same interpretations as the English counterpart, also with a syntactic anaphor. This prediction is correct: example (12), containing sentence (11a) as the first member of the comparison, has the same interpretive possibilities as the English example (5).[5]

(12)   La Maria es defensa a si mateixa millor que la Gertrudis.
           Mary   RF defends herself   better than Gertrude

     a. 'Mary defends herself better than Gertrude (defends herself).'

     b. 'Mary$_i$ defends herself better than Gertrude (defends her$_i$).'

     c. 'Mary defends herself better than (she defends) Gertrude.'

---

[5]Some speakers of Catalan require that the single NP in the elliptical clause be introduced by the preposition *a* in order for it to have the object interpretation of (12c). (Structures with an elliptical predicate are one of the contexts that favor or require the use of this preposition introducing animate accusative objects.) Thus, for such speakers interpretation (12c) is only possible if sentence (12) is given in the following form:

(i)   La Maria es defensa a si mateixa millor que **a** la Gertrudis.
        Mary   RF defends herself   better than A Gertrude

      'Mary defends herself better than (she defends) Gertrude.'

What is important to note is that this disambiguating strategy is only available when there is an accusative object in the nonelliptical clause, as in (i). So, if the object *a si mateixa* is removed from (i), the sentence becomes ungrammatical. In other words, the object interpretation of the NP of the elliptical clause is not available in a sentence like (4), even if we try to force it by introducing that NP with the preposition *a*, as in (ii):

(ii)   *La Maria es defensa millor que **a** la Gertrudis.
         Mary   RF defends better than A Gertrude

      'Mary defends herself better than (she defends) Gertrude.'

Thus, (11a), with an anaphoric object, contrasts with (11b), with a-structure binding, with respect to the range of interpretations they give rise to, as we see comparing (12) and (4). This contrast is explained because (12), with a syntactic anaphor coreferential with the logical subject in the nonelliptical clause, does not involve a-structure binding; the reflexive clitic merely functions as a marker of this coreference. Therefore, the two arguments of the predicate have distinct linking indices, which requires them to map onto different syntactic functions (consequently with different semantic representations). This allows the single NP in the elliptical clause to be interpreted either as the subject or as the object; and, when it is interpreted as the subject, the object may retain the referential index (or R-IX) of the nonelliptical clause or acquire a new one in the elliptical clause, thus accounting for both the sloppy and the strict readings.

The contrast between (4) and (12), which follows naturally from the dual function attributed to the reflexive clitic in Catalan (as an a-structure binding morpheme and a marker of coreference), is completely mysterious for the pronominal approach. If, as proposed in Moore 1991, (11a) and (11b) both have a syntactic anaphor in object position and only differ in that the anaphor has phonological content in the former but is silent in the latter, that contrast has no natural explanation.[6] It is clear then that the fact that the reflexive clitic can cooccur with a syntactic anaphor (in Catalan and Spanish) is not an argument for

---

[6]One could not attribute this contrast to the presence vs. absence of phonological content in the object position even by stipulating that the absence of phonological content in object position precludes the possibility of using that argument in a clause with an elliptical verb. This stipulation would predict that a sentence like (i), with a pronominal object clitic, should only allow the subject interpretation of the NP of the elliptical clause, since it is analyzed according to Moore 1991 as having a phonologically null NP in object position agreeing with the clitic.

(i)   La Maria el   defensa millor que   (a) la Gertrudis.
        Mary   him ACC defends better than   A   Gertrude

'Mary defends him better than Gertrude.'

But this sentence allows the same two interpretations as the English translation, in particular, the one where *Gertrude* is the object: "Mary defends him better than she defends Gertrude." Furthermore, one could not even restrict that stipulation to phonologically null anaphors, given the facts of the Chicheŵa reflexive prefix discussed in Sells, Zaenen and Zec 1987, and Mchombo 1993. This reflexive prefix would have to be like the Romance reflexive clitic in Moore's 1991 theory in agreeing with a null anaphor in object position: however, as shown in the references cited, the Chicheŵa reflexive prefix allows the same interpretations in elliptical constructions as the English anaphors. In the present theory, the Chicheŵa reflexive prefix (unlike the Romance reflexive clitic and the Chicheŵa reciprocal suffix) is a syntactic anaphor, and, like an object marker in Chicheŵa, a morphologically incorporated pronoun that bears the grammatical function object.

analyzing it as an anaphor (or a morpheme that agrees with an anaphor) but for analyzing it as a morpheme signalling alternatively coindexation (in the technical sense intended here) and coreference of a logical subject and a co-argument.

7.3 Further Consequences

Having argued that the reflexive clitic in Catalan is not a valence reducing morpheme if and only if it cooccurs with a syntactic anaphor (such as *si mateix*), reflecting the coreference relation encoded by the reflexive clitic in the (9b) option, the following prediction is made: a reflexivized dyadic verb taking a syntactic anaphor as its object does not behave like an intransitive verb. This conclusion is already supported by the evidence discussed in the previous section: the single NP of an elliptical clause in Catalan can only be interpreted as the object of a reflexivized verb when this verb is used transitively in the nonelliptical clause, that is, with an anaphoric object. In addition, this analysis predicts that a verb taking a syntactic anaphor as an object should show none of the signs of valence reduction attributed to the reflexive clitic in section 3.2, to which we now turn. We will not discuss NP extraposition, as it can only be clearly illustrated in French and French lacks the clitic doubling function of the reflexive clitic, or past participle agreement, since a past participle agrees with a clitic bearing an object function, but the reflexive clitic is not an object either as an a-structure binding morpheme or as a marker of coreference. The relevant evidence in Catalan is nominalizations and case marking in causative constructions.

Having a syntactic anaphor as an object following a nominal based on a reflexivized infinitive is unacceptable, as we see in (13) (cf. the acceptable form (3.13a) without the anaphoric object).

(13)   *El sàtir observava amagat el   despullar-se   a si mateixes
          the satyr observed hidden the undress INF-RF themselves

          sorollós de les nimfes.
          noisy   of the nymphs.

          'The satyr was observing concealed the noisy undressing of
          themselves by the nymphs.'

Given that only intransitive verbs in Romance can be nominalized in their infinitive form, the ungrammaticality of (13) follows from the assumption that the reflexive clitic in its clitic doubling function does not intransitivize the dyadic verb with which it combines.

Regarding case marking in causative constructions, the facts involving an anaphoric object of the embedded predicate turn out to be apparently inconsistent with the expectation that such a predicate should behave like a transitive verb.[7] To understand the nature of the problem, it will be useful to consider first the facts of Italian. In this language, when a dyadic predicate embedded in a causative construction has a reflexive interpretation, the case marking on the nonanaphoric object depends on whether the reflexive interpretation is conveyed by a syntactic anaphor or not. There seem to be two dialects in Italian, one that allows the predicate embedded in the causative construction to take the reflexive clitic, and one that doesn't. The former dialect is illustrated in (14), from C. Rosen 1988:174, and the latter is illustrated in (15), based on Burzio 1986:404, 421. Examples (14a) and (15a) contain an embedded predicate involving a-structure binding, signalled by the reflexive clitic in the former, and morphologically unmarked in the latter. Examples (14b) and (15b) contain the syntactic anaphor *se stesso* as an object of the embedded verb.

(14) a. Quell'episodio rischia di far -lo   /*gli odiar-si.
        that incident risks to make him ACC DAT hate RF

   b. Quell'episodio rischia di far -gli   /*lo odiare se stesso.
        that incident risks to make him-DAT ACC hate   himself

   'That incident is likely to make him hate himself.'

(15) a. Maria ha fatto accusare Piero.
        Maria has made accuse   Piero

   b. Maria ha fatto accusare se stesso a Piero.
        Maria has made accuse   himself   to Piero

   'Maria made Piero accuse himself.'

Whereas in (14a) and (15a) the nonanaphoric object (the only object, since the embedded predicate involves a-structure binding) is expressed as an accusative object, in (14b) and (15b), where it cooccurs with the anaphoric object *se stesso*, it is expressed as a dative object. On the assumption that the nonanaphoric object in these examples is the causee (the logical subject of the embedded predicate), the case alternation conforms to the generalization that the object causee is dative when it cooccurs with an accusative object, and is accusative otherwise.

In contrast with the Italian facts, what we find in Catalan is that the presence of an anaphoric object in the embedded predicate does not affect the case marking on the nonanaphoric object. This object

---

[7] I am grateful to John Moore (personal communication) for raising this potential objection to the present theory and for sharing his informant consultations with me, which coincide with the facts that I present here.

is accusative whether there is an anaphoric object or not, as the following examples illustrate. This is particularly clear in (17), where the nonanaphoric object is expressed as a pronominal clitic. (Notice that in these examples, as in previous examples involving reflexivized predicates embedded in causative constructions, the reflexive clitic is optional.)

(16) a. He   fet   rentar(-se) en Ferran (a si mateix).
       I have made wash   RF Ferran   himself

       'I made Ferran wash himself.'

    b. He   fet   defensar(-se) en Ferran (a si mateix).
          I have made defend   RF Ferran   himself

          'I made Ferran defend himself.'

(17) a. { L'   /*Li }   he   fet   rentar(-se) (a si mateix).
       him ACC/ him DAT I have made wash   RF   himself

       'I made him wash himself.'

    b. { L'   /*Li }   he   fet   defensar(-se) (a si mateix).
          him ACC/ him DAT I have made defend   RF   himself

          'I made him defend himself.'

Given the Italian facts in (14)–(15), the Catalan results in (16)–(17) are quite unexpected. If, as in Italian, the nonanaphoric object in the Catalan examples (16)–(17) is the causee, the fact that it is not a dative, but an accusative, object would be inconsistent with the case marking generalization if the anaphoric object were also accusative.

However, it is clear that the anaphoric object in (16)–(17) is not an accusative, but a dative, object. If it were accusative, these sentences would exemplify a situation not attested anywhere else in the language: a clause containing two accusative objects. In addition, examples like (16) reflect the unmarked order of objects in Romance, in which the accusative object precedes the dative object. (Compare with the Italian (15b), which also reflects this unmarked order, although the accusative object there is the anaphoric phrase.) Reversing the order of objects, as in (18), corresponding to (16), yields marginal to unacceptable results.

(18)   ??He   fet $\begin{Bmatrix} \text{rentar} & \text{(-se)} \\ \text{defensar} & \text{(-se)} \end{Bmatrix}$ a si mateix (a) en Ferran.
        I have made wash/defend RF   himself   to Ferran

        'I made Ferran wash/defend himself.'

The contrast between (16) and (18) follows from a general word order constraint visible in any double object construction in Romance, including noncausative constructions with nonanaphoric objects, such as (19).

This follows, as argued in 5.2.3, from the assumption that the dative phrase is a PP and from the linear precedence principle that requires an NP, such as an accusative object, to precede a sister XP of a different category. (19a), where the accusative NP *en Ferran* precedes the dative PP *a la Gertrudis*, complies with this principle; (19b), where the order of the two objects is reversed, does not.

(19) a. He   presentat en Ferran a la Gertrudis.
       I have introduced Ferran   to Gertrudis

    b.??He   presentat a la Gertrudis en Ferran.
        I have introduced to Gertrudis   Ferran

    'I introduced Ferran to Gertrudis.'

The conclusion that the anaphoric object *a si mateix* in (16)–(17) is a dative object can only be reconciled with the principles of case assignment and with the argument structure of causative constructions by assuming that that object is the causee. If it is the causee, it is assigned dative case in the presence of an accusative object: since the nonanaphoric object in (16)–(17) is accusative, it follows that the anaphoric object, the causee, should be dative. According to this, the thematically most prominent argument of a predicate, its logical subject, may be expressed as a syntactic anaphor that takes a thematically less prominent argument as its antecedent: an apparently unusual situation.

Recall that the Case Assignment Convention (5.43) assigns dative case (the feature value [DAT +]) to the thematically more prominent of two direct functions that does not map onto the external argument, with the unmarked nondative case being the default specification for direct functions. This principle determines the right case pattern not only with underived predicates that take two direct functions excluding the external argument, but also with causative complex predicates, as we saw in chapter 6. The causee is expressed as an object when it is coindexed with the internal (or P-P) argument of the causative predicate in (6.3). This predicate combines with a dyadic predicate such as *rentar* 'wash' to yield the complex a-structure and its associated grammatical functions shown in (20). Notice that the internal argument of the 'cause' predicate and the logical subject of 'wash' are coindexed; as with coindexing triggered by an a-structure binding morpheme, these coindexed arguments must map onto the same grammatical function. The assignment of grammatical functions to arguments is predicted by the FMT, and the assignment of case features is determined by the Case Assignment Convention (5.43).

(20)

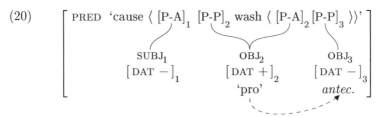

(20) represents the structure corresponding to sentences like (16)–(17), in which the dative causee is expressed as a syntactic anaphor (*si mateix*) that takes the accusative object as its antecedent. The discontinuous line with an arrowhead in (20) signals the relationship between the anaphor and its antecedent (with the arrow pointing to the antecedent). What is apparently unusual about this relationship is that the antecedent is thematically less prominent (the internal argument or patient of 'wash') than the anaphor, which corresponds to the logical subject of the predicate. However, this aspect of the anaphoric relationship in (20) is not peculiar to causatives: noncausative constructions in Romance involving a dative and an accusative object in which one of the objects is anaphorically related to the other, it is always the dative object that is the anaphor, and the dative object is thematically more prominent than the accusative object. Taking the ditransitive verb *presentar* 'introduce' of (19), we see that the dative object can be a syntactic anaphor referentially dependent on the accusative object, but not viceversa. The anaphoric expressions *a si mateixos* and *l'un a l'altre* are indistinct for dative and accusative case; we know that they must be dative in (21) because they cooccur with the accusative object clitic *els*, and not with the dative *els hi*.[8]

(21) { Els   /*Els hi } he   presentat   a si mateixos/l'un a l'altre.
      them ACC/ DAT   I have introduced themselves   each other

    'I have introduced them to themselves/each other.'

Thus, the a-structure of the verb *presentar*, which takes a goal and a theme internal arguments, has the goal internal argument positioned more prominently than the theme internal argument, as required by the

---

[8] Whereas the use of the reciprocal expression *l'un a l'altre* in (21) raises no problem of interpretation, the reflexive expression *a si mateixos* in this example is pragmatically odd, as with the English translation 'I introduced them to themselves'. This is because one can normally only introduce someone to someone else. However, if one does not know that John and Bill are Mr. Smith and Mr. Jones and one suggests to John and Bill that they should meet Mr. Smith and Mr. Jones, they might object that one would be introducing them to themselves. The same can be said in Catalan, showing that sentence (21) with the reflexive expression is not ungrammatical, only pragmatically unexpected.

thematic hierarchy (2.20). By the FMT and convention (5.43), the object corresponding to the goal argument is assigned dative case. As we see in the structure in (22), the thematically lower object is the antecedent of the thematically more prominent object.

(22)

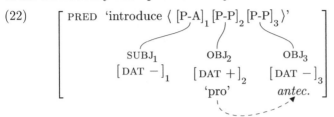

Comparing the causative structure (20) with the noncausative structure (22), we see that in both it is the dative object that can be referentially dependent on the accusative object, and not viceversa. A possible reason for this is that, in the hierarchy of syntactic functions, a dative object (an object with a marked case feature) is lower than an accusative object (an object with an unmarked case feature). The proposal made in (2.54) merely states that direct functions are more prominent than obliques, and a subject is more prominent than a nonsubject, but does not say anything about the relative prominence of objects. Let us assume that a further ranking is imposed among grammatical functions appealing to morphological case (in languages where morphological case distinctions are used): a function with an unmarked case feature is more prominent than one with a marked case feature. The result is that a nondative (or accusative) object is more prominent than a dative object, as in the hierarchies of Keenan and Comrie 1977 and Perlmutter and Postal 1974. If a syntactic anaphor (in Catalan, at least) is required to take a more prominent syntactic function as its antecedent, it follows that an accusative object qualifies as an antecedent for a dative object, but not viceversa. Therefore, the causee in a structure like (20), because it is a dative object, can be anaphorically dependent on the accusative object, even though the latter is thematically less prominent than the former.[9]

---

[9]It remains to be seen why Italian differs from Catalan with respect to anaphoric binding in ditransitive causative constructions, as shown in (14)–(15) vs. (16)–(17), but not in other ditransitive constructions, such as (21) (see Rizzi 1986a:504 for similar examples in Italian). It seems that two competing generalizations operate in Italian: on the one hand, as in Catalan, the requirement that the antecedent of an anaphor be more prominent on the GF hierarchy than the anaphor, and, on the other hand, the requirement that, if a direct function involved in an anaphoric relation is a logical subject, as a maximally prominent argument at a-structure, it be the antecedent of a less prominent argument. In case the two principles conflict, the latter overrides the former in Italian (although not in Catalan), accounting for the

The evidence presented in this section confirms the prediction that the reflexive clitic in Catalan has a valence reducing effect except when it cooccurs with a syntactic anaphor in object position. This conclusion was already supported by the facts discussed in the previous section involving elliptical constructions, where a reflexivized verb with a syntactic anaphor in object position behaves unlike the same verb without the syntactic anaphor and like the nonreflexivized form of the verb. It is further validated by the failure of a reflexivized verb with a syntactic anaphor to be nominalized, just like any transitive verb. The facts of causative constructions raise the puzzle that the case marking on an object in a causative construction is unaffected by the presence or absence of a cooccurring anaphoric object, and thus appear to indicate that the transitivity of the base predicate is unchanged by having an object expressed as a syntactic anaphor or not having it. These facts are best analyzed by assuming that the single object of a causative based on a reflexivized dyadic predicate is the expression of the causee (as well as of the other bound argument), but the same object is not the expression of the causee when it cooccurs with an anaphoric object, since the latter is the expression of the causee. Thus, we account for the fact that, in both cases, by the general Case Assignment Convention the nonanaphoric object is nondative, and the anaphoric object, when it is used, is dative. The seemingly unusual analysis that the thematically more prominent argument is not the antecedent when the binding relation holds between two objects turns out to be not specific to causative constructions, but the general situation in Catalan: an accusative object may antecede a dative object, but not viceversa, even though the dative object is thematically more prominent than the accusative object.

---

situation in (14)–(15), where the causee, as the logical subject, is the antecedent of the anaphor. There is evidence independent of causative constructions that suggests that this account is correct. In other constructions where the logical subject is a direct function but not a grammatical subject, Italian has the logical subject as the antecedent of an anaphor, whereas Catalan has the grammatical subject as the antecedent. This can be illustrated with the verb *piacere* 'like' in Italian, and the verb *agradar* 'like' in Catalan, both of which take an experiencer logical subject expressed as a dative object and a thematically lower theme expressed as the subject. Whereas the dative logical subject is the antecedent in the Italian example (i), from C. Rosen 1988:27, it is the anaphor in the Catalan example (ii).

(i)   A Mario piace solo se stesso.   (Italian)
        to Mario likes only himself

        'Mario likes only himself.'

(ii)   En Ferran s' agrada només a si mateix.   (Catalan)
       Ferran   RF likes   only   to himself

       'Ferran likes only himself.'

7.4   Reciprocal Readings with "Inversion" Verbs

Reflexivized constructions in Romance allow a reciprocal, as well as a reflexive, interpretation. As noted by Higginbotham (1980), and further discussed by Heim, Lasnik, and May (1991), by Williams (1991), and by Dalrymple, Mchombo, and Peters (1994) (henceforth Dalrymple et al. 1994), among others, reciprocal constructions in English give rise to various readings when the antecedent of the reciprocal expression is an anaphoric pronoun. Following Dalrymple et al. 1994, an English example like (23) is ambiguous, having the two paraphrases in (24).

(23)   John and Bill think they defeated each other.

(24) a.   John thinks: John and Bill defeated each other.
        Bill thinks: John and Bill defeated each other.

   b.   John thinks: John defeated Bill.
        Bill thinks: Bill defeated John.

In (24a), the pronoun *they* of (23) has a coreferential interpretation, whereas in (24b) it has a bound variable interpretation. Interestingly, Dalrymple et al. 1994 show that reciprocal verb forms in Chicheŵa, containing the reciprocal suffix *-an*, give rise to the same interpretations as their English counterparts with the syntactic anaphor *each other*. Thus, the Chicheŵa translation of (23), given in (25) (from Dalrymple et al. 1994), also has the two readings in (24).

(25)   John ndí Bill a-ku-gáníz-a   kutí a-na-gónj-éts-an-a.
       John and Bill 2s-PR-think-FV that 2s-PST-lose-CAUS-REC-FV

       'John and Bill think that they defeated each other.'

   Mchombo 1992, 1993, Dalrymple et al. 1994, and Alsina 1993 argue that the reciprocal morpheme in Chicheŵa is a valence reducing morpheme and show that the combination of the reciprocal morpheme with an otherwise transitive verb stem is an intransitive verb. Given this, and the claim that the Chicheŵa reciprocal morpheme signals a binding relation between two arguments of a predicate, like the Romance reflexive clitic, it is clear that it should be analyzed as an a-structure binding morpheme (see Alsina 1993 for further arguments). This means that there is only one syntactic function corresponding to the two bound arguments of the reciprocalized verb form in (25), the subject, which, in this example, is encoded as the subject marker functioning as a pronoun. What is important to note is that, whether the reciprocal semantics is expressed by means of syntactic anaphor that bears a syntactic function, as in English, or by means of an a-structure binding morpheme, as in Chicheŵa, there is an asymmetry in the interpretation of the two semantic participants involved in the binding relation.[10] This asymmetry is reflected in the fact that both the English sentence (23) and the Chicheŵa sentence (25) lack the reading in (26).[11]

(26)   * John thinks: Bill defeated John.
         Bill thinks: John defeated Bill.

It is easy to see why this asymmetry exists in English. When the syntactic function that provides the interpretation for the bound argument (the pronominal subject in (23)) is interpreted as a bound variable, giving rise to what Dalrymple et al. 1994 refer to as the "wide scope" reading of the reciprocal, exemplified in (24b), the variable, x, provided by the pronoun, identical to that of its antecedent, fills the argument role that corresponds to the pronoun. Thus, the arguments linked to the subject of *defeat* and to the subject of *think* in (23) (pronoun and antecedent respectively) are interpreted as the same variable. The reciprocal anaphor *each other* must be interpreted as another variable, y, distinct from that of its antecedent, occupying the argument role that corresponds to the anaphor. Since the pronoun is the subject and the reciprocal anaphor is the object in (23), and these syntactic functions correspond to the agent and patient arguments of the predicate *defeat* respectively, we obtain the semantic representation in (27a), not the one in (27b).

(27) a.
$$\underset{\text{THINK}(x, \text{ DEFEAT}(\overset{|}{x}, \overset{|}{y}))}{\text{ag pt}}$$
b. *
$$\underset{\text{THINK}(x, \text{ DEFEAT}(\overset{|}{y}, \overset{|}{x}))}{\text{ag pt}}$$

The fact that the same asymmetry also exists in Chicheŵa (namely, that the Chicheŵa example (25) has the "wide scope" reading in (24a), but not that in (26)) is perhaps somewhat surprising given the assumption that the subject of the reciprocalized verb in (25) is the expression of both arguments of the predicate. In other words, the bound variable interpretation of the pronominal subject of (25) yields the semantic representation in (27a), and not that in (27b), just as in English. Given the analysis of the reciprocal morpheme in Chicheŵa as an a-structure

---

[10] I am grateful to Mary Dalrymple, Sam Mchombo, and Stanley Peters for discussing this point with me. The ideas about the semantics of reciprocals that follow are a loose adaptation of Dalrymple et al. 1994.

[11] The claim being made is that it is not possible to assign the reading in (26) to an English sentence like (23) or a Chicheŵa sentence like (25) as its sole interpretation, unlike what happens with each of the two readings in (24). In other words, such sentences cannot mean that John thinks that Bill defeated John, and Bill thinks that John defeated Bill, without also meaning that John thinks that John defeated Bill, and Bill thinks that Bill defeated John.

binding morpheme, which entails that one single syntactic function will map onto two arguments of a predicate, we cannot say, as Dalrymple et al. 1994:161 do, that "[b]oth the English pronoun *they* and the Chicheŵa incorporated subject pronoun *a-* are interpreted as a variable, x, which is filled into the semantic argument role to which the pronoun is linked." In the present theory, the Chicheŵa incorporated subject pronoun of a reciprocalized verb form is linked to both bound arguments; consequently, if the variable that the pronoun is interpreted as were to fill the two argument roles to which the pronoun is linked, we would get a representation like (28), which is not the intended result.

(28) DEFEAT(x, x)

Furthermore, we do not want this variable simply to fill either of the argument roles to which the pronoun is linked, assigning a distinct variable to the remaining argument role, since that would give us the two representations in (27). Since a-structure binding is an operation on the argument structure, it seems reasonable to capture the asymmetry in (27) by appealing to the a-structure asymmetry between the two arguments involved in a-structure binding. This can be done by rephrasing the interpretation procedure as follows:[12]

(29) A (bound variable) pronoun is interpreted as a variable, x, which is filled into the *most prominent* argument role to which the pronoun is linked.

Adding this restriction (that the variable is filled into the most prominent argument to which the pronoun is linked) has no effect on the interpretation of constructions with a reciprocal syntactic anaphor, as in English, since the pronoun is linked to only one argument. However, it achieves the desired result for the interpretation of reciprocal constructions marked by a-structure binding, as in Chicheŵa. Since the bound pronominal subject of the reciprocalized clause in (25) is linked to the two argument roles of the predicate, the interpretation procedure in (29) requires the variable corresponding to the pronoun to fill the more prominent of the two arguments it is linked to, namely, the agent. In

---

[12]Since this interpretation procedure is not designed to account only for the reciprocal cases, we cannot require the variable to be filled *only* into the most prominent argument role to which the pronoun is linked. The reflexive interpretation that the Romance reflexive clitic allows is also accounted for by the interpretation procedure (29); in this case, however, the same variable fills both argument roles to which the pronoun is linked, giving a representation like (28). The difference between the reflexive and the reciprocal interpretation of reflexivized verbs is whether the lower argument in the a-structure binding relation is filled by the same variable as the higher argument or by a different one, which corresponds to the reflexive and the reciprocal interpretations respectively.

order to obtain the reciprocal interpretation, we have to assign a distinct variable to the remaining bound argument. Hence, we account for the grammaticality of the interpretation in (27a), and we rule out (27b).

If the asymmetry represented in (27) is to be captured at the level of a-structure, rather than at some other syntactic level, we have a potential source of evidence to distinguish between the a-structure binding approach and alternative approaches to the same phenomenon that treat the reciprocal morpheme as a syntactic anaphor. What we need is the kind of predicate that exhibits a mismatch between a-structure and syntactic functions in that the most prominent argument (at a-structure) does not map onto the most prominent syntactic function. These are what we can call "inversion" predicates using the RG terminology. Unfortunately, Chicheŵa (to my knowledge) lacks such predicates. The Romance languages, on the other hand, do have such predicates, represented by verbs such as *agradar* 'like' in Catalan (*piacere* in Italian, *gustar* in Spanish, etc.). As argued in chapter 5, *agradar* has a logical subject (the experiencer) that does not map onto a grammatical subject, while its less prominent co-argument (the theme) may be the grammatical subject. Since the reflexive clitic in Romance allows a reciprocal meaning, reflexivized inversion verbs with a reciprocal semantics may provide the desired evidence.

First, we have to show that, independently of inversion verbs, reflexivized constructions in Romance have the same range of reciprocal interpretations as their Chicheŵa and English counterparts and exhibit the requisite asymmetry with a bound variable pronoun. A sentence like (30) favors (or only allows) the bound variable interpretation of the controlled subject of the reflexivized verb in a reciprocal use, and can be paraphrased as (31a), but not as (31b).

(30) En Ton i la Clara han promès separadament ajudar-se
      Ton and   Clara have promised separately   to help RF

      tant   com poguessin.
      as much as   they could

      'Ton and Clara promised separately to help each other as much as they could.'

(31) a. Ton promised to help Clara.
         Clara promised to help Ton.

     b. * Ton promised that Clara would help Ton.
           Clara promised that Ton would help Clara.

This evidence reveals that, given the assumption that the subject of a reflexivized verb like *ajudar-se* is linked to the two argument roles of the predicate, the interpretation procedure in (29), which is sensitive to a-structure prominence, derives the right semantic representation for a sentence like (30). However, this evidence is equally consistent with the assumption that the reflexive clitic is (or binds) a syntactic anaphor in object position: the subject is interpreted as a variable that occupies the argument role that it is linked to (the agent or logical subject), while the anaphoric object, in order to yield a reciprocal semantics, is interpreted as a variable distinct from the former and fills the argument role that the object is linked to.

The crucial evidence that distinguishes between these two approaches is provided by reflexivized inversion verbs. An inversion verb like *agradar* in (32a) appears to project the same syntactic structure as a verb like *escriure* 'write' in (32b): both take a subject and a dative object.

(32) a. En Ton li   agrada molt, a la Clara.
          Ton her DAT likes   much to Clara

      'Clara likes Ton very much.'

      b. En Ton li   escriu sovint, a la Clara.
          Ton her DAT writes often   to Clara

      'Ton often writes to Clara.'

However, these two types of verbs have been argued to differ in important ways (for example, by Perlmutter (1984) within RG, and by Belletti and Rizzi (1988) within GB). Within the present approach they differ in that the noninversion verb (*escriure*) has an external argument as its logical subject, which maps onto the grammatical subject, whereas the inversion verb (*agradar*) has an internal argument as its logical subject, which does not map onto the grammatical subject. The reason why the logical subject of the inversion verb does not map onto the subject function is that, being an internal argument, it maps onto a direct function, not necessarily a subject, just like its co-argument; being the thematically more prominent of two direct functions, it is assigned dative case by the Case Assignment Convention (5.43); bearing dative case, it is incompatible with the subject function, according to the Nondative Subject Constraint (5.50), leaving its co-argument as the sole argument that may map onto the subject function. The mapping of arguments to functions for the verbs in (32a) and (32b) is given schematically in (33a) and (33b) respectively.[13]

---

[13]Note that the English equivalent of the inversion verb *agradar* is a noninversion verb: 'like' is syntactically identical to a verb like 'see' in having a subject and an object in the active form with the subject mapped onto an external argument. An inversion verb is characterized by having the prominence relations among arguments

(33) a.

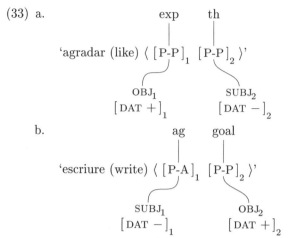

b.

Notice that the single internal argument in (33b) is assigned dative case because of its thematic role, goal, as required by (5.43). (*Escriure* is a predicate that can take a theme internal argument in addition to the goal. Whether that argument is present in the a-structure or not when it is not expressed as a syntactic function is irrelevant here.)

The two verbs in (32) can combine with a reflexive clitic with a reciprocal semantics. If the subject of these reflexivized (reciprocal) forms is a null pronominal, it can be interpreted as a bound variable, giving rise to the "wide scope" reading of the reciprocal. With the inversion verb *agradar* in (34), we obtain, in addition to the "narrow scope" reading in (35a), the "wide scope" reading in (35b), but we do not obtain the "inverted" reading in (35c).[14]

(34)   En Ton i   la Clara m' han dit que s' agraden molt.
        Ton and   Clara me have said that RF like   much

    'Ton and Clara told me that they like each other very much.'

(35) a.   Ton and Clara told me: "We like each other very much."

    b.   Ton told me: "I like Clara very much."
          Clara told me: "I like Ton very much."

---

at the level of argument structure "reversed" at the level of syntactic functions. Therefore, the observations that apply to *agradar* do not necessarily apply to 'like'.

[14] A Spanish example equivalent to (34) is given in Heim, Lasnik, and May 1991: 89, fn. 17, containing the inversion verb *gustar* 'like'. That example is followed by a sentence that favors the "wide scope" reading of the reciprocal. Similarly, adding a clause like *tot i que no s'ho han confessat mai* 'although they have never confessed it to each other' to (34) would also favor the "wide scope" reading in (35b).

c. * Ton told me: "Clara likes me very much."
Clara told me: "Ton likes me very much."

With the noninversion verb *escriure* in (36), we also obtain the "narrow scope" reading in (37a) and the "wide scope" reading in (37b), but not the reading in (37c).

(36)   En Ton i   la Clara m' han dit que s' escriuen sovint.
        Ton and   Clara me have said that RF write   often

        'Ton and Clara told me that they often write (to) each other.'

(37) a.   Ton and Clara told me: "We often write to each other."

     b.   Ton told me: "I often write to Clara."
           Clara told me: "I often write to Ton."

     c. * Ton told me: "Clara often writes to me."
           Clara told me: "Ton often writes to me."

The reciprocalized forms of the inversion verb and of the noninversion verb have the same types of readings, as reflected in (35) and (37) respectively. This follows from the assumptions that the morpheme responsible for the reciprocal semantics performs a-structure binding, an operation on the a-structure, and consequently that the asymmetry between the two bound arguments (which accounts for the contrasts (35b) vs. (35c) and (37b) vs. (37c)) is to be captured at the level of a-structure, as stated in (29). Notice that, whereas there is a different mapping of arguments to functions for the two verbs in their nonreflexivized forms, since in one case the logical subject maps onto an object and in the other case it maps onto the subject, as shown in (33a) and (33b) respectively, the same mapping obtains for their reflexivized forms, as we see in (38). With both *agradar* in (38a) and *escriure* in (38b), the two bound arguments map onto the subject. In (38a), since there is only one direct function, the Case Assignment Convention (5.43) cannot assign it dative case, and it is assigned the default nondative. In (38b), there is also one single direct function, which, being the expression of the external argument, cannot be assigned dative case, and so is also nondative.

(38) a.

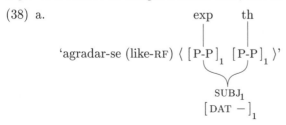

b.

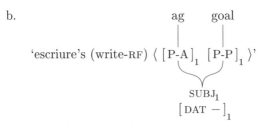

If the subject of these predicates is a pronoun interpreted as a bound variable, necessary for the "wide scope" reading of the reciprocal, the interpretation procedure in (29) requires the bound variable to fill the more prominent argument that the pronoun is linked to, that is, the logical subject in both (38a) and (38b). In order to obtain a reciprocal interpretation, the other (less prominent) bound argument must be filled in by a distinct variable. Thus, we account for why inversion verbs do not yield the "inverted" reading (35c) when reciprocalized; instead, they yield the "noninverted" reading (35b), paralleling the behavior of reciprocalized noninverted verbs, which yield (37b), but not (37c).

The facts of reciprocalized inversion verbs would not be adequately accounted for if the reflexive clitic were assumed to be (or bind) a syntactic anaphor in object position. This assumption would derive the right interpretations for the noninversion verb, since the reflexive clitic would be assumed to be (or bind) the dative object, which, as an anaphor, would be bound by the subject external argument. If the pronominal subject is interpreted as a bound variable in an example like (36), the anaphoric object, in order to give the reciprocal interpretation, is interpreted as a distinct variable, accounting for the readings in (37). Things are different with the inversion verb: if the syntactic anaphor (realized as or bound by the reflexive clitic) is the dative object here too, taking the subject as its antecedent, it will be the experiencer argument (the dative object) that will be referentially dependent on the theme argument (the subject). This assumes the phrase structure given in (39a).[15] Thus, if the pronominal subject is interpreted as a bound variable, it will be the theme that is interpreted as a variable identical to that of its antecedent, while the experiencer is interpreted as a distinct variable, incorrectly yielding the "inverted" reading in (35c), instead of the good reading in (35b).

---

[15]If one were to adopt the Belletti and Rizzi's 1988 analysis of "psych"-verbs, the structure in (39a) would be the s-structure that results from moving the theme argument from its d-structure position as sister of V to the subject position at s-structure. This derived structure would satisfy the binding requirements of the anaphor in the dative object position.

(39) a.

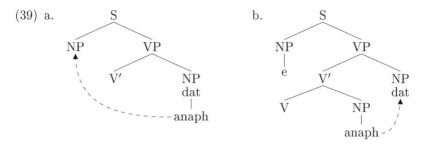

b.

Alternatively, adopting the structure proposed in Belletti and Rizzi 1988 for "psych"-verbs and assuming that anaphors can be bound at d-structure, the theme would be the syntactic anaphor taking the experiencer as its antecedent, as shown in the structure in (39b). While this would give the right readings, it incorrectly predicts that the experiencer, being assigned "inherent" dative case (according to Belletti and Rizzi 1988), should be realized as a dative object, and not as a subject, as it actually is. As we see in (39b), the only nonanaphoric NP is the dative object.

In sum, the interpretations of reciprocalized inversion verbs in Catalan constitute further evidence for treating the reflexive clitic in Catalan as an a-structure binding morpheme, a morpheme that performs an operation on a-structure, rather than as a syntactic anaphor (or the morphology that licenses a syntactic anaphor), as has been predominantly assumed.

7.5 Discussion

The facts presented in this chapter provide additional support for the theory of a-structure binding proposed here, and prove to be particularly problematic for the pronominal approach to the reflexive clitic proposed in Rizzi 1986b, Moore 1991, and Fontana and Moore 1992, among others. The evidence involving elliptical constructions reveals the need to distinguish anaphoric binding (involving syntactic anaphors such as English *himself*) from a-structure binding at all syntactic levels of representation (c-, f- and a-structure). To assume that a structure with the reflexive clitic contains a syntactic anaphor and merely differs from a structure with an overt syntactic anaphor such as *himself* in the morphological or phonological properties of the anaphor (morphologically dependent vs. independent, or phonologically null vs. overt) loses the possibility of accounting for the contrast between the two brought out in elliptical constructions. Section 7.1 illustrates this contrast comparing the English syntactic anaphors and the Catalan reflexive clitic, and section 7.2, arguing that the reflexive clitic in Catalan functions as a marker of coreference when cooccurring with a syntactic anaphor, shows that, in Catalan, structures with a syntactic anaphor contrast with structures involving a-structure binding in just the expected way.

The facts discussed in section 7.3 involving syntactic anaphors in causative constructions support an argument structure approach not only to reflexive cliticization, but also to causative constructions in Romance. The standard GB analysis of causative constructions assumes that the embedded predicate projects its arguments in the syntax (at d-structure) in the same way as it does in a main clause. According to this analysis, then, the causee is in many cases a subject in the syntax. This analysis is required by the pronominal approach to the reflexive clitic: since this approach proposes that the reflexive clitic (or the empty object that it binds) must be bound by a subject in its governing category, and the reflexive clitic can appear attached to the verb embedded in the causative construction expressing a binding relation between the causee and another argument of the embedded predicate, the causee must be a subject in order to license the reflexive clitic. However, the assumption that the causee is a subject is very difficult to reconcile with the evidence in 7.3 that shows that the causee can be expressed as a syntactic anaphor that takes a thematically lower argument as its antecedent. In the standard GB analysis of causatives, the causee would be a subject and the thematically lower argument an object; having the former be bound by the latter is a clear violation of the Binding Theory of GB.

In an argument structure approach to causatives, such as the one outlined here, the anaphoric dependency of the causee on a thematically lower argument is not a problem because the causee is not a subject, as argued in chapter 6 of this study and Alsina 1992b, 1993, among others. The causee, as a dative object, takes an antecedent that is more prominent in the GF hierarchy, such as an accusative object.

Section 7.4 explores the range of reciprocal interpretations with reflexivized verbs, focusing on inversion verbs. The facts reveal an asymmetry in the interpretation of the bound arguments in reciprocal constructions. The a-structure binding analysis of the reflexive clitic, which is the marker of reciprocity, predicts that this asymmetry should be captured at the level of a-structure. The range of readings with reciprocalized inversion verbs indicates that this asymmetry must indeed be captured at the level of a-structure. Treating the reflexive clitic as a syntactic anaphor would not allow us to capture this asymmetry at this level, and would lead to incorrect results.

8

Conclusions

Many current syntactic theories assume that each predicate has a syntactic representation that constrains its complement-taking abilities and that is invariant across the various uses and morphologically related forms of the predicate. This is what we can refer to as the argument structure. However, not all theories that make this assumption agree as to the nature of that representation and its relation to other syntactic representations. There are two competing views in current linguistic theory with respect to the representation of argument structure and its relation to other levels of representation (or types of information): on the one hand, the view that proposes to represent argument structure as a phrase structure that is related to other syntactic levels also represented as phrase structures; and, on the other hand, the view that proposes to represent argument structure as a structure formally distinct from other syntactic structures related to them by correspondence principles. After showing what the consequences of assuming the former view are, I will proceed to recapitulate the evidence presented in this study that argues against those consequences and supports the alternative view of argument structure.

8.1 The CURT, the PEAR, and the 1-1 Match

A very prevalent position within the GB framework assumes that all syntactic information has to be encoded in the form of a phrase structure representation. Consequently, as the argument structure expresses syntactic information, it follows within that approach that it must be encoded in phrase structure terms. Since the arguments of a predicate have alternative morphosyntactic realizations (as in basic vs. passive vs. causative vs. reflexivized forms of the predicate), the phrase structure representation of the argument structure may be considerably removed from the representation of the morphosyntactic expression of arguments.

Thus, it is assumed by most GB practitioners that d-structure is the syntactic representation of argument structure. Through movement transformations and other principles of the theory, the phrase structure configurations of arguments at d-structure are mapped onto their surface forms also encoded in phrase structure terms.

The idea that argument structure is represented in phrase structure terms at d-structure has a number of important consequences, which can be summarized as the following three:

I. Each predicate projects a uniform d-structure; in other words, each argument of a predicate has a constant d-structure representation: the hypothesis of the *Configurationally Uniform Representation of Theta-roles* or *CURT*.

II. Properties of arguments, such as their prominence relations and the argument type, are encoded as phrase structure configurations: the *Phrase-structure Encoding of Argument Relations* or *PEAR*.

III. There is a one-to-one correspondence between arguments and syntactic constituents that bear a θ-role at d-structure; in other words, a given syntactic constituent cannot correspond to more than one argument of a predicate, and vice versa: the *1-1 match*.

These consequences arise because the d-structure is required to fulfil the main functions of the argument structure: being the invariant representation of predicates underlying their alternative surface realizations (consequence I), specifying the *prominence* and *type* of the arguments (consequence II), and specifying the *number* of arguments of a predicate (consequence III). By "type" I refer to the distinctions between direct and indirect arguments, generally represented at d-structure as the distinction between NP arguments and PP arguments, and between external and internal arguments, generally represented at d-structure as subject and objects respectively. So, if an argument is assumed to be an internal argument, it will be represented as an object at d-structure (an NP sister of V or, in some cases, V′ depending on particular theories); and if an argument is assumed to be an external argument, it will be represented as a subject at d-structure (an NP external to the VP or in the specifier of VP, also depending on particular theories).

The CURT is a necessary consequence of the assumption that d-structure represents argument structure and that the argument structure of a predicate must be largely invariant for the various uses of the predicate. For example, if a verb like *defend* is assumed to take two arguments, these two arguments are assigned to specific configurations at d-structure and are assigned always to the same d-structure positions. In addition, these positions are significant inasmuch as they identify one of the arguments as the external argument and the other as an internal argument, as required by the PEAR, which relies only on phrase structure to represent different types of arguments and their relative prominence. Thus, a verb like *defend* is assumed to project always a d-structure in which the internal argument is encoded as an object and the external argument is encoded as a subject if at all. (There is currently a debate within GB as to whether the external argument is syntactically realized or not in passive forms; it nevertheless is commonly accepted that, when the external argument is syntactically realized, it is realized as a subject.) By the CURT, this d-structure is posited even in cases, such as passive forms, where the internal argument does not appear morphosyntactically realized as an object, but as a subject. The assumption that the subject of the passive form of *defend* is an internal argument is expressed by the PEAR by having this argument represented as a d-structure object. Thus, if an argument manifests properties attributed to internal arguments, it will have to be represented as an object, at least at d-structure; likewise, if an argument manifests properties characteristic of external arguments, it will be encoded as a d-structure subject.

The 1-1 match, the one-to-one correspondence of arguments and θ-role bearing syntactic constituents, arises as follows. If d-structure is the syntactic representation of argument structure, the number of arguments must be the same as the number of θ-role bearing syntactic constituents at d-structure. A mismatch between the number of arguments and the number of syntactic constituents that express these arguments cannot arise because, given that conception of argument structure, an argument *is* (or is defined as) a syntactic constituent that bears a θ-role. The idea of a single syntactic constituent corresponding to two different arguments is a conceptual impossibility in that approach because arguments are represented by syntactic constituents: if there is only one syntactic constituent, it cannot correspond to more that one argument.

8.2   For an Autonomous Argument Structure

In this study I have argued for and motivated a notably different conception of argument structure, one in which argument structure is not represented in phrase structure terms, but is represented as an information structure formally and conceptually distinct from those structures that encode information about surface grammatical functions and the surface arrangement of syntactic constituents. The argument structure in this conception is related to the levels of structure that it interfaces with by principles of correspondence. In order to implement this conception of argument structure and its relation to other levels of syntactic structure,

I have adopted the general framework of LFG, which posits the existence of several formally distinct simultaneous levels of representation related by principles of correspondence. The evidence presented in this study supports the conception of the autonomy of argument structure, the view that argument structure (a-structure) is a level of representation that encodes information distinct from and nonisomorphic with that of any other level or representation. In particular, as a level of representation that constrains the syntax, it is distinct from syntactic levels of representation that encode information about syntactic category, dominance relations, and linear precedence (c-structure) or about syntactic function, agreement relations, case, etc. (f-structure). The various case studies examined here constitute evidence for the autonomy of argument structure and against the phrase structure representation of argument structure characteristic of GB.

Reflexivized Constructions The facts of the Romance reflexive clitic provide direct evidence against the CURT, the PEAR, and the 1-1 match, the main consequences of the assumption that argument structure is represented in phrase structure. The analysis of these facts in terms of the theory of a-structure binding highlights the autonomy of a-structure since a-structure binding entails a mismatch between arguments (the units at a-structure) and their morphosyntactic expressions (represented at f-structure and c-structure). Through a-structure binding, two arguments, which are bound, map onto the same syntactic function, and, therefore, to the same morphosyntactic expression. Thus, instead of having one syntactic function corresponding to every argument of a predicate, a-structure binding implies that it is possible for one single syntactic function to correspond to two different arguments. In addition, since it is important to identify a given syntactic function as an internal or an external argument in order to determine certain of its syntactic properties, the conclusion that a particular syntactic function may be at the same time an external argument and an internal argument indicates that it is impossible to represent these notions as distinct phrase structure configurations, contrary to what is held by the PEAR. We are also led to reject the 1-1 match, since the number of arguments and the number of argument bearing syntactic constituents needn't match, and the CURT, since it does not seem possible to posit an invariant phrase structure encoding of the argument structure.

The 1-1 match has often been enforced even in theories that don't assume that the argument structure should be encoded in phrase structure, but assume instead the autonomy of argument structure. Many versions of LFG, for example, adopt Function-Argument Biuniqueness, proposed by Bresnan (1982a), according to which one argument cannot be assigned to more than one syntactic function, and one syntactic function cannot be assigned more than one argument, which has the effect of enforcing the 1-1 match. This principle is similar in spirit to the Theta-Criterion of Chomsky 1981 within GB. While it might appear that in order to abandon the 1-1 match, as the facts of the Romance reflexivized construction require, all that is necessary is to eliminate or replace Function-Argument Biuniqueness in LFG and the Theta-Criterion in GB, abandoning the 1-1 match has entirely different consequences in the two frameworks. In LFG, eliminating Function-Argument Biuniqueness, making it possible to have two arguments mapped onto the same syntactic function, has no major consequence for the theory, except for allowing a situation required by empirical evidence. In GB, on the other hand, abandoning the 1-1 match entails not only eliminating or restating the Theta-Criterion, but also giving up the idea that the argument structure can be encoded in phrase structure terms: one of the major functions of the argument structure is expressing the number of arguments that a predicate takes; if this information cannot be expressed in phrase structure terms, then clearly the phrase structure cannot be used to encode the argument structure.

Allowing a many-to-one correspondence between arguments and syntactic functions raises no problem in the present theory because of the simultaneous accessibility of the two levels of representation in which arguments and syntactic functions are encoded (a-structure and f-structure respectively). Given this design feature of the theory, a situation in which a syntactic function maps onto only one argument is distinguished from a situation in which the same syntactic function maps onto two arguments. Because notions such as internal argument and external argument are represented at a-structure, it is possible to tell, for example, whether a given syntactic function is (mapped onto) an internal argument or not, regardless of whether it is a subject or an object. Consider a dyadic predicate such as *defensar* 'defend', which has an external argument and an internal argument: in its nonreflexivized form, its subject does not map onto the internal argument, but only onto the external argument, as the internal argument maps onto the object; but in its reflexivized form, the subject does map onto the internal argument, as well as onto the external argument, and there is no object corresponding to the internal argument.

For most versions of GB, on the other hand, allowing a many-to-one correspondence between θ-roles and syntactic positions raises important difficulties, as it is inconsistent with the assumption common in GB that the argument structure is represented in phrase structure terms at d-structure. Not only would the phrase structure not represent the *number* of arguments of the predicate, as required by the 1-1 match, but it would not be able to represent the *prominence* and *type* of the arguments, as required by the PEAR. If structures such as (1) were allowed (as I claim must be allowed, since (1) is merely the phrase structure representation of a reflexivized construction corresponding to (4.7)), neither the number nor the prominence and type of the arguments would be represented.

(1)

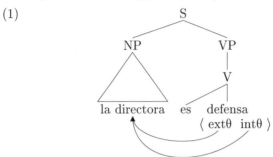

For example, we need to be able to tell that the subject NP in (1) is an internal argument, although it is not represented as an object at d-structure or any other level, as required by the PEAR. Therefore, we cannnot tell simply by inspecting the structure in (1) that the subject is an internal argument (as well as an external argument). This requires abandoning the standard view in GB that a-structure has the function of constraining or determining the syntactic representation at d-structure and plays no other role in the syntax. We have to assume that notions such as external and internal argument are represented at a-structure and that a-structure is a level of representation autonomous from other syntactic levels of representation and parallel to them.

Another important consequence for GB that the facts of the Romance reflexivized construction lead us to is the abandonment of the CURT, the conception that each θ-role of a predicate is assigned to a uniform position in the phrase structure. (A strong version of this idea is stated as the "Uniformity of Theta Assignment Hypothesis," or UTAH, of Baker 1988a.) As we see comparing a structure like (1) with one in which the nonreflexivized form of the same verb is used, the patient or theme internal θ-role of the verb is assigned in one case to a subject position and in the other case to the object position. Abandoning the hypothesis of the configurationally uniform representation of θ-roles would have major consequences in GB. For example, there would no longer be a principled motivation for the transformational treatment of passive: if an internal θ-role can be assigned to subject position, as in (1), then there is no reason to assume that, in a passive form, the internal θ-role is assigned to an object, which subsequently becomes a subject. The analysis of the Romance reflexive presented here has shown that an internal θ-role must be assigned to the subject position (together with the external θ-role) when the verb combines with an a-structure binding morpheme. If the theory allows the internal θ-role to be assigned to the subject position, it is unclear what would prevent this when the verb combines with the passive morpheme.

The conclusion that the phrase structure cannot adequately encode the argument structure has far-reaching consequences for prevalent conceptions of the syntax-semantics interface in GB. In GB it is crucial for θ-roles to be encoded in a uniform way in phrase structure in order to allow the LF (Logical Form) component to interpret the θ-role information correctly; if this encoding cannot be uniform, problems will arise with the semantic interpretation. If an internal θ-role (in an a-structure binding construction) is not assigned to the object position, but to the subject position, as argued in this study, the LF component will not be able to tell whether that θ-role has been assigned.

Case Marking The analysis of morphological case and case marking in Romance proposed in this study also raises problems for the idea that argument structure is represented in phrase structure, in particular, for the PEAR. It is argued that in some instances whether an object is assigned dative or accusative case can be determined on the basis of the semantics—goal objects are assigned dative case. However, it is also shown that this semantic basis for the assignment of case does not provide a complete account of the distribution of case features on objects. The proposal advanced here relates the assignment of dative case to the relative prominence at a-structure of the objects involved: the more prominent of two direct functions that is not the external argument is assigned dative case. One could think of recasting a-structure prominence in phrase structure in such a way that more prominent arguments asymmetrically c-command less prominent arguments. This means that a goal, experiencer or beneficiary object would asymmetrically c-command a theme or patient object, just like a subject asymmetrically c-commands an object. We, thus, might be able to capture the difference in case assignment between two object arguments by appealing to this asymmetry in their phrase structure configuration. Now, the notion of c-command is referred to by other principles of grammar, in particular, those that concern the binding theory. When we consider phenomena involving binding, we find that the assumption that the dative object asymmetrically c-commands the accusative object leads to incorrect predictions. We would expect that a dative object should be able to antecede an anaphoric accusative object, and not the other way around, but what we find is that the accusative object may be the antecedent, not the dative object. Example (2) (=(7.21)) illustrates this point.

(2) { Els   /*Els hi } he   presentat a si mateixos/l'un a l'altre.
     them ACC / DAT   I have introduced themselves   each other

     'I have introduced them to themselves/each other.'

This example shows that anaphoric binding would require the accusative object to be more prominent than the dative object. Quantifier binding, on the other hand, would require both kinds of objects to be equally prominent, since either one can bind the other, as we see in (3). In (3a), the pronominal in the accusative object is bound by the quantified dative object *a cada sol·licitant*, whereas, in (3b), the pronominal in the dative object is bound by the quantified accusative object *cada carta*.

(3) a. Vaig enviar el seu$_i$ certificat a cada sol·licitant$_i$.
         I PAST send his$_i$ certificate to every applicant$_i$

         'I sent every applicant his certificate.'

     b. Vaig enviar   cada carta$_i$ al seu$_i$ destinatari.
         'I (PAST) sent every letter$_i$ to its$_i$ addressee.'

In a quantifier binding relation between a dative and an accusative object, we would expect that only the former could be the binder, if prominence relations among arguments were expressed solely in terms of c-command, as a dative object would be assumed to asymmetrically c-command an accusative object. Thus, we would incorrectly predict an example like (3b) to be ungrammatical.[1]

What this shows is that a-structure prominence cannot be represented as the same kind of prominence relations that are needed to account for anaphoric binding phenomena. We need two different prominence scales for arguments, as has been argued at various points in this study, one determined by the hierarchical ordering of arguments at a-

---

[1] It would not improve the situation to assume that the accusative object asymmetrically c-commands the dative object, because we would leave an example like (3a) unaccounted for. Furthermore, that would make it impossible to account for case assignment in causative constructions by a general principle of case assignment. The causee of a transitive base verb, which is marked with dative case, is standardly assumed in GB to asymmetrically c-command all other arguments of the base verb. Thus, we would not be able to account for case assignment in both causative and non causative constructions by appealing to prominence among arguments. In addition, as has been shown in chapter 6, the dative causee behaves like any dative object with respect to quantifier binding, that is, it can be bound by a quantified accusative object.

structure and the other determined by a hierarchy of syntactic functions, in which subjects are most prominent, objects are more prominent than obliques, and nondative objects are more prominent than dative objects. Neither of the two prominence scales can be reduced to the other and each is relevant for different phenomena. Thus, the a-structure prominence is relevant for case assignment. The f-structure prominence is relevant for binding of anaphors, since an anaphor must be bound by a more prominent argument according to the GF hierarchy. This accounts for the fact illustrated in (2) that a dative object may not bind an accusative object, even though the former is the more prominent argument at a-structure. Quantifier binding is sensitive to both kinds of prominence: a pronoun may be a variable bound by a quantified argument that is more prominent either at a-structure or at f-structure than the argument that contains the bound variable. Thus, when we get a mismatch between the two prominence scales, as with dative and accusative objects in Romance, we predict the possibility of alternative binding relations: the dative object is the more prominent argument at a-structure and therefore qualifies as a binder; the accusative object is the more prominent argument at f-structure and therefore also qualifies as a binder. For this reason, we have the two binding relations illustrated in (3). This constitutes clear evidence against the PEAR, the attempt to define argument structure relations in phrase structure.

Causative Constructions The facts of causative constructions in Romance can be seen as providing persuasive evidence against the CURT and the PEAR. The assumption of these two hypotheses, namely, that each predicate has a uniform phrase structure representation of its argument structure and that this representation encodes significant properties of arguments, leads to the conclusion that a particular argument of a predicate that is analyzed in some cases as an external argument and, therefore, as a d-structure subject must always be realized in this way, unless it can be argued not to be syntactically realized at all, as in passive forms. The effect of this in the analysis of causative constructions is that a predicate that is analyzed as taking an external argument in noncausative constructions must be assumed to have its logical subject (the causee) realized as a subject also in causative constructions.[2] Thus, what looks in all respects like an object is being analyzed as a subject. As pointed out in chapter 6, the problem with this analysis is not only

---

[2]Note that there may be some mechanism that allows the logical subject role of the base predicate not to be assigned to any syntactic position. It is commonly assumed that, when the causee is realized as an oblique (a *per*-phrase in Catalan), it is not a subject at any level of representation, because it is not an argument, but some kind of adjunct.

that the causee behaves in no way like a subject, but that analyzing it as a subject makes incorrect predictions in several respects. The analysis of the causee as a subject wrongly predicts that the causee should be able to launch floating quantifiers, like other subjects, and that it should not be able to be bound by a quantified object, just like subjects in general, as demonstrated in 6.3. This analysis also predicts that it should be able to function as an antecedent of an anaphoric object and that it should not be able to take an object as an antecedent; the facts discussed in section 7.3 indicate that the opposite is true.

These facts lead us to analyze the object causee not as a subject, but as an object, rejecting the CURT and the PEAR. In spite of the fact that the logical subject of *llegir* 'read' is analyzed as an external argument and a subject in the noncausative sentence (4a) (=(6.6a)), it is not analyzed as a subject, but as an object, in the causative sentence (4b) (=(6.6b)). This shows that linguistic theory has to accept the conclusion that the same θ-role (or argument) can be assigned to different positions in the phrase structure, as shown in (5)

(4) a. El nen   llegeix   un poema.
        'The boy is reading a poem.'

    b. El mestre   fa   llegir un poema al nen.
        the teacher makes read a poem   to-the boy

        'The teacher is making the boy read a poem.'

(5) a.

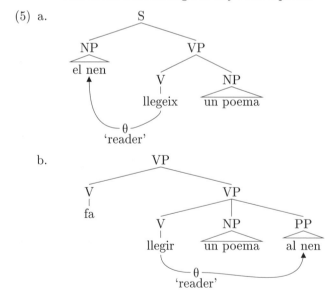

    b.

For example, in the noncausative construction (4a), the agent or 'reader' θ-role would be assigned to the subject position, as in (5a), whereas in the causative construction (4b), the same θ-role would be assigned to an object position, as in (5b). (For convenience, I use an extremely simplified phrase structure for these representations, in which the subject position is the NP sister of VP and both the accusative and dative objects are represented as sisters of V. The observation that the same θ-role is assigned to two distinct phrase structure configurations applies just as well if we assume that the subject position is the sister of I′ or the specifier of VP or any other position.)

Accepting the conclusion that the same θ-role can be assigned to two entirely distinct phrase structure configurations, as illustrated for the 'reader' or agent θ-role of *llegir*, implies rejecting the CURT and the PEAR, and, consequently, the assumption that argument structure can be represented in phrase structure. If each θ-role of a predicate does not have a configurationally uniform representation, contra the CURT, but has various possible phrase structure representations, it follows that the phrase structure cannot fulfil the function of providing an invariant representation that underlies the alternative syntactic manifestations of each predicate. The alternative assignments of the 'reader' θ-role to phrase structure positions in (5) show that the phrase structure fails to represent the relevant argument relations, which is required by the PEAR: the 'reader' θ-role is the logical subject of the predicate, a direct argument and not an internal argument, but this information is not captured in the causative structure (5b), where that θ-role is assigned to the same position as an internal argument that is not a logical subject can be assigned to. Thus, another crucial function of the argument structure cannot be captured in phrase structure terms.

8.3 Autonomous Levels of Representation

The facts just reviewed constitute strong support for the position proposed in this study according to which the argument structure is an autonomous level of representation that constrains other levels of representation by correspondence principles. By formalizing the a-structure in a vocabulary distinct from that used for encoding grammatical functions and surface constituency, the a-structure can fulfil the various functions that it is assumed to have: providing an invariant representation of the arguments of each predicate, expressing syntactically significant relations and distinctions among the arguments of a predicate, and denoting the number of arguments of a predicate. The a-structure is the interface of the two main modules of the grammar, namely, the lexicon and the syntax. In this respect, the a-structure is both a lexical and a syntactic level or representation, in that it constitutes the information that lexical items bring into the syntax to determine the syntactic functions they may be associated with.

On the lexical side, the a-structure is in a correspondence relation with what is known as the Lexical Conceptual Structure or LCS (see Jackendoff 1990), whose representations allow the definition of thematic roles. The correspondence between the LCS and the a-structure is mediated by the thematic hierarchy (see Grimshaw 1990), which imposes an ordering on the units of the a-structure according to the thematic role that they bear at LCS, and the assignment of P-Role specifications to those units on the basis of their semantic entailments (adapting Dowty 1991). On the syntactic side, the a-structure interfaces with the level of representation that encodes syntactic functions, that is, the f-structure. The a-structure information is not stated in terms of syntactic functions (such as subject or object, or even a featural decomposition of such functions), although it directly constrains the assignment of syntactic functions to arguments. Arguments (in the a-structure) are put into correspondence with syntactic functions (in the f-structure) by the Functional Mapping Theory or FMT. Syntactic functions, in turn, are the grammatical categories that mediate the correspondences between arguments and overt morphosyntactic expressions; the latter are represented in the c-structure. Syntactic functions, which are autonomous in that they are not defined in terms of other categories of the theory, such as phrase structure categories, have their correspondence with the latter constrained by principles of function-category association. The overall picture of the theory that emerges from this factorization of information into autonomous levels of representation can be schematized as in (6).

(6)   LEXICON | SYNTAX

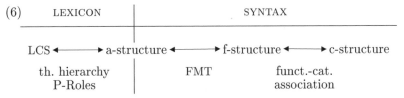

An important feature of this proposal is that it allows us to account for syntactic function alternations without assuming changes in the assignment of syntactic functions to arguments. This is possible, on the one hand, because arguments do not specify syntactic function information, and, on the other hand, because the principles of the FMT may refer to underspecified syntactic functions. Since the association between arguments and syntactic functions is not pre-specified (i.e., is not lexically specified for each argument), it is possible for the same argument to map alternatively to one syntactic function and to another. One of the ways in which alternations in the assignment of syntactic functions to arguments arise is through predicate composition, the operation by which the a-structures of two predicates combine into one. Derived predicates, such as passivized, causativized, or reflexivized predicates, are analyzed as the result of composing a base or complete predicate with the appropriate incomplete predicate. The FMT applies to a derived predicate in the same way as it does to the corresponding base predicate; however, since the a-structures of the two predicates are different, the syntactic functions assigned to a particular argument in the two cases may be different.

The assumption that syntactic functions are not only autonomous from both arguments and phrase structure information, but are decomposed into features that group them into natural classes of syntactic functions (direct vs. oblique functions, and subject vs. nonsubjects) is another important element in the analysis of syntactic function alternations. This featural decomposition enables one of the mapping principles to refer to an underspecified syntactic function, a direct function unspecified as to whether it is a subject or not. The various principles of the FMT will allow or require this direct function to be specified in one way or the other depending on the a-structure involved. This assumption, in particular, the assumption that an internal argument is mapped onto a direct function plays a crucial role in the alternation that typically affects an internal argument in an active/passive pair: whether the internal argument is mapped onto an object, as in the active form, or onto a subject, as is generally the case in the passive form, depends on other principles of the theory, such as the Subject Condition. The same idea accounts for the syntactic difference between a reflexivized predicate and its nonreflexivized counterpart. The syntactic functions assigned to an external argument and to an internal argument are nondistinct: the external argument is assigned to the subject function, which is a direct function ([obl−, subj+]), and the internal argument is assigned to a direct function that is unspecified for the subject feature ([obl−]). Since the mapping constraints imposed on the internal argument are a (proper) subset of those imposed on the external argument, the two sets of constraints can be combined so that the syntactic function assigned to both arguments is the same—a subject. This is the situation we find in a-structure binding constructions, which argues for having syntactic functions (not defined in terms of phrase structure) mediate the correspondence of arguments with morphosyntactic expressions and for having subjects and objects grouped as a natural class of syntactic functions—direct functions. The c-structure (or morphosyntactic) representation of an argument is constrained by the syntactic function of the argument, whether it is a direct or an indirect function, and, if direct, whether it is further specified as a subject or a nonsubject.

The modular conception of the theory schematized in (6) suggests that not all levels of structure have direct access to the information at all other levels of structure, in other words, that there is some degree of compartmentalization. The picture in (6) suggests that, while there is a close interaction between the LCS and a-structure, between a-structure and f-structure, and between f-structure and c-structure, there should not be any direct interaction between any other pair of structures in (6).

Consider first the possibility of interaction between the LCS and f- or c-structure. The idea that a-structure is the interface between lexical semantics and syntax implies the hypothesis that whatever lexical semantic information is relevant for the syntax has to be encoded in a-structure; lexical semantic information that has no translation in a-structure terms is hypothesized to be inaccessible to syntax, unless it is mediated by morphology, as stated in 2.2.1. Determining what information is represented in a-structure is important because that is the information that the syntax (i.e., syntactic principles not signalled by morphology) may refer to and is constrained by. The present study has formulated a precise and restrictive hypothesis as to the kind of information that the a-structure contains. For example, as in Grimshaw 1990, it is proposed that a-structure contains no information about thematic roles; this proposal, combined with the hypothesis that the other syntactic levels have no direct access to the LCS, entails that the syntax cannot make reference to thematic roles. Whether this conclusion is correct still needs to be proved by showing that syntactic phenomena that have been claimed to be sensitive to thematic roles can be analyzed (or are best analyzed) without allowing the syntax to refer to thematic roles. There is empirical evidence supporting this conclusion (for example, in Alsina 1993).

The schema in (6) also suggests that there should not be direct interaction between a-structure and c-structure, in other words, that a-structure constrains the representation of f-structure, which in turn constrains the c-structure, but a-structure and c-structure do not directly constrain each other. However, although the principles that constrain the c-structure (such as the principles of function-category association) generally refer to the syntactic function of a constituent rather than to its status in the a-structure, the possibility that the a-structure may directly constrain the c-structure or viceversa cannot be excluded. In fact, this study presents an instance in which the c-structure constrains the a-structure: in causative constructions (and other complex predicates) in Romance, two c-structure nodes jointly determine the representation at a-structure throught predicate composition. Other instances of direct interaction between a-structure and c-structure would include word order facts that are constrained by the hierarchical ranking of arguments at a-structure (as in Kiparsky 1987, Alsina 1994a, 1994b, among others). Nevertheless, the formal representation of a-structure within the theory presented here does not rule out such interactions. The assumption that a-structure is part of f-structure as the value of the feature PRED, together with the assumption that the c-structure may refer to features of the f-structure, implies that the c-structure may access information in the a-structure. The precise extent of this interaction is yet to be determined. It is to be hoped that future research will shed further light on the types of interactions that exist among the various modules or levels of representation in the model in (6).

Bibliography

Ackerman, Farrell. 1992. On the Domain of Lexical Rules: Hungarian Causatives and Wordhood. In *Approaches to Hungarian, Vol. 4: The Structure of Hungarian*, ed. István Kenesei and Csaba Pléh, 9–35. Szeged: JATE.

Aissen, Judith. 1979. *The Syntax of Causative Constructions*. New York: Garland. [1974 Harvard University dissertation.]

Alsina, Alex. 1992a. On the Argument Structure of Causatives. *Linguistic Inquiry* 23:517–555.

————. 1992b. The Monoclausality of Causative Constructions in Romance. Ms., Stanford University, Stanford, Calif.

————. 1993. Predicate Composition: A Theory of Syntactic Function Alternations. Doctoral dissertation, Stanford University, Stanford, Calif.

————. 1994a. Bantu Multiple Objects: Analyses and Fallacies. *Linguistic Analysis* 24:153–174.

————. 1994b. Passive Types and the Theory of Object Asymmetries. *Natural Language and Linguistic Theory*, to appear.

————. 1995. A Theory of Complex Predicates: Evidence from Causatives in Bantu and Romance. In *Complex Predicates*, ed. Alex Alsina, Joan Bresnan, and Peter Sells, to appear. Stanford, Calif.: CSLI Publications.

————. To appear. Where's the Mirror Principle?. In *Levels, Principles and Processes: The Structure of Grammatical Representations*, ed. Wynn Chao and Geoffrey Horrocks. De Gruyter.

Alsina, Alex, and Sam A. Mchombo. 1991. Object Extraction and the Accessibility of Thematic Information. In *Proceedings of the Seventeenth Annual Meeting of the Berkeley Linguistics Society*, 15–29. Berkeley Linguistics Society, Berkeley, Calif.

————. 1993. Object Asymmetries and the Chicheŵa Applicative Construction. In *Theoretical Aspects of Bantu Grammar*, ed. Sam A. Mchombo, 17–45. Stanford, Calif.: CSLI Publications.

Andrews, Avery. 1985. The Major Functions of the Noun Phrase. In *Language Typology and Syntactic Description. Volume 1: Clause Structure*, ed. Timothy Shopen, 62–154. Cambridge: Cambridge University Press.

————. 1990. Unification and Morphological Blocking. *Natural Language and Linguistic Theory* 8:507–557.

Aoun, Joseph. 1985. *A Grammar of Anaphora*. Cambridge, Mass.: MIT Press.

Baker, Mark. 1983. Objects, Themes, and Lexical Rules in Italian. In *Papers in Lexical-Functional Grammar*, ed. Lorraine Levin, Malka Rappaport, and Annie Zaenen, 1–45. Bloomington, In.: Indiana University Linguistics Club.

————. 1985. The Mirror Principle and Morphosyntactic Explanation. *Linguistic Inquiry* 16:373–416.

————. 1988a. *Incorporation: A Theory of Grammatical Function Changing*. Chicago: University of Chicago Press.

————. 1988b. Theta Theory and the Syntax of Applicatives in Chicheŵa. *Natural Language and Linguistic Theory* 6:353–389.

Baker, Mark, Kyle Johnson, and Ian Roberts. 1989. Passive Arguments Raised. *Linguistic Inquiry* 20:219–251.

Belletti, Adriana. 1988. The Case of Unaccusatives. *Linguistic Inquiry* 19:1–34.

————. 1990. *Generalized Verb Movement: Aspects of Verb Syntax*. Torino: Rosenberg & Sellier.

Belletti, Adriana, and Luigi Rizzi. 1981. The Syntax of *ne*: Some Theoretical Implications. *The Linguistic Review* 1:117–154.

————. 1988. Psych-Verbs and θ-Theory. *Natural Language and Linguistic Theory* 6:291–352.

Bennis, Hans. 1986. *Gaps and Dummies*. Dordrecht: Foris.

Bordelois, Ivonne. 1988. Causatives: From Lexicon to Syntax. *Natural Language and Linguistic Theory* 6:57–93.

Brame, Michael. 1976. *Conjectures and Refutations in Syntax and Semantics*. New York and Amsterdam: Elsevier North Holland.

Bresnan, Joan. 1976. Nonarguments for Raising. *Linguistic Inquiry* 7: 485–501.

————. 1978. A Realistic Transformational Grammar. In *Linguistic Theory and Psychological Reality*, ed. Morris Halle, Joan Bresnan, and

George A. Miller, 1–59. Cambridge, Mass.: MIT Press.

———. 1980. Polyadicity: Part 1 of a Theory of Lexical Rules and Representations. In *Lexical Grammar*, ed. Teun Hoekstra, Harry van der Hulst, and Michael Moortgat, 97–121. Dordrecht: Foris. [Printed with revisions as Polyadicity in *The Mental Representation of Grammatical Relations*, ed. Joan Bresnan, 149–172. Cambridge, Mass.: MIT Press. 1982.]

———. 1982a. Control and Complementation. In *The Mental Representation of Grammatical Relations*, ed. Joan Bresnan, 282–390. Cambridge, Mass.: MIT Press.

———. 1982b. The Passive in Lexical Theory. In *The Mental Representation of Grammatical Relations*, ed. Joan Bresnan, 3–86. Cambridge, Mass.: MIT Press.

———. 1994a. Category Mismatches. Paper presented to the plenary session of the 25th Annual Conference on African Linguistics at Rutgers University on March 26, 1994.

———. 1994b. Linear Order vs. Syntactic Rank: Evidence from Weak Crossover. In *Papers from the Thirtieth Regional Meeting, Chicago Linguistics Society*, to appear. Chicago Linguistics Society, University of Chicago, Chicago, Ill.

———. 1994c. Locative Inversion and the Architecture of Universal Grammar. *Language* 70:72–131.

Bresnan, Joan, Per-Kristian Halvorsen, and Joan Maling. 1985. Logophoricity and Bound Anaphors. Ms., Stanford University, Stanford, Calif.

Bresnan, Joan, and Jonni M. Kanerva. 1989. Locative Inversion in Chicheŵa: A Case Study of Factorization in Grammar. *Linguistic Inquiry* 20:1–50.

———. 1992. The Thematic Hierarchy and Locative Inversion in UG. A reply to Paul Schachter's comments. In *Syntax and Semantics 26: Syntax and the Lexicon*, ed. Eric Wehrli and Tim Stowell, 111–125. San Diego, Calif.: Academic Press.

Bresnan, Joan, Ronald Kaplan, and Peter Peterson. 1986. Coordination and the Flow of Information Through Phrase Structure. Ms., Center for the Study of Language and Information, Stanford University, Stanford, Calif.

Bresnan, Joan, and Sam A. Mchombo. 1987. Topic, Pronoun, and Agreement in Chicheŵa. *Language* 63:741–782.

———. 1995. The Lexical Integrity Principle: Evidence from Bantu. *Natural Language and Linguistic Theory* 13:181–254.

Bresnan, Joan, and Lioba Moshi. 1990. Object Asymmetries in Comparative Bantu Syntax. *Linguistic Inquiry* 21:147–185.

Bresnan, Joan, and Annie Zaenen. 1990. Deep Unaccusativity in LFG. In *Grammatical Relations: A Cross-Theoretical Perspective*, ed. Katarzyna Dziwirek, Patrick Farrell, and Errapel Mejías-Bikandi, 45–57. Stanford, Calif.: CSLI Publications.

Burzio, Luigi. 1986. *Italian Syntax: A Government-Binding Approach.* Dordrecht: Reidel. [Revision of 1981 MIT dissertation.]

Butt, Miriam. 1995. *The Structure of Complex Predicates in Urdu.* Stanford, Calif.: CSLI Publications. [Revision of 1993 Stanford University dissertation.]

Butt, Miriam, and Tracy H. King. 1991. Semantic Case in Urdu. In *Papers from the Twenty-seventh Regional Meeting, Chicago Linguistics Society*, 31–45. Chicago Linguistics Society, University of Chicago, Chicago, Ill.

Centineo, Giulia. 1986. A Lexical Theory of Auxiliary Selection in Italian. *Davis Working Papers in Linguistics* 1:1–35.

Chicerchia, Gennaro. 1989. A Semantics for Unaccusatives and its Syntactic Consequences. Ms., Cornell University, Ithaca, New York.

Chomsky, Noam. 1970. Remarks on Nominalization. In *Readings in English Transformational Grammar*, ed. Roderick A. Jacobs and Peter S. Rosenbaum, 184–221. Waltham, Mass.: Ginn.

———. 1981. *Lectures on Government and Binding.* Dordrecht: Foris.

———. 1982. *Some Concepts and Consequences of the Theory of Government and Binding.* Cambridge, Mass.: MIT Press.

———. 1986. *Knowledge of Language: Its Nature, Origin, and Use.* New York: Praeger.

———. 1993. A Minimalist Program for Linguistic Theory. In *The View from Building 20: Essays in Linguistics in Honor of Sylvain Bromberger*, ed. Samuel J. Keyser and Kenneth Hale, 1–52. Cambridge, Mass.: MIT Press.

Dalrymple, Mary. 1993. *The Syntax of Anaphoric Binding.* Stanford, Calif.: CSLI Publications. [Revision of 1990 Stanford University dissertation.]

Dalrymple, Mary, Sam A. Mchombo, and Stanley Peters. 1994. Semantic Similarities and Syntactic Contrasts Between Chicheŵa and English Reciprocals. *Linguistic Inquiry* 25:145–163.

Davies, William, and Carol Rosen. 1988. Unions as Multi-Predicate Clauses. *Language* 64:52–88.

Demonte, Violeta. 1987. C-Command, Prepositions, and Predication. *Linguistic Inquiry* 18:147–157.

Di Sciullo, Anna-Maria, and Sara T. Rosen. 1990. Light and Semi-Light Verb Constructions. In *Grammatical Relations: A Cross-Theoretical Perspective*, ed. Katarzyna Dziwirek, Patrick Farrell, and Errapel Mejías-Bikandi, 109–125. Stanford, Calif.: CSLI Publications.

Di Sciullo, Anna-Maria, and Edwin Williams. 1987. *On the Definition of Word*. Cambridge, Mass.: MIT Press.

Dowty, David. 1991. Thematic Proto-Roles and Argument Selection. *Language* 67:547–619.

Duranti, Alessandro and Ernest R. Byarushengo. 1977. On the Notion of "Direct Object". In *Haya Grammatical Structure (Southern California Occasional Papers in Linguistics no. 6)*, ed. Ernest R. Byarushengo, Alessandro Duranti, and Larry M. Hyman, 45–71. Los Angeles: University of Southern California Press.

Feldman, Harry. 1978. Passivizing on Datives in Greek. *Linguistic Inquiry* 9:499–502.

Fillmore, Charles. 1968. The Case for Case. In *Universals in Linguistic Theory*, ed. Emmon Bach and Robert Harms, 1–90. New York: Holt, Rinehart and Winston.

Foley, William A., and Robert D. Van Valin. 1984. *Functional Syntax and Universal Grammar*. Cambridge: Cambridge University Press.

Fontana, Josep M., and John Moore. 1992. VP-Internal Subjects and *se*-Reflexivization in Spanish. *Linguistic Inquiry* 23:501–510.

Gibson, Jeanne, and Eduardo Raposo. 1986. Clause Union, the Stratal Uniqueness Law, and the Chômeur Relation. *Natural Language and Linguistic Theory* 4:295–331.

Givón, Talmy. 1984. *Syntax: A Functional-Typological Introduction*. Amsterdam: John Benjamins.

Greenberg, Joseph. 1966. *Language Universals*. The Hague: Mouton.

Grimshaw, Jane. 1982. On the Lexical Representation of Romance Reflexive Clitics. In *The Mental Representation of Grammatical Relations*, ed. Joan Bresnan, 87–148. Cambridge, Mass.: MIT Press.

———. 1986. A Morphosyntactic Explanation for the Mirror Principle. *Linguistic Inquiry* 17:745–749.

———. 1988. Adjuncts and Argument Structure. Lexicon Project Working Paper #21. Cambridge, Mass.: The Center for Cognitive Science, MIT.

———. 1990. *Argument Structure*. Cambridge, Mass.: MIT Press.

Grimshaw, Jane, and Elisabeth Selkirk. 1976. Infinitival Noun Phrases in Italian. Ms., University of Massachusetts, Amherst.

Gruber, Jeffrey S. 1965. Studies in Lexical Relations. Doctoral dissertation, MIT, Cambridge, Mass. [Reprinted in 1976 as part of *Lexical Structures in Syntax and Semantics*. Amsterdam: North-Holland.]

Guasti, Maria Teresa. 1990. The *faire-par* Construction in Romance and in Germanic. In *Proceedings of the West Coast Conference on Formal Linguistics* 9, ed. Aaron L. Halpern, 205–218. Stanford, Calif.:CSLI Publications.

Guéron, Jacqueline. 1985. Inalienable Possession, PRO-Inclusion and Lexical Chains. In *Grammatical Representation*, ed. Jacqueline Guéron, Hans-Georg Obenauer, and Jean-Yves Pollock, 43–86. Dordrecht: Foris.

Halvorsen, Per-Kristian. 1983. Semantics for Lexical-Functional Grammar. *Linguistic Inquiry* 14:567–615.

Heim, Irene, Howard Lasnik, and Robert May. 1991. Reciprocity and Plurality. *Linguistic Inquiry* 22:63–101.

Higginbotham, James. 1980. Reciprocal Interpretation. *Journal of Linguistic Research* 1:97–117.

———. 1985. On Semantics. *Linguistic Inquiry* 16:547–593.

Hoekstra, Teun. 1984. *Transitivity: Grammatical Relations in Government-Binding Theory*. Dordrecht: Foris.

Hyman, Larry M., and Sam A. Mchombo. 1992. Morphotactic Constraints in the Chicheŵa Verb Stem. In *Proceedings of the Eighteenth Annual Meeting of the Berkeley Linguistics Society*, 350–364. Berkeley Linguistics Society, Berkeley, Calif.

Hyman, Larry M., and Karl Zimmer. 1975. Embedded Topic in French. In *Subject and Topic*, ed. Charles N. Li, 191–211. New York: Academic Press.

Isoda, Michio. 1991. The Locality Condition of Argument-Structure Operations. Ms., Wacom Co. Ltd., and CSLI, Stanford University, Stanford, Calif.

Jackendoff, Ray. 1972. *Semantic Interpretation in Generative Grammar*. Cambridge, Mass.: MIT Press.

———. 1987. The Status of Thematic Relations in Linguistic Theory. *Linguistic Inquiry* 18:369–411.

———. 1990. *Semantic Structures*. Cambridge, Mass.: MIT Press.

Jaeggli, Osvaldo. 1982. *Topics in Romance Syntax*. Dordrecht: Foris.

———. 1986a. Passive. *Linguistic Inquiry* 17:587–622.

————. 1986b. Arbitrary Plural Pronominals. *Natural Language and Linguistic Theory* 4:43–76.

Joseph, Brian. 1979. Raising to Oblique in Modern Greek. In *Proceedings of the Fifth Annual Meeting of the Berkeley Linguistics Society*, 114–128. Berkeley Linguistics Society, Berkeley, Calif.

Joshi, Smita. 1989. Logical Subject in Marathi Grammar and the Predicate Argument Structure. In *Proceedings of the West Coast Conference on Formal Linguistics* 8, 207–219. Stanford, Calif.:CSLI Publications.

————. 1993. Selection of Grammatical and Logical Functions in Marathi. Doctoral dissertation, Stanford University, Stanford, Calif.

Kameyama, Megumi. 1984. Subjective/Logophoric Bound Anaphor *zibun*. In *Papers from the Twentieth Regional Meeting, Chicago Linguistics Society*, 228–238. Chicago Linguistics Society, University of Chicago, Chicago, Ill.

————. 1985. Zero Anaphora: The Case of Japanese. Doctoral dissertation, Stanford University, Stanford, Calif.

Kaplan, David. 1971 [1989]. Demonstratives. *Themes from Kaplan*, ed. Joseph Almog, John Perry, and Howard Wettstein, 481–563. New York: Oxford University Press, 1989.

Kaplan, Ronald, and Joan Bresnan. 1982. Lexical-Functional Grammar: A Formal System of Representation. In *The Mental Representation of Grammatical Relations*, ed. Joan Bresnan, 173–281. Cambridge, Mass.: MIT Press.

Kaplan, Ronald, and John T. Maxwell. 1988. Constituent Coordination in Lexical-Functional Grammar. In *Proceedings of COLING 1988*, 303–305. Budapest.

Kaplan, Ronald, and Annie Zaenen. 1989. Long-Distance Dependencies, Constituent Structure, and Functional Uncertainty. In *Alternative Conceptions of Phrase Structure*, ed. Mark Baltin and Anthony Kroch, 17–42. Chicago and London: the University of Chicago Press.

Kayne, Richard. 1975. *French Syntax*. Cambridge, Mass.: MIT Press.

Keenan, Edward L. 1976. Towards a Universal Definition of Subject. In *Subject and Topic*, ed. Charles N. Li, 303–333. New York: Academic Press.

Keenan, Edward L., and Bernard Comrie. 1977. Noun Phrase Accessibility and Universal Grammar. *Linguistic Inquiry* 8:63–99.

Kiparsky, Paul. 1973. Elsewhere in Phonology. In *A festschrift for Morris Halle*, ed. Stephen Anderson and Paul Kiparsky, 93–106. New York: Holt, Rinehart and Winston.

————. 1982. Lexical Phonology and Morphology. In *Linguistics in the Morning Calm*, ed. I.-S. Yang, 3–91. Seoul: Hanshin.

————. 1983. Word-Formation and the Lexicon. In *Proceedings of the 1982 Mid-America Linguistics Conference*, ed. Frances Ingemann, 3–29. Lawrence: University of Kansas.

————. 1985. Some Consequences of Lexical Phonology. *Phonology Yearbook* 2:82–138.

————. 1987. Morphology and Grammatical Relations. Ms., Stanford University, Stanford, Calif.

Kroeger, Paul. 1993. *Phrase Structure and Grammatical Relations in Tagalog*. Stanford, Calif.: CSLI Publications. [Revision of 1991 Stanford University dissertation.]

Larson, Richard K. 1988. On the Double Object Construction. *Linguistic Inquiry* 19:335–392.

Legendre, Géraldine. 1986. Object Raising in French: A Unified Account. *Natural Language and Linguistic Theory* 4:137–183.

————. 1989. Inversion with Certain French Experiencer Verbs. *Language* 65:752–782.

————, 1990a. French Causatives: Another Look at *faire-par*. In *Grammatical Relations: A Cross-Theoretical Perspective*, ed. Katarzyna Dziwirek, Patrick Farrell, and Errapel Mejías-Bikandi, 247–262. Stanford, Calif.: CSLI Publications.

————. 1990b. French Impersonal Constructions. *Natural Language and Linguistic Theory* 8:81–128.

Levin, Beth and Malka Rappaport Hovav. 1995. *Unaccusativity: At the Syntax-Lexical Semantics Interface*. Cambridge, Mass.: MIT Press.

Levin, Lorraine. 1986. Operations on Lexical Forms: Unaccusative Rules in Germanic Languages. Doctoral dissertation, MIT, Cambridge, Mass.

Li, Yafei. 1990. X^0-Binding and Verb Incorporation. *Linguistic Inquiry* 21:399–426.

Lois, Ximena. 1986. Les groupes nominaux sans déterminant en espagnol. Ms., Université de Paris VIII.

Lonzi, Lidia. 1985. Pertinenza della struttura tema-rema per l'analisi sintattica. In *Theme-Rheme in Italian*, ed. Harro Stammerjohann, 99-120. Tübingen: Gunter Narr.

Lunn, Patricia, and Janet A. DeCesaris. 1981. The Case of the Changing Clitic in Spanish and Catalan. In *Current Research in Romance Languages*, ed. James P. Lantolf and Gregory B. Stone, 108–117. Bloomington, In.: Indiana University Linguistics Club.

Marantz, Alec P. 1984. *On the Nature of Grammatical Relations*. Cambridge, Mass.: MIT Press.

Martin, Robert. 1970. La transformation impersonnelle. *Revue de Linguistique Romane* 34:377–394.

McCloskey, James. 1984. Raising, Subcategorization, and Selection in Modern Irish. *Natural Language and Linguistic Theory* 1:441–485.

Mchombo, Sam A. 1992. Reciprocalization in Chicheŵa: A Lexical Account. *Linguistic Analysis* 21:3–22.

———. 1993. On the Binding of the Reflexive and the Reciprocal in Chicheŵa. In *Theoretical Aspects of Bantu Grammar*, ed. Sam A. Mchombo, 181–207. Stanford, Calif.: CSLI Publications.

Miller, Philip H. 1991. Clitics and Constituents in Phrase Structure Grammar. Doctoral dissertation, University of Utrecht.

Mithun, Marianne. 1984. The Evolution of Noun Incorporation. *Language* 60:847–893.

Mohanan, K. P. 1982. Grammatical Relations and Clause Structure in Malayalam. In *The Mental Representation of Grammatical Relations*, ed. Joan Bresnan, 504–589. Cambridge, Mass.: MIT Press.

———. 1983. Functional and Anaphoric Control. *Linguistic Inquiry* 14: 641–674.

———. 1986. *The Theory of Lexical Phonology*. Dordrecht: Reidel. [Revision of 1982 MIT dissertation.]

———. 1989. On the Representation of Theta Role Information. Ms., Stanford University, Stanford, Calif.

Mohanan, Tara. 1994. *Argument Structure in Hindi*. Stanford, Calif.: CSLI Publications. [Revision of 1990 Stanford University dissertation.]

———. 1995. Wordhood and Lexicality: Noun Incorporation in Hindi. *Natural Language and Linguistic Theory* 13:75–134.

Moore, John. 1990. Spanish Clause Reduction with Downstairs Cliticization. In *Grammatical Relations: A Cross-Theoretical Perspective*, ed. Katarzyna Dziwirek, Patrick Farrell, and Errapel Mejías-Bikandi, 319–333. Stanford, Calif.: CSLI Publications.

———. 1991. Reduced Constructions in Spanish. Doctoral dissertation, University of California, Santa Cruz.

O'Neill, Patrick F. 1990. Case Marking in Icelandic and Ancient Greek. Ms., Stanford University, Stanford, Calif.

Ostler, Nicholas. 1979. Case Linking: A Theory of Case and Verb Diathesis Applied to Classical Sanskrit. Doctoral dissertation, MIT, Cambridge, Mass.

Perlmutter, David. 1971. *Deep and Surface Structure Constraints in Syntax.* New York: Holt, Rinehart and Winston.

————. 1978a. Impersonal Passives and the Unaccusative Hypothesis. In *Proceedings of the Fourth Annual Meeting of the Berkeley Linguistics Society*, 157–189. Berkeley Linguistics Society, Berkeley, Calif.

————. 1978b. The Unaccusative Hypothesis and Multiattachment: Italian Evidence. Paper presented to the Harvard Linguistics Circle, May 9, 1978.

————. 1983. Personal vs. Impersonal Constructions. *Natural Language and Linguistic Theory* 1:141–200.

————. 1984. Working 1s and Inversion in Italian, Japanese and Quechua. In *Studies in Relational Grammar 2*, ed. David Perlmutter and Carol Rosen, 292–330. Chicago: University of Chicago Press.

————. 1989. Multiattachment and the Unaccusative Hypothesis: The Perfect Auxiliary in Italian. *Probus* 1:63–119.

Perlmutter, David, and Paul Postal. 1974. Lectures on Relational Grammar. Summer Linguistic Institute of the Linguistic Society of America, University of Massachusetts, Amherst.

————. 1983. Some Proposed Laws of Basic Clause Structure. *Studies in Relational Grammar 1*, ed. David Perlmutter, 81–128. Chicago: University of Chicago Press.

Picallo, M. Carme. 1984. The Infl Node and the Null Subject Parameter. *Linguistic Inquiry* 15:75–102.

————. 1990. Modal Verbs in Catalan. *Natural Language and Linguistic Theory* 8:285–312.

Picallo, M. Carme. 1991. Nominals and Nominalizations in Catalan. *Probus* 3:279–316.

Pinkham, Jessie. 1974. Passive and *faire-par* Causative Construction in French. Senior essay, Harvard University, Cambridge, Mass.

Pollard, Carl, and Ivan A. Sag. 1987. *Information-Based Syntax and Semantics, Vol. 1: Fundamentals.* Stanford, Calif.: CSLI Publications.

————. 1991. An Integrated Theory of Complement Control. *Language* 67:63–113.

————. 1992. Anaphors in English and the Scope of Binding Theory. *Linguistic Inquiry* 23:261–303.

————. 1993. *Head-Driven Phrase Structure Grammar.* Stanford, Calif.: CSLI Publications and Chicago: University of Chicago Press.

Rappaport, Malka, and Beth Levin. 1989. Is There Evidence for Deep Unaccusativity in English? An Analysis of the Resultative Constructions. Ms., Bar Ilan University and Northwestern University.

Reed, Lisa. 1991. The Thematic and Syntactic Structure of French Causatives. *Probus* 3:317–360.

Rhodes, Richard. 1990. Ojibwa Secondary Objects. In *Grammatical Relations: A Cross-Theoretical Perspective*, ed. Katarzyna Dziwirek, Patrick Farrell, and Errapel Mejías-Bikandi, 401–414. Stanford, Calif.: CSLI Publications.

Riemsdijk, Henk van, and Edwin Williams. 1986. *Introduction to the Theory of Grammar*. Cambridge, Mass.: MIT Press.

Rigau, Gemma. 1988. Strong Pronouns. *Linguistic Inquiry* 19:503–511.

Rizzi, Luigi. 1986a. Null Objects in Italian and the Theory of *pro*. *Linguistic Inquiry* 17:501–557.

———. 1986b. On Chain Formation. In *Syntax and Semantics 19: The Syntax of Pronominal Clitics*, ed. Hagit Borer, 65–95. New York: Academic Press.

Rosen, Carol. 1983. Universals of Causative Union: A Co-Proposal to the Gibson-Raposo Typology. In *Papers from the Nineteenth Regional Meeting, Chicago Linguistics Society*, 338–352. Chicago Linguistics Society, University of Chicago, Chicago, Ill.

———. 1988. *The Relational Structure of Reflexive Clauses: Evidence from Italian*. New York: Garland. [1981 Harvard University dissertation.]

———. 1990a. Rethinking Southern Tiwa: The Geometry of a Triple-Agreement Language. *Language* 66:669–713.

———. 1990b. Italian Evidence for Multi-Predicate Clauses. In *Grammatical Relations: A Cross-Theoretical Perspective*, ed. Katarzyna Dziwirek, Patrick Farrell, and Errapel Mejías-Bikandi, 415–444. Stanford, Calif.: CSLI Publications.

Rosen, Sara Thomas. 1989. Argument Structure and Complex Predicates. Doctoral dissertation, Brandeis University, Waltham, Mass.

Rothstein, Susan. 1983. The Syntactic Forms of Predication. Doctoral dissertation, MIT, Cambridge, Mass.

Rouveret, Alain, and Jean-Roger Vergnaud. 1980. Specifying Reference to the Subject: French Causatives and Conditions on Representations. *Linguistic Inquiry* 11:97–202.

Rugemalira, Josephat M. 1993. Bantu Multiple "Object" Constructions. *Linguistic Analysis* 23:226–252.

Safir, Ken, and Tim Stowell. 1988. Binominal *each*. In *Proceedings of NELS 18*, 429–450. GLSA, University of Massachusetts, Amherst.

Sag, Ivan. 1987. Grammatical Hierarchy and Linear Precedence. In *Syntax and Semantics 20: Discontinuous Constituency*, ed. Geoffrey J.

Huck and Almerindo E. Ojeda, 303–340. New York: Academic Press.

Salvi, Giampaolo. 1983. L'infinito con l'articolo e la struttura del SN. *Rivista di Grammatica Generativa* 8:197–225.

Sanfilippo, Antonio. 1990. Clitic Doubling and Dislocation in Italian: Towards a Parametric Account. *Edinburgh Working Papers in Cognitive Science* 6:169–194.

Sells, Peter. 1988. Thematic and Grammatical Hierarchies: Albanian Reflexivization. In *Proceedings of the West Coast Conference on Formal Linguistics* 7, 293–303. Stanford, Calif.:CSLI Publications.

Sells, Peter. 1991. Disjoint Reference into NP. *Linguistics and Philosophy* 14:151–169.

Sells, Peter, Annie Zaenen, and Draga Zec. 1987. Reflexivization Variation: Relations between Syntax, Semantics, and Lexical Structure. In *Working Papers in Grammatical Theory and Discourse Structure*, ed. Masayo Iida, Steve Wechsler, and Draga Zec, 169–238. Stanford, Calif.: CSLI Publications.

Shieber, Stuart M. 1986. *An Introduction to Unification-Based Approaches to Grammar*. Stanford, Calif.: CSLI Publications.

Simpson, Jane. 1983. Topics in Warlpiri Morphology and Syntax. Doctoral dissertation, MIT, Cambridge, Mass.

Smith, Henry. 1992. Restrictiveness in Case Theory. Doctoral dissertation, Stanford University, Stanford, Calif.

Solà, Jaume. 1992. Agreement and Subjects. Universitat Autònoma de Barcelona doctoral dissertation.

Sportiche, Dominique. 1988. A Theory of Floating Quantifiers and its Corollaries for Constituent Structure. *Linguistic Inquiry* 19:425–449.

Suñer, Margarita. 1988. The Role of Agreement in Clitic-Doubled Constructions. *Natural Language and Linguistic Theory* 6:391–434.

Tellier, Christine, and Daniel Valois. 1993. Binominal *chacun* and Pseudo-Opacity. *Linguistic Inquiry* 24:575–583.

Torrego, Esther. 1984. Determinerless NP's. Ms., MIT, Cambridge, Mass.

Van Valin, Robert D. 1990. Semantic Parameters of Split Intransitivity. *Language* 66:221–260.

Van Valin, Robert D. 1991. Another Look at Icelandic Case Marking and Grammatical Relations. *Natural Language and Linguistic Theory* 9: 145–194.

Vergnaud, Jean-Roger. 1974. French Relative Clauses. Doctoral dissertation, MIT, Cambridge, Mass.

Viaplana, Joaquim. 1980. Algunes consideracions sobre les formes pronominals clítiques del barceloní. *Anuario de Filología* 6:459–483.

Villalba, Xavier. 1992. Case, Incorporation, and Economy: An Approach to Causative Constructions. *Catalan Working Papers in Linguistics* 2:345–389.

Wheeler, Max. 1979. *Phonology of Catalan*. Oxford: Blackwell.

Williams, Edwin. 1980. Predication. *Linguistic Inquiry* 11:203–238.

———. 1981. Argument Structure and Morphology. *The Linguistic Review* 1:81–114.

———. 1991. Reciprocal Scope. *Linguistic Inquiry* 22:159–173.

Zaenen, Annie. 1983. On Syntactic Binding. *Linguistic Inquiry* 14:469–504.

———. 1993. Unaccusativity in Dutch: Integrating Syntax and Lexical Semantics. In *Semantics and the Lexicon*, ed. James Pustejovsky, 129–161. Dordrecht: Kluwer.

———. In preparation. Nominal Arguments in Dutch and WYSIWYG LFG. Ms., Xerox PARC, Palo Alto, Calif.

Zaenen, Annie, Joan Maling, and Höskuldur Thráinsson. 1985. Case and Grammatical Functions: The Icelandic Passive. *Natural Language and Linguistic Theory* 3:441–484.

Zagona, Karen. 1982. Predication and the Interpretation of Causative Complement Subjects. In *Current Research in Romance Languages*, ed. James P. Lantolf and Gregory B. Stone, 221–231. Bloomington, In.: Indiana University Linguistics Club.

Zubizarreta, María Luisa. 1985. The Relation Between Morphophonology and Morphosyntax: The Case of Romance Causatives. *Linguistic Inquiry* 16:247–289.

———. 1987. *Levels of Representation in the Lexicon and in the Syntax*. Dordrecht: Foris.

Zucchi, Alessandro. 1993. *The Language of Propositions and Events: Issues in the Syntax and the Semantics of Nominalization*. Dordrecht: Kluwer. [University of Massachusetts, Amherst, dissertation.]

Index

1-1 match 266–268. *See also* correspondence
  evidence against it 268–270

Ackerman, Farrell 183
active-passive
  alternation 6, 7, 48, 78
  commonality 53
actor 124
adjunct 21, 45, 46, 49, 55–57, 59. *Also* ADJ, XADJ
  optionality 57
agreement
  and null subjects 28
  and *there* constructions 73
  on past participles 94–97, 122, 211
    in French 96
    in Italian 96
Aissen, Judith 187
Albanian 18
Alsina, Alex 18, 21, 29, 37, 43, 51, 121, 165, 182, 186, 188, 198, 201, 202, 203, 222, 255, 264, 278, 279
anaphor 239
  binding of 9. *See also* anaphoric binding
  syntactic 14, 152, 237–242
anaphoric binding 14, 274
Andrews, Avery 19, 125
Aoun, Joseph 186, 208

appositions 166
arguments 35. *See also* thematic: roles
  coindexation of 116
    marked option 117
  direct 41, 42, 117
  hierarchical ordering of 39
  indirect 41, 42
  phrase structure representation of 7, 11
  prominence ranking of 7, 9, 12, 35, 36, 41, 273, 279
  representation of 120
  unexpressed 46
  vs. adjuncts 56
argument-adjunct 55, 56. *See also* oblique, passive:oblique
argument structure 16. *See also* a-structure
  main functions of 266
  phrase structure encoding of 8
attribute-value matrix 18
auxiliary selection 125, 243
  default 125
  in French 97, 98
  in Italian 97–99, 124–126
a-structure 1, 7–9, 11, 12, 16, 38, 48, 77–79
  as PRED value 38, 43
  asymmetry 257
  autonomy of 9, 14, 233, 234, 275
  complex 42, 142

definition 34
interface between the lexicon and
    syntax 275
interface with f-structure 276
interface with LCS 276
intuitive idea 4–7
lexical information 7
operation 41, 117
prominence ranking at 273
role of 14, 35, 275
semantic constraints on 34
semantically based 44, 63
syntactic information 11
underspecified 51
a-structure binding 13, 14, 116–
    121, 144, 177, 237, 241, 263,
    268, 277
    and passive 136–138
    and raising verbs 140
    co-argument condition on 140–
    142, 221, 222
    interpretation under ellipsis 241
    reciprocal affix in Chicheŵa 255
    no suppression 144
    valence reducing effect 144
    vs. anaphoric binding 237–242,
    263, 264

Baker, Mark 8, 20, 110, 138, 139,
    168, 186, 208, 270
Bantu 29, 121, 138, 139, 169
bare indefinite NP 104–107, 129,
    133
    nonspecific interpretation 129
    not a subject 106
    postverbal 105
Belletti, Adriana 8, 37, 39, 82, 101,
    102, 104, 107, 129, 225, 259,
    262, 263
Bennis, Hans 20
binding
    between objects 254, 264
    in elliptical constructions 14
    theory 239
Bordelois, Ivonne 187, 196, 208
Brame, Michael 64

Bresnan, Joan 7, 10, 11, 15, 18, 19,
    21, 23, 24, 28, 29, 30, 35, 36,
    39, 43, 46, 51, 59, 64, 67,
    109, 115, 138, 155, 156, 157,
    158, 159, 160, 168, 175, 244,
    269
Burzio, Luigi 83, 98, 99, 100, 107,
    124, 135, 140, 141, 142, 143,
    186, 187, 208, 249
Burzio's Generalization 83
Butt, Miriam 27, 175
Byarushengo, Ernest R. 29

case
    accusative 27, 122, 123
    assignment 169
        a-structure basis of 13
    dative 13, 122
        marked case value 161
    default 13
    ergative 27
    marking 13, 249, 271
        in causatives 86–88, 122, 190–
        193, 248
    morphological 13, 14, 149, 160
    quirky 171
Case (abstract) 14. *See also* GB
    inherent 129, 168, 169
    partitive 129
    structural 168, 169
Case Assignment Convention 174,
    181, 190–193, 199, 205, 251–
    254, 259–261
Catalan 1–4, 28, 81–96, 98–101,
    104–113, 118, 123, 124, 126,
    130–133, 136, 137, 139–142,
    149–169, 171–174, 176–180,
    185, 187, 189, 190, 192–199,
    201–207, 210–221, 223–228,
    231–234, 237–254, 258–264,
    272, 274
Categorial Unification Grammar 82
category 27
    empty 59
    lexical 17
    major 27

minor 23, 25
nominal 27
phrasal 17
prepositional 28
causative 122
and idioms 211
and inalienable possession 211
based on a ditransitive verb 192
based on an intransitive verb 190
based on an optionally transitive verb 193
based on a transitive verb 191
coercive 226
constructions (in Romance) 14, 185, 273. *See also* case: marking, reflexivized verbs: causatives of
and a-structure binding 222, 249
biclausal analysis 207
complex a-structure 14, 188, 235
linear order in 205
monoclausal analysis 14, 186, 188, 208, 234
passive of 187, 200
c-structure to f-structure mapping 204
permissive 225
predicate 126
a-structure 188
internal argument of 221
reflexivized 211, 220–223
causee 14, 127. *See also* floating quantifiers, quantifier binding
and control 212, 231
as a d-structure/initial subject 207–209, 211, 276
as a logical subject 14, 209, 223–232
as an anaphor 252
morphological case alternation. *See* case:marking

not a grammatical subject 207–209, 220, 223
object/oblique alternation 194, 195, 198, 225
omission of 88, 99, 100, 126, 197
Centineo, Giulia 124
Chicheŵa 19, 118, 121, 157, 168, 169, 188, 222, 244, 247, 255–258
Chierchia, Gennaro 224
Chomsky, Noam 7, 11, 20, 46, 82, 92, 115, 155, 221, 269
clitic
agreement features 96
as affix 137, 151
doubling of objects 151, 237, 243
optional 244
first and second person 116
in causatives 87
in participles 100
object 123
as agreement marker 244
as pronoun 244
pronominal 82, 86
bearing a GF 92
reflexive. *See* reflexive clitic
topic-anaphoric 157
Coherence 46, 49, 52, 55, 64, 66, 68, 70, 71, 75, 76, 119, 131
COMP, XCOMP 21, 65. *See also* syntactic function
Complete Functional Complex (or CFC) 221
Completeness 45
Comrie, Bernard 67, 253
configurational 27, 28
Configurationally Uniform Representation of Theta-roles. *See* CURT
Consistency. *See* Uniqueness
Constraint on Sharing of F-Structures 61, 62, 69, 71, 119, 121
control ("equi") 67
an anaphoric relation 230
condition 229

in passive clauses 228
not by nonarguments 230
coordination 168
correspondence (between levels)
arguments and c-structure 50
not one-to-one (many-to-one) 2,
13–14, 120, 146
one-to-one 1, 3, 13, 266. *See
also* 1-1 match
principles. *See* mapping:princi-
ples
prominence mismatch between
arguments and syntactic
functions 258–260, 273
semantic roles and morphosyntactic expressions 50
co-argument 41, 117
condition 117, 118
co-linking 23, 24
CURT (Configurationally Uniform
Representation of Theta-
roles) 266–268, 270. *See also* UTAH
evidence against it 268, 273–275
c-command 67
c-structure (constituent structure)
11, 12, 16, 17, 21, 23, 31, 77
annotated 21–23
licensing. *See* syntactic func-
tion:licensing
C-structure Encoding of Direct
and Indirect Functions 29

Dalrymple, Mary 9, 44, 116, 166,
239, 255, 256, 257
DAT(IVE) ± 160, 163, 164
Davies, William 208
DeCesaris, Janet A. 162
Demonte, Violeta 155, 167
discourse function (DF) 21, 30, 57–
62, 79
ditransitive verbs 133
and subject selection 111
Di Sciullo, Anna-Maria 5, 138,
186, 208
Dowty, David 40, 41, 129, 276

Duranti, Alessandro 29
d-structure 7–12
syntactic representation of argument structure 266

ellipsis 240, 241, 246, 247
Elsewhere Condition 125
English 18, 19, 27, 30, 49–77, 81,
84, 132, 156, 213, 216, 230,
237–243, 246, 247, 252, 255,
256, 258, 259, 263
en-cliticization (or *ne*-cliticization)
107–109, 133
in Italian 108
unaccusative diagnostic 108
equation
functional. *See* functional annotation
constraining 175
expletive (expletive function) 45,
47, 57, 71, 72, 79, 124, 131,
132. *See also* syntactic func-
tion:nonthematic
chain 73
il (French) 85
it (English) 72
last resort 76
subject 230
there (English) 57, 72–77, 132
external argument 9, 12, 39–42, 44,
48, 65, 135
External Argument Mapping Principle 44, 48, 68, 70, 119, 120,
127

factorization 16, 77
Feldman, Harry 181
Fillmore, Charles 36
Final 1 Law 20. *See also* Subject
Condition
floating quantifier 154, 214–217
and causee 213, 216, 217
and object clitics 217
and the VP-internal subject hypothesis 216
subjecthood diagnostic 215

FMT (Functional Mapping Theory) 43, 45, 46, 48–50, 52, 53, 55–57, 61, 64, 71, 78, 118, 130, 131, 175, 199, 209, 234, 235, 251, 276, 277
  mapping principles 64, 75, 133, 189, 200, 221, 222
focus (FOCUS) 21, 57, 58. *See also* discourse function
Foley, William A. 10, 36
Fontana, Josep M. 82, 135, 139, 263
FORM feature 73
French 85–87, 96–98, 101, 107, 122, 137, 141, 143, 151, 154, 167, 187, 193, 195, 208, 213–216, 227, 229, 230, 248
Function-Argument Biuniqueness 46, 47, 77, 115, 268, 269
function-category association 50, 53, 54, 58, 60, 61, 66, 78, 278. *See also* mapping
subject/nonsubject asymmetry 27, 28, 204
functional annotation 21, 22, 30, 59. *Also* equation
Functional Mapping Theory. *See* FMT
f-command 67, 69, 156
  vs. c-command 156
f-structure (functional structure) 11, 12, 16, 18, 21, 23, 31, 34, 77
  as a mathematical function 18
  as a value 25
  conditions on 21
  inclusion of 26, 31
  interface between a- and c-structure 78
  licensing of 25
  principles internal to 51, 52, 54, 55
  semantically empty 71
  sharing of 59–61, 63, 64, 66, 67, 69, 75. *See also* Constraint on Sharing of F-Structures

notation 61, 66, 69
structural asymmetry 62

GB (Government-Binding) 7, 9, 10, 12, 14, 20, 82, 100, 115, 120, 160, 185, 207–209, 213, 215, 216, 223, 232, 259, 264, 265–272
  Binding Theory 82, 97, 244, 264
  Case Theory 163, 168, 183
gender 123
GF hierarchy. *See* syntactic function:hierarchy of
Gibson, Jeanne 208
Givón, Talmy 36
governing category 155
  minimal 155
grammatical function (GF). *See* syntactic function
Greek 69, 181
Greenberg, Joseph 161, 162
Grimshaw, Jane 5, 7, 9, 10, 37, 38, 39, 51, 55, 57, 82, 84, 85, 86, 90, 93, 94, 98, 103, 109, 110, 111, 124, 134, 135, 136, 138, 144, 171, 180, 225, 232, 276, 278
Gruber, Jeffrey S. 36
Guasti, Maria Teresa 196
Guéron, Jacqueline 82

Halvorsen, Per-Kristian 44, 155, 240
Haya 29
head 17, 23, 25
  lexical 25, 27
Head-driven Phrase Structure Grammar 82, 239
head-initial 203
Heim, Irene 116, 255, 260
Higginbotham, James 5, 116, 255
Hindi-Urdu 27
Hoekstra, Teun 124
Hyman, Larry M. 117, 195, 196

Icelandic 180, 181, 182
idiom 68

impersonal construction 124. *See also* inversion, passive: impersonal
include 67
internal argument 9, 12, 39–42, 44, 48, 58, 65
Internal Argument Mapping Principle 44, 46, 48, 75, 119, 120, 127
inversion
    construction 130, 131, 230. *See also* impersonal construction
    locative 30
    verbs (or predicates) 258–263
        reciprocalized 262
        reflexivized 258
Irish 69
Isoda, Michio 117, 200
Italian 28, 82, 87, 89, 90, 92, 96–102, 104, 107–109, 124–126, 128, 129, 131, 140–143, 145, 154, 187, 188, 195, 203, 208, 222, 224, 225, 242, 243, 249, 250, 253, 254, 258

Jackendoff, Ray 7, 10, 36, 43, 54, 56, 65, 109, 142, 146, 147, 159, 166, 199, 225, 276
Jaeggli, Osvaldo 103, 110, 139, 167
Japanese 117
Johnson, Kyle 110, 139
Joseph, Brian 69
Joshi, Smita 9, 19, 37, 40, 41, 223

Kameyama, Megumi 155
Kaplan, David 239
Kaplan, Ronald 11, 15, 18, 21, 23, 46, 59, 168, 175
Kanerva, Jonni M. 10, 18, 29, 36, 43, 51
Kayne, Richard 85, 86, 107, 143, 151, 154, 187, 193, 194, 195
Keenan, Edward L. 19, 67, 253
Kichaga 138, 139
King, Tracy H. 175

Kiparsky, Paul 9, 10, 18, 36, 125, 136, 160, 223, 279
Kroeger, Paul 38, 202

Larson, Richard K. 156
Lasnik, Howard 116, 255, 260
Latin 167
Legendre, Géraldine 85, 122, 194, 227, 229, 230, 231
level of representation 7, 9, 15, 16, 21, 22, 34, 38, 77
    acessibility 9
    modular conception 278
Levin, Lorraine 18
Levin, Beth 18, 39, 106, 108
Lexical Conceptual Structure (or LCS) 34, 146, 276
lexical entry 22
Lexical Integrity Hypothesis 15
Lexical Mapping Theory (LMT) 43
Lexical Phonology and Morphology 136
lexical semantic structure 8. *See also* Lexical Conceptual Structure
Lexicalist Hypothesis 92. *See also* Lexical Integrity Principle
lexicalist theory 15
LFG (Lexical-Functional Grammar) 11, 15, 16, 18, 20–22, 35, 38, 43–47, 58, 59, 61, 65, 66, 73, 77, 115, 166, 175, 183, 201, 202, 239, 244, 268, 269
light verb 203. *See also* predicate: incomplete
Li, Yafei 186, 208
linear precedence 168
    principle 204, 251
linker 10, 43. *See also* syntactic function
linking
    constraints on 10. *See also* mapping:principles
    shown by coindexation 22–24
    shown by connecting lines 22, 23

theory 10, 11
locality 117
Logical Form (LF) 7, 8, 12, 271
logical subject 12, 36, 39, 40, 42, 51, 53–55, 89, 116, 135, 177, 223
and control 227
as anaphor 251
as antecedent 225–227
as dative object 229, 259
modifiers of 109–111, 133
oblique expression of 55
reflexive 224
vs. grammatical subject 37, 209
Lois, Ximena 104
long distance dependencies 58, 62. *Also wh*-movement
Lonzi, Lidia 108
Lunn, Patricia 162

Malayalam 19, 30
Maling, Joan 155, 180, 181, 182
mapping 11–13. *See also* Uniqueness of F-Structures
of a-structure to f-structure (arguments and syntactic functions) 43, 45, 48, 49, 57, 59, 61, 118
not one-to-one 47
one-to-one 46
of c-structure to f-structure 21, 22, 24, 25, 30, 32–34, 47, 60, 63, 73, 74, 76, 130, 132. *See also* function-category association
asymmetries 24
mathematical function 24
lexical head 25
many-to-one 24
Part-Whole Parallelism 26, 31, 68
part-whole relations 26
phrasal node 25
principles 24, 27, 29
principles 11, 16, 22, 77, 175, 180

semantics to a-structure 38
theory 43
Marantz, Alec 82, 186, 208
Marathi 18, 41
Martin, Robert 85
May, Robert 116, 255, 260
Maxwell, John T. 168
McCloskey, James 69
Mchombo, Sam A. 15, 18, 19, 37, 43, 116, 117, 157, 244, 247, 255, 256, 257
Miller, Philip H. 137, 151, 193
mirror principle 138
Mithun, Marianne 36
Mohanan, K. P. 17, 19, 30, 37, 67, 136
Mohanan, Tara 15, 20, 27, 37, 175, 223, 228
Moore, John 82, 88, 135, 139, 186, 208, 221, 244, 247, 249, 263
Morphological Blocking Principle 125
Moshi, Lioba 18, 29, 43, 138
multiattachment 85, 145, 146
resolution 146
multilevelled theory 15

nominalizations 2, 89–94, 122
of infinitives 89, 248
expression of arguments 90
no subject 93
transitivity 89, 93
not with pronominal clitics 91
of reflexivized verbs 90
nonargument 57, 62, 72, 124, 125. *See also* expletive, syntactic function:nonthematic
nonconfigurational 27
Nondative Subject Constraint 180, 181, 259
nonthematic. *See* syntactic function:nonthematic
NP extraposition (in French) 85, 86, 122
nucleus 20, 76, 155
number 123

objective 29
objects (OBJ) 13, 60, 65
  accusative 112
  as antecedents 252, 253
  as controllers 230
  canonical position of 106
  dative 29, 112, 141, 142, 260
    as direct functions 150–160
    as PPs 166
    vs. nondative 160
  direct 13
  indirect 13, 149. *See also* case:
    dative, object:dative
  multiple 47
  nonthematic 76
  relative order of 250
  relative prominence of 253
  types of 21
oblique (OBL) 21, 39, 40, 43, 46, 48,
    55. *See also* adjunct, pas-
    sive:oblique
  argument 56
  not subject to Coherence 49
  obligatoriness 55, 56
  optionality 45, 54, 56, 57
obl(ique) ± 19, 29, 44
Ojibwa 19
one-to-one. *See* correspondence
O'Neill, Patrick F. 181
Ostler, Nicholas 36

participial
  absolute 101
    in Italian 128
    unaccusative 102
    unergative 102
  constructions (in Italian) 100–
    102, 128, 129
  morphology 136
passive 35, 83, 180. *See also* ac-
    tive-passive
  and controllers 228
  and subject selection 112
  impersonal 107, 109, 188
  morpheme 51, 53, 139
    a-structure 51

morphology 48, 50, 71
oblique 29, 46, 48, 53–55, 194,
    225
  and oblique causee 196
  optionality 54
  of double object constructions
    150
  of raising verb 70
  syntactic structures 52
    no empty category 53
PEAR (Phrase-structure Encod-
    ing of Argument Relations)
    266–268, 270, 271
  evidence against it 268, 270,
    273–275
Perlmutter, David 18, 20, 40, 67,
    85, 98, 100, 107, 109, 145,
    154, 208, 253, 259
Peters, Stanley 116, 255, 256, 257
Peterson, Peter 168
Phonetic Form (PF) 8, 12
Phrase-structure Encoding of Ar-
    gument Relations. *See*
    PEAR
Picallo, M. Carme 90, 107
Pinkham, Jessie 198
Pollard, Carl 24, 57, 64, 67, 212,
    239
Portuguese 28, 98
Postal, Paul 18, 20, 67, 208, 253
PRED feature: absence of 73
predicate
  base 51
  complex 53, 142, 188
    formed in the syntax 202
    functionally double-headed 203
  derived 51
  incomplete 51, 116, 118, 188,
    201
  c-structure position 202
  secondary 158
Predicate Argument Structure (or
    PAS) 35. *See* a-structure
predicate composition 12, 14, 51,

116, 118, 126, 136, 186, 188, 200, 201, 235, 279
in the syntax 201–203
prepositions as case-markers 29
Projection Principle 11
Extended 20
pronominal approach 82, 84, 86, 88, 94, 95, 99, 115, 135, 145, 263
pronoun
  bound variable 255–257, 262
  coreferential 154, 255
  resumptive 156
  strong 156
  topic-anaphoric 157
Proto-Agent (P-A) 40
  classification 41
  semantic entailments 40
Proto-Patient (P-P) 40
  semantic entailments 40
Proto-Role (P-Role) 40, 278
  classification 38, 40–43, 57, 117
PS (phrase structure) tree 17
"psych"-verbs 176, 262, 263. *Also* experiencer verbs
  vs. passive verbs 229

quantifier binding 155, 272
  and objects 218
  and the causee 217–220
  subject/object asymmetry 217

raising 67, 124
  function 57, 62, 63, 66, 68, 79
    direct 63, 69, 70
    licensing 64, 68, 72
    subject 64
  to object 68, 76
  to oblique 69
  verb 63, 139
    VP complement of 64, 65
    passivization of 70
Raposo, Eduardo 208
Rappaport (Hovav), Malka 39, 106, 108
reciprocal

affix (morpheme) 117, 121, 138, 255
in Bantu 139
semantics 116, 258
  interpretation procedure 257
  thematic asymmetry 256
  "wide scope" reading 256, 260, 261
  with a-structure binding 258
verb 138
  passivized 138
Reed, Lisa 208, 215
referential index 239
reflexive
  in Chicheŵa 247
  in English 81
  semantics 116
reflexive clitic (in Romance) 13, 81, 116, 136–139, 237, 238, 240, 241, 268
  as a syntactic anaphor 82, 84, 94
  as object 83
  as suppression 82
    of the external argument 83
  binding at a-structure 84, 121.
    See also a-structure binding
  clitic doubling use 14, 242–248
  in causatives 100, 211
  no suppression 111
  not a syntactic anaphor 97, 98
  not an argument/GF 90–94
  reflexive and reciprocal interpretations 242
  two functions 245–247
  unaccusative properties 123
  valence reducing morpheme 82, 83, 85–97, 102, 113, 121–123
  with unaccusative verbs 141
reflexivized constructions 1, 13, 14, 47, 81–114, 268–271. *See also* pronominal approach, unaccusative approach, unergative approach
  based on causatives 220
  based on inversion verbs 258

external argument subject 83, 114
internal argument subject 114
mapping to grammatical functions 120
reciprocal interpretation 14, 81, 116, 255–263
reflexive interpretation 81, 116, 257
reflexivized verbs 124–126, 177
  causatives of 99, 100, 126–128
  in participial absolutes 102
  nominalizations of 90
  not unaccusatives 103
  subject selection 112
  unaccusatives 98–103
  unergatives 129
restructuring verb 203. *See also* predicate:incomplete
RG (Relational Grammar) 18, 20, 85, 100, 145, 146, 160, 207, 208, 209, 213, 227, 232, 258, 259
  object relations 183
Rhodes, Richard 19
Riemsdijk, Henk van 82
Rigau, Gemma 156, 158
Rizzi, Luigi 8, 37, 39, 82, 97, 99, 107, 135, 138, 139, 140, 141, 225, 253, 259, 262, 263
Roberts, Ian 110, 139
Romance 1, 13, 14, 28, 81, 84, 85, 90, 104, 139, 144, 147, 149, 197, 199–201, 203, 207, 220, 222, 226, 233, 234, 241, 242, 247, 248, 250, 252, 255, 258
Rosen, Carol 19, 85, 98, 100, 101, 102, 107, 109, 141, 145, 194, 208, 222, 232, 243, 249, 254
Rosen, Sara T. 7, 82, 84, 94, 97, 103, 124, 135, 136, 144, 186, 187, 203, 208, 221
Rothstein, Susan 109
Rouveret, Alain 208, 230
Rugemalira, Josephat M. 29

Runyambo 29

Safir, Ken 213
Sag, Ivan 24, 57, 64, 67, 212, 239
Salvi, Giampaolo 90
Sanfilippo, Antonio 82
secondary predication 158
  of objects 158
  not of obliques 159
Selkirk, Elizabeth 90
Sells, Peter 18, 117, 240, 241, 247
semantic information: only accessible to morphology 38
semantic selection 37
semantic structure (s-structure) 44
Shieber, Stuart M. 24
Simpson, Jane 18
sloppy reading 241, 242, 247
Smith, Henry 182
Solà, Joan 131
Solà, Jaume 104, 105
Southern Tiwa 19
Spanish 28, 87, 88, 98, 100, 104, 124, 131, 141, 154, 158, 159, 162, 166, 167, 187, 188, 195, 203, 208, 242, 244, 245, 247, 258, 260
Sportiche, Dominique 216
Stowell, Tim 213
strict reading 241, 242, 247
subcategorization 45, 78
subject (SUBJ). *See also* bare indefinite NP
  dative 181
  grammatical 39
  marked choice 124
  maximally prominent 228
  not dative 179
  /object alternation 189
  obligatoriness 20
  properties of 19, 20
  "pro-drop" (or null subject) languages 85, 104, 132
  uniqueness 20, 21
  verb agreement 130

Subject Condition 20, 26, 34, 48, 52, 64, 68, 70, 71, 75, 76, 119, 120, 125, 130, 131, 132, 175, 180, 181, 189, 199, 277
subj(ect) ± 19, 28, 44
Suñer, Margarita 154, 159, 166, 167
superior 62, 66, 67, 69, 71, 75
suppression 10, 51–54, 56, 71
  notation 51
syntactic function 10, 18. *Also* grammatical function
  alternations 4, 6, 12, 15, 48, 78, 276–278. *Also* grammatical function changing
  assignment 39, 53
    lexical vs. syntactic 43
    sensitive to case 27
    to a-structure 52
    to c-structure nodes 27
  atomic 18
  attribute 21, 47
  autonomous 277
  c-structure constraints 27, 28
  direct 18, 39, 43, 117. *Also* term
    as antecedent 225, 226
  direct vs. indirect 18, 19, 29, 45, 53, 110
  discourse. *See* discourse function
  featural composition 18–20, 29, 44, 277
  hierarchy of 67, 69, 71, 229, 253, 273. *Also* GF hierarchy
  idiomatic 71. *See also* syntactic function:nonthematic
  in-clause 21, 58, 59
  indirect. *See* oblique
  interface category (between arguments and morphosyntactic expressions) 43, 277
  licensing 26, 45, 46, 71
    c-structure licensing 61, 74–76, 132

f-structure licensing 64, 68, 75, 76
  natural classes 18, 19, 29, 277
  nonthematic 45, 47, 49, 57, 62, 66–69, 71, 72, 75, 78. *See also* expletive, nonargument
    licensing 68, 69, 71
    not in a-structure 72
    phonologically null 28
  subject vs. nonsubject 18, 19, 20
  types 21
  underspecification 276
syntax-semantics interface 2–5. *See also* a-structure
s-structure 8, 9, 12
  mapping to 8

Tagalog 38
Tellier, Christine 213, 214
term 18. *See* syntactic function: direct
thematic
  hierarchy 36, 38, 41, 147, 228, 276
  information 37, 38, 43
    not in a-structure 38, 278
    reference to 37
    sensitivity to 37
  roles 36, 37. *Also* theta-roles, θ-roles
    abbreviations 36
    hierarchy of 36. *Also* thematic:hierarchy
Theta-Criterion 46, 115, 269
theta-structure (θ-structure) 7, 8. *See also* a-structure
Thráinsson, Höskuldur 180, 181, 182
topic (TOPIC) 21, 30, 57, 58. *See also* discourse function
  relative pronoun 157
Torrego, Esther 104
Transformational Grammar (TG) 7. *See also* GB

unaccusative 40, 42, 83, 98, 106,

122, 123, 125, 130, 177, 224, 232
and object agreement 131
diagnostics 103, 104, 108
verbs 140
in participial absolutes 102
with reflexive clitics 141, 142
unaccusative approach 83, 94, 95, 98, 99, 103, 115, 145
undergoer 124
unergative 40, 84, 98, 106, 122, 126, 177
in participial absolutes 102
unergative approach 84, 99, 111, 145
unification. *See* Uniqueness
uniform phrase-structure representation of argument roles (hypothesis of) 4, 11, 207. *See also* CURT
Uniqueness 20, 21, 24, 48. *Also* Consistency, unification
Uniqueness of F-Structures 47, 49, 60, 61, 69, 78, 119, 121
unrestricted 29
UTAH (Uniformity of Theta Assignment Hypothesis) 270

Vallduví, Enric 108
Valois, Daniel 213, 214
Van Valin, Robert D. 10, 36, 103, 124, 182
Vergnaud, Jean-Roger 167, 208, 230
Viaplana, Joaquim 161
Villalba, Xavier 206, 208, 211, 212, 219, 220

Wasow, Tom 241
Wheeler, Max 162
wh-movement. *See* long distance dependencies
Williams, Edwin 5, 7, 9, 39, 82, 138, 186, 208, 255

X′ theory 17, 22, 28, 31, 203

Zaenen, Annie 18, 20, 39, 40, 43,
59, 180, 181, 182, 240, 241, 247
Zagona, Karen 208
Zec, Draga 240, 241, 247
Zimmer, Karl 195, 196
Zubizarreta, María Luisa 99, 134, 159, 160, 186, 187, 208, 225
Zucchi, Alessandro 89, 90, 92